transforming the frontier

BRAM BÜSCHER

transforming the frontier

PEACE PARKS AND THE POLITICS
OF NEOLIBERAL CONSERVATION
IN SOUTHERN AFRICA

DUKE UNIVERSITY PRESS   DURHAM AND LONDON   2013

© 2013 Duke University Press

All rights reserved

Printed in the United States of America
on acid-free paper ∞

Designed by Heather Hensley

Typeset in Scala by Keystone Typesetting

Library of Congress Cataloging-in-Publication Data
Büscher, Bram, 1977–
Transforming the frontier : peace parks and the politics of
neoliberal conservation in southern Africa / Bram Büscher.
p   cm
Includes bibliographical references and index.
ISBN 978-0-8223-5404-8 (cloth : alk. paper)
ISBN 978-0-8223-5420-8 (pbk. : alk. paper)
1. Transfrontier conservation areas—Africa, Southern.
2. Biodiversity conservation—Africa, Southern. 3. Ecotourism—
Africa, Southern. 4. Neoliberalism—Africa, Southern. I. Title.
S934.A356B87   2013
333.720968—dc23   2013003133

TO STACEY

contents

preface

> "Where to travel" and "what is worth seeing there"
>
> is nothing but a way of saying in plain English what
>
> is usually said under the pompous Greek name of
>
> "method," or, even worse, "methodology."

Bruno Latour, *Reassembling the Social*

Whether "method" and "methodology" are pompous words or not, I believe that the metaphor of traveling is a good way to describe the research journey that led to this book and the arguments contained in it. The journey started in 2002 when an initial backpacking expedition through southern Africa exposed me to the concept of a Transfrontier Conservation Area (TFCA). The area in this case was the Great Limpopo Transfrontier Park, the southern African showcase, which, according to a poster at an entrance to the Kruger National Park, was to connect South African, Mozambican, and Zimbabwean conservation areas. The excitement about this new development was palpable. During a three-day safari in the Kruger, I saw many maps, posters, and signs heralding this new frontier in conservation. Conservation, the message seemed to be, was finally going to pay its dues and take care of biodiversity *and* people on a massive new scale. The Great Limpopo, in particular, was going to reestablish old animal-migration routes, and this "world's greatest animal kingdom" would also bring in more tourists and economic benefits to local communities. But that was not all.

TFCAS were also going to enable southern African nations to cooperate more amicably and more effectively. According to the slogan of one organization that appeared on all the posters, TFCAS are "the global solution" and thus required a fitting name: "peace parks."

Peace parks, and how they are implicated in contemporary frontiers of conservation, are the topic of this book. When starting the research for this book in the framework of my dissertation research, I—quite naively, I must admit—thought of frontiers mostly as international borders. But as my research journey progressed, the concept steadily acquired more connotations, many of which feature prominently in the ensuing account. As I became more aware of these connotations, my research journey was shaped by the widening and discovery of frontiers. First I recognized that I should not limit myself to the showcase Great Limpopo if I wanted to gain a deeper understanding of transfrontier conservation dynamics in southern Africa. During my initial exploratory field visit to southern Africa in late 2003, I realized that regional differences in TFCA practices were immense and that the global and regional spotlight on the Great Limpopo actually kept these from sight. Besides, its grand claims were already being investigated by a number of scholars (something that became poignantly clear when I had to wait in line for an interview with the responsible staff member at South Africa's Department of Environmental Affairs). A chance encounter led me to consider the mountainous Maloti-Drakensberg TFCA between Lesotho and South Africa. During the late 1990s and early 2000s, the region was abuzz with scholarly activity on community-based natural resource management and a big conference on this topic was organized in Johannesburg, which I attended. There I met the Lesotho coordinator for the Maloti-Drakensberg project, who invited me to join him and Lesotho's environment minister on a trip to the eastern highlands of the country to thank local communities for their participation in the project. He wanted to show me that they took local communities seriously.

Lesotho—that tiny, sovereign "historical accident" in the middle of South Africa—proved quite an experience. After driving a 4x4 over rocky roads, passing many small villages with stone and traditional houses, wading through a river that according to my travel companions could rise so quickly following rains that we could be stuck for days if we did not depart in time, we finally arrived in Tlhanyaku village. The scene was vivid. Many villagers, wrapped in traditional Basotho blankets, sat on a grassy patch waiting for the "ceremony" to begin. The dignitaries were first brought to a community center, where food was being prepared. Before any formal activity could start, everybody first needed to eat chicken and *moroho*, the local vegetable staple. This took a while, and once the ceremony finally commenced, the minister had not even spoken for five minutes when the rains began. It was a mere drizzle at first, so she continued explaining to the local people how the massive five-year Maloti-Drakensberg Transfrontier Project (MDTP) depended on their cooperation. The goal was to conserve the fragile mountain ecosystem along with the project's South African counterparts. The minister insisted that although the project was complex and politically difficult, it could succeed if they, the local people, participated in it, owned it. They, after all, were the real stewards of the mountain grasslands and the sources of some of the region's major rivers. Moreover, they would directly benefit from the project. After all, its second objective was to stimulate development through nature-based tourism. Then, it truly began to pour. The minister cut her speech short and we rushed to the cars. The meeting was over. We had to get back across the river because the minister could not get stuck in this remote place. As we sped off and left the villagers behind in the rain, I reflected on what the minister had said about the intervention and its challenges and knew I had found, in Bruno Latour's words, "where to travel."

The next thing was finding out what was worth seeing there and how to go about this. One thing was clear from the start: I wanted to combine long-term ethnographic field research with an eye for structural power. Approaching empirical realities in this way led me to agree with Alexander Wendt that "just as social structures are ontologically dependent upon and therefore constituted by the practices and self-understandings of agents, the causal powers and interests of those agents, in their own turn, are constituted and therefore explained by structures" (1987, 359). Obviously, this approach had repercussions on different levels. Above all, it forced me to look for, and often transcend, the frontiers between academic disciplines, methodological traditions, theoretical dispositions, and empirical realities. This seemed to be the only way to capture the political ecology of it all: to connect and analytically unravel the broader, regional power relations behind transfrontier conservation and the ethnographic realities of the MDTP; the space that Tanya Li (2007) terms the "witches brew," the situated practices of real-world actors.

Traversing methodological, theoretical, and disciplinary frontiers takes time, and as the implementers of the MDTP were coming to grips with the implementation of the intervention, I was coming to grips with studying them doing so. My research strategy, particularly from 2005 to 2007 when I spent most of my time in the field, came close to what Latour states about interactions in the field: "Any given interaction seems to *overflow* with elements which are already in the situation coming from some other *time*, some other *place*, and generated by some other *agency*. . . . Thus, if any observer is faithful to the direction suggested by this overflow, she will be led *away* from any given interaction to some *other places, other times*, and *other agencies* that appear to have moulded them into shape" (Latour 2005, 166; emphasis in the original).[1]

Over time, while I was becoming better aware of both the overall trans-frontier conservation context and the politics of the MDTP, it became easier to be "led away." This knowledge of the overall context also helped in making informed decisions about where to be led away to. Following Li (2007, 28), I argue that this ethnography of particular "conjunctures" forms a valuable method to come to a more holistic picture of the overall "constellation," provided—of course—that the conjunctions are selected carefully.

Central to these conjunctions is getting access to the social relations and spaces where discourses, practices, relations, and interventions are produced, felt, lived, and interpreted. Long-term ethnographic field research enabled me to get access to and study many project papers, plans, maps, memos, meetings, and activities. To complement this, I interviewed nearly all the important individuals in the MDTP, as well as many key figures in the regional transfrontier conservation scene in southern Africa. Moreover, I used the Internet to collect documentary evidence. Many actors these days leave their traces online, which can provide interesting additional information. As a corrolary, it proved hard to disconnect from the social relations in the field, and, in fact, I did not want to (even if I could, see Ferguson 2006, 66–68). I tried to maintain relations of critical engagement throughout the entire period while retaining the right to interpret the data. This process and its contradictions are well understood by David Mosse: "while fieldwork has changed beyond recognition—becoming ever more intensely social—ethnographic writing (interpreting, objectifying and textualising) remains a solitary process that disembeds knowing from its relationships, denying (to varying degrees) the social its claim to power, to ownership, to negotiation" (2006, 4).

But even this process can to some extent be made part of one's methodology. I tried to do so by sending notes of our conversations to interviewees so they could check my interpretations. This often led to new data and further engagements. As such, my research is in line with a shift in development studies from work based on critical disengagement (e.g., Escobar 1995; Ferguson 1994) to more-recent ethnographic research committed to critical engagement with development agents (e.g., Lewis et al. 2003; Li 2007; Mosse 2004, 2005).[2] Ultimately, however, and despite continuous engagement with informants, I retained the right to interpret the data. This is necessary to guarantee a critical approach, which "distinguishes critical theory from problem-solving theory, where the latter takes for granted the framework of existing power relations and institutions and is concerned with the smooth functioning of the system. By contrast, critical theory calls the very framework into question and seeks to analyze how it is maintained and changed" (Ford 2003, 121; see also Cox 1981). "Critical," then (like the term "politics") does not mean "negative." Yet it often connotes this with the people involved in a scholar's research. I hope, therefore, that this book will show that a balance between "critical" and "engagement" can lead to findings that are ethnographically robust yet attentive to structural power, and why this is highly necessary.

After the first year of my fieldwork, finding this balance—and dealing with its tensions—was vital to realize what became the main objective of the book: to study peace parks as a contemporary manifestation of the neoliberal governance of conservation. During this first year, I discovered that the neoliberal element is crucial; it is neoliberal conservation that is the true frontier of contemporary global conservation. The argument in the book centers on an effort to more clearly define the politics of neoliberal conservation, which coalesces around dynamics of consensus, antipolitics, and marketing. Specifically, I will argue that the politics of contemporary neoliberal conservation revolves around the framing of contradictory realities in consensus terms, which curtails the space for open discussion of different and divergent interests through various tactics of antipolitics and actively markets solutions and institutions in order to acquire and induce legitimacy, acceptance, and ownership. This argument implicates the popularization of what could be called the "postmodern frontier," namely an epistemological struggle over what constitute construction and reality with regard to nature, conservation, and development.

These modes of politics are arguably broader than conservation; they often seem to be a general feature of the global neoliberal political economy. But nature conservation is salient here, as conservation actors try to convince audiences that our lives are still steeped in and dependent on biophysical, natural realities. The central conclusion, therefore, holds that this epistemological struggle in conservation is set to become one of the major struggles of our time; a struggle that will define the relations between humans and their natural environments for the foreseeable future. The book's relevance transcends southern Africa: it is an attempt to define and understand the contemporary frontiers of conservation and the ways in which these are changing under the influence of political-economic pressures. At the same time, the southern African context is critical; actors from this region have been crucial in influencing transfrontier conservation globally, and the context embeds the study in ethnographic and material realities that give it place-based relevance. The frontiers of conservation transcend particularities of space and place, yet they can only be understood through these particularities and their associated material and discursive contexts, conditions, and struggles.

Acknowledgments

The biggest joy of traveling is meeting people and hearing their stories. During the travels that led to this book I have met and heard many. I am grateful first and foremost to those who spent time talking to me, teaching me, and giving me insight into their lives. I have tremendously enjoyed all the engagements throughout and after my research for this book, and I hope the account does justice to these engagements, even though I know some of my informants will be critical about my desire to call the framework into question and to analyze how it is maintained and changed. I respect this fully, which is one important reason why I made the informants anonymous except for those who explicitly gave me permission to use their real names. Another reason is that the book is ultimately not about my informants but about broader social and political-economic structures that they were struggling with as much as I was (and still am). An understanding of these structures requires working through these struggles, but they should not be personalized in the process. I ask of the reader, especially those knowledgeable about the study area, to bear this in mind.

Besides those who were "subjected" to my study, I owe a great debt of gratitude to all those who facilitated, cooperated, and helped me with my research and made my various stays in the region so much nicer. Thanks to

Maxi Schoeman, Hussein Solomon, Anton Du Plessis, Gerhard Wolmarans, Roland Henwood, Rina Du Toit, Marieta Buys, and all my colleagues at the Political Science Department of the University of Pretoria; the vu University master's students Julia Wittmayer, Inge Droog, Bartjan Bakker, and Chris Büscher; my colleagues and friends at the Centre for Environment, Agriculture and Development at the University of KwaZulu-Natal, Monique Salomon, Maxwell Mudhara, Rob Fincham, Thabile Khuboni, Zanele Shezi, Gail du Toit, Michael Malinga, and Senzo Mthethwa, who passed away much too early on 18 May 2007; at PLAAS, Ben Cousins, Ursula Arends, Frank Matose, Barbara Tapela, Mafaniso Hara, and Moenieba Isaacs; Munyaradzi Saruchera; André du Toit; and all the others who helped in ways big and small.

The research for this book would not have been possible without the amazing support from various organizations in the Netherlands. Many thanks to Jan Willem Gunning, Jacques van der Gaag, Jeroen van Spijk, and the Amsterdam Institute for International Development, which provided the seed funding to get the research going. My academic home during the research was the Department of Social and Cultural Anthropology of the vu University Amsterdam. I want to thank all my colleagues at the department for their collegiality, great lunch meetings, discussions, and the stimulating environment. Extra special thanks go to the various members of the management team for all their support, André Droogers, Ina Keuper, Oscar Salemink, Ton Salman, and Freek Colombijn; Erella Grassiani and Tijo Salverda; and the very efficient secretariat, Anouk, Marleen, and Annet. I am also grateful to other colleagues at the Faculty of Social Sciences, too many to mention here with one exception: a special thanks to Dean Bert Klandermans. During my Ph.D. studies, I worked part-time at another institute of the vu University Amsterdam: its Centre for International Cooperation. They enabled me to participate in the types of projects that I also ended up studying, which provided me with invaluable additional insights. In the nearly six years I worked there, I greatly enjoyed the interaction with a very talented team of colleagues, most especially those in the Natural Resource Management unit and the many colleagues in the Netherlands and abroad with whom I worked on several projects. I cannot name them all, but have to mention Chris Reij, Wendelien Tuyp, Sabina di Prima, and my two very dear mentors, William Critchley and Stephen Turner.

Two more institutions deserve special credit. The first is my current academic home: the Institute of Social Studies of the Erasmus University Rotterdam. Thanks to all my colleagues and students over the years for support, collegiality, and a truly stimulating environment. Extra special thanks to my colleagues in the agriculture and environment specializations, Murat Arsel, Max Spoor, Jun Borras, Lorenzo Pellegrini, and Ben White, and all other colleagues—current and previous—in staff group IV. I need to mention Linda Hererra here separately; she encouraged me tremendously while she was still at the institute. The second is my academic home away from home: the University of Johannesburg in South Africa, especially the Department of Geography, Environmental Management and Energy Studies. I am indebted to many colleagues and friends for their support, but none more so than Harold Annegarn, who has given me the most ideal environment, facilities, and support to broaden my (post-Ph.D.) academic and intellectual horizons.

As is clear by now, this book developed out of my Ph.D. project, and I owe an immense amount of gratitude to my dissertation supervisors: Ton Dietz, Henk Overbeek, and Bernhard Venema. I could not have wished for a more supportive and intellectually stimulating supervisory team. Many thanks also to James Ferguson, James McCarthy, Rosaleen Duffy, Mohamed Salih, Robert Fincham, Anton Du Plessis, and Oscar Salemink for stimulating comments and questions, and playing a very special and supportive role during my Ph.D. trajectory and defense.

While the current book developed from my dissertation, it has dramatically changed and—so I hope—improved since I defended it in early 2009. In this process, I have been supported by many colleagues and friends, whose generosity, humor, intellectual engagement, and wisdom have all left their marks on the book. Rosaleen Duffy, Dan Brockington, Wolfram Dressler, James Ferguson, Michael Schoon, Sander Chan, Eric Deibel, William Critchley, and Murat Arsel read (parts of) the manuscript and critically commented on previous versions. I cannot thank them enough. Jim Igoe and Paige West read the manuscript several times; their engagement with the manuscript has gone far beyond what can be expected from colleagues, and I am deeply indebted to them for their astute comments, advice, and insight.

Of course, a manuscript not only depends on those who read it and provide comments, but also on those who are part of the intellectual and amicable context within which it develops. These are truly many, and I cannot even begin to name all of those I am in one way or another indebted to. At the risk of missing some people, I do have to mention some names. I am incredibly fortunate to be part of an international group of scholars with whom I share a broader agenda of studying the political economy of conservation. This group seems to be growing every day, but here I want to specifically mention Dan Brockington, Wolfram Dressler, Rosaleen Duffy, Rob Fletcher, Jim Igoe, Katja Neves, Sian Sullivan, and Paige West. Colleagues such as these are special and I truly feel that this book is part of the bigger project we are all involved in, even though the mistakes in it can only be attributed to me. Other dear friends and colleagues—besides the ones previously mentioned—with whom I have discussed the arguments contained in the book include Philip Quarles van Ufford, Webster Whande, Elna de Beer, Max Spoor, Ken MacDonald, Catherine Corson, Frank Matose, and Aysem Mert.

There is one more person who deserves special credit: my editor at Duke University Press, Courtney Berger. Her faith in the project, astute comments along the way, and continuing support throughout truly brought this book to where it is now. Courtney, I cannot begin to tell you how much I learned from you. This book would never have been possible without your support and guidance; thank you. At Duke, I also want to acknowledge Christine Choi and all other staff who have been invaluable in getting the manuscript through the various editorial stages.

Finally, I would like to thank my family and friends all around the world for their love and support over the years—you all know who you are and what you mean to me. A special word of thanks to my parents, Henk and Lenny Büscher, for their unwavering support, love, and inspiration. I dedicate this book to my wife, Stacey Büscher-Brown. All of this would not make sense without her; she is the love of my life.

While this completes the acknowledgments of people I have met, worked with, befriended, and am close to, I want to end by acknowledging a group of people that I am not sure I have met, and perhaps do not even know: the reviewers of my articles over the years. I have learned much from their constructive and engaged feedback, for which I am grateful. This is therefore also a good place to acknowledge the journals where some portions of this book were published earlier. Portions of chapters 2 and 7 originally appeared as "Seeking Telos in the 'Transfrontier': Neoliberalism and the Transcending of Community Conservation in Southern Africa," *Environment and Planning A* 42 (3): 644–60; and "Derivative Nature: Interrogating the Value of Conservation in 'Boundless Southern Africa,'" *Third World*

Quarterly 31 (2): 259–76. Earlier portions of chapter 5 originally appeared in "Anti-politics as Political Strategy: Neoliberalism and Transfrontier Conservation in Southern Africa," *Development and Change* 41 (1): 29–51. Finally, small portions of several chapters appeared earlier in Bram Büscher and Wolfram Dressler, "Commodity Conservation: The Restructuring of Community Conservation in South Africa and the Philippines," *Geoforum* 43 (3): 367–76; and Bram Büscher and Michael Schoon, "Competition over Conservation: Governance, Cooperation and Negotiating Transfrontier Conservation," *Journal of International Wildlife Law and Policy* 12 (1): 33–59.

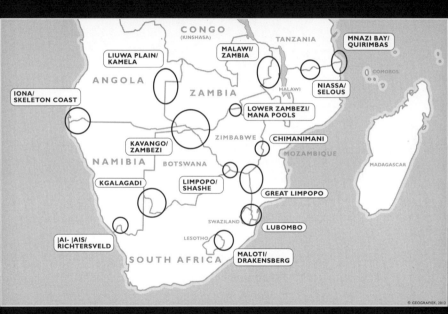

MAP 1 Southern African region indicating existing and potential Transfrontier Conservation Areas © GEOGRAFIEK, 2012.

MAP 2 Maloti-Drakensberg Transfrontier Conservation and Development Area ©
GEOGRAFIEK, 2012.

FRONTIERS OF CONSERVATION

"The global solution": this is the appealing slogan of one of the most powerful conservation actors that promotes transfrontier conservation areas or "peace parks," large conservation areas that aim to protect biodiversity and stimulate development across international boundaries. Peace parks have become a global phenomenon. Over the past fifteen years, they have been established throughout the world and "generated a tremendous enthusiasm in the conservation community" (Mittermeier, Kormos, Mittermeier, Sandwith et al. 2005, 41). Promoted by Conservation International, the World Conservation Union, and other members of the conservation establishment, peace parks have quickly become an important conservation paradigm because "the transboundary element can act as a multiplier, greatly amplifying the benefits protected areas already provide." These benefits include: "moving across political boundaries to protect a transboundary ecosystem in its entirety" and "reuniting communities divided by borders or allowing mobile peoples to move across their traditional territories more easily" (41). But that is not all. Peace parks add yet another element to the conservation package, namely "the capacity to reduce tensions or even to help resolve conflicts between countries, in particular those stemming from boundary disputes." It is this peace-making dimension, according to proponents, that "enlarges the range of benefits parks provide in a significant way" and "also provides powerful evidence for one of the central tenets of conservation—that protected areas are not only necessary to secure the planet's ecological integrity but, more broadly, that they are an essential component of any healthy, peaceful, and productive society" (41).

In this book, I am equally interested in why peace parks have become such a popular conservation paradigm and have created such incredible enthusiasm in the conservation community. My approach is different from that of the conservation establishment, however. While I am fascinated by the answers given and will critically investigate these in the book, I am concerned more with why actors in the conservation community feel that they must portray transfrontier conservation so jubilantly. Or why others, in this case the South African nongovernmental organization (NGO) Peace Parks Foundation, believe that peace parks are "the global solution." Transfrontier conservation areas are not simply promoted. They are presented as the new telos of conservation; conservation the way it should be. In its peace parks incarnation, so the message goes, conservation moves beyond being a vehicle to safeguard biodiversity and help rural communities prosper. It now also aims to bring peace to nations. To *all* nations, according to Nelson Mandela, the former president of South Africa and a patron of the Peace Parks Foundation: "I know of no political movement, no philosophy, no ideology, which does not agree with the peace parks concept as we see it going into fruition today. It is a concept that can be embraced by all. In a world beset by conflict and division, peace is one of the cornerstones of the future. Peace parks are a building block in this process, not only in our region, but potentially in the entire world."[1]

We know from scholarly work that conservation and development solutions are usually framed so that they are attractive to (potential) donors (see Ferguson 1994; Mosse 2005). This, however, does not explain why advocates of peace parks have amplified their discourse to such grandiose proportions or try to position protected areas more broadly as an "essential component of any healthy, peaceful, and productive society." Moreover, this jubilation seems strangely out of place. Protected areas have—on the whole—done little to halt global biodiversity loss, which became abundantly clear from the 2010 Global Biodiversity Outlook (Secretariat of the Convention on Biological Diversity 2010). Protected areas also hold a poor social record, particularly in southern Africa, the book's region of concern. Displacements, racialized dispossession, and lack of access to resources are all intimately connected to the historical development and contemporary governance of protected areas and conservation more broadly (see W. Adams and Hutton 2007; Brockington, Duffy, and Igoe 2008; Dowie 2009; Galvin and Haller 2008; Hughes 2010). If peace parks greatly amplify the benefits of parks, might they equally amplify their shady aspects? And if so, how does this fit with the amplified jubilation that peace parks have brought to conservation?

In the tradition of political ecology, one of my foundational assumptions is that we cannot begin to address these questions and the broader issues they give rise to without placing conservation squarely within historically informed political-economic and social contexts and associated power constellations across interconnected scales and locales. It is these contexts and constellations that have framed and influenced the societies that conservation so eagerly wants to be an essential component of (and, in fact, has always been). Moreover, they have evolved dialectically with broader nature-society relations over time, thereby preconfiguring and structurating how conservation is practiced, perceived, and legitimated.

Two historically specific but intertwined sets of political-economic and social contexts are especially important for my analysis. First, the demands of a postcolonial society have rendered the "de facto extraterritorial" or "extra-sovereign" status that many parks occupy in (southern) Africa more fragile but certainly not prostrate (Mbembe 2000, 284).[2] Some areas are still protected from society, but this no longer means that they can ignore societal interests as they did during colonial times.[3] In southern Africa, community-based natural resources management has been—and to some degree still is—the political umbrella under which these demands have been articulated most forcefully (see Hulme and Murphree 2001). The second context relates to the demands of the global neoliberal political economy. These, too, have drastically changed conservation. While conservation and capitalism share a long and intertwined history, neoliberalism is truly reconstituting conservation as a tool for the expansion of capital and, in doing so, reconfiguring its ideals, practices, and representations (see, e.g., Arsel and Büscher 2012; Büscher 2009; Igoe, Neves, and Brockington 2010). In short, the book investigates how conservation actors and transfrontier interventions in southern Africa keep conservation legitimate in and functional to a postcolonial, neoliberal political economy.[4] Furthermore, I seek to understand the politics involved in this process and the social and material struggles to which they give rise.

I fuse ethnography and political economy to understand the complex structures and agencies that influence these processes and struggles. This combination of methods is powerful. It heeds structural political-economic questions about "control over the means of production and the structures of law and force that support systemic inequalities" while simultaneously paying attention to the contingent nature of things (Li 2007, 11). According to Paige West, this "is particularly important if one takes seriously Karl Marx's argument about the universalizing tendency of capital but if one also sees the evidence of local articulations with capital as more creative and diverse than Marx anticipated" (2006, 266). My entry point is an in-depth conceptual engagement with neoliberalism.[5] Neoliberalism "has become nearly hegemonic in the most powerful national and international arenas over the past two decades," and it needs to be engaged if political economy is to be taken seriously (McCarthy 2005, 996).[6]

This is especially the case for environmental conservation where many organizations and actors feel marginal compared to "big" global politics around trade, energy, and security. I heard this complaint often: politicians do not see or understand the value of conservation. It is not taken seriously as a "big issue," while my informants believe it ultimately eclipses all other concerns. Conservation, they told me, needs to become a competitive land-use option, a market where the value of nature's "services" would be visible and clear. Above all, I was told, conservation needs to be economically profitable, otherwise politicians and stakeholders were not going to care. Conservation actors truly felt that they had to "sell nature to save it" (McAfee 1999). This sense of political ranking adds impetus to conservation actors' drive to appease the dominant paradigm. Neoliberal conservation is the new frontier—one that conservation actors worldwide are eager to conquer.[7]

Peace parks are important tools in this conquest. Their enlistment of many new actors to the cause of conservation testifies to their ability to turn contradictory political-economic realities into reified and attractive win-win propositions. This ability is the hallmark of the politics of neoliberal conservation. Thus, while neoliberal conservation reality is characterized by (racialized) dispossession, inequality, and persistent and accelerating environmental degradation (see Dowie 2009; Ferguson 2006; Gibson 1999; Kovel 2002; Secretariat of the Convention on Biological Diversity 2010; Sullivan 2006), neoliberal conservation discourse "moves beyond a world of win-win solutions to a world of win-win-win-win-win-win-win (or win[7] if you like) solutions that benefit: corporate investors, national economies, biodiversity, local people, Western consumers, development agencies and the conservation organisations that receive funding from those agencies to undertake large interventions" (Igoe and Brockington 2007, 435).

But we must take that argument further. One of the main tenets of the book is that in a neoliberal political economy tensions between material realities and reified representations are political opportunities that must be exploited to gain competitive advantage. Transforming the frontier is not optional in a neoliberal political economy; it is a necessity. In order to gain legitimacy, credibility, and support in the conservation marketplace, actors must exploit the cracks between constructions and realities of complex and contradictory socio-ecological dynamics. This is what many conservation agents do in their struggle to influence conservation and development dynamics in particular settings. I follow them and their stakeholders in this struggle, and in the process I analyze peace parks as contemporary manifestations of the neoliberal governance of conservation and development in southern Africa and the contradictions and struggles they unleash and conceal.

Reified Representations and Contradictory Realities

The dynamics of environmental degradation, biodiversity loss, and continued legacies of racial inequality make the translation from contradictory realities to jubilant discourses awkward. It frustrates many conservation and development professionals tremendously. One of my informants complained around mid-2005, "in conservation you feel you are playing catch-up all the time." He and his colleagues constantly had to "tiptoe through the socioeconomic agendas." It's better if conservation changes its message, and presents it more forcefully, he believed: "more doom-and-gloom messages so that people will listen." But neither he nor the intervention he worked for put this into practice. In a postcolonial neoliberal context, legitimacy in conservation and development is rarely obtained through the doom and gloom that always lurks around the corner. The orientation is "future positive" (see Edwards 1999; Mosse 2005), attuned to our "time zone of amazing promises" (Haraway 1997, 41).

An example from 9 March 2005 illustrates this. After having received a million euros from a Dutch lottery, the Peace Parks Foundation's (PPF) chief executive and a program manager visited the Dutch embassy in Pretoria, South Africa, to present the foundation's mission, goals, and operations. Through a contact at the embassy, I was able to attend the presentation. The program manager said, "Peace parks developed out of African history." He explained that the Berlin Conference of 1884–85 divided Africa among colonial powers, completely disregarding ethnicities and animal migration routes. For a long time, even after independence, African borders could not be discussed, but the billionaire Anton Rupert dared to do so when he met with the Mozambican president Joaquim Chissano in 1990 to explore possibilities for a cross-border park between South Africa and Mozambique. These plans eventually led to the founding of the PPF in 1997, with the aim of stimulating and supporting the establishment of transfrontier conservation areas across southern Africa. But the chief executive said, "peace parks are not necessarily for the protection of biodiversity; they are mostly for development" because "tourism is the biggest supplier of jobs." While admitting that biodiversity conservation is the main objective, the chief executive confided in us that "after a while you find out that people are more important than the environment."

As the presentation continued, we were told that the PPF exists chiefly to make space for peace parks, help with facilitation, and train wildlife rangers. Facilitation means to "oil the government machinery" and "fix what is broke" by supplying governments with staff, technical aids, and advice. Visibly proud, the PPF representatives told us that most southern African presidents act as the foundation's patrons, while Mandela is both a cofounder and an honorary patron. On the PPF's request, Mandela even traveled to Asia to explore possibilities for a peace park between North and South Korea. Intrigued, I shared my experience some years earlier of traveling the border of the region's flagship peace park: the Great Limpopo Transfrontier Park between Mozambique, South Africa, and Zimbabwe. Along its borders live many different peoples, among them the Tsonga. Several Tsonga men told me that they knew the PPF and lamented that as members of a poor community, they do not "have access to Thabo Mbeki" (the then South African president) and cannot "send Nelson Mandela anywhere." The PPF's chief executive agreed that the five million people living next to the Great Limpopo in South Africa were not yet benefiting and that "this is a problem." He then mentioned how proud he was of the community projects in the Mozambican Limpopo National Park: "In Limpopo, the community engagement process is easier. They can decide if they want to stay, and be fenced in, or move out." He was aware that the resettlement process in Limpopo, backed by the World Bank, is highly controversial, and added that "there just aren't many better ways of doing it." He quickly moved on to another topic. What is important according to him is that "politicians just love the peace parks concept: It has everything, conservation, development, it is green. They love signing the contracts."

Supported by global business elites interested in nature conservation and driven by a deeply neoliberal outlook, the PPF wields enormous power over the regional peace parks agenda, including over the national ministries and conservation parastatals officially responsible for implementing and governing individual TFCAS (see Büscher and Dietz 2005; Draper, Spierenburg, and Wels 2004; Ramutsindela 2007; Schoon 2009; Wolmer 2003). The exposé also illustrates the politics at play when reified representations confront contradictory realities. In what I will refer to as the "peace parks discourse," most conspicuously endorsed by the PPF, difficult questions on contradictory material realities are seen as disruptive and thus preferably avoided. I am interested in the politics involved in how proponents of peace parks like the PPF negotiate the tensions between reified representations and contradictory realities. Moreover, I ask why and how the dominant peace parks discourse is supported, reinterpreted, or resisted by other actors in transfrontier conservation.

This is crucial because the peace parks discourse is but one representation of the promises of transfrontier conservation. While regionally dominant and attractive for international donors, it relates only precariously to individual transfrontier conservation interventions. One of these is the Maloti-Drakensberg Transfrontier Project (MDTP), the intervention of my ethnographic focus. Initiated to protect globally significant biodiversity and stimulate local development through ecotourism in the high mountains between Lesotho and South Africa, the Maloti-Drakensberg is somewhat of an outlier in the regional peace parks picture. It does not boast the so-called typically African wildlife experiences, focusing instead on landscapes and less spectacular taxa. In its implementation, the Maloti-Drakensberg Transfrontier Project also differed. It was funded by the Global Environment Facility as a single, massive cross-border intervention (as opposed to the often multiple interventions involved in other TFCAS), the PPF was only marginally involved, and many implementers were not very charmed by the peace parks discourse. Yet, while the dominant discourse was regarded with suspicion, the contradictory dynamics and practices behind the peace parks discourse featured equally in the Maloti-Drakensberg. A brief empirical illustration from 2007 testifies.

Malefiloane is a small village in Lesotho's Botha-Bothe district. One of the community facilitators for the Maloti-Drakensberg Transfrontier Project introduced me to the members of Balala lihloliloeng me o phele Malefiloane, which translates to "conserving biodiversity to earn a living" or "we conserve to live out of what we conserved." This local handicraft group established by the transfrontier project consisted of twenty-two people but this day there are only five. The community facilitator informed me that the group was going to discuss its constitution. The group needed a constitution, with the chief's stamp of approval, to open a bank account to store the group's earnings. The community facilitator introduced me and asked the group how the drafting of the constitution and the bylaws went. According to one member, they "made progress." We were also informed that the group had asked the chief and the community council for a place to hold meetings, especially when it rained. It would be ideal for them to build a little shelter with wood from the area, which they could purchase from their savings. The group was also into saving and credit modalities: every time they sell something they should put 10 percent into the group's account "to keep the group going," according to the facilitator.

When the meeting finished, the community facilitator said that her job is very challenging. She has to do a lot more than just facilitating. Sometimes she comes to a meeting and finds some of the women crying because they have been beaten by their husbands ("then you have to drop your agenda"). Another time, conflict arose when everyone wanted to individually start selling handicrafts to Liphofung, the nearby cultural center. She managed to resolve it and keep the group together. The community facilitator had a vision about where she wanted to take the group, but "with the people's level of education and the culture it is very difficult," she told me. Just to explain financial percentages is a big thing, as is dealing with money in general. It is also difficult to deal with interpersonal relationships. Telling the truth when someone is not functioning can be hard, especially when people are related. All these things make the facilitator's job very challenging. What added to her frustration was that members of the head office of the Maloti-Drakensberg Transfrontier Project in Maseru, Lesotho, did not understand the situation: "They think that training is enough. For them it means that part of the work plan or action plan has been fulfilled." Moreover, she added, "They think that when you have trained people they are empowered, but in reality it is not like that. For real empowerment you must make sure you have local leadership, accountability, and independent action, and this takes a long time." According to the facilitator, people talk about capacity building so easily, as if it's something you can do in bits and pieces, but "this is a process." She further complained that many people in the head office don't want to attend the group's meetings because they have so many other meetings or because "the food at this meeting is not good enough."

In this and other occasions, the community facilitator tried to show me what happens when discourses on community-based transfrontier conservation confront the complexities and messiness of everyday local life. The ethnographic richness, intricacies, and contradictions of local life in the Maloti-Drakensberg form a stark contrast to the grand narratives and global solution of the peace parks discourse. Yet both are part of the frontiers of conservation. In investigating these dynamics, I am especially interested in the political practices they entail. Recent "aidnography" has been attentive to these practices through ethnographic research committed to close but critical engagement with conservation and development agents (see Lewis et al. 2003; Mosse 2004, 2005; Quarles van Ufford, Giri, and Mosse 2003). I have also sought to engage with proponents of transfrontier conservation and implementers; chapters 3 to 7 analyze the politics the implementers of the Maloti-Drakensberg Transfrontier Project employed to negotiate material realities and reified representations and how other actors responded with their own political strategies. However, adding up these political practices will not lead to an exposition of the infinite variety of interests and strategies that actors hold or deploy. Rather, I will show that these political practices—in all their variety—are deeply influenced by political-economic structures.[8] If neoliberal conservation is the frontier of conservation; this book dissects the politics involved in transforming the frontier.

Frontier Politics

Frontiers, clearly, connote much more than parks across borders. They are peculiar spaces, separating the usual from the unusual and the possible from the impossible. A frontier is "an edge of space and time: a zone of not yet—not yet mapped, not yet regulated" (Tsing 2005, 29). Frontiers are the moments that new knowledge is created and that open minds to new possibilities, new ways of thought, and different practices. The frontier, therefore, cannot be just a border. It will always be a space on its own, riddled with contradictions and struggles, mired in ambiguities and uncertainties. It is this space that allows the negotiation of the inherent tensions between material realities and reified representations.

Conceptualizing frontiers in this way has major implications. It means that opening new frontiers is a profoundly political act, tied up with interests and shaped by power constellations. Indeed, I argue that the negotiation of frontiers occurs as a particular set of political practices. This sets the book apart from related interventions, particularly in anthropology and development studies. While many authors ultimately stress the partial, limited, and refractory nature of their ethnographic observations, I emphasize the structural features to which I believe my ethnography directed me. This is why I argue for ethnographic research that links different levels of abstraction, has a special eye for power relations, and combines agency with structure. Only in this way can the book account for neoliberalism's diversity of contextualized and place-particular hybridizations and say something about the remarkable congruencies in how neoliberalism embeds itself in the conduct of governing social-ecological change. This has nothing to do with trying to "identify hidden motives" behind observations (Li 2007, 9). Rather, I emphasize that ethnographic interventions are political and part of the frontier politics that they investigate. Yes, we must always acknowledge that "local articulations with capital are more creative and diverse than Marx anticipated" (West 2006, 266), but we cannot not hide behind this fact. It is in this vein that I will conclude the book by going back to the politics in political ecology in order to give fresh impetus to a positive politics that critically engages with neoliberal solutions and interventions while opening space to think about just and sustainable futures.

This is not straightforward, and the scale of the challenge should be appreciated. After all, frontiers have special significance in a neoliberal political economy. Neoliberalism needs frontiers. For all its idiosyncrasies and contradictions, neoliberalism, and in fact the wider capitalist system, has proven remarkably resilient and able to overcome resistance. This is not to say that neoliberal expansion is linear or without boundaries. Rather, neoliberal capitalism is able to deal with its own systemic boundaries, because both its excesses and its alternatives can be turned into new sites for commodity production (see Hartwick and Peet 2003; Harvey 2010; Kovel 2002). To put it stronger still: neoliberal capitalism thrives on frontiers. It thrives on the borders between the known and the unknown, the possible and the (yet) impossible; this is the source of its "crazy vitality" and dynamism and the reason why Marx paid homage to capitalism (Berman 1988, 92; Thrift 2005).

Fuse this dynamic with the "disorderly" and violent demands and constitutions of African postcolonial societies and it becomes even clearer that opening up new frontiers is deeply political (see, e.g., Chabal and Daloz 1999; Mbembe 2001, 88). In a study of transfrontier conservation in southern Africa, this above all means dealing with dynamics of racial inequality and questions of sovereignty implied by the notion of the transfrontier. Conservation, David Hughes forcefully argues, "continues to produce the aesthetics, symbols, and fables of white privilege" (2010, 133; see also Kepe 2009). What started as violent, "racialized dispossession" of "African property and personhood" in the context of colonial rule and white occupation of large tracts of land continues to starkly influence affairs and relations to this day (D. S. Moore 2005, 12), particularly as many whites in southern Africa and abroad persist in favoring African nature over African people (Hughes 2010). In the case of the Maloti-Drakensberg Transfrontier Project between South Africa and Lesotho, this dark shadow appeared many an instance: from Sotho fear that South Africa was going to "steal" more land to racialized struggles between the white-dominated South African and black Lesotho project-implementation teams (see chapter 4).

In addition to being imbued with racialized histories, transfrontier conservation denotes new spatial ordering: the reorganization of the regulation and governance of nature and people in particular places. This implies sovereignty, not just the prerogative of states within political boundaries but—following Achille Mbembe (2001, 78–79)—the subjectivities and disciplinary tactics created to control and direct people. In this way, peace parks extend and modify earlier ideas and practices around community-based conservation (CBC). CBC emerged in the 1970s and 1980s as a response to colonial top-down fortress-conservation models that excluded people from protected areas (see Hulme and Murphree 2001; Kusters et al. 2006; Ros-Tonen and Dietz 2005). This conservation discourse, built on ideals of respect for indigenous knowledge, awareness of historical injustices, and the compatibility of human development and conservation of nature, matured when neoliberalism was becoming increasingly hegemonic, making it likely, in James McCarthy's words, that CBC discourses were "influenced by the larger policy environment in which they developed" (2005, 996). The result is a continuous amalgamation of mixed "institutional forms and political agendas" that favor particular constructions of governance of conservation and development around faith in markets to assign roles to communities, the state, and other stakeholders (998). Transfrontier conservation builds on and further transforms these institutional forms and political agendas to create novel subjectivities and disciplinary tactics in postcolonial neoliberal spaces.

Such are the frontiers of contemporary neoliberal conservation: approached, transcended, and transgressed in highly uneven and contradictory ways; imbued with historical and contemporary dynamics of race and sovereignty and related issues of citizenship and democracy. Such are therefore the conditions in which frontier politics in transfrontier conservation is played out.

Neoliberal Conservation

The starting point for my framework of frontier politics is an in-depth conceptualization of neoliberalism. This conceptualization is in line with an understanding of frontiers as spaces that allow for the negotiation of the tensions between material realities and reified representations and hence the central contradiction in neoliberal conservation that emanates from the above discussion. It is a metacontradiction, and one that I define as the core of the current politics of neoliberal conservation, namely the ability of its proponents to produce and favor discourses seemingly free of contradictions while they saturate its practices. Now, the fact that there is a difference between rhetoric and reality when it comes to (neoliberal) conservation has been well established (see Benjaminsen and Svarstad 2010; Büscher and Dressler 2007). The more interesting question is how neoliberalism is able to survive, even thrive, despite major contradictions and crises. This question animates the frontier politics that my conceptualization of neoliberal conservation will lead to.

Neoliberalism is notoriously hard to define. Many scholars prefer to speak of a neoliberalization process rather than a "generic" or "fixed and homogenous" neoliberalism that can be attributed causality (Castree 2008b, 137; see also Brenner, Peck, and Theodore 2010; Peck 2010). A key element of neoliberalization that comes out of this literature is its variegated character: "it produces geoinstitutional differentiation across places, territories and scales; but it does this systematically, as a pervasive, endemic feature of its basic operational logic" (Brenner, Peck, and Theodore 2010, 328). As Noel Castree reminds us, the point is to abstract from theory and practice generic modalities—"variants or hybrid forms"—that can aid and direct our understanding of the fundamentals of the neoliberalization of nature seen across the globe (2008a, 157; see also 2008b). Two such modalities of neoliberalism's operational logic are competition and commodification (see Harvey 2005; McDonald and Ruiters 2005). Neoliberalization from this perspective requires that an increasing amount of life's facets become embedded in competitive markets and subject to trade in monetary terms. This does not necessarily involve coercion: "In contemporary times, neoliberal rationality informs action by many regimes and furnishes the concepts that inform the government of free individuals who are then induced to self-manage according to market principles of discipline, efficiency, and competitiveness" (Ong 2006, 4). Hence, the dynamic of the market (ideally) forces its participants to discipline themselves to do what is required to remain competitive in selling their product (which increasingly includes one's agency and identity).

Clearly, neoliberalism is many things to many people and thus often causes conceptual confusion (McCarthy and Prudham 2004). Neoliberalism is at the same time an ideology, a politics, a discourse, a system of rules and regulations, and much more. James Ferguson (2010) rightly criticizes the many "uses of neoliberalism," as well as the often-fuzzy analyses to which these lead. Moreover, as Becky Mansfield (2004) points out, neoliberalism must not be attributed more coherence and dominance than is justified. The focus should be on understanding what Neil Brenner and Nik Theodore (2002) term "actually existing neoliberalism," or the inherent unevenness and contradictions in the neoliberalization of actual spaces, processes, and relations, such as the construction, governance, and marketing of peace parks. To facilitate this focus and for purposes of analytical clarity, I make a distinction between neoliberalism as a system of rule with particular modes of devolved governance and neoliberalism as a political ideology with particular modes of political conduct. While this move is not unfamiliar among scholars (e.g., Li 2007), the tendency is to focus on governmental techniques rather than political conduct. I aim to emphasize the latter, although it should be clear that the two are deeply intertwined and dialectically co-constituted in practice.

Modes of Devolved Governance

To illustrate the concept of devolved governance, a glimpse at the area of my ethnographic focus, the Maloti-Drakensberg, is useful. This area is an immensely complicated socio-ecological space. Mountainous, with abrupt and major differences in height, the region is known for its ruggedness, spectacular landscapes, and rare indigenous fauna and flora. The Zulu people refer to the area as uKhahlamba (the "barrier of spears"), while the

Afrikaans term "Drakensberg" means "dragon mountains." Both names give a sense of the ecology of the area and the people who live there. Life in the barrier of spears takes many, often challenging, forms, shaped by the ebbs and flows of seasons, intricate socio-ecological dynamics, custom, tradition, different (ideas about) modernities, and very particular postcolonial forces and structures. Influencing the governance of these dynamics is equally challenging. In evaluating their options to stimulate productive conservation and development outcomes, the implementers of the Maloti-Drakensberg Transfrontier Project stressed that many governance methods were on the table: "flagged areas need not become fenced nature reserves, as there are a range of 'tools' in the conservation tool box: protected areas, conservancies, stewardship agreements, incentives and education programmes can all help in achieving the targets."[9] Even though many South African Transfrontier Conservation Area (TFCA) implementers privately preferred state-led, top-down conservation measures, they made sure that devolved and participatory governance mechanisms were stressed in their communication to the outside. Two distinctly neoliberal devolved-governance mechanisms became especially important: tourism and payments for environmental services (see chapter 7).

I conceptualize devolved governance as the induced self-regulation of public affairs by governmental and nongovernmental actors according to general, structural principles. Often operationalized as "incentives," "education," "benchmarking," or "capacity building"; many of these principles have been around for a long time, but in later chapters I show that devolved governance practice is changing quickly. In the international relations literature, it is argued that the historical context of this change is a shift from *government* to *governance,* indicating the increased levels of power of nonstate actors vis-à-vis the state, and therefore the necessity for more-devolved and hybrid methods of rule (Rosenau and Czempiel 1992).[10] Related to southern Africa, this development finds further roots in colonial forms of direct and indirect rule that still influence contemporary postcolonial governance (Mamdani 1996). It is in this context that neoliberalism was able to thrive as a system of rule; one that has long been and continues to be strongly endorsed by many dominant state, interstate, and private actors (see Harvey 2005; Peck 2010).

Hence, contrary to authors such as James Rosenau (1997) who see little normative implication in this shift, the increased number of (influential) actors has led to a very specific and normative type of governance system—

that of devolved neoliberal governance. Modalities of capitalist markets, such as commodification and competition, thus became the (self)regulatory, structural principles for (rational economic) behavior, both in the private sector and—crucially—in the public sector and civil society (see Ayers 2006; McDonald and Ruiters 2005). Competition is supposed to work as an incentive that stimulates producers of goods and services toward supplying the best product for the lowest price. Neoclassical economic logic stipulates that if the latter is not achieved, competition will force producers out of business. This logic has increasingly been transposed to conservation, rendering the legitimacy and right of existence of biodiversity increasingly subject to (economic) demand. In Kathleen McAfee's words, "Nature would earn its own right to survive through international trade in ecosystem services and permits to pollute, access to tourism and research sites, and exports of timber, minerals, and intellectual property rights to traditional crop varieties and shamans' recipes" (1999, 133). Making this work, however, requires new regulatory and disciplinary mechanisms, as well as a state that guarantees their enforcement. In neoliberal discourse, this is referred to as an "enabling environment," which signifies state reregulation rather than the deregulation so often associated with neoliberalism (see Castree 2008b; Heynen et al. 2007).

An interesting way to conceptualize commodification begins with the philosophical roots that neoliberalism shares with other forms of liberalism—a move not often made in the literature on the neoliberalization of the environment (Barnett 2005; but see Castree 2010).[11] According to Richardson (2001, 1), neoliberalism and liberalism share similar visions of "a world of peaceful democracies" and equality between individuals yet harbor distinctly dissimilar ways of dealing with different (incompatible) values. Whereas liberalism would lean toward finding an absolute answer to resolving conflicts of value (and reinstating control and order) through political judgment or military action, neoliberalism turns inherent or use values into exchange values and lets the market decide (see McDonald and Ruiters 2005). Those values that can muster market buy-in remain politically and socially legitimate, pushing other values that are less able to establish a clientele to take a backseat (West 2006, 212–13).[12] This ostensible economic equalization and subsequent market prioritization of political and social values through commodification might well be regarded as a second "great transformation," as it penetrates the human consciousness and experience to such a level that it is seen as the "normal" or "natural" state of affairs (see Harvey 2005; Polanyi 2001). In turn, this links in with the Foucauldian notion of disciplinary power about which Carolan states that it "now seeks to transform, not merely punish, by embedding within the subject what was formerly an external mechanism of control" (2005a, 366). In other words, neoliberal modes of devolved governance are being consolidated as the hegemonic social norm in terms of rules and regulations (see Gill 1995; Igoe, Neves, and Brockington 2010), which in the (southern) African context builds on more-established yet contradictory (post)colonial forms of direct and indirect rule (Mamdani 1996). In turn, the pursuit of this hegemonic social norm requires the concomitant development of particular modes of political conduct.

Modes of Political Conduct

Underlying the neoliberal ambitions to establish a new system of rule are two assumptions. The first is that neoliberalism has entered a new frontier and differs from when it was considered to be most visibly dominant during the 1980s and early 1990s. The second assumption relates to neoliberalism's "blatant universalism" (Richardson 2001, 1).[13] Discussing these assumptions clarifies why it is important to identify particular modes of political conduct. Regarding the first point, many scholars make a distinction between the structural adjustment and Washington Consensus neoliberalism of the 1980s and early 1990s and the consolidated neoliberalism of the mid-1990s and 2000s. Henk Overbeek, for instance, postulates several important moments in "the process of global restructuring and the neoliberal ascendancy" (1999, 248–49). He argues that 1980s neoliberalism should be seen as a "constructive" project, imposing structural adjustment, privatization, liberalization, and so on, while the 1990s saw the hegemonic consolidation of neoliberalism as "the global rule of capital" (248–49). Similarly, Jamie Peck and Adam Tickell argue that

> there seems to have been a shift from the pattern of deregulation and dismantlement so dominant during the 1980s, which might be characterized as "roll-back neoliberalism," to an emergent phase of active state-building and regulatory reform—an ascendant moment of "roll-out neoliberalism." In the course of this shift, the agenda has gradually moved from one preoccupied with the active *destruction and discreditation* of Keynesian-welfarist and social collectivist institutions (broadly defined) to one focused on the purposeful *construction and consolidation*

of neoliberalised state forms, modes of governance, and regulatory relations. (2002, 384, emphasis in original)

In essence, Peck and Tickell emphasize what was already mentioned,
namely that state-driven neoliberal reregulation has increasingly replaced
1980s neoliberal deregulation. A key issue therefore is the role of the state
in contemporary neoliberalism and the dissolving of the public-private
divide (Clarke 2004). In relation to Africa, Alison Ayers argues that "the
neoliberal project 'conceals its own massive use of state power, transnational and local, for the construction of civil society in its own image,'"
meaning that "the reconstitution of the public and private domains is
undertaken actively by state managers and is predominantly about reorga-
nizing (rather than bypassing) states" (2006, 328).[14] The reorganization of
the state, in turn, fits well with and has in fact enabled Graham Harrison's
(2005b) notion of a "positive-sum" view of governance, held by actors such
as the World Bank, which highly influenced how the Maloti-Drakensberg
Transfrontier Project was conceptualized and implemented.

The active reconstitution of the state and the public realm in neoliberal
terms directly relates to the second assumption. Both liberals and neoliberals are unapologetically universal in their ambitions: they believe that
(neo)liberal tenets in theory and practice hold true for all people. The
aspiration is for the global neoliberal constitution of society—a project that,
despite a highly uneven historical geography (Peck 2010, 20), so far has
succeeded remarkably well: "Neoliberalism has become hegemonic as a
mode of discourse. It has pervasive effects on ways of thought to the point
where is has become incorporated into the common-sense way many of us
interpret, live in, and understand the world" (Harvey 2005, 3). Yet, in
agreeing with this argument, one must simultaneously emphasize the
struggles inherent in neoliberal progression: "Neo-liberalism is not a constituted project implemented in the world economy, a thing that fills structures. As a political reality, neo-liberalism is *both* a broad strategy of restructuring *and* a succession of negotiated settlements, of concessions to
the rigidities and dynamics of structures, as well as the political possibilities of the moment" (Drainville 1994, 116; emphasis in the original). While
not denying neoliberalism's structurating effects, André Drainville, and
others like Becky Mansfield (2004) and Jamie Peck (2010), cautions for the
reification of neoliberalism and urges us to understand concessions to
neoliberal ideology and practices and how its progression adapts to re-

sistance. This is especially important in an African postcolonial context, where there are "distinct limits to the process of subjection," and it must "be admitted that Africa's affiliation to the bourgeois ethos remains uncertain and varies enormously from one area to another" (Bayart 2009, Li, 103; see also Ferguson 2006, 82).

Now we can identify the frontier politics that structures the book's critical analytical framework of neoliberal transfrontier conservation. Present-day neoliberalism should be conceptualized as a disciplining sociopolitical order, but one in which resistance and struggle are inherently entrenched, so particular political strategies are necessary to deal with this resistance and struggle. Based on my empirical analysis, I argue that the politics of neoliberal conservation hinge on three modes of political conduct: consensus, antipolitics, and marketing.

Consensus, Antipolitics, and Marketing

In conservation and development discourses, there is a persistent emphasis on the idea and concept of consensus. Many UN initiatives boast that they enjoy consensus,[15] and referring to peace parks as "the global solution" is clearly entrenched in consensus thinking. Where does this emphasis on consensus come from? I suggest that because there is actually less universal consensus as people increasingly have the potential power, tools, and information to follow their own individual conduits, that the rhetorical need for consensus becomes greater. After all, if one cannot bluntly force subjects into submission or if systems of rule are compromised by "escape clauses," such as sociospatial fluidity or weak enforcement (which is of course especially the case in postcolonial Africa; see Bayart 2009), three political courses of action are available to try and retain control over governance processes: actually creating consensus, making people believe that there is consensus, or positing consensus as a discursive umbrella to forge through particular political agendas. Since we can discard the first option as an illusion, my focus is on the latter two. This is obviously overly simplistic. Brute force is still often used, and many actors do try to bring about global consensuses, which is exemplified by other incessant governance buzzwords such as "institutionalization," "benchmarking," and "best practices" (Büscher and Mutimukuru 2007). Yet if one accepts that absolute (universal) consensus cannot be achieved, then political analysis has to focus on "consensus as make-believe" and "consensus as smokescreen."

To start with the latter, there is substantial evidence of actors (ab)using consensus oriented-discourses as a conceptual smokescreen so as to facilitate their own political agendas (see Büscher and Dietz 2005; Olivier de Sardan 2005).[16] In particular, consensus ideals are often used to strengthen the self-reinforcing dynamics of neoliberal devolved governance. Gerhard Anders explains how this works when he discusses the "global consensus on good governance and development":

> This consensus is phrased in the language of economic theory and legitimised by scientific rationality. Good governance and ownership are not presented as superior ideological concepts or desirable goals, but as inevitable solutions or tools to address problems that are of a technical nature. One set of tools, conditionality, creates possibilities to insert another set of tools, such as civil service reform or measures against corruption. Together they form an interlocking ensemble of self-controlling sub-systems that make other alternative forms of policy making impossible and even unthinkable. (2003, 55)

Consensus discourses also habitually end up obscuring the often-substantial differences between planned objectives and the actual effects of interventions, a dynamic very familiar to scholars working on conservation and development (see, e.g., Cornwall and Brock 2005; Dressler 2009; Goldman 2005). As we shall see in the discussions on the implementation of the Maloti-Drakensberg Transfrontier Project in chapter 4, consensus discourses can even obscure wildly divergent interpretations of the same intervention by teams working closely together.

But this point must be taken further. In line with neoliberalism's universalism, proponents increasingly fuel the belief that contradictory realities can actually disappear. There is a latent acceptance of pluralism based on the assumption that this pluralism is destined to disappear through appropriately planned and implemented technocratic governance.[17] An example is the Commission on Global Governance's definition of global governance as "the sum of the many ways individuals and institutions, public and private, manage their common affairs. It is a continuing process through which conflicting or diverse interests may be accommodated and cooperative action taken." In a review, Henk Overbeek argues that "by exclusively emphasizing the co-operative element this definition in fact eliminates any possible connotation of domination and force, which of course is also part of 'governance'" (2005, 39). He criticizes the commission for falling into the "pitfall of pluralism": "taking the plurality of actors, interests and partial structures . . . as being the essence of things, and as being essentially undetermined, unbiased, 'neutral,' rather than seeing this plurality as set in a wider hierarchical configuration of social power" (39–40). Overbeek calls this a "depoliticizing tendency," a familiar notion in conservation and development (39).

Many scholars have tried to understand why conservation and development interventions are so often subject to "depoliticizing tendencies," focusing predominantly on associated techniques of rationalizing and rendering technical what is in fact political (see, e.g., Ferguson 1994; Li 2007).[18] Nicholas Rose aptly captures the crux of the neoliberal bent on rationality and technicalization when he states that "the strategies of regulation that have made up our modern experience of 'power' are thus assembled into complexes that connect up forces and institutions deemed 'political' with apparatuses that shape and manage individual and collective conduct in relation to norms and objectives but yet are constituted as 'non-political' " (1996, 37). Hence, we are talking of antipolitics, which I argue, following Andreas Schedler (1997), is another important mode of neoliberal political conduct.

Antipolitics is a form of (denying) politics, which I define as the mediation and contestation of different interests and power struggles. Crucial, therefore, is that politics be constituted by language, communication, and deliberation (Marden 2003; Schedler 1997).[19] In Peter Marden's words, "Essentially though, it [politics] is to recognize and promote discursive contests, to uphold or contest political decisions, to contest dominant hegemonic metaphoric language that disguises alternatives or constrains choice, and finally, to recognize that decisions are made within larger discursive frames that define the parameters of the problems and the possible solutions; to have less is to deny politics" (2003, 234). More important, politics does not necessarily constitute something "bad," a point of view that aroused some observers to call for antipolitics (and "antipoliticians") as a completely separate sphere that has nothing to do with formal politics (Konrád 1984). Politics can also be a constructive engagement (Büscher and Wolmer 2007). Similarly, rationality and technocracy—two favorite recipients of political-ecology criticism—are also not necessarily negative or narrow. They can be interpreted and are often operationalized as such, but they can also be the opposite: a communicative, democratic rationality and technocracy that aims to reduce error without stifling social dynamism and creativity (Barry, Osborne, and Rose 1996).[20]

Antipolitics, in sum, is the political act of doing away with politics. Often this is done through rationalization and technocratization, but in order to grasp the full import of this political mode, it is crucial to propose a broader conceptualization. I find this in the work of Schedler (1997), who, inspired by Jürgen Habermas, distinguishes four types of antipolitics (see also Marden 2003, 235): instrumental, amoral, moral, and aesthetic antipolitics. Instrumental antipolitics comes close to Habermas's scientization of politics in the sense that it wants all decisions to be made by technocratic experts and based on rational cost-benefit analyses. Instrumental antipolitics does not regard political resistance as serious, as this must stem from irrational ignorance. The road is thus open for technocratic engineering of the social world and the smothering of democratic politics and deliberation. Amoral antipolitics relates to the privatization of the public domain. It regards a person as a utility-maximizing homo economicus whose interests and preferences should be clear from what makes the most commercial and economic sense. Politics becomes a strategic power game whereby rational choice prevails. Conservation and development literature has predominantly focused on these two types of antipolitics, especially its most famous example: James Ferguson's study of a development project in Lesotho that he likened to an "anti-politics machine" (Ferguson 1994).[21]

The third type, moral antipolitics, replaces "procedural normative arrangements with material norms" (Marden 2003, 235) thereby stifling political debate. In other words, ethics and morals are seen as constituted on (quantifiably) immutable goals and outcomes, and disagreement with proposed (material) norms is seen as "amoral" or even "treason" (235). Compromise becomes superfluous because "ethical norms" are derived outside of human ethical and moral consideration. A good example of this type of antipolitics is the reliance on econometrics and statistics to design what are basically moral and normative policies (see Strange 1970, 308). Finally, aesthetic antipolitics stifles democratic politics by substituting words for images, theater, and drama. Democratic politics becomes trivialized as it is represented by the visual rather than the deliberative or communicative. In Marden's words, "this is the triumph of the symbolic over verbal communication, the virtual over the actual and the ritual over the experience of learning. This is a form of 'bread and circuses' and the spectacle of politics which is regarded as a coloniser because of its potential to replace important elements of public life and *vita activa* with layers of stimulation such as expressions of emotion over plausible argument" (2003, 235).[22]

The political modes of consensus and antipolitics form the first steps toward the contemporary construction of reified representations in conservation and development. Proponents and implementers of transfrontier conservation go to great lengths in using these representations to construct and legitimate neoliberal interventions that aim to address contradictory realities by denying their contradictory nature. But denying the contradictory nature of conservation and development realities in order to forward a political agenda does not mean they disappear. Contradictions and struggles are inherent in neoliberal expansion, and analysis should therefore also be focused on how neoliberal's progression adapts to resistance. This leads us to the third mode of neoliberal political conduct: marketing.

Marketing, simply stated, is the exercise of increasing the likelihood that consumers choose your product, thereby enhancing one's "competitive advantage" in the marketplace. It is distinct from public relations, which is to increase or secure political and social legitimacy for an organization's policies and activities.[23] While this distinction is important, the two are often hard to disentangle in empirical reality. For example, when members of the PPF visited the Dutch embassy, their goal was to seek legitimacy for the peace parks concept and also quite literally for stakeholders to buy into it. In other words, legitimacy in the conservation and development marketplace often works as a commodity, because the (perceived) legitimacy of one's activities helps to generate donor resources (see, e.g., Mosse 2005). In the case of the PPF, the staff members' visit to the Dutch embassy was directly related to the many millions of euros that they receive from the Dutch Postcode Lottery (Nationale Postcode Loterij).[24] Consequently, I conceptualize marketing to also encompass issues of securing legitimacy.

Public sector organizations have of course long employed marketing tools and discourses usually associated with the private sector in order to attract investment, legitimacy, and attention or to instigate behavioral change. In fact, many colonial discourses depended on similar techniques to feign legitimacy or civilized rule (Mbembe 2001). Under neoliberalism this has been further stimulated and generally accepted as necessary and normal. As Nigel Thrift notes, "the language of economics has become common linguistic currency, making it increasingly difficult to conceive of the world in any terms except those of a calculus of supply and demand" (2005, 4). Hence, many public or nonprofit organizations increasingly see their citizens, target audiences, or members as customers and markets, rendering their manipulation necessary to obtain or maintain legitimacy and sell products and services.[25]

But, one may ask, even in contemporary neoliberal governance there is still the need to maintain democratic legitimacy, meaning that relevant stakeholders need to be involved and consulted on their own terms and not necessary on those of the social marketer. In today's hypercompetitive world, however, people's own terms are elastic and continuously targeted by (private or public) entrepreneurs. The idea of marketing, then, comes close to Paul Cammack's "imposition of consent": "the purposive action of human agents bent upon establishing the hegemony of a particular social form of organisation of production is presented as if it were the natural outcome of abstract forces too powerful for humanity to resist. The specific logic and limits of the policies proposed are obscured, and the intention that forms of participation and decentralisation should serve to embed the domestic and global disciplines of capitalist reproduction is concealed" (2003, 48).

Interestingly, while commodification on a global scale has long been recognized as a sociological fact and given labels such as the "McDonald-ization of society" (Barber 1995), the concepts of marketing and public relations are still rather marginal to critical social science (Van der Westhuizen 2005).[26] However, the social and political pervasiveness of marketing structures and techniques can be seen, for example, in the use of metaphors in advertising. According to Roland Bleiker, "these semantic structures permit the expression of a societal consciousness in which metaphors . . . seem to lose their metaphorical dimensions because they appear natural in the context of a speech environment that has already objectified hierarchical representations of political realities" (2000, 233). Thus, we encounter the political essence of marketing: stimulating those semantic structures that make people consciously forget the metaphorical dimensions of marketing speak, and instead think of a product, service, or political argument as the natural, embodied choice. There is acute irony here. The postmodern critique that language and metaphors are never neutral, objective, or able to depict reality has proven to be the ultimate strategy with which consensus around neoliberal systems of rule is promoted.

All of this has been enabled and further reinforced by rapid developments in information and communication technology. Studies on globalization and the information age generally agree that the current intensity and exponential growth of information fundamentally alters social fabrics around the world (see Castells 1996; Eriksen 2001). This further influences the semantic structures that induce disciplinary power. Tony Porter captures this well when he talks about "the increased speed and intensity with which new abstract knowledge is transformed into routine unquestioned practices which can then be taken as commonsense reality" (1999, 138). He distinguishes "two characteristic features of this knowledge structure. The first effect is ontological: there is an increasing tendency to negotiate or rework the fabric of understandings that constitute our notion of what is real. The second is decentralizing: this reworking becomes effective not through centralized controls and directives but through its acceptance and reproduction at the micro-level" (138). Neoliberal conservation works in a similar fashion; particular modes of political conduct mask and stimulate the reproduction of neoliberal governance on the micro-level. Marketing is crucial because it is focused on reworking "the fabric of understandings that constitute our notion of what is real," the effects of which are becoming increasingly visible in empirical reality.

Outline of This Book

By outlining the three modes I am not to stating that neoliberal political conduct is straightforward and blindly follows this model. This is a nonexclusive framework; the concepts of consensus, antipolitics, and marketing are not the only contemporary politics of neoliberal conservation. Rather, I argue that the core of the politics of neoliberal conservation converge around these concepts or can be better understood through them. Moreover, these politics represent the "political possibilities of the moment" (Drainville 1994, 116), and they are therefore likely to change when contextual circumstances change. In what follows, I will not only provide evidence for the salience of these frontier politics, but also their limits in ethnographic settings. The guiding thread for this task is fairly straightforward: chapters 1 and 2 discuss the regional southern African history and politics of peace parks, while chapters 3 to 7 delve into the ethnographic particularities of the Maloti-Drakensberg Transfrontier Project between Lesotho and South Africa.

Specifically, chapter 1 situates conservation within the context of colonial and postcolonial political-economic histories of southern Africa and shows how this context has influenced the political mobilization and legitimation of transfrontier conservation. Chapter 2 analyzes how these historical characteristics fuse with postcolonial neoliberalism to influence the contemporary regional politics and governance of peace parks. The concepts of consensus, antipolitics, and marketing are given their first empirical flesh here by showing how they have enabled transfrontier conservation to massively amplify, and so give new meaning to jubilant win-win conservation discourses and their neoliberal constitution.

Chapters 3 to 7 examine how the Maloti-Drakensberg Transfrontier Project tried to keep conservation legitimate in and functional to a postcolonial neoliberal political economy in order to reach its twin objectives of conservation of globally significant biodiversity and development through ecotourism. Chapters 3 and 4 deal with the consensus struggle and analyze the process of governing the Maloti-Drakensberg Transfrontier Project and its effects on international cooperation. The focus in chapter 3 is on the process of reducing the massively complex socio-ecological dynamics of the Maloti-Drakensberg into a fundable intervention that could count on a consensus by important stakeholders. Chapter 4 centers on those primarily responsible for implementation, the South African and Lesotho project coordination units (PCUs), and how they struggled to deal with each other and their divergent interpretations of this consensus. Chapter 5 widens the analysis to investigate how the PCUs dealt with these differences toward the outside in order to convince stakeholders to buy into their interpretation of the project. I will analyze the different (anti)political strategies used by the PCUs as well as the political reactions that these elicited from important stakeholders. Together these strategies and reactions culminated in a highly contradictory governance reality in that the implementation of the Maloti-Drakensberg project started focusing more on abstract discourse and planning rather than on-the-ground realities.

Chapter 6 examines this governance reality by analyzing the politics of implementing a project on the level of discourse and planning. This is the core of the marketing struggle and the way that different stakeholders tried to influence the long-term vision for (and material realities of) the Maloti-Drakensberg through the manipulation of abstraction. Chapter 7 shows how these struggles over reified representations are underpinned by the promotion of devolved neoliberal conservation-governance strategies of payments for environmental services and tourism. At the same time, the chapter grounds the analysis by showing the contradictory realities and material consequences of what happens when the implementation of neoliberal conservation is increasingly focused on the level of discourse rather than practice—a dynamic I refer to as the "bubble of neoliberal conservation."

The book's concluding chapter outlines the broader implications of the contemporary politics of neoliberal conservation. The most important implication is the popularization of what might be called the "postmodern frontier," namely a struggle over what is reality and how this reality is constructed (Castree and Braun 1998). This epistemological struggle in conservation, I will argue, has become one of the major struggles of our time and will define the relations between humans and nature for the foreseeable future. At the same time, the conclusion returns to political ecology, arguing that current neoliberal modes of political conduct could be opened up for more progressive ends and that not every frontier set for us by the neoliberal political economy has to be overcome.

chapter one

FORGING (TRANS)FRONTIER SPACES

"At the 1884 Berlin Convention, Africa was dealt like a pack of
cards to the colonial powers. The national boundaries proclaimed at this time cut across tribal and clan groupings and
animal migration routes, thereby fragmenting eco-systems
and led to biodiversity being destroyed. Transfrontier conservation areas or 'peace parks' are a way to 'link' those protected
areas that are divided by an international boundary" (Myburgh
2005). This quote by the CEO of the Peace Parks Foundation is
often used in the marketing of transfrontier conservation.[1]
Based on the recognition that African borders are artificial and
superimposed colonial constructs, popular support is easily
garnered through a discourse centered on righting the wrongs
that these borders have caused. To many proponents and their
followers, it makes intuitive sense to undo boundaries through
the establishment of peace parks and so "correct" the mistakes
of history. Yet, just as it is not easy to forge boundaries, they—
and their effects—are not easily undone. The forging of the
frontiers that made peace parks possible gave birth to particular postcolonial spaces that continue to have strong bearings
on contemporary southern African realities. Moreover, "once
brought into the world, space is always in process of becoming
something else and contributing to the production of other
spaces, objects, and subjects" (West 2006, 27). In order to
understand the complex spaces, objects, and subjects currently

targeted by transfrontier conservation interventions, we need to analyze how they—and the relations between them—were forged and transcended over time. Not only is this necessary so as to appreciate the historical circumstances that these interventions confront and transform, it is also crucial to understand the politics of neoliberal transfrontier conservation. After all, what makes modes of politics *political* is directly related to how actors conceive, narrate, and act on the historical constitution and transformations of spaces, objects, and subjects.

The popular history of transfrontier conservation devotes little attention to these complex constitutions and transformations and how they have influenced the contemporary postcolonial constellation. It is usually confined to how the United States and Canada proclaimed the first official peace park in 1932—the Waterton-Glacier International Peace Park, established foremost to celebrate the friendship between the two countries (Sandwith et al. 2001). While this historical precedent serves to indicate a longer-term rationale behind peace parks, the idea was not actively entertained in international conservation until it resurfaced in the 1980s and rose to global prominence during the 1990s. In this global rise, North American and southern African actors took a leading role. Frederick Jackson Turner, the American historian who gave the frontier a prominent place in explaining American culture and mentality, would surely argue that it is no coincidence that these regions with long frontier histories are infatuated by the idea.[2] This, however, is too simplistic. Frontier histories matter, but it is the way in which histories are conceived and acted on that shape present and future political possibilities. From this perspective, southern Africa's status as a heartland of transfrontier conservation makes sense: the future promises and hopes embodied in the peace parks concept provide a convenient alternative to the many injustices related to (southern) Africa's turbulent past and artificial boundaries. Or rather: it is a sanitized version of this past that all but begs the grandiose vision of peace parks—"the global solution"—to transcend it. In doing so, it enables proponents of peace park to manage the contradictory postcolonial spaces, subjects, and objects molded by this past, easing the forging and transcending of a new frontier.

As we will see in the following chapters, the politics of neoliberal conservation build on and amplify this strategy. The purpose of this chapter is to show that the contradictions concealed by these political strategies have deep roots in the historical development of a postcolonial political economy centered on struggles over race, sovereignty, and dispossession. More specifically, the chapter has two objectives. First, it traces the historical political economy within which postcolonial southern African state boundaries and sovereignties were forged. This political economy is a mix of settler colonialism, racial capitalism, and institutionalized segregation that still characterizes the region today (see Ferguson 2006; Mamdani 1996; Mbembe 2001; D. S. Moore 2005). Special emphasis will be on the circumstances that led to Lesotho becoming a sovereign nation-state and thus the first roots of the Maloti-Drakensberg transfrontier conservation area. Second, the chapter will situate and analyze the idea of conservation in this constellation to show how the rise and prospects of transfrontier conservation are deeply embedded in historical political-economic dynamics and ideas about spaces, objects, and subjects.

Conservation and Turmoil in the Hinterland

Southern African frontier history is well studied, especially how from the mid-seventeenth century on, Dutch, English, and other settlers increasingly extended and conquered the frontiers between them and indigenous peoples in the search for agricultural opportunities.[3] Less well known is the role that conservation played in this constellation. William Beinart argues that "comments and debates about environmental degradation are evident surprisingly early in the history of European settlement. They arose from the emerging understandings of the environment, from the experience of farmers, and from international scientific advances that framed environmental problems in new ways" (2003, 64). In turn, Beinart continues, these "scientific ideas were closely linked to mid-Victorian colonial notions of progress, agricultural improvement, and economic growth"; notions that often triggered and officially justified repressive colonial action (64).[4]

Changes in Europe led to the British taking over the Cape Colony in 1795 and finally obtaining sovereignty (in the eyes of other European powers) in 1814. Establishing control in the turbulent eastern frontier—a sign of "progress"—proved a major predicament for the British, especially as they and other settlers increasingly came into (violent) contact with Xhosa peoples living in what today is the Eastern Cape province. These settlers, particularly the Dutch descendants or Afrikaners, saw British attempts at establishing order as an infringement on their rights, most notably the right to slavery, which the British abolished in 1833. Their subsequent Great Trek to free themselves from British control coincided with other upheavals that were to shape the region. Important here is the coming into being of Lesotho as a result of specific historical developments in which the Great Trek and the "movement of peoples" were central.

When the Afrikaners started their trek north and eastward around 1835, a massive movement of peoples had already been under way for some time. Under Shaka kaSenzangakhona's leadership, the Zulu kingdom had launched aggressive military campaigns against other peoples, creating such havoc that the era later became known as the Difaqane (times of trouble). In response to the Zulu's actions and around their core territory of what is Zululand today, other peoples tried to hold their ground. The boundaries between them had always been relatively flexible, characterized by negotiation and struggle. This changed with the arrival of colonizers who acted "from two fundamental principles—exclusive ownership and physical boundaries—that together constitute enclosure and a territorial paradigm" (Hughes 2006, 8). Hence, "in seizing the landscape, frontiersmen both define territory and place a premium upon its control" (8). The Great Trek added a major impetus to the colonial control of territory and the multiple (social, material, spiritual) dispossessions of native populations in the region. Obviously, this is not how the colonizers saw it; as the Afrikaner Boers (farmers) enclosed and territorialized the areas between the Vaal and Caledon (the Orange Free State) and the Limpopo and Vaal Rivers (the Transvaal) they regarded the land as *territorium nullius* where "the settler inherits no real responsibility" toward native peoples (Mbembe 2001, 183).

This is not to say the settlers confronted "passive recipients" (Hart 2002, 52). Remarkably, in between these forces, the Sotho people under Chief Moshoeshoe's leadership managed to lay the foundations of present-day independent Lesotho. In the late eighteenth century, when Moshoeshoe was born, most of the Basotho people did not live in the area we now know as Lesotho but north of the Caledon River and in the Maloti Mountains between the Orange and Caledon Rivers;[5] land eyed by the Boers. Moshoeshoe, recognized as one of Africa's most cunning diplomats, led his people's defense from the mountain stronghold of Thaba Bosiu, not far from present-day Maseru. Although he was able to stave off many attacks from Boer commandos, he also realized that he could not hold them back forever and asked the British for protection (Gill 1993). Partly out of pity but also for fear that the newly established republics might grow too powerful,

Britain agreed. On 12 March 1868, Basutoland was annexed to the empire; its physical boundaries were defined by the British and the Orange Free State without Basotho involvement. In the process, the Basotho ceded much land to the Boers, land that is still referred to as "conquered territory" (Coplan 2001). The Basotho people had established the foundations for their sovereignty, but at a price: they were landlocked and driven into the mountains, dispossessed from their most fertile lands. Yet, "throughout the 1870s Lesotho retained its position as the granary of neighbouring communities" (Thabane 2002, 106). Fifty years later, the situation had changed drastically. Due to import tariffs from the Orange Free State, Lesotho's agriculture had "collapsed, and with it Lesotho's food self-sufficiency" (Thabane 2002, 112). Overall, the nation had become little more than a labor reserve for South Africa. To understand how this happened, one has to turn to the emerging regional political economy.

Foundations of a Political Economy

Despite all the upheaval, many earlier concerns of Cape life continued to dominate the regional political economy, prominent among these were the issues of agriculture, stock, and environmental degradation. Beinart argues that "by the mid-nineteenth century," "a concern for the balance of nature, and the loss of species was linked to a critique of Cape Pastoral practices" (2003, 77). These practices revolved around overstocking, cutting trees, and competing for natural resources, particularly grazing lands (99), and they defined frontier dynamics for a considerable period: "The characteristic Southern African frontier, whether early in the southwestern Cape or 150 years later in the Transvaal and Namibia, was one where stock farmers searching for new land interacted with Africans, who themselves were generally in possession of cattle and/or sheep. With few exceptions the colonists fought the Africans in order to capture grazing ground or stock, not to control trade routes or agricultural land" (Ross 1981, 212).

Nevertheless, while this early transfrontier movement was about stock and grazing lands, agricultural and environmental concerns never trailed far behind. Indeed, they "had become associated with attempts to intensify settlement and agriculture, as part of the broader priority of colonial development" (Beinart 2003, 99). This colonial political economy—built on notions of "progress, agricultural improvement, and economic growth"— was intimately connected to the land and its resources. In turn, this triggered mechanist, scientific, and romantic images and ideas about nature and the land (Beinart 2003, 66), themes that are still very much part of the current political economy of (transfrontier) conservation in the region.

The discovery of diamonds near Kimberley in 1866 and gold near modern-day Johannesburg twenty years later changed this constellation dramatically. Raw capitalist development arrived and turned southern Africa on its head. Profit seekers from around the globe descended on the mining areas; black Africans from across the continent flocked to the region for labor. The emergent white-dominated capitalist political economy left few African communities untouched that "had previously preserved their independence" (Thompson 2001, 108), creating stark class differences and a black urban proletariat and further entrenching racial, ethnic, and gender inequalities throughout the region (Hart 2002). The mineral discoveries also further stimulated the territorial paradigm and colonial need to control land. By the end of the century, the four white polities—the Cape and Natal under the British crown and the Boer republics of Transvaal and Orange Free State—had subjected all African peoples in their territories, laying the foundations for intensified colonial oppression and apartheid.[6] The unionization and formal independence of South Africa in 1910 further reinforced the marginality of black, mixed (colored), and Indian peoples, despite the fact that they remained the absolute majority. Lesotho, although not part of the union, did not escape this fate and became a dependent and peripheral element within white-dominated South Africa.

With these developments, the dominant contours of the postcolonial political economy of southern Africa were put in place. According to Patrick Bond, this entails the "minerals-energy complex" as the "core quarter of the economy," combined with other core features such as the lack of production of "intermediate capital goods" and "basic needs industries", and a focus on luxury goods (2000, 18; based on Fine and Rustomjee 1996). These tenets were further bolstered under apartheid and institutionalized in extreme forms, leading to the increasing concurrence of class and racial hierarchies.[7] Blacks, coloreds, and Indians were not "merely" further marginalized under apartheid; their suppression became ever more violent, the curtailing of their freedom ever more extreme. In this way, the apartheid government was able to further reinforce the region's political economy, essentially entrenching earlier institutional segregation and associated race and class structures and degrading its neighboring countries to labor reserves (Mamdani 1996). Lesotho was especially vulnerable; its hard-won sovereignty became effectively meaningless other than as a relative safe haven for antiapartheid activists. In fact, according to James Ferguson, "Lesotho's sovereign status was accepted by the international community more as a response to its status as an ex-British colony than as an endorsement of any internal capabilities to function economically or politically" (2006, 55).

Within this wretched constellation, it would seem that land and environmental issues were of little concern. Nothing is further from the truth. Land was a central pillar of the racist, capitalist political economy, and agriculture and conservation were the apartheid states' prime articulations with the land. Agriculture was most important,[8] and one of the central strategies for whites to ground "racialized rule in spatial practices" (D. S. Moore 2005, 13). White farming sought to make the land "productive" and by so doing produce (sociopolitical) spaces to control and discipline black subjects. At the same time, whites increasingly started romancing the land and setting big chunks aside for conservation by designating them protected areas (see Hughes 2010). This signaled a change in the rationale behind conservation from the preceding period: an almost exclusive focus on combating degradation gave way to a strategy built around Garden of Eden symbolism and practical concerns around the survival of species (Igoe 2004). Both articulations with the land were reflective and constitutive of a broader space-making exercise that defined the relations between objects and subjects along narrowly circumscribed social, political-economic, and racial lines (see, e.g., Neumann 2004, 822–23).

That is not to say that these projects did not clash on occasion. South Africa's most famous protected area, the Kruger National Park, provides a good example. On the one hand, the park was born out of an (elite) white need for the preservation of an ideal space that people had emotionally and politically attached themselves to. On the other hand, many people at the start of park's development early in the twentieth century were unsure whether to sacrifice possibilities for industrialization and commercial farming for a protected area (Carruthers 1995, 47). The Afrikaner lower classes, especially, needed to be convinced that a protected area was a legitimate use of land, and proponents of the park developed large public relations campaigns to garner support. With the adoption of the name of the former president of Transvaal Paul Kruger symbolically linked to a national park, the connection between the developing political economy and the protected area was sewn (Carruthers 1995, 47).

Conservation, in a sense, became the mirror image of industrialized commercial agriculture in the colonization of southern Africa, especially the union. In both cases, whites further grounded their control over the region through the construction of particular ideas and associated spatial practices about what entailed legitimate land use, whereby "African attitudes and interests were ignored or over-ridden" (Carruthers 1995, 65). These ideas, in turn, were steeped in and influenced by a science based on notions of "progress, agricultural improvement, and economic growth": "In the late years of the nineteenth century, the much trumpeted universality of conservation was legitimated by reference to an international scientific community. It was this, in particular, that allowed the colonial state to use the righteous language of conservation and to confine and regulate the activities of peasant farmers in the marginal lands to which they were becoming increasingly restricted" (Grove 1989, 187).

Ultimately, coercive, fortress conservation was but one part in a wider process of the partitioning, enclosing, and making productive of land whereby whites sought to relieve themselves of "restraint on material possibility" (Weaver 2003; see also Peluso 1993). The paradoxical irony of this tendency combined with the material and spatial conservation ethic, which was ever more seen through the eyes of tourism (Carruthers 1995), was little recognized.

Conserving a Wretched Constellation

How then were these land uses and the political-economic space that they functioned within preserved, rationalized, and legitimized, particularly with respect to African peoples? The blunt way was through what Roderick Neumann refers to as "no development without tears" (1998, 68). To explain the point, he quotes a commissioner in the colony of northern Tanganyika who stated that "Africans should understand that the loss of their land . . . is an inevitable part of the price [they] must pay for [their] advancement" (70). This, of course, was a much more widely accepted way of thinking in the colonies.[9] In early to mid-nineteenth century in Indonesia, the Dutch governor General van den Bosch similarly referred to the Javanese as "permanent minors who would require the ongoing tutelage of a disciplinary state" (quoted in Li 2007, 37).

The other tactic was that colonial discipline and interference were said to be good for the "lethargic peoples" (Mudimbe 1988, 137). This became known as the "dual mandate," coined by Lord Frederick Lugard in 1922 to defend and show the "value of British rule" (1965, 617; see also Mamdani 1996). He argued "that Europe is in Africa for the mutual benefit of her own industrial classes, and of the native races in their progress to a higher plane; that the benefit can be made reciprocal, and that it is the aim and desire of civilised administration to fulfill this dual mandate." Similarly, the mission of saving Africa's wilderness was increasingly seen as good for colonizers and the colonized. The colonizers could take resources out of and recreate (i.e., hunt) in the so-called Garden of Eden, whereas the colonized could become civilized by losing their dependence on subsistence living and learning how to become part of the modern market economy (see W. Adams 2004; Brockington, Duffy, and Igoe 2008; Mudimbe 1988).

With protected areas at its core, nature conservation became a matter of law enforcement through a "fences and fines" approach, whereby conservation interests trumped those of local people (W. Adams and Hutton 2007). Obviously, in the framework of the dual mandate this was not recognized until much later. Even after decolonization fortress conservation persisted, the financial argument of foreign exchange brought in by Western tourists who wanted to visit "untainted" African nature convinced many postcolonial governments to continue colonial-style conservation policies (see Brockington, Duffy, and Igoe 2008; Garland 2008). Nevertheless, "the social impact of PAS [protected areas] began to be widely recognized in the 1970s. The idea that parks should be socially and economically inclusive slowly began to become part of mainstream conservation thinking" (W. Adams and Hutton 2007, 150). By this time, the initial optimism over postcolonial promises and prospects had largely died down and, along with the broader development climate, a more people-oriented approach to conservation emerged. Western donors and African leaders could no longer—at least in rhetoric—keep local people away from the resources they often depended on for their livelihoods (Duffy 2010).

While southern Africa is often seen as the cradle of community-based conservation due to high-profile programs such as CAMPFIRE (Community Areas Management Programme for Indigenous Resources) in Zimbabwe, ADMADE (Administrative Management Design for Game Management Areas) in Zambia and LIFE (Living in a Finite Environment) in Namibia, the situation in South Africa was different.[10] Until the early 1990s, conservation in South Africa was strictly a white affair and fortress conservation was as stringent as ever. And even though beginning in 1978 the apartheid state was in constant crisis, it went to great lengths to conserve the wretched constellation (Thompson 2001). One of the most prominent examples in this respect is directly related to this book, namely South Africa's aggressive attempt to control Lesotho's water resources to buttress the racist regional political economy and guarantee inputs for white industrial development. This attempt not only illustrates the type of struggles over race, sovereignty, and dispossession that characterized this political economy but also directly structured and shaped the roots of the Maloti-Drakensberg transfrontier conservation area and the intervention aimed at its establishment.

In the 1950s, the South African government commenced negotiations with the Lesotho government about a scheme that ended up being the Lesotho Highlands Water Project (LHWP). This project was meant to alleviate the rapidly increasing demands for water in the industrial heart of South Africa—the then Pretoria-Witwatersrand-Vereeniging area, now the Gauteng province—through a system of dams and associated tunneling infrastructure. Several feasibility studies were conducted in the 1970s and early 1980s—the time when relations between Lesotho and South Africa soured rapidly. Upon independence in 1966, the ruling party in Lesotho, the Basutoland National Party, was convinced that the best way to deal with the apartheid regime was through conciliatory diplomacy rather than outright condemnation. This changed in the 1970s. Leabua Jonathan, Lesotho's dictatorial prime minister, learned that an antiapartheid stance brought in more goodwill and development aid than South Africa could offer. But not only did he become more vocal in his condemnation of the apartheid regime, he also started offering support to the African National Congress (ANC), triggering two violent raids on ANC cadres in Maseru by South African security forces and a swift worsening of relations (Gill 1993). South Africa's reaction to Jonathan's new tactics was the "economic strangulation of Lesotho in December 1985" (Thabane 2000), leading to a South Africa–backed military coup d'état in January 1986. The Lesotho Highlands Water Treaty between Lesotho and South Africa was subsequently agreed upon and signed remarkably swiftly—in October 1986. So swiftly, in fact, that Anne Marie De Jonge Schuermans, Jacob Helbing, and Roman Fedosseev contend that "given the significance of the treaty and the complexity of the project, it is difficult to imagine that the two governments—one brand new—could have finalized negotiations in such a short period of time without a level of discussion and agreement prior to the coup. It can be argued that one ulterior motive for supporting the coup was to secure access to

Lesotho's water" (2004, 5). Regardless, construction on the dams began in 1987 and the first water delivery to South Africa was in 1998.

From the start of the LHWP, the project was mired in controversy. If the circumstances that led to the LHWP treaty were dubious, its implementation had far graver consequences (see Horta 1995; Mwangi 2007; Schmitz 1992; Thabane 2000). Of course this is not what the governments of South Africa and Lesotho or the agencies funding the LHWP emphasized. From the start they employed classic "dual mandate" rhetoric by portraying "the Treaty as one of mutual benefit" (Mwangi 2007, 9). This continued even after apartheid as a World Bank press release from 1998 indicates: "The Lesotho Highlands Water Project provides a major source of development for Lesotho," said Pamela Cox, the World Bank country director for Lesotho and South Africa. "It also represents the lowest-cost alternative for water supply to the Gauteng Province. This is an excellent example of regional collaboration for mutual benefit achieving truly win-win solutions to urgent issues facing both countries."[11] The evidence, however, points in the opposite direction. Although the project brought Lesotho royalties and economic growth, study after study argued that the negative impacts of the dams and the associated flooding were massive. These include inadequate compensation for the majority of resettled communities, severe environmental degradation (Mwangi 2007), considerable loss of land and livelihoods (Thabane 2000), and a highly unequal distribution of the benefits between the two countries in South Africa's favor (Horta 1995; Schmitz 1992). Moreover, the money flowing into Lesotho was mostly absorbed by elites, while the Lesotho Highlands Development Authority started functioning as a "state within a state" due to the project's disproportionate size relative to the rest of the economy (Horta 1995, 229).

While these effects became obvious quite early on in the LHWP's development, they were recognized only much later (albeit to a limited extend, because the post-1994 democratic regime in South Africa maintained the project). In later chapters, this history will be taken further as the transfrontier conservation area takes over where the LHWP stopped: the conservation of the water sources that feed the dams and ultimately supply Johannesburg and Pretoria. Important here is to emphasize that from the mid-1970s, the global context these developments were taking place within changed dramatically, and that the LHWP and other measures to conserve the wretched constellation could not halt the apartheid government from collapsing. Spurred on by these dynamics, the southern African region went through massive change once more. Honest expectations arose that the dominant regional political economy could be transformed.

Breaking Boundaries?

In the new postcolonial development climate that emerged in the 1970s, it was increasingly accepted that conservation and development were extremely complex processes that could not be planned and administered in a top-down fashion (see Chambers 1983; Critchley 2000). The democratic post-1994 South African government used similar rhetoric to try and transform a political-economic space that had been in the making for several centuries. Environmental sustainability and conservation again proved significant. As South Africa sought to regain international credibility after apartheid, the new government actively used the seemingly nonpolitical issue of environmental sustainability to assert its place in the international diplomatic realm, among others, by organizing the 2002 World Summit on Sustainable Development (Death 2010, 2011). Furthermore, nature-based tourism became one of South Africa's prime strategies for stimulating growth and foreign investment (Wells 1996). All this put even more pressure on South Africa to take community-based conservation (CBC) seriously,[12] with due implications for the postcolonial context in which the embryonic peace parks agenda emerged (Büscher 2010c).

The still-central principles of community-based conservation developed during the late 1970s and early 1980s. Their basis was a shift in thinking about local people's participation in conservation as something "bad" to something good and even necessary (see W. Adams and Hulme 2001; Fabricius and Koch 2004). Clark Gibson and Stuart Marks, for example, argued that "conservation will be more successful at the local level when rural residents possess significant legal claims over wildlife resources and its management" (1995, 942). To a limited degree, ideas about (local) sovereignty were being rethought; states were regarded with mistrust and communities were increasingly recognized as entities possessing traditional, historical sovereignty over their surrounding natural resources. It was further recognized that most developing countries did not have the capacity to effectively guard protected areas, so local communities were better seen as allies than enemies (Brosius, Tsing, and Zerner 2005). Lastly, as the overwhelming majority of biodiversity is found outside protected areas, it was argued that local communities needed to be taken seriously as stakeholders in the effort to protect the biodiversity they live with (W. Adams and Hulme 2001). In sum, management of natural resources became comanagement (see Borrini-Feyerabend et al. 2004; Venema and van den Breemer 1999), and old boundaries that long defined landscapes, races, habits, governance systems, and sovereignties were thought to be dissoluble.

These principles have rendered CBC hegemonic in international and national policy circles, a position it still enjoys today (Blaikie 2006, 1954). Yet again, as with the postcolonial political economy that envelops CBC, transformation proved elusive and the failings of CBC with respect to conservation and development were increasingly noted (see Barret and Arcese 1995; Gibson 1999; Wunder 2001). Edmund Barrow and Marshall Murphree argue that two main factors account for this: the unwillingness of African governments to adapt to CBC and decentralize power and the "core motivational direction behind CBC policy, planning and action," which was often still "fortress oriented" (2001, 28). This is not to say that the scholars espousing these critiques denounced CBC completely.[13] Instead they sought its limitations in practice with an aim at improvement. These lively debates across scholarly and policy boundaries during the late 1990s and early 2000s were influential regionally, especially among young black scholars, policymakers, and conservation professionals, including Lesotho's implementation team of the Maloti-Drakensberg project.

At the same time, more-fundamental criticism emerged. So-called neoprotectionists believe that CBC detracts from the conservation objective and argue that a return to top-down, fortress styles of management is imperative to save biodiversity (Oates 1999; Terborgh 1999).[14] Despite their marginal recognition in mainstream conservation discourses and strong criticism from CBC-oriented scholars, neoprotectionist ideas remain influential and continue to inform the conservation and natural resource management practices of many conservation actors (Büscher and Dietz 2005). This was the case for many in the South African implementation team of the Maloti-Drakensberg project, a situation that, as we shall see, led to two project teams speaking similar rhetoric but diverging widely in terms of their practical operationalization.

The Hybridization of Critiques and Practices

The above implicit sequence from fortress conservation to CBC is simplistic yet fairly standard in the general conservation literature. In southern Af-

rica—and globally—a myriad of complex conservation-development discourses and practices exist and have long existed. Criticisms and reflections continuously influence conservation practices and discourses in
multifarious ways. These, however, usually leave the wider political economy, or the "framework of existing power relations and institutions" un-
changed (Ford 2003).[15] But then again, so do those critiques that are explicitly aimed at the wider political economy. Part of the problem is that any
knowledge, including scientific knowledge, is part of and influenced by the
political economy it engages (see Carolan 2006; Castree and Braun 1998).
The irony is that CBC has shown itself to be remarkably comfortable with
the newer neoliberal incarnations of the segregated capitalist political
economy in which colonial fortress conservation thrived.

This contradiction is not exceptional, and perhaps it is even paradigmatic
of the broader postcolonial South African context. Two years after apartheid's collapse in 1994, the new ANC government replaced the decentral-
ized and developmental Reconstruction and Development Programme with
the neoliberal Growth, Employment and Redistribution agenda (GEAR) (see
Alexander 2002, 49; Hart 2002). GEAR radically changed the ANC's policy
outlook by tying social spending to economic growth, reneging on redis-
tributive targets, and focusing more on building an enabling environment
to attract foreign direct investment than guaranteeing service delivery to
the poor (Bond 2000). Similarly, the government's CBC commitment was
gradually tied into a broader rural strategy that relied on capital-intensive
farming, market-based land distribution mechanisms to counter the massive dispossession of land under colonialism and apartheid, and tertiary
sector alignment where rural dwellers would become less dependent on
land and resource-based livelihoods and more dependent on selling services, especially to the tourism industry. This policy outlook has been heavily criticized for its failure to meaningfully tackle societal inequality and
access to resources, land, and services, but that has had little impact on
policy so far (see Cousins 2007; Dressler and Büscher 2008; Fay and James
2009; Walker et al. 2011).

The shift from critiques of colonial capitalism to alignments with postcolonial neoliberal capitalism has not, despite its own criticisms, impeded
much on the legitimacy of CBC and GEAR discourses. Piers Blaikie hints at
this when he states that "scepticism and criticism have appeared now for
about fifteen years—too long a period to invoke policy lag as a reason for
the popularity and continuation of CBNRM [Community-Based Natural Re-

source Management] projects and programs" (2006, 1954). He argues that the success of CBNRM

> is reproduced within a network of multi-lateral and bi-lateral agencies, international NGOs, in-country NGOs and a limited number of senior government officials in recipient countries. The discursive power of the theoretical benefits to environment and community of CBNRM, the need to proclaim success to other international audiences, and the diffuseness and range of the social and environmental objectives, all lie behind representations of this "success." Success, in turn, is defined in ways that will allow it to be found. Success stories prevail against criticism that comes from other quarters (particularly local people who have experienced CBNRM, and independent commentary from scholars). (Blaikie 2006, 1954)

While accurate insofar as the discourse of CBC is concerned, the emphasis on the "discursive power of the theoretical benefits" does not in itself explain the continued legitimacy of CBC approaches. Two crucial characteristics of neoliberalism need to be taken into account to accurately assess CBCs legitimacy and success.

First, missing in Blaikie's argument is the way that neoliberals continuously amalgamate mixed "institutional forms and political agendas" that favor particular constructions of devolved governance of conservation and development around faith in markets to assign roles to communities, the state, and other stakeholders (McCarthy 2005, 998). This is an effective strategy to ensure that access to and possession of biodiversity and natural resources will favor those who can back up their entitlements most effectively (see Dietz 1996). Behind the "discursive power of the theoretical benefits" of CBC, then, many material power struggles take place that may (deliberately) contradict community-based principles, yet they are legitimated by those same principles. Hence, increasingly contradictory and hybrid realities are not merely concealed but actively managed and exploited through win-win discourses. The deeper understanding of this contradiction is precisely what requires an investigation into the politics of neoliberal conservation, or into the way that interests and demands are actively managed and manipulated under the banner of jubilant conservation and development discourses.

Second, Blaikie does not account for the central role of frontiers in neoliberal politics or how actors under neoliberalism deal with the limits to exploiting the tensions between contradictory realities and reified win-win constructions. Despite its continuing dominance and alleged success, CBC has reached these limits and lost much of its initial glow after a continuous barrage of criticism and failures in practice (Dressler et al. 2010). In other words, CBC is no longer as hegemonic as it is often portrayed and it is increasingly less of an ideal platform upon which to build hybrid "institutional forms and political agendas." By virtue of its ability to deal with its own contradictory practices, however, neoliberalism can rise above itself, most poignantly by opening up new frontiers. Part of opening up new frontiers is eclipsing former frontiers, to use the ambiguities and contradictions of past solutions for the political legitimation of future promises. Transfrontier conservation has proven to be an excellent tool to forge such a new frontier. By adding the peace component, proponents of transfrontier conservation have tried to eclipse allegedly simple and increasingly criticized CBC models (Büscher 2010c). Indeed, the failures, contradictions, and disappointments of this older conservation model have become fertile ground for jubilant peace parks promoters to reignite the "crusading energy of current environmentalism" (Nelson 2003, 67).

This argument brings us back to the ways in which particular spaces become something else and contribute "to the production of other spaces, objects, and subjects" (West 2006, 27). Transfrontier conservation is such a something else; it was brought into being by—among others—the historical productions of spaces, objects, and subjects discussed in this chapter. In turn, these historical productions enable us to understand the rise of transfrontier conservation in the postcolonial neoliberal political economy.

The Rise of Transfrontier Conservation

In 2003, William Wolmer remarked that "what at first sight appears to be a rather surprising coalition of interests has rapidly rallied around the recent concept of Transboundary Natural Resource Management" (2003, 261). Despite the mixed results of many community-based conservation-development initiatives, southern Africa's strong commitment to transfrontier conservation means that the region is promoting these initiatives on a greater scale than ever before. Many conservation actors have jumped on the bandwagon, realigning their activities and interests to fit the new banner (Magome and Murombedzi 2003). The popular starting point for transfrontier conservation in the region is commonly attributed to the personal, philanthropic commitments of the late South African business tycoon Anton Rupert, who established the Peace Parks Foundation (PPF) in 1997. Criticizing this tendency, Maano Ramutsindela provides a more legible, historically informed explanation in his book, *Transfrontier Conservation in Africa: At the Confluence of Capital, Politics and Nature* (2007). He shows that the rise of transfrontier conservation was intimately linked with the emerging postapartheid political economy.

The key element in Ramutsindela's argument is the history of how the PPF's predecessor, the Southern African Nature Foundation (SANF), married conservation and capital. Originally founded by Rupert as the unofficial South African chapter of the World Wildlife Fund (WWF), the SANF became a highly successful conservation NGO, active in many countries in the region. According to Ramutsindela, "the most defining character of SANF was that it was strongly linked to the business sector" (2007, 56). Facilitated by Rupert's extensive business network, the SANF successfully persuaded South African and international companies during the 1980s to support the organization financially, which simultaneously strengthened their own image. Considering the decaying state of apartheid, companies were eager to be associated with a different future South Africa, which, as was becoming clear, was going to be ruled by the black majority. The link with nature conservation made sense, as it conjured up sentiments of going back to a real or unspoiled South Africa before colonization and apartheid.[16] Besides, the new black majority government needed to be convinced that nature conservation—Transfrontier Conservation Areas (TFCAS) in particular—were crucial to postapartheid economic reconstruction (Ramutsindela 2007, 58). This was skillfully done by the SANF by pointing out the growth potential of nature-based tourism.

The SANF, however, was not to be the vehicle to continue promoting these plans. In 1995 it was subsumed under WWF International, who disallowed the organization to continue its operations in countries that neighbor South Africa. But as Ramutsindela shows, these operations were the nuclei of future TFCAS and therefore crucial for the promotion of transfrontier conservation and associated business interests. A new vehicle was needed, and in 1997, Rupert, with Nelson Mandela and Prince Bernhard of the Netherlands, founded the PPF, an NGO devoted to the establishment of peace parks. The official objectives of the PPF are to raise and allocate funds for the establishment of TFCAS, identify and purchase land for transfrontier conservation, and to promote the development of TFCAS on a commercial basis (Hanks 2000). The PPF, based on the networks and methods built up by the SANF, gained strong political and business support, including from the heads of state of eight southern African nations as honorary patrons and twenty-one wealthy patrons organized in the PPF's Club 21. According to PPF's 2001 annual report, "Club 21 is an international trust, which aims to have at least 21 members who will each *donate $1 million or its equivalent to the work of the Foundation. It is thus a club for those concerned with peace through conservation in the 21st Century*" (Peace Parks Foundation 2002, 15). Rupert and the PPF, particularly John Hanks, its first CEO,[17] were also essential in getting other donors, such as the World Bank, the German Development Bank, and USAID, interested in the peace parks concept (Hanks 2000). In 1996 the World Bank, through the Global Environment Facility, offered Mozambique a US$5 million grant for the Transfrontier Conservation Area Pilot and Institutional Strengthening Project, with the objective to "test new approaches to exploit the synergies between conservation and community development in very poor areas where income earning opportunities are limited" (World Bank 1996, 14).[18]

But while community conservation dominated the rhetoric of the PPF and the World Bank, the big picture was never lost. In the words of Hanks:

> To produce sustained economic growth, African countries must create and maintain an enabling environment for investment. The world economic system is highly competitive and market based, and Africa has been largely marginalized in recent years in attracting significant inflows of long-term foreign direct investment. In 1998, the Secretary-General of the United Nations called attention to the importance of focusing attention on multi-country infrastructure projects for the development of shared natural resources. . . . TFCAS not only meet this requirement, but can also open up new opportunities for private/public sector partnerships and help to restore investor confidence in a continent increasingly perceived as lacking in transparency and accountability and trapped in a syndrome of dependency. (2003, 143)

One thing is clear: TFCAS are promoted with rigor and backed by substantial financial means by a great variety of actors, especially white business elites linked to the PPF. Yet, while the PPF has been crucial in pushing the southern African TFCA agenda, it is part of a larger coalition of interests, including donors, others NGOS, and—perhaps most important—the regional states whose cooperation was vital to bring transfrontier conservation into being. Together these actors have ensured that transfrontier conservation has been firmly embedded within regional and global political economies and—crucially—that the dominant postcolonial neoliberal political economy was firmly embedded in the peace park concept.

Forging Transfrontier Spaces

I have tried to build a picture of the complex historical political-economic spaces in which transfrontier conservation in southern Africa was born, conceptualized, and is currently implemented. Due recognition was given to the discourses and representations of these spaces and the way they worked to situate objects and subjects under historical conditions of racial dispossession and struggles over sovereignty and territory. But we must move beyond this in order to heed David Harvey's remark that there is "a key difference in the deployment of the concept of space as an essential element in a materialist project of understanding tangible geographies on the ground and the widespread appropriation of spatial metaphors within social, literary and cultural theory" (2006, 129). Hence, to move from spatial metaphors to "tangible geographies on the ground," we need to briefly introduce the actual material geographical places and the peoples and ecologies that reside there (see, e.g., West 2006, 7). This is necessary to give ethnographic and empirical depth to the forging of transfrontier spaces.

The material geographical places that feature most prominently in the following chapters are the six TFCAS considered to be making the most progress in southern Africa (Kgalagadi Transfrontier Park, Great Limpopo Transfrontier Park [GLTP], Maloti-Drakensberg Transfrontier Conservation and Development Area, |Ai-|Ais-Richtersveld Transfrontier Park, Limpopo-Shashe TFCA, Lubombo TFCA). Table 1.1 compares their main features. Interestingly, South Africa's dominant role in the regional political economy is reflected in the table; it is involved in all TFCAS considered to be "progressing seriously" (Van Amerom and Büscher 2005, 166). However, since Marloes Van Amerom developed this table in 2005, many TFCAS between other southern African countries have seen major investments, particularly the massive Kavango-Zambezi TFCA between Angola, Botswana, Namibia, Zimbabwe, and Zambia, with an official treaty signed on 18 August 2011 at a Southern Africa Development Community summit in Luanda, Angola.[19] Despite this, the six TFCAS involving South Africa remain firmly in the lead due to South Africa's superior organizational capacity and financial means, and also because many of the push factors that kept the pace of transfrontier conservation high emanated from South Africa.[20] An important recent

TABLE 1.1 Stages of development per transfrontier conservation area

NAME	PARTICIPATING COUNTRIES	PROGRESS TO DATE	TFP	TFCA	LEVEL OF PROGRESS
Kgalagadi Transfrontier Park	South Africa, Botswana	Treaty signed (12 May 2000)	✓		Established
Great Limpopo Transfrontier Park/ Area	South Africa, Zimbabwe, Mozambique	Treaty signed (9 December 2002)	✓		Advanced (South Africa and Mozambique) Medium (South Africa and Zimbabwe)
Maloti-Drakensberg Transfrontier Conservation and Development Area	South Africa, Lesotho	Memorandum of Understanding signed (11 June 2001); subsidiary agreements		✓	Advanced
|Ai-|Ais-Richtersveld Transfrontier Park	South Africa, Namibia	Treaty signed (1 August 2003)	✓		Advanced
Limpopo-Shashe TFCA	South Africa, Botswana, Zimbabwe	Memorandum of Understanding signed (22 June 2006)		✓	Fairly advanced
Lubombo TFCA	South Africa, Mozambique, Swaziland	Trilateral Protocol signed (22 June 2000); subsidiary protocols		✓	Fairly advanced

Source: Adapted and updated from Van Amerom 2005, 68.

push factor was South Africa hosting the 2010 FIFA World Cup, where TFCAS played a major role in enticing tourists to cross South Africa's boundaries and ensuring that neighboring countries would also benefit from the soccer spectacle (Büscher 2010b).

All this, of course, is not to say that the forging of TFCAS, even backed by so many powerful actors, was straightforward. Each of the six TFCAS is a complicated space on its own, where the general historical dynamics have worked out differently and produced different contemporary circumstances and dynamics. A particularly crucial difference in the development of TFCAS has been whether, like with the GLTP, Kgalagadi, and |Ai-|Ais/Richtersveld, they are built around existing protected areas that can be connected as transfrontier parks or whether they revolve around the more complex format of stimulating conservation, development, and international cooperation across a variety of land-tenure arrangements next to protected areas, such as commonage areas, private land, and so forth. This is the case with the Maloti-Drakensberg, Lubombo, and Limpopo/Shashe TFCAS.

Arguably, the most straightforward situation has been the conjoining of South Africa's Kalahari Gemsbok National Park and Botswana's Gemsbok National Park into the Kgalagadi Transfrontier Park,[21] Africa's first officially declared transfrontier park, on 12 May 2000. This was important symbolically as it greatly stimulated the regional transfrontier movement, but little changed on the ground. A harsh desert landscape characterized by its famous red dunes, the Kgalagadi has, unlike other TFCAS, never seen a physical border other than the Nossob River and a symbolic line of stones in certain parts, while coordination of management had been in existence since 1948. This made the declaration of the Kgalagadi Transfrontier Park relatively easy compared to other transfrontier endeavors, such as the flagship GLTP (Schoon 2009).[22]

The GLTP links together Kruger National Park in South Africa, Limpopo National Park in Mozambique, and Gonarezhou National Park in Zimbabwe, as well as the interconnecting areas.[23] Due to its flagship status, many actors have tried hard to keep the pace of developments in the GLTP high. The former South African environment minister Valli Moosa, for example, wanted to see the prestigious peace park come to fruition before the end of his term in 2004. In 2000 he demanded that the GLTP International Technical Committee prepare drafts of a conceptual plan, an action plan, and a trilateral agreement for the Great Limpopo within a year. In contrast, the committee had proposed a minimum of two years for proper stakeholder consultation, especially with the many local communities in and around the proposed TFCA.[24] Although the Zimbabwean and Mozambican ministers accepted Moosa's demand, technical issues around border security and control only led to the signing of the international treaty that established the GLTP on 9 December 2002. A treaty, however, does not guarantee adherence. While the Zimbabwean government has consistently stated its support for the GLTP, its involvement has in reality been mired in difficulties to the extent that it repeatedly threatened the entire project (Duffy 1997; 2006b).[25] As a consequence, the development of the GLTP focused mainly on connecting the Kruger and Limpopo National Parks.

All six TFCAS mentioned in table 1.1 have treaties, memoranda of understanding, or various protocols in place that are supposed to coordinate governance action across borders. A treaty or protocol, however, is only a small step in forging transfrontier spaces. They are both the outcomes and determinants of complicated politics around (historical) struggles over land and resources, the political economy of regional southern African sovereignties, domestic political struggles, the differential expectations of involved actors, and the nature of the ecologies and biodiversity targeted by a specific TFCA. It is these types of politics, set within historical and contemporary conditions (and the way that actors conceive and act on these conditions), that determine the potential of and prospects for transfrontier conservation and the peoples and ecologies that reside there. The following chapters show how these politics revolve around struggles over consensus, antipolitics, and marketing. This chapter has shown that these modes of political conduct are not new. They have been around in various guises that are reused, reignited, and reemphasized by different actors in particular political constellations across the African continent and beyond. What makes them particularly salient now is their combined strength in the context of the neoliberal postcolony.

chapter two

NEOLIBERAL AMPLIFICATIONS

On 16 August 2006, the 7:00 p.m. news bulletin on South African Broadcasting Service 3 reported as one of the main stories that the Giriyondo border post between South Africa and Mozambique in the Great Limpopo Transfrontier Park (GLTP) had been opened that day. The station aired the presidents Thabo Mbeki of South Africa, Robert Mugabe of Zimbabwe, and Armando Guebuza of Mozambique jointly cutting the ribbon that separates the Kruger National Park from the Limpopo National Park. Speeches were made heralding the consensus between the leaders on how the new border post symbolizes the unity of the three countries in conservation, and all the development benefits that will accrue from this. Mbeki explicitly mentioned how the GLTP, and other Transfrontier Conservation Areas (TFCAS), would "be a major tourist attraction before, during, and after the 2010 World Cup." Following the formal festivities, the three presidents move straight to Maseru, Lesotho, to attend a Southern Africa Development Community (SADC) heads of state summit. According to the news bulletin, the leaders again discussed how regional development could best accrue from the 2010 FIFA World Cup.

The news bulletin showed that during the twenty-first century's first decade, the transfrontier conservation movement in southern Africa had become a locomotive on full steam. In a relatively short time, transfrontier conservation had not only been accepted at the highest political level but was seen as strategically important for the prestigious World Cup. The chapter analyzes the political strategies and struggles involved in acquiring this legitimacy on the regional level. It begins by exploring how dominant actors tried to create and operationalize a political consensus over the direction of the peace parks discourse, placing special emphasis on the role of the state and the highly uneven and contradictory realities resulting from this process. This, however, did not deter proponents to temper their claims about peace parks. To the contrary: I will argue that through the political strategies of antipolitics and marketing, the already-grandiose peace parks discourse and its claims were amplified to even grander proportions. Peace parks are presented as a model of meaning to which people can attach their identities and fortunes as well as the telos—the end state or natural order—of conservation. The chapter discusses the implications of this neoliberal amplification by outlining how the peace parks discourse has become a derivative, almost completely divorced from the contradictory realities of transfrontier conservation, and how, in relation to popular spectacles such as the World Cup in 2010, it creates value out of nature in ways that are constitutive of the regional political economy.

Practicing the Peace Parks Discourse

In the shift from fortress to community conservation, mistrust of state intervention, community sovereignty, and decentralization of power were key in conservation debates (see Hulme and Murphree 2001; McCarthy 2005). In turn and despite ambiguous results in practice, these attitudes and values were strongly defended against neoprotectionist approaches that advocated top-down state intervention, particularly in southern Africa (Büscher and Dressler 2007). Transfrontier conservation presents an interesting twist because many actors again had to give the state a more central role in conservation discourse and practice. After all, so argue governments, the formal international treaties, protocols, and memorandums of understanding necessary for transfrontier conservation can only be negotiated and concluded by the representatives of sovereign nations. This reasoning strongly influenced the way key proponents started practicing the emerging peace parks discourse.

However, actors other than national governments continuously facilitate, encourage, take over, or discourage transfrontier cooperation. And even though there still has to be an official agreement between two or three sovereign states to bring a peace park into being, formal sovereignty has clear limits in empirical reality (see also Corson 2011). For one, it was Anton Rupert, a businessman and wildlife patron, who in 1990 started pressing the then president of Mozambique, Joaquim Chissano, about the development of the GLTP. More importantly, local people have been and are still managing resources across borders outside official state-proclaimed transfrontier conservation areas. This can cause conflicts of interests, which was clear from my interview with a Department of Environmental Affairs and Tourism (DEAT) staff member who complained that communities in the |Ai-|Ais-Richtersveld Transfrontier Park (TFP) were behaving problematically, "because they feel it is their park." Specifically, his irritation dealt with the fact that "they also talk to the Namibian side and thereby bypassing the government, which they can't do."[1] Finally, we can point to the Kgalagadi TFP, where transfrontier conservation has always been a de facto reality because harsh environmental conditions have seldom respected human-made borders.

Despite this, proponents of transfrontier conservation are keenly aware of the importance of state involvement (Duffy 2006b). An actor with the resources and networks to follow up on this is the Peace Parks Foundation (PPF). According to its CEO during a meeting at the Dutch embassy in Pretoria, South Africa, in March 2005, the management of PPF is concerned mostly with access to and space for peace parks, and facilitation and training to support their development. Facilitation meant to "oil the government machinery and so fix what is broke." Significantly, the PPF has oiled the government machinery by funding the appointment of staff working solely on TFCAs in nearly each ministry of environment or tourism in southern Africa. According to a PPF document:

> Based on the tremendous success PPF had with the secondment of a TFCA Technical Advisor to South Africa's Department of Environmental Affairs and Tourism, it is now planned to create a network of similar positions throughout the SADC region within each of the conservation agencies. One of the biggest requirements to promote the TFCA concept is continuity. Through appointing a person dedicated to focus on TFCA issues with the support of PPF assisting technically, logistically and financially a great impact can be made on various fields but most importantly at a political level to influence and empower decision-makers. (Peace Parks Foundation 2002, 5)

In addition to staff, the PPF also supplies relevant ministries with technical and financial resources, maps, and overview documents, and it brings governments and other actors together by organizing and financing conferences and workshops: "In this way, not only has the PPF direct political access by contributing a wide variety of resources, they also have an edge in directing policy because they can influence part of the content, as the resources they offer are directly being used by 'their' officers in the various departments to make decisions in the policy process" (Büscher and Dietz 2005, 5). This content, obviously, is not free of value. The PPF makes it perfectly clear that it combines conservation with business goals, and that peace parks need to be "properly managed" to "achieve their economic potential" through tourism.[2] The PPF boasts that it supports TFCA business plans that "provide a comprehensive package of business and investment opportunities"; training courses where "entrepreneurship (business and financial management) and tourism as a generic subject form part of the curriculum"; and the Leadership in Conservation in Africa initiative where "the idea is that industry leaders should advise on how to bring business principles to bear on the way nature parks are managed, and for their companies to become more directly involved in conservation."[3] Besides, the PPF had initiated programs related to carbon trading and to create markets around payments for ecological services.[4]

The reasons why the PPF can do this and exert enormous influence on the transfrontier conservation agenda in southern Africa are its enormous financial power and its wide-ranging network of influential (business) elites across the world. Interpreting this dynamic, Malcolm Draper, Marja Spierenburg, and Harry Wels argue that "through the TFCAS the PPF manages to foster cohesion between the old—mainly white—and new political and business elites in post-apartheid South Africa . . . by developing a new 'Super-African' identity based on bonding with nature" (2004, 343). While there is merit in this argument, it only partially explains the consensus around transfrontier conservation. Instead, I argue that this strategy by the PPF should be seen as a conscious political move to construct a dominant discourse that favors broader neoliberal devolved governance in line with the postcolonial political economy. This peace parks discourse is the logical outcome of the historical process where big business aimed to secure its future legitimation after apartheid by investing in nature (Ramutsindela 2007). The peace parks discourse consists of the familiar transfrontier conservation elements (international cooperation, community development, and biodiversity conservation), but with a particular emphasis on finding harmony between capitalism and nature, predominantly through nature-based tourism.

Establishing a discourse as dominant requires practical action though. And from a practical viewpoint, states are vital in the overall critical mass needed to get things done in transfrontier conservation. The state functions as a transfrontier conservation focal point, and elite bonding (between the new black elites that dominate the southern African governments and the business elites backing the PPF) then serves to tie different interests to particular agendas. Thus, besides the human, financial, and technical resources that the PPF bestows on southern African states, it consciously and deliberately builds and maintains very strong links to top officials, including all heads of state and many top civil servants at ministries and state conservation agencies. According to the former PPF chief executive during his presentation at the Dutch embassy, these contacts regularly help to overcome "bureaucratic hurdles." In one specific instance, when the PPF wanted to get something done but the regional SADC was taking too long, it "called in [President] Mbeki to get the SADC logjam surpassed." During the same presentation, the CEO also mentioned how it was PPF's idea to "send" Nelson Mandela, one of the PPF's founding patrons, to South Korea to talk about a peace park between South and North Korea, something that would have created an enormous global boost for TFCAS.

The obvious point is that there are not many people who can "call in Mbeki" to do something or "send Mandela" to go somewhere. During fieldwork along the border of the Kruger National Park in November 2003, I spoke with people from resident Tsonga communities who were complaining about exactly that. Sitting on the porch of a brick house in one of the many dusty settlements along the border of the park, a middle-aged Tsonga man complained that unlike the PPF, community members there cannot step into Mbeki's office to ask him for favors, for example to protect them from the dangerous wildlife that regularly escape from the park and pose a threat to their livestock, vegetable gardens, and lives. He sarcastically added that while the PPF is keen to conserve these dangerous animals, its managers do not live with them.

The bottom line here is the importance of material resources or networks that can make a difference in how transfrontier conservation spaces are shaped (see MacDonald 2010). According to Donald Moore, this relates to Henri Lefebvre's notion of "space as a 'social relationship inherent to property relationships,' especially those securing land and environmental resources" (2008, 258; see also Lefebvre 1991). The PPF, through its resources and networks, is central in the property relationships that shape transfrontier conservation spaces in southern Africa—more so than any other actor, especially rural people living in and around TFCAS. And it makes very strategic use of this position, as another ethnographic example from research in November 2003 illustrates.[5] Halfway through my interview with the then senior manager of transfrontier conservation at South Africa's Department of Environmental Affairs—conducted behind closed doors—the PPF GIS (geographic information system) technician burst into the office and started talking to the senior manager, seemingly without noticing me. He needed the senior manager to look at some maps of TFCAS and make a decision on which ones to distribute. Only after he was finished talking and laying out the maps on the table we were sitting at did my host have a chance to introduce me. It was only then, at least five to ten minutes after he had come in, that the PPF technician acknowledged my presence by jovially shaking my hand, handing over his business card and offering me some maps.

The very fact that the PPF employs its material resources and networks to put the peace parks discourse into practice shows how the regional political economy is reflected in the southern African transfrontier conservation movement: both are largely dominated by white business interests, with the explicit inclusion of black political elites. This does not mean that the PPF has unrestrained access to all important actors or does not have to take into account those with less access or material possibilities. In a postcolonial context where community conservation and the South African transformation process have reinforced each other, heeding to community needs is vital and in its official public relations the PPF is master in doing so, particularly by referring to the benefits brought by tourism. Yet these too are far from straightforward.

Community Dilemmas

During the presentation at the Dutch embassy, the CEO mentioned that peace parks are "not necessarily for the protection of biodiversity, but mostly for development," and later added that "after a while you find out that people are more important than the environment." Whether this was genuine or hollow rhetoric is a contested issue. In academic circles the latter view has the upper hand and evidence for it is certainly available.[6]

After stating that it is all about people, the CEO hardly talked about communities in his presentation; he instead focused on animal relocations and veterinary diseases, which he believed would become the most important issues in the coming decade for the PPF.[7] Likewise, Randy Tanner notes that the PPF has given its critics "good reason to be skeptical" (2003, 83). His quotes from an interview with a PPF project manager bear strong resemblance to the colonial discourse of the dual mandate:

> For community representatives to participate on the actual management of a national park is something unfair to the community themselves. In most cases the people that are appointed to manage a national park have gone and done years of studying to gain a tertiary education. They're well qualified. . . . I know a lot of critics are advocating for it [community involvement], but in my mind it is the same as having someone living next to an airport come and sit next to the air traffic controller. . . . You can't make them air traffic controllers. (Quoted in Tanner 2003, 83)

The issue of community participation in TFCA management is highly contentious. As local communities do not represent a sovereign state or command the resource and network power of the PPF, they have little say in the international negotiations that establish TFCAs. This is ironic because—unlike the PPF—some communities actually own parts of TFCAs, most notably the Makuleke community, which owns the northernmost section of the Kruger National Park. The Makuleke people were particularly indignant when they, as owners of the land, were not taken seriously in negotiations on the GLTP (Robins and van der Waal 2011). Even when the international coordinator of the GLTP at the time, together with some consultants, pressed for more time for community involvement or granting community members a say in top-level meetings, he was refused.[8] Particularly ironic is that this refusal came from Valli Moosa, the then South African minister for environmental affairs and tourism, who regularly praised transfrontier conservation for bringing prosperity to the poor (Moosa 2002). What his reasons were are not clear, but one informant reckoned that pressure from donors and organizations such as the PPF, the amount of public relations that had already gone into the GLTP, and Moosa's desire to attach his name to a successful megaproject, caused him to shortchange promised stakeholder-consultation processes, sending a clear signal that communities were not taken very seriously.[9]

The GLTP also provides an ample illustration of the problematic implementation of the promised community benefits of TFCAS through the further sedimentation of "fragmented forms of sovereignty" (Mbembe 2000, 284; see also Spierenburg, Steenkamp, and Wels 2006). First, the South African government decided in January 2009 that all outstanding Kruger land claims by communities—covering nearly the entire park—would be dealt with by "equitable redress" rather than restoring land rights.[10] After the successful Makuleke land claim,[11] the government and South African National Parks became worried they might lose a "national and international asset." They therefore decided to seek alternative ways to address the history of community deprivations around the establishment of the Kruger National Park (see Carruthers 1995). Needless to say, this sedimentation of colonial sovereignties infuriated the other thirty-eight communities who had outstanding land claims.[12] Second, in Mozambique, concurrent with the relocation of animals from the Kruger National Park to the Limpopo National Park, discussions about the removal of communities intensified. A resettlement policy framework was developed that claimed that local people were extensively consulted (Huggins et al. 2003) while important actors involved in the process continued to proclaim that the resettlement would be voluntary (Milgroom and Spierenburg 2008). Community members, when questioned by researchers, challenged the claims that they were extensively consulted and that they agreed to be relocated (Refugee Research Programme 2002, 3). Jessica Milgroom and Marja Spierenburg, in an assessment of the resettlement process, state that "interviews with residents in four villages designated to be resettled suggest that many feel that outside the park they will not have access to resources that hitherto have been key to their livelihood security. They are concerned about not having access to suitable land for agriculture, and facing a lack of forest resources and reduced grazing land" (2008, 440). While reckoning that resettlement procedures are never straightforward, they conclude that at best the fate of park residents should be described as "induced volition."[13] Finally, community-park relations in Gonarezhou National Park in Zimbabwe were also historically ambiguous, but here local communities decided to break through colonial sovereignties, and "invade" the park, thereby threatening Zimbabwe's participation in the GLTP (Duffy 2006b).[14]

In all, research points out that the GLTP—like other TFCAS—is (so far) unable to fulfill its promise to redress historical injustices and create sufficient community benefits (see Schoon 2009; Thondhlana, Shackleton, and Muchapondwa 2011; Wolmer 2003). In fact, as the resettlement from the Limpopo National Park shows, local people might equally be worse off. Another such case relates to how open borders are focused on animals and tourists rather than local people, which "is ironic since discussions about transboundary conservation benefits highlight their potential to remove 'artificial borders' and restore 'historical links'" (Jones 2005, 273). In the Lubombo TFCA, for instance, the plan was to connect various reserves situated along the borders of southern Mozambique, South Africa, and Swaziland via a corridor along the international border to facilitate wildlife movement. This plan would have affected local livelihoods in South Africa, and as for communities, "social access to family and friends in Mozambique is a unique, yet important, resource that cannot be easily replaced or substituted" (273). Hence, Jennifer Jones argues that "if potential designs for the conservation corridor include separating the community from the border by a fenced protected area, residents will lose this access if other provisions are not made" (273). Ultimately, provisions were made, but the corridor established in 2011 still constrains local people more than the alternative would and gives priority to the free movement of animals.[15]

Tourism: The Holy Grail

If community consultation and cross-border linkages are problematic, what about the benefits that local people are said to receive from nature-based tourism? After all, tourism is generally posited as the "holy grail," capable of tying together all the different goals of contemporary (transfrontier) conservation (see Carrier and Macleod 2005; Duffy 2002; Fletcher 2011). Tourism is constructed as if it necessitates conservation, because it is (charismatic, large) wildlife and landscapes that draw most tourists to the region. And, nature-based tourism is expected to bring economic growth, jobs, and development, as the official "Brand South Africa" tourism website asserts: "Nama communities living in and around the |Ai-|Ais/Richtersveld Transfrontier Park are set to reap the benefits of the treaty. The disadvantaged Richtersveld population, comprising the Kuboes, Sanddrift, Lekkersing and Eksteenfontien communities, heavily reliant on a mining industry which is scaling down, is set to reap sustainable jobs from tourism growth."[16] Also, tourism is assumed to catalyze international cooperation. Tourism requires a stable political climate, and international cooperation is thus required if the region is to remain attractive to tourists. This became especially apparent from the continuous hype and expectations around the World Cup in South Africa in 2010, which was believed to bring benefits to the entire region (Department of Environmental Affairs and Tourism 2005). All in all, tourism is seen as the glue that binds the different goals of TFCAS together. It is therefore no surprise that it features prominently in the peace parks discourse and that investments in TFCAS are spent largely on tourism infrastructure.

Yet again, transfrontier conservation realities are a far cry from this rhetoric. In the GLTP,

> progress to develop tourism has been constrained by different levels of infrastructure and capacity within the three countries [Mozambique, South Africa, and Zimbabwe] to realise their objectives, areas of political instability, land tenure issues, and addressing the needs of existing inhabitants of the area. Constraining the strategic plan for the entire TFCA, animal health implications of merging wildlife populations of the three countries have yet to be fully investigated and resolved—especially with regard to their potential contact with livestock. No real constraints to tourism investment were identified in South Africa, but it was clear that the situation was less favourable in Zimbabwe and Mozambique. (Spenceley 2005, 53)[17]

Anna Spenceley addresses a crucial issue that is also recognized by other scholars (see Duffy 2006b; Schoon 2009; Van Amerom 2005), namely that South Africa has enormous advantages when it comes to benefiting from tourism because its infrastructure is far superior to that of its neighbors. The crux of the matter is that most TFCAS will be accessed from the South African side, with excursions into the other countries, which will not bring substantial increases in tourism revenues. In fact, neighboring countries have argued that they could even end up paying more for tourism than receiving from it, as they do share in the burden of developing tourism infrastructures (Van Amerom 2005). Moreover,

> even if Mozambique and Zimbabwe would successfully develop tourism facilities on their side of the Great Limpopo and attract substantial tourism, chances are that much of the income generated by ecotourism on their territories would leak back to South Africa. Its dominant position on the regional tourism market, coupled with the fact that TBPAS are modelled on free market principles, gives South Africa an important edge over its neighbours to earn from ecotourism in TBPAS, even in adjacent territory. (Van Amerom 2005, 157)

Marloes Van Amerom makes the important point that it is mainly white South African and foreign companies that have the capacity to cater to the demands of tourists. They are therefore likely to win tourism-related tenders in neighboring countries or just expand their operational territory into these countries, funneling back most of the revenues to South Africa or overseas. This is a good example of a capitalist space built around property relations that further fragments postcolonial sovereignties and thus governments' abilities to address historical injustices and dispossessions (reducing them instead to "the contractual legal authority that can legitimate the extractive work of transnational firms" [Ferguson 2006, 207]). In sum and in spite of the rhetoric, the tourism market is set to benefit those (overwhelmingly white) market leaders much more than (poor) local people, a state of affairs recognized the world over (see Duffy 2002; Fletcher 2009; West and Carrier 2004). In fact, tourism might even harm people due to evictions and the closing of borders or, in Mark Dowie's words, "permanently indenture" them "as park rangers . . . , porters, waiters, harvesters, or, if they manage to learn a European language, ecotour guides" (2009, xxvi).

Cracks beneath the Discourse?

Clearly, there are major cracks beneath the neoliberal peace parks discourse of harmony between conservation, development, and capitalism. While states argue that they are the only official negotiating partners, communities that own the land beg to differ but end up having no say, and actors that do not own any part of TFCAS or cannot lay historical claims to the land do have tremendous influence. Also, some actors clearly benefit (much) more than others. This begs the question, who is needed for what consensus? Is there indeed "elite pacting" whereby members of the elite agree on a certain course of action regarding TFCAS, including the tacit exclusion of the nonelite (see Draper, Spierenburg, and Wels 2004)? Or is reality more nuanced, and can one distinguish differing alliances and consensuses? I argue that because of its resources and networks, the PPF has so far been able to dominate the discourse, but other more-marginal discourses exist that compete with the PPF while leaving the neoliberal undercurrents of the dominant discourse unchallenged.[18] Discourses tie actors to certain sets of ideas, which frame space for action. And it is exactly this space for action that in response to growing contradictions and struggles over consensus becomes more narrowly defined. The task at hand then is to show how neoliberal discourses are legitimated in the face of contradictions in practice. First, however, we must briefly examine how solid the consensus around the dominant peace parks discourse and associated practices really is.

We have seen how less influential actors in transfrontier conservation, such as the communities in the GLTP, contest the discourses and practices produced by the PPF to little avail, due (mainly) to lack of resources and networks. Other actors, for instance in the nongovernmental sector, do have resources and networks. Perhaps not on the same scale as the PPF, but they are influential nonetheless. Two prominent examples, Conservation International and the International Union for Conservation of Nature (IUCN), both contested the idea that the PPF provides good "conceptual and practical leadership."[19] According to the then (South African) cochair of the IUCN Transboundary Protected Areas Taskforce, the IUCN should be the home for leadership with respect to TFCAS in the region. The regional director at Conservation International stated that there is a lack of leadership with respect to TFCAS in southern Africa. He mentioned that the chairs of the IUCN Transboundary Protected Areas Taskforce are too busy to adequately fulfill a leadership role and create consensus. According to him, the PPF should have done this, but he likens the organization to a balloon: it does not have the content and falls "hopelessly short of intellectual guidance." Other impossibilities for leadership according to him are the regional government body SADC, which does not have the capacity, and his own Conservation International, which is "quietly doing its thing" and would not be fit to lead.[20] In short, these NGOs active in transfrontier conservation in the region are critical of the peace parks discourse put forward by the PPF, but do not have the time, resources, or ambition to provide leadership themselves.

What about the state? Obviously, southern African states, despite being intensely lobbied by other actors, have resources (albeit often limited) and networks and contain plenty of intelligent staff members, many of whom are not automatically charmed by the images promoted by the PPF. In the South African DEAT offices in Pretoria, for example, I often heard employees in the biodiversity conservation branch complain about the influence of the PPF on their colleagues in the TFCA department and the ways they portray peace parks as the epitome of conservation. At the same time, employees grumbled that under the influence of the PPF, the focus of the TFCA department was often "more on tourist and border infrastructure" than the core mandate: biodiversity conservation.[21] Yet the way that South African government departments have been restructured in the last decade or so makes them increasingly dependent on seductive "public-private partnerships." Many government departments have seen massive reorganizations that increasingly align them with private-sector neoliberal operating principles (see Castree 2008b; McDonald and Ruiters 2005). Add to this that many postcolonial states in southern Africa are "weakly governed" and severely underresourced and it again becomes clear that sovereignty in assessing and implementing policy proposals for the public good can be severely compromised (Ferguson 2006, 207).[22] This process is further reinforced by another group of actors that seems elusive but is crucial in legitimizing and stabilizing particular discourses while at the same time ensuring that these are practically operationalized in neoliberal terms: consultants.

Consulting Conservation

To stress the importance of consultants in transfrontier conservation, one only has to look at the budget of one of the many projects aimed at establishing TFCAS. The World Bank's final implementation completion report for a "Transfrontier Conservation Areas Pilot and Institutional Strengthening Project," in Mozambique between 1997 and 2002, noted total costs of US$4.69 million, of which $2.09 million was spent on "technical assistance, training and studies" and $1.43 million on "incremental operating costs" (World Bank 2004, 26).[23] Both involve mostly consultant or World Bank staff services, which gives these actors leeway in operationalizing discourses. This, however, is rarely acknowledged publicly. Consultants' services are often taken for granted, thought to be "neutral" and therefore not worthy of notice. Moreover, the information provided by consultants is rarely out in the public domain. Contracts between consultants (firms) and their clients often state that the clients may not publicly disclose any of the information provided without authorization.[24] All this makes the researcher's job more difficult, as trust needs to be gained from informants before they (are willing to) disclose documents that provide valuable information about the framing of discourses and the management of contradictions.

Consultants are some of the main contributors to the (rather voluminous) trail of documents—which I will refer to as the paper/policy trail— produced to turn transfrontier conservation ideas into reality. An emphasis on the paper/policy trail is important because it reveals much about practices of politics and administration (Quarles van Ufford, Giri, and Mosse

2003, 14–17). Several interviewees on the policy level admitted this openly when we were talking about career and personal development, ambition, interpersonal relations, and, especially, the political legitimation and consensus purposes of policy and paper. Paper/policy is the lubricant that enables practices of politics and administration to take place and—more importantly—to shape them in particular directions. Interestingly, if one glances at some of the documents produced, it is remarkable that despite the diversity, so many themes, methods, proposals, and even wordings are the same or similar, especially in the more-public documents like treaties and protocols. General policy language is used in these, for example around the stated benefits of TFCAs. These are constructed around the familiar themes of tourism, biodiversity protection, harmonization of policies, social and economic development, and international cooperation, among others. It is only further down the paper trail that one discovers subtleties and specificities around various TFCAs and comparisons become harder.

Because of the sheer amount of existing policies, legislation pieces, and guidelines, many donors or governments do not even have an overview of what they need to take into account, so they ask consultants to provide this for them. One such consultancy report is by Development Alternatives Inc. from Nelspruit, South Africa. The report was prepared for the USAID Regional Center for Southern Africa. It said, "The study reported here was undertaken to assist in the creation of an enabling policy environment in and among the three countries [South Africa, Mozambique and Zimbabwe]. It examines some of the levels of policies governing Transboundary activities among the three nations, and in particular regarding the Great Limpopo Transfrontier Park (GLTFP) and the Transfrontier Conservation Area (GLTFCA)" (Buzzard 2001, 1). These and similar reports are plentiful and many have similar conclusions: namely that more, better, and simpler policies are needed and should be reviewed continuously and "translated into practice on the ground" (57–58). In fact, the title of the frequently cited annex A in the report, "Key Policy Issues Affecting the Implementation of the GLTFP and GLTFCA and Proposed Actions," refers to a "need for TFCA policies" (57).[25]

This excessive focus on policies is not shared by all consultancy reports. Many technical, thematic, or other reports have been produced around TFCAs, but the point here is that consultants are important not only because of what they produce but also because of the social-political functions they fulfill. Particularly in relation to the state, these functions are significant and revolve as much around issues of legitimacy for specific political agendas as they do around filling capacity gaps. Consultants are thus especially crucial in the politics of consensus in neoliberal conservation, because their labors often contribute to the belief that contradictory realities can actually disappear.[26] But this is not all. Consultants also bring with them a particular way of working, namely according to private-sector operating principles such as cost recovery, competitive bidding, cost-benefit analysis, and performance-targeted salaries. After all, consultants are part of the private sector, and in their service to the public sector they stimulate the public-private fusion already so desired by states and donors. In practice this means that consultancies help to ensure that "a wide variety of non-business institutions become subject to a discipline primarily designed for capitalist enterprise" (Van der Pijl 1998, 161). In other words, in the very (micro)production of their services, consultancies guarantee a further neo-liberalization of the state (and this is not even taking into account the fact that consultants' reports often recommend market-based strategies to many of the problems and issues that the state sought an answer for).

Neoliberal Undercurrents, the State, and Consensus Struggles

This begs the question, do states actually want to challenge these neo-liberal undercurrents? The above discussion shows that this is not the case. Recalling Jamie Peck and Adam Tickell (2002), transfrontier conservation should be seen in the context of where contemporary neoliberalism has progressed to, from its rollback in the 1980s to the rollout variant in the 1990s and 2000s, implicating not only the (public transfers to the) private sector but also the actual neoliberalization of the state. David Moore, with reference to Africa, describes this process as follows: "If the era of 'structural adjustment' economic policies of the 1980s and earlier 1990s meant attempts to 'get the prices right' and to hack away indiscriminately at the state, then we are now in the age of 'getting the state right' to implement the same goals as before" (1999, 64). Transfrontier conservation is thus remarkably in line with these recent developments in neoliberal practice, which brings the state back in.[27] This is not to suggest that neoliberalism's ambivalence toward the state is gone, or that the state is a monolithic actor. Rather, neoliberals, such as the members of the PPF, now recognize the need to have the official representative of a sovereign space as a partner in the neoliberal constitution of conservation and development.

This, in turn, should be seen in the broader South African political-economic context where, as Patrick Bond (2000) has convincingly argued, both black and white elites have actively subjected themselves to the global neoliberal project during the 1990s. The (accepted) soothing of the state by the PPF should therefore be seen as recognition of the important role attributed to state apparatuses as tools for the further entrenchment of neoliberal practices. While the common argument for state emphasis in TFCA development is that nation-states are the only actors with international negotiation powers, I argue that in a swiftly neoliberalizing economy that places tremendous emphasis on the importance of tourism, the state plays a vital role in providing services such as security, international investor confidence, a legal framework, and infrastructure. Getting the state to support neoliberal policies and internalize neoliberal political conduct fuels a continuous deepening of neoliberalization across society (see Fletcher 2010). The real frontier transcended by the transfrontier trend is therefore the public acceptance of the important role of the state in stimulating conservation as a neoliberal project.

Taking stock of the analysis so far, how do we characterize the political consensus struggle over transfrontier conservation on the regional southern African level and its neoliberal disposition? On the one hand, consensus about transfrontier conservation practice is far from present in southern Africa. On the other hand, there is a pragmatic convergence around (or little resistance to) the dominant peace parks discourse. I suggest, therefore, that the consensus struggle is a struggle to socially regulate the production of transfrontier conservation as well as the actors involved in terms of carving out accepted ways to behave. These behaviors, although divergent in interests, practices, and even discourses, operate within a narrow space of action that does not challenge the underlying status quo that mirrors the wider neoliberal, racial political economy of the region.[28] The way that this social regulation works is that public values (like societal care for biodiversity) are increasingly transformed into tradable, more commercially oriented values (such as environmental services) that can be ranked by market mechanisms (Kovel 2002, 166). This favors those who can compete the best, which is an inherent part of neoliberal devolved governance.

Elites, such as the PPF, are typically best able to compete in a neoliberal enabling environment, but this is not always the case. By creating appealing consensus discourses, the neoliberalization of transfrontier conservation becomes a process stimulated and legitimated from above and below (see, for example, Taylor 2003). The TFCA paper/policy trail is a good illustration, especially down the line, where contextual, historical, and other differences become bigger but similarities in discourse remain striking. Consequently, the paper/policy trail very much embodies the devolved part of increasing self-regulation within a free-market context, a point that is especially clear with respect to consultants. Self-regulation alone though does not uphold consensus over the peace parks discourse. It needs constant proactive grooming and strategic interventions so that the contradictions in transfrontier conservation practice remain manageable. Consensus as neoliberal political conduct is therefore also a struggle to maintain a critical mass of actors that uphold the superiority of market-based strategies to tackle public problems. But to enable this consensus to deeply enter into the social conscious, other political strategies are necessary. In the face of contradictions, the trick is to amplify the consensus discourse to even grander proportions.

Seeking Telos in the Transfrontier

Because the word "transfrontier" denotes political international relations, one should expect a highly politicized intervention process in which TFCA implementation is pursued. However, in line with other interpretations of conservation and development interventions (see Bebbington 2005; Ferguson 1994), TFCAS are portrayed as technical, nonpolitical, and indeed antipolitical. A case in point is the discourse employed in the book *Transboundary Conservation: A New Vision for Protected Areas*, authored by several members of the conservation establishment, that I quoted in the beginning of the introduction. This is the complete paragraph from which I took the quotes:

> How can we explain the tremendous increase in the number of transboundary protected areas in the last few decades? And why has this phenomenon generated such tremendous enthusiasm in the conservation community? The answer is that the transboundary element can act as a multiplier, greatly amplifying the benefits protected areas already provide. Transboundary conservation area initiatives allow conservationists to operate at a larger scale, moving across political boundaries to protect a transboundary ecosystem in its entirety, rather than stopping at political borders that rarely correspond to natural systems. By the same token, a TBCA [Transboundary Conservation Area] can create

unique social opportunities; for example, by reuniting communities divided by borders or allowing mobile peoples to move across their traditional territories more easily. TBCAS also add an enticing political dimension to conservation, which is the capacity to reduce tensions or even to help resolve conflicts between countries, in particular those stemming from boundary disputes. This peace-making dimension enlarges the range of benefits parks provide in a significant way. It also provides powerful evidence for one of the central tenets of conservation —that protected areas are not only necessary to secure the planet's ecological integrity but, more broadly, that they are an essential component of any healthy, peaceful, and productive society. (Mittermeier, Kormos, Mittermeier, Sandwith et al. 2005, 41)

It is a beguiling paragraph, albeit a fairly accurate reflection of the broader gray literature that posits transfrontier conservation as the new frontier. What is striking, first, is that the political dimension of TFCAS is squarely equated with peace making. That few (social) scientists would equate politics with peace making is an understatement. Nonetheless, this idea undergirds the entire *peace* parks discourse.[29] Second, the excerpt praises the multiple positive effects of TFCAS—in the environmental, social, and the political realms (see, e.g., Hanks 2000). TFCAS supposedly bring positive contributions, "greatly amplifying the benefits protected areas already provide." Naturally, this is marketing speak, because in the real world the benefits of transboundary protected areas are all but clear-cut. Finally, protected areas in the excerpt are molded as a new all-embracing teleology of health, peace, and productivity, with the adjective "transboundary" being the latest stage in the molding process.

This last element, in particular, is important in the politics of neoliberal transfrontier conservation. The previous focus was on the mobilization of support for, and defining, a consensus around the peace parks discourse— outside of which one is regarded a radical or outsider. The next step is for the discourse to become normalized into the unconscious. This entails both abstract and practical strategies. The more abstract antipolitics struggle is over purging transfrontier conservation of political content. The argument that I will advance is that proponents of TFCAS, especially the PPF, try to construct transfrontier conservation as a model of meaning to which people can attach their identities and fortunes and as the telos of conservation and development more generally (Büscher 2010c).

The background to this argument is Daniel Brockington, Rosaleen Duffy, and Jim Igoe's statement that "Marx was correct that liberal capitalism alienated people from the environment in ways that ecological connections were no longer evident to them" (2008, 197). Marx's overall assertion, evidently, was much broader than the environment. In a capitalist world, he argued, where in principle everything can be commodified, general alienation continuously deepens. This in turn leads to loss of meaning as meaningful attachment gives way to commercial rationality (see Arvidsson 2005; West 2006). Jean Baudrillard takes this point further and argues that in our hyperreal information society, information "exhausts itself in the act of staging communication" and that "rather than producing meaning, it exhausts itself in the staging of meaning" (1994, 80). But in true capitalist fashion, and as Brockington and colleagues show, this does not deter entrepreneurs from exploiting this new space by reattaching meaning to and engagement with commercial products through consumption. Nowhere is this better understood than in contemporary private-sector marketing, where the sole objective is to tie products in with personality attributes, passions, personal emotions, and so forth, in order to hook clients on a deeper level (Arvidsson 2005). There seems to be no actor in transfrontier conservation that understands this better than the PPF, an organization originating from and rooted in big business (Ramutsindela 2007). In its pursuit to establish and legitimate peace parks, I argue that the PPF, along with other actors, employs all the familiar marketing moves of contemporary advertising and public relations to make TFCAs meaningful to stakeholders. How then does this work in political terms?

To being with, if politics is about the mediation and contestation of interests and power struggles, the peace parks discourse tries to avoid this by trying to take everything related to conservation and development into account. Looking at the lists of criteria and principles that donors and stakeholders want conservation and development schemes to attend to peace parks seem to be the epitome of what can be asked of interventions. Besides the conservation of nature and reduction of poverty, they are supposed to facilitate participation, enhance ownership, empower communities, enrich international cooperation and peace, reunite and reinvigorate cultures, stimulate spirituality, encourage economic growth and tourism, educate, form partnerships, boost security, adhere to good governance, and so forth. The conservation and development teleology seems complete and ready to compete. Crucially, whereas states are often seen as the prime focal

FIGURE 2.1
Peace Parks
Foundation logo.

points from which to expect these noble objectives, the shift to devolved governance under the neoliberal state in an already-fragmented postcolonial context gives many actors possibilities to fill the governance voids (see Ferguson 2006). Next, these actors need to start more consciously and strategically behaving as part of a political arena in which they have to compete for popular support to justify their existence and interventions. The way to do this is similar to classic consensus building: gather as many people as possible under unifying, all-embracing, and seemingly uncontestable concepts, premises, and promises. The PPF does exactly this, and rather bluntly so. Its official slogan, "the global solution" (see fig. 2.1), intends to convey the idea that the peace parks concept is as perfect as conservation and development constructions can be and is implementable and appropriate across the globe. Another example is the extremely strategic use that the PPF makes of its patrons, especially Mandela, a former president of South Africa. Mandela is one of the most recognizable and respected people in the world and to have him as founding patron, regularly endorsing PPF activities and initiatives, probably guarantees the highest buy-in one could get from any endorsement.

Interestingly, not all PPF staff members always agree with the way the organization conceptualizes peace parks, but most are still admirers of its founder, Rupert, and believe that he "gave them" the tools to make their common "dream" a reality.[30] In fact, the PPF uses Rupert himself as a tool to present peace parks as a model of meaning, as Rupert's life is portrayed as arguably the most significant life that can be lived. Nowhere is this clearer than in a fancy brochure dedicated to Rupert's life, titled "An Idea That Binds: How Anton Rupert's Philosophy of Co-existence and Partnership Culminated in Peace Parks."[31] In it, Rupert is portrayed as a role model: a hard worker, successful business entrepreneur, and patron of nature who remains humble despite his enormous successes in life. The brochure starts by extolling Rupert's resistance against apartheid based on his "philosophy of co-existence between man and man, and man and nature": "The policy of apartheid stymied the development of the entire Southern Africa. When Rupert's philosophy of co-existence was discussed in the South African parliament in 1966, he was accused of trying to establish Hong Kongs and Singapores in South Africa! If only South Africa had done so way back in 1966. . . . !'"

The brochure moves on to praise Rupert's achievements in nature conservation by founding World Wildlife Fund South Africa and how this "culminated" in the "global solution" of peace parks. Different aspects of peace parks are explained in grandiose style, after which the brochure ends by quoting some of Rupert's practical philosophies and wisdoms in life.[32] These portrayals of Rupert do not only come from the PPF. Many other people, especially after his passing in January 2006, described him in similar terms.[33] The point is not whether Rupert's alleged successes are factually and contextually correct, although it should be obvious that there are large contradictions in a "benevolent conservation tycoon" who made most of his fortune during apartheid from cigarettes, liquor, and luxury goods, many of which depend on mining and natural-resource extraction (Spierenburg and Wels 2010). The crux is that Rupert is portrayed as a role model, whose entire life was meaningful in multiple ways. In an interview, the former PPF chief executive stated that Rupert was "the catalyst, by example": "His whole life has been taking an idea and putting it into a real venture, and he's applying those things to his conservation activities. I am his arm, his weapon" (Weaver 2001, 9). In sum, the direct link between Rupert's exemplary life and peace parks serves to construct the latter as models of meaning, through which people can obtain new hope in conservation, development, peace, Africa, and so on.[34]

There are plenty of other examples besides the PPF, but the point is clear.

Peace parks are presented as all embracing ideological, even spiritual, models of meaning that combine the Garden of Eden with business sense, both of which are seen as natural to humans. In this vein it is apt to heed Peter Marden's point that "the spiritual centre of contemporary life in modern capitalist society is deemed by the protagonists to be corporate in origin, and is itself, one manifestation of the deification of the market and the triumph of anti-politics" (2003, 185). Yet the inverse of this argument might also illustrate why the construction of peace parks as a model of meaning is an antipolitical strategy. One could argue that, instead of TFCAS forming "the global solution" to social, environmental, political, and economic problems, they are the solution to many of the social, political, economic, and environmental contradictions in conservation interventions today. In short: the more intense the politics, the more intense the antipolitics (Büscher 2010a). As it becomes more difficult and complex to maintain order and govern change in a globalized world, it becomes equally difficult and complex to formulate and develop answers in terms of governance structures. Antipolitical strategies are therefore not only necessary for building political consensus, they are increasingly the sole option to at least discursively adhere to neoliberal contradictions in practice.

All of this is not to say that TFCAS are merely discursive constructions to deal with the contradictions of our time. It makes (biological, managerial) sense that ecosystems across borders are looked at and managed holistically, that often previously disadvantaged communities living in or near these areas have a say in the management of TFCAS, and that more-regular cooperation between countries could enhance understanding. Yet, when implemented and legitimated the neoliberal way, these issues are increasingly torn between the enormous expectations of peace parks as discursive models of meaning and the contradictions described above. A practical strategy is needed to keep peace parks manageable, credible, and competitive in the face of many other models in the conservation and development marketplace, both in its implementation and in terms of political legitimation and mobilization: marketing.

The Marketing and Consumption of Transfrontier Conservation

I have likened marketing to strategies that aim to gain competitive advantage in a marketplace. Marketing, however, does not stop with the promotion of a certain product. It entails the active influencing of consumer choices, preferably to the point that the choice becomes embodied and internalized. As such, marketing and politics are closely related. Both are processes that mediate and try to influence decisions and interests in the public sphere and are usually informed by a certain ideological attitudes (whether implicit or explicit). One could argue that the main difference is that marketing focuses on a specific product rather than political ideals or a political agenda, but even these boundaries are becoming blurred, which is why I speak of marketing as a political strategy. If peace parks, as political constructs, are "products," then their promotion is inherently political, especially when on a more abstract level they are posited as antipolitical.

What then are the most-important elements of the marketing of peace parks, particularly in terms of the practical strategies that aim to create legitimacy and political buy-in? Typical practical activities are flyers, brochures, leaflets, websites, commercials in magazines, and the like. In many government departments in southern Africa, for example, brochures are available for each of the six major peace parks, hailing their ecological features, cultural importance, and tourism opportunities. These brochures seemingly originate from national governments as they include official department staff and contact details, yet they actually say they are "sponsored by Peace Parks Foundation." Other more-personalized activities are, inter alia, fundraisers, personal chats, and presentations with the aim of selling peace parks (such as the presentation at the Dutch embassy in 2005). In one way or another, these activities aim to enhance the consumption of peace parks. They are aimed at the wider public as well as individual decision makers, donors, conservationists, influential businesspeople, and politicians. The CEO of the PPF specifically mentioned during the meeting at the Dutch embassy that the peace parks concept works well with politicians due to its "feel-good" character. According to him, politicians love "shaking hands" when opening peace parks, as it brings good publicity. Consequently, most of these activities revolve around the one practical strategy that markets peace parks like no other: tourism.

Recall that (nature-based) tourism is often portrayed as the holy grail in transfrontier conservation and development. Now consider Rupert's comments in the PPF's *Annual Review 1999*: "Sinking beneath the weight of war and survival and of exploding populations searching for living space are Africa's designated protected areas, the crown jewels of a tourism industry which has the potential to provide a sustainable way of life." He further adds: "Poverty stricken Africa desperately needs alternatives to subsistence living, and the creation of jobs from tourism gives these"

(Peace Parks Foundation 2000, 2). According to the second issue of *Peace Parks Quarterly* from 1998, "Visitors are drawn by the outstanding natural beauty and wildlife of the [southern African] region. Conservation areas, and peace parks in particular, will provide that product. While peace parks will not provide the whole recipe for a multi-destination visit, they will be focused on the main ingredient—wildlife." The same article adds that "tourism is under-exploited in southern Africa," and that the branding of Africa should revolve around "Africa, the cradle of mankind, confident host to a wealth of wildlife and proud of its heritage as the custodian of some of the most precious treasures in the world."[35]

These remarks are typical of the PPF's strategy to amplify the marketing of tourism as the ultimate answer to the complex links between poverty, the conservation of wildlife and biodiversity, and economic growth in (southern) Africa. In this amplification, dual-mandate style racial and colonial stereotypes resurface with a vengeance. Consider Rupert's words once again: "Embedded deep in the psyche of man is the oldest symbol of all, the Garden of Eden. This is a place of peace and reflection free from divisive barriers and physical constraints. Affluent Western man needs for the health of his soul to take time off from the frenetic treadmill of his existence to return to the Garden for refreshment and contemplation, and the growth of tourism to wilderness areas endorses this" (Peace Parks Foundation 2000, 2). Combined with his other remark about "poverty stricken Africa," it is clear that Rupert sees wilderness-based tourism as a way for the "affluent Western man" (not woman) to cleanse his tired soul and for poor black Africans to earn some money serving whites. Whereas black Africans need to be taken off the land to make a living (Africa "desperately needs alternatives to subsistence living"), whites apparently need the land to make life tenable. All of this supports David Hughes's argument that "contemporary conservation dabbles in nostalgia for the colonial past" and "continues to produce the aesthetics, symbols, and fables of white privilege" (2010, 133). Although critical research continues to debunk these fables (see Duffy 2010; Singh and van Houtum 2002), it is remarkable that the racial, gender, and cultural prejudices so strongly embedded in the southern African political economy not only persist in the peace parks discourse but form the basis of its marketing.

When seen in the broader history of South Africa's political economy, these remarks by Rupert (and similar remarks by others) further suggest that conservation is a space-making exercise, as whites try to reassert "a continental space commensurate with a particular white history and hope for the future" (Hughes 2005, 161). This history and hope entail an African landscape based on the "myth of wild Africa" (J. Adams and McShane 1996), whereby Eurocentric visions of a borderless natural Africa and Christian visions of whites "saving Africans from themselves" play a dominant role (see Hughes 2010; Nelson 2003; Neumann 1998). Although these mythological and religious aspects of transfrontier conservation are important—as they are in other regions of the world (see Slater 2002)—this is only part of the story. Or, rather (and put somewhat impudently), they are the grease in the wheels of political consensus creation. The more important element is the coming together of the end of apartheid, the neoliberalization of South Africa and the country's associated desire to integrate into the global economy, and the role of whites (see Alexander 2002; Ramutsindela 2007).

In short, the neoliberalization of the South African economy made it possible for those with a head start in the private sector—especially whites —to take advantage of and fortify their positions (Bond 2000). This became even more marked when labor opportunities in the public sphere diminished and many highly skilled whites made the switch to the private sector. Although formally under pressure to cater to previously disadvantaged groups, the position of whites in the economy actually became stronger due to their necessity in maintaining and extending South Africa's global competitiveness, something the government of the African National Congress had committed itself to through its Growth, Employment and Redistribution GEAR policy (Bond 2000).[36] In line with this, South Africa had to start breathing the "culture of neoliberalism," which involved promoting a "political strategy that emphasized the liberty of consumer choice, not only with respect to particular products but also with respect to lifestyles, modes of expression, and a wide range of cultural practices" (Harvey 2005, 42). Marketing is central in this.

On the microlevel, one can easily see by walking around any one of the malls that are mushrooming throughout the country that South Africa has quickly adapted to this culture. On the macrolevel, the neoliberal pressure shines through in the need to make southern Africa competitive in the global market by focusing on its products with a comparative advantage (Van der Westhuizen 2005). One of the most important of these is tourism, and the trick is to make the product stand out by marketing it more aggressively, more openly, and in line with so-called lifestyles, modes of expression, and cultural practices and desires. From this perspective, it makes sense that those who do the marketing (mostly South African whites) and those who are targeted (mostly white European and American tourists, but also potential business partners) find each other in the theme that intuitively appeals to them both: the Garden of Eden, or the myth of wild Africa.[37] Hence, the significance is not just whether they actually believe in or long for this. The point is that the Garden of Eden is a useful marketing tool that further entrenches, stimulates, and broadens business interests associated with peace parks, while at the same time keeping inconvenient and contradictory realities out of sight.[38]

But marketers do not leave it at that. In addition to hiding inconvenient and contradictory realities, marketing actively engages in the (re)interpretation of realities so that they are (re)aligned to fit the marketers' stories. In other words, marketing is focused on spectacle or "a social relation that is mediated by images" (Debord 1967, 4). Jim Igoe has argued that Guy Debord's ideas about spectacle are extremely relevant for contemporary neoliberal conservation and that research should address "the ways in which this spectacle mediates social relationships and human-environment relationships" (2010, 382). Regarding TFCAS, one way to do this is through the opportunistic use of celebrities or sports events to create and further amplify the desired representations and images (Van der Westhuizen 2005).

The 2010 World Cup Spectacle

As was clear from the SABC 3 news bulletin, the relevant recent event that stood out by triggering new marketing activities around TFCAS is the 2010 World Cup.[39] Where tourism in general is already seen to hold endless amounts of benefits, the World Cup seemed to amplify benefits and expectations even further (DeMotts 2009). A poster at the DEAT offices in South Africa referred to tourism resulting from the World Cup as "South Africa's new gold" (see fig. 2.2). South Africa did have plenty reasons to promote tourism around the World Cup in this way. In their bid to host the cup, the South African government promised to spread the benefits to the wider region. In turn, the PPF and DEAT actively tried to construct transfrontier conservation as vital in this objective. They produced a strategy in 2005 that aimed to launch TFCAS as the prime vehicles to realize these regional benefits (Department of Environmental Affairs and Tourism 2005).

"Why TFPS and TFCAS?," asks the strategy document. The answer: "FIFA showcases soccer, TFCAS showcase Africa." The document adds: "This view

FIGURE 2.2 Tourism is South Africa's new gold.

was based on the realisation that apart from being home to Africa's unique attractions, wildlife (fauna and flora), beautiful landscapes, culture and history, TFPS and TFCAS have the distinct advantage of having in place co-ordination and collaboration mechanisms that can be used to take advantage of the 2010 event. Consolidation of transfrontier initiatives therefore provides an opportunity to create Africa's premier international tourism destination" (Department of Environmental Affairs and Tourism 2005, 4).

But in order to share the benefits with neighboring countries, tourists would need to travel to all these countries. According to the PPF this was no problem: "One drawcard will be the chance to visit nine countries in five days. That includes Namibia, Lesotho, Zambia, Zimbabwe, Mozambique, South Africa, Botswana and, potentially, Angola, as a tourist attraction

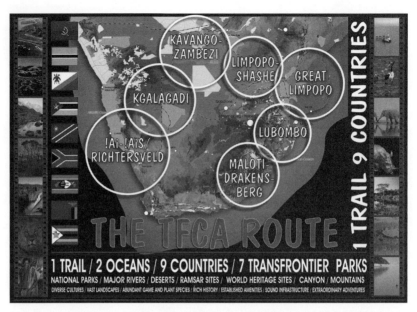

FIGURE 2.3 The proposed TFCA route for 2010 from a DEAT report.

during the 2010 Soccer World Cup."[40] Accordingly, the DEAT and the PPF developed the TFCA route (see fig. 2.3), presenting the various TFCAS as situated in a logical route along a single trail (naturally adorned by Garden of Eden images of African wildlife, landscapes, and one San person in traditional clothing).

Clearly, this idea of visiting nine countries in five days is ambitious at best and a plain illusion at worst, a point even made by DEAT staff officers in the 2010 TFCA section.[41] Yet the contradictions between what is marketed and whether it can be achieved did not deter the PPF, DEAT, and others from repeating the regional benefits that would come from the World Cup—and the need for peace parks to achieve them—over and over. In fact, this is why a 2010 TFCA section within the DEAT was created in the first place. And this section truly amplified the marketing around TFCAS to grandiose proportions. Its prime strategy to make local and regional wildlife and communities benefit from the World Cup was to launch the massive Boundless Southern Africa marketing campaign around TFCAS (see DeMotts 2009). While I was traveling in South Africa six months before the start of the World Cup, this campaign seemed omnipresent. Through free tourism booklets at the international airports, Internet advertising, investor conferences, and even an expedition along the TFCA route by the famous South African adventurer Kingsley Holgate, the Boundless Southern Africa campaign team was keen to emphasize that "the World Cup event will not only benefit South Africans but southern Africa and Africa as a whole."[42]

At the launch of the Boundless Southern Africa brand in May 2008, the South African deputy minister of environmental affairs and tourism, Rejoice Mabudafhasi, said, "The merit of a single brand for TFCAS cannot be overemphasized enough, primarily because TFCAS are the key tourist attractions and value offerings that link our respective countries. Indeed, they are Southern Africa's unique draw card. In this regard, the nine Southern African countries unanimously support the 'Boundless Southern Africa' brand as a means of showcasing the Trans-frontier Conservation Areas (TFCAS) which straddles [sic] the South African Development Community (SADC) region."[43] The aim, then, according to a promotional brochure, "is to make Boundless Southern Africa an independent and sustainable marketing brand that initiates, promotes and ensures a consistent contribution to conservation, community development and sustainability. As a recognised transfrontier marketing brand, it will be trusted by consumers. The Boundless brand will honour, protect and promote the rural environmental and cultural heritage."[44]

The importance attached to branding transfrontier conservation is evident from these quotes: it is the agency of the brand that is expected to showcase TFCAS and to "honour, protect and promote the rural environmental and cultural heritage." On top of that, according to a brochure that advertised investment opportunities, "Boundless Southern Africa makes the transfrontier conservation areas a very viable profit opportunity for potential investors."[45] TFCAS are seen as crucial "value offerings" (in Mabudafashi's word), but only insofar as they are supported by an "independent and sustainable marketing brand," as the brochure points out. It is the brand that shows tourists, private investors, and other stakeholders why nature and poor rural communities are valuable. Phrased differently, the brand "allows" nature and communities to be valued in the global marketplace. Elsewhere I refer to this as "derivative nature," in that "nature and rural communities . . . are increasingly becoming 'underlying assets' for what has become the primary source of value of neoliberal conservation, namely idealized images within the realms of branding, public relations and marketing" (Büscher 2010b, 261). Thus, the World Cup spectacle allowed dominant actors in the southern African TFCA scene, most notably the PPF and DEAT, to amplify the peace parks discourse to the extent that there is simply no representational space left for contradictory realities.

The politics of marketing has turned TFCAS into the ultimate commodities. They have fulfilled Debord's prediction that "the fetishism of the commodity . . . attains its ultimate fulfillment in the spectacle, where the real world is replaced by a selection of images which are projected above it, yet which at the same time succeed in making themselves regarded as the epitome of reality" (1967, 19). Consider once more Mabudafhasi's words at the launch of the strategic branding of TFCAS: "The FIFA 2010 Soccer World Cup brings along a range of business, investment and tourism opportunities for our region and the African continent at large. We have a chance here to shape the image of Southern Africa in a way that we may not have again. It is therefore critical for the region and the continent at large, to formulate and implement strategies that will enable the realisation of these opportunities."[46] The chance is not to shape the reality of southern Africa but—more important—its image. Conservation has quickly become one of the strategies that the deputy minister talked about, which gives us a clearer understanding of its value. In this logic, the value of conservation becomes conserving the derivative of nature, and its commercial exploitation, through marketing, branding, and public relations.

In the context of spectacle and derivative nature, the peace parks discourse starts acquiring a new meaning altogether. The discourse suggests that the contradictory realities actually become less important as the "true value" of conservation increasingly lies in idealized derivative marketing. Take the following lines in a business-sponsored brochure about peace parks: "Africa's natural wealth is an economic factor of the first order. Cross-border parks are unique attractions and will draw large numbers of new visitors. With just one visa these will now be able to visit the parks in their entirety, experiencing Africa in its 'aboriginal' state, free of borders and bureaucracy and showing only minimal traces of human intervention."[47] It does not matter whether this is actually true or not,[48] or whether there are some absurd contradictions in the statement.[49] It serves the marketing purpose.

This type of marketing is drenched in racial, colonial fables but has stark consequences for real people, as the aforementioned resettlement policy framework for the Mozambican part of the Great Limpopo illustrates. According to this framework, there are two basic options for the local people living in the Limpopo National Park: staying in the park (either fenced in or not) or resettlement to an area outside the park. The framework recognizes the adverse impacts that fencing will have on the socioeconomic opportunities and the general freedom of movement of the local people, but it does not regard staying in the park unfenced as a good alternative:

> The implications of this option for the Park potential would again depend greatly on the number of people remaining in the Shingwedzi river basin. If the number were small, their impact on the Park as a conservation area would be very limited. Nevertheless, for the potential of the LNP [Limpopo National Park] as a tourist destination this option would be less desirable than concentration in enclaves, as the free movement of people would, in the eyes of many people, reduce the attractiveness of the Park as a wilderness safari area. (Huggins et al. 2003, 31)

In the end and despite the rhetoric about the importance of local people, this is the point that lingers: the very presence of local people in a peace park reduces the "attractiveness of the Park as a wilderness safari area," and thus ultimately reduces the experience for tourists and therefore the profits that businesses make out of tourism.[50]

Conclusion

Peace parks in southern Africa are thoroughly reflective of and embedded in the regional political economy. This in itself does not make them neoliberal. In this chapter, I have shown that it is the concomitant politics of constructing and marketing consensus discourses in spite of increasingly contradictory realities that make transfrontier conservation in southern Africa a truly neoliberal project. Peace parks proponents do not merely ask stakeholders to (literally and figuratively) buy into TFCAs; they have amplified this discourse to market a belief in TFCAs as model of meaning and the telos of conservation. That these proponents, in particular the Peace Parks Foundation, the South African government, and several others, do so in spite of the inherently and increasingly contradictory realities, reveals neoliberalism as a political ideology—among its other guises—and reminds one of Geoff Mulgan's statement about the grand ideologies of the twentieth century: "The grander the story, it seems, the grander have been the unintended consequences. The greater their claim to intellectual coherence across a range of fields, the less has been the likelihood that any ideology will survive unscathed" (1994, 23). It seems that the peace parks discourse wanders a well-trodden path.

More concretely, I have started to put flesh on the framework of the politics of neoliberal conservation and the concepts of consensus, antipolitics, and marketing. The consensus struggle serves to socially regulate the production of transfrontier conservation as well as the actors involved in terms of carving out accepted ways of behavior that, although divergent in interests, practices, and discourses, do not challenge the underlying neoliberal status quo. But for a discourse to be lifted above situated contradictions, special efforts are necessary, most especially and paradoxically, to amplify the discourse to huge, derivative proportions. Hence, in the face of overwhelming political intensities, the trick is to posit transfrontier conservation as antipolitical—in this case as a model of meaning to which people should attach their fortunes, and that can function as "the global solution." The paradox, as noted by Philip Quarles van Ufford, Ananta Kumar Giri, and David Mosse is that the contemporary politics and administration of development (and conservation) is "bereft of meaning," while "moral choices become important political assets of specific agencies, constituting their 'symbolic capital' in the marketplace" (2003, 16–17). This links in with the third mode of neoliberal politics, that of marketing, which I conceptualize as the more practical strategy to regionally constitute the peace parks discourse as dominant, and so ensuring the deeper neoliberalization of conservation and development. Through strategies of neoliberal devolved governance such as nature-based tourism, in combination with major, spectacular events such as the 2010 World Cup, the peace parks discourse radically relocates value and attention from contradictory realities to reified representations.

chapter three

COMPRESSING REALITY

The focus on consensus, antipolitics, and marketing as modes of neoliberal political conduct provides new ways of understanding conservation and its embedment in the regional southern African political economy. Yet, if this framework is to hold, we need to delve deeper into the "witches brew" and connect the (as of yet) abstract strategies of consensus, antipolitics, and marketing to the ethnographic lifeworld of an intervention (see Li 2007). This chapter and the ones that follow do so by analyzing the Maloti-Drakensberg Transfrontier Conservation and Development Area between South Africa and Lesotho. From a regional perspective, focusing on the Maloti-Drakensberg is ideal to study the strength of the argument because it is somewhat of an outlier in the southern African transfrontier conservation landscape.

First, the influence of the Peace Parks Foundation (PPF) on the Maloti-Drakensberg is marginal compared with other Transfrontier Conservation Areas (TFCAS). The PPF offered its services, but these were only accepted on the Lesotho side and on a small scale.[1] Second, the Maloti-Drakensberg is the one TFCA that does not chiefly revolve around protected areas. It is true that the South African uKhahlamba-Drakensberg Park is a dominant presence, but much less so than protected areas in other TFCAS. Third, the Maloti-Drakensberg differs from the regional transfrontier conservation picture because it is one of the few TFCAS not focused on wildlife and charismatic megafauna. It cannot boast the more traditional images around the myth of wild Africa that is so familiar and important in tourism marketing. Fourth and last, the establishment of the Maloti-Drakensberg TFCA has been effected by a single massive intervention, the Maloti-Drakensberg Transfrontier Project (MDTP). In contrast, other TFCAS have usually seen multiple (large) interventions, funded by different sponsors and with stronger involvement from government and the PPF. This is not to say that the MDTP received more money (it did not, especially in comparison to the Great Limpopo), but the work done to establish the TFCA was concentrated in one intervention.

By the time the MDTP started early 2003, there had been more than twenty years of preparation. During this time, many actors had developed high hopes for the multimillion-dollar project to finally bring the plethora of conservation, development, and cooperation benefits that had become associated with it. The timing and context in 2003 appeared to be just right: relations between Lesotho and South Africa had greatly improved since the end of apartheid;[2] increasing desire for formalized cooperation on the Maloti-Drakensberg Mountains joined with the quickly rising transfrontier conservation movement in southern Africa, leading to increased donor attention and the area's designation as a peace park; South Africa had recently hosted the World Summit on Sustainable Development and established a reputation on environmental matters that needed to be upheld (see Death, 2011); the South African economy—especially the tourism sector—was booming and the Maloti-Drakensberg area had become a standard ingredient in tourists' itineraries; the Drakensberg area had been proclaimed a World Heritage Site three years prior; and, finally, the project did not have to start from scratch because the years of preparation laid much of the groundwork. The MDTP, so it seemed, "just" had to provide the icing on the cake.

The planners foresaw challenges too. The MDTP's appraisal report for the project was especially worried about the stalling of legal and administrative processes, disagreement on area designations, ineffective community participation, and lack of acceptance of grazing protection and antipoaching measures (World Bank 2001a; 2001b, 34). Other potential challenges concerning strained bilateral relations or ineffective leadership were thought to be modest or negligible. All challenges were deemed surmountable by putting in place "risk-minimizing measures." In short, everything seemed lined up for a successful intervention.

Toward the end of the project it became clear that the MDTP had not lived up to the high expectations. The project had worked out very differently than planned and the many benefits either did not transpire or did so in a different way and to a different extent than desired. To reflexive practitioners and those familiar with the conservation and development literature, this comes as no surprise; it is the rule rather than the exception (see, e.g., Dressler 2009; Ferguson 1994; Li 2007; Mosse 2005; Nustad 2001; Olivier de Sardan 2005). The main purpose of this and following chapters is therefore not to show that there is a difference between policy and practice in the MDTP. After all, development scholars have convincingly pointed out that "policy goals come into contradiction with other institutional or 'system goals' such that policy models are poor guides to understanding the practices, events and effects of development actors, which are shaped by the relationships and interests and cultures of specific organizational settings" (Mosse 2004, 663; see also Quarles van Ufford 1988).

Hence, we need to move beyond thinking about transfrontier conservation in terms of policy and practice, and especially in terms of a gap that need to be bridged. In line with much anthropological and geographical literature, we need to look at transfrontier conservation as a political arena where different actors and organizations embody and stimulate different practices, events, effects, interests, and cultures (see Mosse 2004; see also Brosius 2006; Prudham 2005; Slater 2002). I will place special emphasis on the interaction between how MDTP implementers increasingly tried to promote neoliberal devolved governance strategies and the associated political strategies they employed for purposes of legitimation and mobilization.

Whereas the next chapter will deal with the project implementation during the actual intervention phase, which lasted from 2003 to 2008, this chapter focuses on the preparation phase leading up to the MDTP. I argue, following David Mosse (2005) and Tania Li (2007), that the purpose of the preparation phase was to compress the reality of multiple "institutional and individual interests and ambitions and optimisms" into a seemingly coherent policy document that portrayed consensus over the subsequent courses of action to be followed by stakeholders (Mosse 2005, 21). This, I will show, is a peculiar technical consensus containing many problematic assumptions. The overall objective of the chapter is to describe the historical political arena in which the MDTP sought to intervene and change so as to better situate and appreciate the political strategies employed during the actual intervention. I will start by giving a brief overview of the MDTP history.

A Brief History of the Maloti-Drakensberg Transfrontier Project

As with many such endeavors, the MDTP started as a combination of a perceived (ecological, material, or ideological) opportunity or threat and the personal interest of several key individuals. Arguably, the main grounds on which the case for the MDTP rests are water and ecosystem conservation (Bainbridge, Motsamai, and Weaver 1991). As narrated in chapter 1, the first roots of the project lie in the 1950s when South Africa commenced negotiations with Lesotho about the Lesotho Highlands Water Project (LHWP). This scheme was meant to guarantee water supply to Pretoria and Johannesburg, South Africa's industrial heartland. A concern over the quality of the water emerged concurrently with South Africa's supply worries. After all, the main river dammed in the LHWP is the Senqu-Orange River, which together with the tributary of the Vaal River, is tremendously important in supplying the region with water (De Jonge Schuermans, Helbing, and Fedosseev 2004). The catchments of the Orange River, however, lie in Lesotho, and to protect them, another arrangement with Lesotho besides the LHWP was needed. This had to be linked to the broader conservation of the mountain ecosystem in the Maloti-Drakensberg, especially because this ecosystem is interconnected and subject to degradation.[3] The first person to champion these ideas in the 1980s was Raymond Williams,[4] who was then working for the Department of Water Affairs and Forestry in Natal, South Africa.[5]

In an interview, Williams recalled that he, as a "mountain man," went to the Drakensberg often and "noticed especially the degradation of the grasslands and the wetlands."[6] He wanted to do something about this, but considering the apartheid context, special care was needed. Williams approached the Ministry of Foreign Affairs and convinced it to allow the Department of Water Affairs—later the Natal Parks Board, where his section was transferred to—to start negotiations with the Lesotho government about the protection of the mountains. After a slow start, a more elaborate program of cooperation with Lesotho developed under the term "intergovernmental liaison,"[7] because "cooperation" remained too sensitive a concept under apartheid. An Intergovernmental Liaison Committee and subcommittees were formed on issues such as agriculture, security, and customs. One of these became the Drakensberg-Maloti Mountain Conservation Programme (DMMCP).

Under the DMMCP, a Joint Technical Committee was established, which commissioned several studies on topics ranging from plant taxonomy and mountain-terrain analysis to socioeconomic issues and data management (Bainbridge, Motsamai, and Weaver 1991, 5). These studies were published between 1987 and 1989. By that time the money for the technical committee was exhausted and many project activities were terminated. While some of the studies were extended beyond 1989, the money problem forced the committee to spend most of the time between 1990 and 1994 looking for new funding. Few donors showed interest until, finally, the European Union committed itself in June 1996 to work toward a preproject, which ran from 1998 to 2001 (European Union and Kingdom of Lesotho 2002). At the same time, the World Bank—who had already been funding projects in Lesotho for some decades, including the Lesotho Highlands Water Project—started showing interest. Thuso Setiloane—a key individual on the Lesotho side who had been involved from the start of the DMMCP—noted that this happened at a consultative donor conference in 1996, where the Lesotho government reported on activities to donors. In our interview, he stated that he was very active in this conference and also talked to representatives from the World Bank about the DMMCP. The representatives, according to Setiloane, first refused, as this was not "how they approached projects." But soon after the conference, they came back with a strong interest.[8]

With regards to why this interest resurfaced so swiftly, Setiloane noted that the MDTP was "transfrontier," a concept that was becoming popular at the time.[9] The World Bank financed the first important workshop in 1997 between officials from Lesotho and South Africa in South Africa's Giant's Castle Nature Reserve, where it was agreed that they would be working toward a bigger TFCA project to be called the Drakensberg-Maloti Transfrontier Conservation and Development Project (Sandwith 1997a, 17). After that conference, frantic interaction took place among Lesotho, South Africa, and the World Bank, which led to another MDTP preproject sponsored by the Japanese government.[10] The Japanese funding was meant to develop the proposal for the MDTP and make sure that all the requirements of the intended funding source, the Global Environment Facility (GEF), were met. This took longer than anticipated. While the proposal was approved by the GEF on 1 February 2000, the actual project started at the beginning of 2003. To understand this and the specific social, political, and institutional configurations we see in the project today, we need to hark back to the broader (post)colonial and political-economic forces shaping the MDTP.

A Watery Momentum

Two main phases stand out in the preparation of the MDTP: the initial conceptualization phase (1982 to the mid-1990s) and the more focused preparation phase (1997 to 2003), which consisted of several-donor funded projects that explicitly intended to lead to an intervention. As with transfrontier conservation more generally, the sheer volume of the paper/policy trail left by the preparation phases makes it impossible to do justice to all the nuances.[11] Important here is how the paper/policy trail leading up to the actual intervention indicates to a large extent who does and who does not belong to the "interpretative policy communities" that tie together— and leave out—particular institutional and individual interests and associated ideas (Blaikie 2006). We must first examine these interests and ideas, and how they together formed the political arena in which the MDTP was to function.

As stated, Williams had for a long time been the driving force behind the idea of cooperation between Lesotho and South Africa to conserve the Maloti-Drakensberg biome. Williams had always loved and spent much time in the Drakensberg Mountains. In fact, he repeatedly mentioned that the mountain ecosystem is different from other ecosystems, and that to work with mountains one has to have an affinity for them. According to Williams, within the main provincial conservation agency in KwaZulu-Natal—then the Natal Parks Board—much of the interest in the mountains depended on whether the responsible person for the Drakensberg understood and cared for the mountains. This was not always the case, he recalled, as "real" wildlife conservation in Natal was often seen as having to deal with rhinos and other charismatic megafauna, especially the big five. Williams mentions that even the famed conservationist Ian Player,[12] at a certain point in his career, got transferred to the Drakensberg and hated it. According to Williams, "Ian was just not a mountain man," and this did not help to get the care and attention that the mountains need.[13]

On the other side of the mountains, in Lesotho, the oral accounts of the history of the MDTP are different in tone. Setiloane, Williams's main counterpart, spoke mostly of the institutions formed, people involved, and workshops held in the process toward the MDTP.[14] He frequently talked about the vision of the South Africans, especially how they pictured the uKhahlamba-Drakensberg Park to be mirrored on Lesotho's side of the border. This, according to Setiloane, would not be possible: the high alpine areas on the Lesotho side are commonage lands, used as summer grazing areas and home to many human settlements. This view is also held by the Lesotho coordinator of the Japanese-funded MDTP preproject: "Seeing threats to their parks . . . coming from Lesotho, they [South Africans] wanted a buffer zone of twenty kilometers all along the border from Botha-Bothe [north Lesotho] to Qacha's Nek [south Lesotho] to protect their resources."[15] These buffer zones had to be International Union for Conservation of Nature category I or II protected areas, the strictest in terms of preservation without human habitation (International Union for Conservation of Nature 1994). But, like Setiloane, the coordinator also noted that on the Lesotho side there were "problems with people using the area." Extensive travels through the eastern Lesotho highlands easily confirm these sentiments. While the mountain ecology seems barren and inhospitable, it supports a considerable number of people who mostly herd livestock but also trade, travel, and use the area to collect natural resources. In the end, the final report of the DMMCP recommended that the higher alpine zone of Lesotho be declared a less strict category VI "managed resource area" (Bainbridge, Motsamai, and Weaver 1991, 2–8).

Interviews and DMMCP reports show that that the initial interest in a collaborative arrangement on the Maloti-Drakensberg area derived mainly from South African interests in biodiversity conservation and water for consumption and industry (see Bainbridge, Motsamai, and Weaver 1991; Quinlan 1995).[16] This interest, however, was articulated most candidly during the 1960s and 1970s. During the 1980s, the conceptualization of the cooperation changed in line with emerging sustainable development and community-based conservation discourses. Consider the following quote from a DMMCP report:

> The policies outlined in this document are directed at long term environmental conservation programmes integrated with human development and educational programmes. Specific attention is paid to conservation of the water resources (in view of the importance of this for the Lesotho Highlands Water Project) and serving the interests of the mountain people who require access to the area for livestock grazing. It is proposed that the area receive specialist management attention, because of the sensitive nature of the environment. It is also proposed that the area receive legal protection as a managed resource area (MRA). Establishment of a MRA would contribute to the conservation of the above resources as well as unique natural communities and other at-

tributes such as scenic values. Application of the MRA concept would bring benefits to the people of Lesotho, as well as the international community. (Bainbridge, Motsamai, and Weaver 1991)

This quote and other sections of the report are some of the stronger statements connecting the LHWP and the MDTP.[17] The importance of water and the LHWP for the southern African political economy, and particularly for South Africa's Gauteng province, can hardly be overstated. According to Anthony Turton, this derives from the fact that "the spatial distribution of people in Southern Africa is generally at variance with the availability of water," and thus "people must come to the water," or "water must come to the people" (2000, 138). Obviously, the latter is preferred and many regional projects were instigated or under way around 2001 to transport water to high-population areas (138). The LHWP is the most complex, most expensive, and most elaborate project, providing a direct supply of water to South Africa's economic heart and providing income for Lesotho (Schmitz 1992).[18] But for the LHWP to succeed in the long term—as explicitly mentioned in its feasibility study (Bainbridge, Motsamai, and Weaver 1991)— conservation of the water catchment areas is vital. We can therefore safely conclude that the main initial reason for the protection of the Maloti-Drakensberg area stems from the importance of water for South Africa's political economy (De Jonge Schuermans, Helbing, and Fedosseev 2004), and that the LHWP and the MDTP were deemed necessary to safeguard the wretched apartheid political economy.

While the report views conservation of the Maloti-Drakensberg as important for the LHWP, it also constructs the intervention as a means to bring benefits to the people of Lesotho and the international community (Bainbridge, Motsamai, and Weaver 1991). The arguments that tie these two together relate to the contentious issues of soil erosion and the (over)grazing of Lesotho's grasslands. First, there is the concern of the "potential silting of the [LHWP] dams as a result of soil erosion in the water catchment valleys which are also the main grazing areas" (Quinlan 1995, 495). Second, these same grasslands are constructed as a vital resource for economic development of local people. Interestingly, Tim Quinlan (1995, 496) argues that this is a turnaround from colonial intervention discourses that considered livestock, not grasslands, to be the critical resource upon which Lesotho's economic prosperity depended. Consequently, the focus on grasslands conservation made the concerns about water and the LHWP politically acceptable within the emerging discourse of community conservation. Additionally, it reinforced the long-held idea that soil and grassland degradation were due to overstocking—as a consequence of Lesotho's common-property tenure system—which was said to imperil Basotho development opportunities and threatening the biodiversity of the area (see Rohde et al. 2006; Showers 1989; Turner 2003).

This last assumption especially informed many interventions and government policies in Lesotho, and the DMMCP was no exception (see Quinlan 1995; Quinlan and Morris 1994). In fact, the lead figure in the DMMCP was still convinced in 2005 that previous interventions based on degradation, tragedy of the commons, and market discourses were right on the mark.[19] He noted, for example, that he believes that the big USAID-funded Land Conservation and Range Development Project in the 1980s was based on successful premises, but that in the end it was ruined by a "sociologist" writing about the "cultural value" of livestock. This "sociologist" was James Ferguson, who wrote what became a highly influential study on development cooperation, titled *The Anti-politics Machine*, which now started to play another interesting role in my research beyond the theoretical arguments that inform my framework on the politics of neoliberal conservation.

In sum, the early conceptualization and legitimation of the MDTP was characterized by several main interests and ideas. First, South Africa took the initiative, chiefly based on its concerns about water and conservation of biodiversity. According to Setiloane, a transfrontier project offered the South Africans a chance of "higher-level institutional protection for the area."[20] Second, the cooperation was conceptualized according to the emerging international discourses on sustainable development and community-based conservation, while at the same time following closely from previous interventions based on rangeland degradation, tragedy of the commons, and market discourses. Third, the accounts of various involved actors showed interesting differences; the South African passion for mountains triggered the early conceptualization of the MDTP, while the Basotho counterparts took a more reactive stance. While this may be a coincidence, the ensuing chapters will show that it reflects broader elements of the political economy, including the issues of race and sovereignty.

Donor Involvement and Cultivating the Intervention

The DMMCP ended in the early 1990s, but it took until the mid-1990s before the European Union and then the World Bank started showing interest in the emerging Maloti-Drakensberg cooperation. By this time, Williams had left the Natal Parks Board and his role was taken over by Trevor Sandwith, who proved to be the new champion behind the initiative. In an interview, Sandwith mentions that like Williams, he is passionate about mountains, especially the Maloti-Drakensberg, and that he made his life from this passion. He emphasized that this is important "because it says something about how these things start and the historical connections that get things going."[21]

After he replaced Williams in 1994, Sandwith had to steer the idea of Maloti-Drakensberg transboundary cooperation through the dramatic political changes that South Africa was experiencing. Considering the massive dispossessions under colonialism and apartheid, land restitution was one of the main items on the South African transformation agenda, and reallocation of protected-area land was one of the potential means (Fay and James 2009). Against these tides, Sandwith defended the MDTP cooperation scheme.

> There is a perception that protected areas are likely candidates for land re-allocation. In the case of the Drakensberg catchment area, there are significant disadvantages to this approach, notably the fragility of the mountain ecosystem and its importance for water production. The alternative approach is to ensure that the use of the land for water production, for nature conservation, sustainable tourism and resource use provides long-term benefits. The Drakensberg-Maloti transfrontier park provides a challenging example for the implementation of an integrated conservation and development programme in a unique and internationally significant region. The alternative is a downward spiral of degradation which would have adverse impacts on the whole sub-region. (Sandwith 1997b, 123)

In a paper that he presented at one of the first major international peace parks conferences,[22] Sandwith displays an acute sense of how the Maloti-Drakensberg project functions in several overlapping and complex political, economic, social, and cultural contexts. He outlines the conflictual history of the region and the difficulties in the political relationship between Lesotho and South Africa, and shows that he is keenly aware of how the sustainable development movement conjoined with the end of apartheid in South Africa to make attention to development, poverty, and land necessary to politically legitimate conservation. The paper also highlights many of the complexities impinging on the cooperation. The most important of these according to Sandwith were a lack of "instruments of international cooperation" between Lesotho and South Africa (such as a memorandum of understanding); the amount of different agencies active in the area; and what Sandwith believes is the "single most significant constraint": the funding necessary for preparation and implementation of the cooperation framework, because "dealing with the different objectives and funding parameters of the major roleplayers has proven to be an enormous challenge" (Sandwith 1997b, 129–30).

With these role players, Sandwith refers to the donors necessary to provide the funding for what had become a complex "multilateral development programme" of a sizable magnitude (Sandwith 1997b, 130). But Sandwith was also aided by several positive dynamics, one of which was—in his words—the "remarkable opportunity afforded by the Peace Parks model" (131). The year 1997 was when the PPF was established and transfrontier conservation was rapidly becoming a popular new trend in conservation. Many donors shifted financing strategies accordingly and actively looked for (potential) peace parks to support (Wolmer 2003).[23] Among these donors was the World Bank, which decided to fund a workshop that sought to actively encourage the Maloti-Drakensberg initiative in terms of funding and practical organization (Sandwith 1997a). This workshop at Giant's Castle in South Africa, held just days before the peace parks conference that Sandwith attended, brought together representatives from all the key players in the preparation phases: the Natal Parks Board (including the then CEO, George Hughes), important Lesotho ministries, the PPF, local NGOs, the Natal Museum, and the World Bank; importantly, Raymond Williams also attended and was extended a "special welcome" for being the person "responsible for a great deal of the planning which had defined the area as a critical one for the long term supply of water in the province" (Sandwith 1997a, 1).

The workshop at Giant's Castle instigated the more focused preparation phase that led to the MDTP. It identified potential funding mechanisms and decided that the GEF would be most suitable for its purposes. The workshop participants adopted the "Giant's Castle Declaration," which endorsed the concept of a "Transfrontier Conservation and Development Area [TFCDA]," and "called upon all interested parties and funding agencies to lend support to achieving the vision of a unique and sustainable TFCDA" (Sandwith 1997a, 29). In terms of the program objectives, all the familiar elements—

biodiversity conservation, community development, tourism, and cultural resources—were included. How to operationalize this general discourse, however, was less clear. Hughes proposed a transboundary biosphere reserve with a key protected area and a buffer zone, while others, including the PPF representative and Williams, stated that the main objective should be a transfrontier park (Sandwith 1997a, 12–13). Sandwith felt that the project's scope should be much broader, and a World Bank representative even stated that the scheme "should not be regarded as just a core protected area but a large area embracing numerous activities ranging from protected area management right down to mining" (Sandwith 1997a, 14).

Another World Bank staff member stressed that it was important that the "Lesotho and South African parties reached consensus on the project concept" (Sandwith 1997a, 14). In the end participants agreed that "the concept of a Peace Park consisting of the protected areas was an important immediate achievement, and that it would lead naturally to a transfrontier conservation and development area" (Sandwith 1997a, 18). By 2008, at the end of the MDTP and more than a decade after the workshop, the "immediate achievement" of an officially declared peace park had not actually been achieved, and few of those involved believed that the consensus and the "win-win situation" they expected materialized according to the optimistic tone of the workshop report (Sandwith 1997a, 14, 30).[24] Again, this is not surprising, and the MDTP should still be judged on its merits. However, the strategy of amplifying optimism and the concomitant raising of high expectations is at least indicative of the ways that donor funding and political legitimacy for such a massive intervention are garnered. Indeed, it was necessary in order to turn the massively chaotic and complex reality of the Maloti-Drakensberg area into a stabilized and coherent set of "systems of interpretation" or "policy models" that could be turned into an actual, fundable intervention (Mosse 2005, 17). The Giant's Castle workshop was a crucial first step. From there, the ensuing years were spent further perfecting the model to fit the GEF mold.

Involving the Global Environment Facility and Developing the Founding Documents

It is not surprising that it took key role players more than five years—from September 1997 to late 2002—to get the MDTP approved and going. In general, getting a GEF project approved is a very time-consuming and complex, if not outright tedious, process.[25] The root cause of this lies in the

GEF's institutional structure and its built-in political dynamics. Basically, the GEF is a financial-allocation mechanism designed to help developing countries meet their obligations under global environmental treaties. It was created in 1991 by donor countries in the Global North (Western Europe, North America, and Japan) but was globally endorsed and officially launched after the 1992 World Summit on Sustainable Development. Donor countries did not want to create a separate institution and asked the World Bank to manage the GEF, who, after initial reluctance, accepted because it saw a chance to "green" its image and shake off some of the environmental criticism it had been receiving (Horta et al. 2002, 4). The World Bank subsequently invited the United Nations Development Programme and the United Nations Environment Programme (UNDP and UNEP) to join as "implementing agencies," albeit as "junior partners" (Horta, Round, and Young 2002, 5). The three implementing agencies together prepare and implement projects.[26]

After widespread dissatisfaction in 1999 with the implementing agencies and overall GEF project performance, the GEF later opened the door to other organizations eager to tap into the GEF purse: the United Nations Food and Agriculture Organization, the United Nations Industrial Development Organization, the International Fund for Agricultural Development, and four regional-development banks (the African Development Bank, the Asian Development Bank, the Inter-America Development Bank, and the European Bank for Reconstruction and Development). These, however, are not implementing but executing agencies, ultimately still answerable to the original three implementing agencies. It is the competition among the implementing (and executing) agencies and their desire to control the biggest part of the GEF pot that makes preparation for and implementation of GEF projects so complicated and tedious (see Horta, Round, and Young 2002; Young 2002).[27] Although several attempts have been made to rationalize the GEF bureaucracy, this has not succeeded so far.

The point of the foregoing was to highlight the political and institutional pressures on the MDTP from its preparation phases through to its implementation. According to Philip Quarles van Ufford (1988), intervention practices are often determined less by the formal goals of the project and rather revolve around system goals: following rules and maintaining administrative order and manageability. The GEF and World Bank both have their contradictory system peculiarities vis-à-vis the projects or the cultures and countries they are involved with (see Goldman 2005). Graham Harrison, for instance, argues that the "Bank's theory of African states politics" differs radically from that of critical interpretations (Harrison 2005b). He argues that the World Bank's theory rests on two pillars: "its basically harmonious view of political change, based in positive sums or at least a convergence of interests; and its desire to promote a complementary relationship between a (reinvigorated) state and an (emerging) market economy" (255).[28] During the workshop at Giant's Castle, World Bank staff members were the ones who kept promoting the forging of this kind of consensus.

Besides the World Bank as implementing agency, the GEF itself also has some peculiar system goals that are crucial in understanding the MDTP. Two project requirements are of particular importance: the incremental cost principle and the principle of global benefits. According to its architects, the GEF was created to fund activities that would have truly global environmental benefits, operationalized as benefits that go beyond national borders. The GEF tries to adhere to this by funding only the incremental costs of projects that make national environmental benefits global. In other words, the GEF adds to national funding for the environment—which can include donor funding—in order to achieve global environmental benefits.[29] Both of these requirements are so conceptually and practically vague that they continue to cause many conflicts over their interpretation (see Horta, Round, and Young 2002; Young, 2002). These conflicts occur on different levels, including the level of projects.

In regards to the MDTP, it took as much time to get the GEF acquisition process completed as it did to actually implement the project. The key in the preparation years was to develop a document that incorporated the concerns, ambitions, and structure goals of the potential implementing agencies in South Africa and Lesotho, the two governments, and all the other stakeholders, while remaining acceptable to the funders. This document became the MDTP Project Appraisal Document (PAD) (World Bank 2001a, 2001b). The PAD, which is consistent with GEF principles, phrases the objective of the project as follows: "The Maloti-Drakensberg transfrontier area encompasses distinct landscape and biological diversity. It is rich in species and high in endemism. However, excessive livestock grazing, crop cultivation on steep slopes, uncontrolled burning, alien invading species and human encroachment threatens this asset. Hence, the GEF objective is to conserve this globally significant biodiversity" (World Bank 2001a, 2).

In line with mainstream conservation-development thinking, the secondary objective flows logically from the first, namely "to contribute to community development through income generation from nature-based tourism, by capacity building for sustainable utilization of the natural and cultural heritage of the project area" (World Bank 2001a, 2). After introducing the objectives, the PAD stresses that the approach to achieve them is a regional one, with the emphasis on "transfrontier ecosystem," "joint management," and creating "economies of scale." The document moreover stresses that the project components are adjusted to the specific situation of each country. For example: "there will be further support to national level institution building for conservation in Lesotho, while this is unnecessary in South Africa" (2). Moreover, the receptive capacity of Lesotho is considered limited and its needs greater; consequently, "the transfrontier nature of the project will ensure that the analysis and resolution of conservation problems will be shared, and the resources and expertise in each country complemented" (2). The incremental cost principle is also explicated:

> The GEF incremental cost contribution of $15.25 million for the two countries together, of which $7.325 goes to Lesotho and $7.925 million goes to RSA [Republic of South Africa], should also be seen in the context of major ongoing support to biodiversity conservation in Lesotho (UNDP: $2.5 million), and support to natural resources and rural income enhancement in the highlands (AfDB [African Development Bank]: $8.4 million). Both are counted here as associated financing, in addition to the Lesotho government contribution ($1.1 million). In RSA, the counterpart contribution is estimated at $16.8m. Most of this represents expenditure for nature conservation by the Kwazulu-Natal Nature Conservation Board. (2–3)

The quote indicates that the PAD reflects Graham Harrison's argument that the World Bank's theory of African state and governance is based on "positive sums" and "convergence of interests" (2005b, 255). There are more examples that could be mentioned here, but the real point of the preparation process is not just the text. Able consultants could have written this in a fraction of the time that it took to get the MDTP accepted. Rather, the five years were—apparently—necessary to build the intervention into the complex social, political, and institutional environments involved in the endeavor. Mosse summarizes the process well: "Most development projects begin as texts, . . . written by a team of project design consultants and aid agency administrators. These statements of policy involve a special

kind of writing that, while preserving the appearance of technical planning, accomplish the social tasks of legitimation, persuasion and enrolment, becoming richly encoded with institutional and individual interests
and ambitions and optimisms" (2005, 21). In turn and through this process, the GEF requirements become part of the political arena targeted by
the MDTP, further complicating and influencing the social-political dynamics during project preparation and implementation.

The Politics of Technical Consensus

The technical process of GEF-proofing the Maloti-Drakensberg project was
so complex that the World Bank sought funding for technical assistance.
The World Bank found this in the Japanese Policy and Human Resources
Development Fund, which "may be used for the purposes of financing
technical assistance and other grant activities in respect of the formulation
and implementation of Bank-supported projects."[30] In April 1998, this
project about appraising a project started with the hiring of two consultants, one from Lesotho and one from South Africa. Their main tasks were
to contract consultancy services, with the aim of generating studies on the
Maloti-Drakensberg area; collating these into a project proposal; and, together with consultants, assisting the receiving countries in fulfilling the
requirements for project approval (Pomela 1998). In general, appraisal
phases for donor projects have a "tendency to turn into an ever-growing
checklist of special issues for investigation" (Pottier 1993, 26), and the
MDTP was no exception. The amount of technical details and operational
requirements is partly why it took five years to get the project started.
These elements of technical legitimation are important to understanding
how the complex Maloti-Drakensberg political economy was interpreted
and accounted for. I highlight and discuss six of them.

First, proposals for conservation and development projects need technical data to back them up. In the case of the MDTP, six consultancy teams
were hired for eleven tasks.[31] These included studies on various aspects of
the ecology, culture, and social-economics of the Maloti-Drakensberg area,
protected area management and development planning, and overviews of
relevant legal and institutional frameworks. According to the Lesotho coordinator I interviewed, these studies made clear "what needed to be done,"
and this "logically" developed into the eight project components of the
MDTP.[32] In short, technical data pervade the message that all the different
aspects of the project have been studied and understood and can be taken

into account. Second, project proposals create legitimacy by being participatory (Cooke and Kothari 2001). By using participatory approaches, the priorities and choices of the project are not those of the planners but becomes those of stakeholders. This in turn gives further credence to the knowledge produced by the studies, because, according to the World Bank, these were generated by using "proven social science research tools" (World Bank 2001a, 72).[33]

Third, projects need to extensively reference international and country policies, regulations, and conventions. On the international level, the Ramsar and World Heritage Conventions were particularly important: if the Maloti-Drakensberg area could be designated as a formal Ramsar site or World Heritage Site, it would not have to deal with the tricky issue of proving global environmental benefits; this would then be considered obvious. On the national level, the project showed its awareness of relevant South African and Lesotho laws and regulations and cited these generously. All of this embedded the project within generally accepted democratic processes, thereby further boosting its legitimacy.

Fourth, projects must make reference to other donor projects to show they are not stand-alone efforts but form part of an integrated and logical set of interventions. The MDTP was preceded by a host of other interventions; the PAD mentions seven supported by the World Bank and three by other agencies. The PAD explicates the "lessons learned" from these other projects and indicates how these are "reflected" in the MDTP's project design (World Bank 2001a, 21). Fifth, Projects have to show that they are not infallible, as that would make them seem unrealistic. Therefore, it must be specified that the risks involved in the project are understood while showing what can be done to mediate or solve them. The MDTP PAD explicates the critical risks in a table (see table 3.1).

Finally, many projects have to adhere to conditions of effectiveness before being approved. For the MDTP, several issues needed to be solved to "guarantee" the project's effectiveness. The majority of these were administrative or financial (project account in place, opening of project bank account, etc.) or related to operational procedures (project coordinators in place, project implementation plan accepted, etc.), and these had to be done according to World Bank stipulations. Other conditions included a signed memorandum of understanding between the Lesotho and South Africa and the official proclamation of Sehlabathebe as a national park by the Lesotho government. Sehlabathebe had already been a nature reserve

TABLE 3.1 MDTP "critical risks" according to the World Bank

RISK	RISK RATING	RISK-MINIMIZATION MEASURE
From Outputs to Objective		
1. Bilateral and domestic administrative dissonance	M	1. Recruitment of sc [Steering Committee] and pccs [Project Coordition Committee] with wide representation
2. Disagreement on conservation priorities among stakeholders	M	2. Thorough technical surveys as basis for priorities; and consultative process
3. Legal and administrative process stalled	H	3. Continued efforts to enhance the environmental dialogue with DEA&T (Pretoria)
4. Disagreement on area designations	S	4. Consultative process with local stakeholders and planning authorities
5. Ineffective conservation management	M	5. Capacity building and local ownership
6. Community participation ineffective	S	6. Consultative process based on local experience
7. Main stakeholders disagree on benefits of project	M	7. Strong communication program
8. Ineffective leadership for domestic and international coordination	M	8. Strict and consultative selection procedure
9. Discontinued constructive bilateral relationships	N	9. Steering Committee leadership
From Components to Outputs		
1. Disagreement on data storage, access to information, supply of data, and surveys	N	1. Demonstration of joint benefits
2. Incompatible regional land-use plans	M	2. Consultation with relevant agencies
3. Skilled staff not available for employment	N	3. Adequate marketing
4. Alien control technically ineffective	N	4. Building on best practice from Cape Peninsula Project and Working for Water
5. Lack of acceptance of effective grazing protection and antipoaching measures	S	5. Community dialogue and mobilization
6. Benefit transfer to community ineffective	M	6. Strict financial procedures
7. Nonacceptance of institutional models	N	7. Dialogue to achieve local ownership
8. Lack of interest in participating in training	N	8. Adequate marketing
Overall Risk Rating	M	

Risk Rating: H (High), S (Substantial), M (Modest), N (Negligible or Low).
Source: World Bank 2001a, 33–34.

for a while, but its status had never been officially proclaimed. Because Sehlabathebe was Lesotho's only protected area at the time, and situated adjacent to South Africa's uKhahlamba-Drakensberg National Park, its official proclamation was considered vital for the MDTP and thus rendered a "condition of effectiveness." These last two conditions were time consuming and were among the reasons why it took from the endorsement of the GEF's CEO on 24 April 2000 to early 2003 to get the actual project started.[34]

These are arguably the main elements that GEF project proposals employ to acquire technical legitimacy. I refer to "technical legitimacy" because all inferences throughout the documents are presented as facts and are not multi-interpretable; they pervade an air of common sense. A closer look at these six elements, however, reveals that they provide mere superficial legitimacy, as many of the assumptions are shaky or even outright false. First, Social science research is always situational and subjective, and much of the data in the documents do not have to be accurate or a good reflection of reality. Interestingly, the reports that came out of the studies do heed these disclaimers, yet there is a fundamental difference between them and the final MDTP PAD. The clearest difference is a completely different epistemological point of departure. Whereas some of the studies show hints of a critical poststructural epistemology, the PAD takes these up in an overtly positivist or positive-sum manner, fitting with Harrison's view of the World Bank (Harrison 2005b).[35]

Second, the proposal continuously talks about being community based and engaging all stakeholders, consequently espousing "participatory" credentials. Although the project proposal in one instance acknowledges that there is a rather "large number of stakeholders" (World Bank 2001a, 40), the idea that all those in or related to the area want to and can be involved in the project vision is pervasive throughout the entire document. Needless to say, this assumption is contentious. James Scott (1985), for instance showed how local communities reappropriate, modify, and transform interventions to suit their ideas about development, culture, and what is socially acceptable. And even if all the local people wanted to be involved, the sheer number could have been deemed too large to say that the project is effectively community based. In fact, this was openly accepted at the start of the project by a South African project implementer. She mentioned that there are 1.5 million people living on the South African side of the MDTP area and that there are far too many to get all of them involved.[36]

Third, referring to international conventions and national policies for democratic legitimacy again leads to questionable territory. Whereas international conventions from organizations such as Ramsar or the World Heritage Centre are quite specific and could provide some credibility for the MDTP area,[37] this certainly is not the case with, for example, the Convention on Biological Diversity or national policies. For South Africa, links are made to very general policy goals, such as "conserving biodiversity" and "building human capacity to manage biodiversity," which of course could legitimize anything (World Bank 2001a, 6). For Lesotho, mention is made of many international conventions and national policies. For most, if not all, of the regulations and laws referred to, it is questionable whether these are really developed by Basotho or by outsiders. The National (Environmental) Action Plans for African countries that accrue from the Convention on Biological Diversity are often financed by donors, and they and Western consultants do much of the conceptualization and actual writing. This is particularly so with Lesotho's National (Environmental) Action Plan and even many of its national policies. Hence, it is questionable whether this type of legitimation is actually democratic or bears testimony to country ownership.[38]

Fourth, a similar logic applies to the common practice of referring to other donor interventions in projects proposals. In the MDTP PAD, these references are very superficial and there seems to be no logic in what points are focused on and why. For example, it is stated about the Lesotho Highlands Water Project that "progress in terms of community involvement, area and initial construction of tourism infrastructure is quite impressive" (World Bank 2001a, 22). This statement runs contrary to many studies that show that there were very serious problems around community resettlements (see, e.g., Horta 1995; Mwangi 2007; Schmitz 1992; Thabane 2000). This is completely neglected as the PAD merely talks of four small "community-based conservation schemes" initiated by the LHWP, which are "of most direct relevance to the current initiative" (World Bank 2001a, 22). This strategic selectivity thus creates superficial legitimacy by only focusing on the project aspects that support the endeavor at hand. Moreover, even with respect to the lessons learned from other projects, it is not clear which ones are reflected in the Maloti-Drakensberg project design and why.[39]

Fifth, the issue of "critical risks," as shown in table 3.1. Nowhere is it explicated how the PAD got to these risks, on what grounds they are rated "high," "substantial," "modest," or "negligible," and why the proposed risk-minimization measures should be sufficient in solving them. It is also interesting to see what is not regarded as a risk. For instance, it is generally assumed that cooperation leads to friendship, and this was therefore not taken up as a risk. But research has shown that this is not a given (see Büscher and Schoon 2009; Van Amerom 2005), and later in the Maloti-Drakensberg project it became apparent that the relations between the two project coordination units were very tense, competitive, and sometimes even unfriendly and antagonistic.[40] Finally, in terms of the conditions of effectiveness, it might be true that without the proper legal and administrative infrastructure, project implementation cannot be effective (leaving aside exactly what "effective" entails). However, the conditions are often presented as sufficient, while it might be safer to assume that they are only necessary for project effectiveness. Many other conditions not mentioned might also be necessary (such as cooperative relations), but these are left out, and in the case of the MDTP they became problematic during project implementation.

All of this builds a clear case for labeling the technical consensus presented in the MDTP PAD as superficial technical legitimacy. But—again—it would be wrong to judge a project or the institution responsible for documenting the project proposal based on text only. After all, "project models have the purpose of conveying precisely the impression of manageability, coherence and rationality that is absent in practice. And as such their orientation is more often upwards (or 'outwards') to validate higher policy goals or justify the allocation of resources than downwards to orientate action" (Mosse 2005, 26). Hence, even though the text might be faulty and superficial and as such never acceptable to a critical social scientist, it was effective: in the end the MDTP was funded and implemented. According to the standards set by the involved actors and within the set of social relations spun around the MDTP preparation, the PAD was sufficient to award the project more than US$15 million over five years. The more important point, however, is that the text alone did not lead to the realization of the intervention. During the five years of preparation, the idea of the MDTP had to be actively marketed through many fast-changing sociopolitical circumstances by continuously acquiring and securing political legitimation.

Marketing Consensus

How can the marketing-consensus process be characterized, who had access to it, and what were some of the events that stood out in terms of creating political legitimization and consensus for the MDTP above and beyond the many texts produced? These questions can only be understood in relation to the massive political-economic changes that southern Africa was experiencing around the time, particularly the conjoining of post-apartheid dynamics, globalization, and neoliberalization (Bond 2000). A postapartheid dynamic that most directly impacted many people's lives is the employment-equity principle that seeks to redress former discriminatory practices regarding labor opportunities.[41] Previously disadvantaged groups—black, colored, and Indian people; women; and people with disabilities—were to be equally represented in "all occupational categories and levels in the workforce,"[42] triggering massive reorganizations in both the public and private sectors. Many previously disadvantaged individuals, especially those with higher education or involved in the struggle to end apartheid, suddenly had a world of opportunities opening up for them. In contrast, for many highly qualified white men, many doors were closing, especially in the public sphere.[43]

The main agency pushing the MDTP proposal, the Natal Parks Board—which became Ezemvelo KwaZulu Natal Wildlife (KZN Wildlife) after restructuring—was not exempt from this dynamic. For several years, it went through a painful reorganization process, culminating in 2004 with the retrenchment of all eight directors—the entire top management under the CEO—of which six were white. In this process, many ambitious (younger) white men left the organization, among them Trevor Sandwith, who until then had done most of the preparation for the MDTP.[44] In fact, Sandwith's boss at the time mentioned in an interview that it was Sandwith who wrote the initial project proposal with guidance and assistance from the World Bank. According to him, it was regretful that Sandwith left, but in the circumstances he could understand that KZN Wildlife "could not hold on to someone with [Sandwith's] caliber."[45] Sandwith's boss, one of the eight directors who was later retrenched, took over from Sandwith. Although his previous role in the project was limited "to get[ting] the political support needed to get the process going," he now had to actually "push the deal through DEAT [Department of Environmental Affairs and Tourism], the KwaZulu-Natal government, and have it signed off."[46]

On the Lesotho side, it was Thuso Setiloane and the Lesotho coordinator for the MDTP preproject who did most of the preparation, and the latter wrote the initial project proposal. According to one informant,[47] the coordinator did not write the proposal according to World Bank standards, and

World Bank staff flew in several times to rewrite parts. What caused the biggest delay on the Lesotho side, however, were the negotiations on project elements and meeting the conditions of effectiveness. In the midst of this process, in 2000, Setiloane left the Lesotho National Environment Secretariat. His successor remembered that the political negotiations for the project took so long that they sometimes forgot that they were still ongoing. Eventually, all conditions were met, but the audit of the feasibility study and the proclamation of Sehlabathebe National Park especially dragged the process.[48]

According to the new principal environmental officer, these two issues took longer than the others because she needed to do everything herself. In the end, she, and by extension the Lesotho government, could not live up to the task and asked for assistance. The PPF was eager to offer its services, especially because the MDTP was the only TFCA including South Africa that they were not yet officially involved in. An unpublished PPF memo announced: "The Kingdom of Lesotho is looking for a champion to assist Lesotho with the process to comply with the prerequisite required by the World Bank to release the project funding and the Peace Parks Foundation has agreed to fund such a position. In this regard, on 3 April 2001, the Cabinet of Lesotho approved the involvement of PPF and the appointment of [Dr. Reinald Du Plessis] to this position."[49]

The principal environmental officer stated that "the PPF was instrumental in getting the MDTP up," adding that "Reinald did all the running" and that he was very "helpful and resourceful."[50] Du Plessis—a white South African geologist—noted that it was hard to meet the conditions for effectiveness because of the fast-changing positions in government.[51] According to him, within the Lesotho government, "as soon as you are efficient, you are promoted," thus indicating a "lack of capacity" in the country. Du Plessis stated that this is quite well known and has even influenced the setup of the MDTP: for the Lesotho project coordination unit, only capable people were hired, who would commit for the full five years.

Interestingly, despite the fact that both countries went through turbulent times with the redressing of labor imbalances high on the agenda, it was white South Africans with a passion for nature who kept the Maloti-Drakensberg cooperation going. In South Africa, Sandwith and his director pushed the project through the authorities, and in Lesotho the PPF—also heavily dominated by white men—and Du Plessis in particular, made sure that the administrative processes did not stall. The World Bank played an equally crucial role, again with white men doing most of the pushing.[52] I do not attribute the role of whites in the MDTP to a longing for a Garden of Eden in Africa but rather to the fact that they were better positioned to lobby for the project in the global conservation and development marketplace, together with a genuine passion for conservation. Evidently, conservation was historically a "white thing" in southern Africa and is often still seen that way (see Hughes 2005; Kepe 2009). Hence, many whites pushing the MDTP had been in government positions that provided privileged access to policymaking and policy-funding networks. Others gained access by being able to pay for it or by forming lobby and interest (nongovernmental) organizations. The PPF is obviously a good example of an organization that combines both.

In sum, it was the relevant government agencies, World Bank staff,[53] hired consultants, and the PPF (albeit only in Lesotho), and especially the white men in these organizations, that operationalized the MDTP and saw to it that it was brokered through all the administrative, bureaucratic processes. What then about other important stakeholders? After all, conservation and development proposals need participation, especially from local communities, to be legitimate. For the MDTP preparation process, however, this was passive rather than active participation. The difference is whether one can forward a political agenda or only respond to one (often in restricted ways that will be discussed in chapter 5). Even though they were referred to often, the "people on the ground" had little to do with the MDTP preparation process, other than being consulted on their priorities (within the framework and language of the project). Thus, even though ownership and participation are official guiding principles, local people hardly feature within the formal system of legitimation of project proposals: if you are not somehow attached to the social relations around the donor network, you are unlikely to run into the proposal process and have any serious influence. Regarding the MDTP, the core people involved from the start remained those principally working on legitimating the MDTP intervention over the five years; all the while cementing their (institutional and individual) relationships (see Schroeder 1999, 371–72).

The frequent visits from World Bank staff to high-ranking government officials illustrate this point. Headway on the project proposal was monitored in technical negotiations between the World Bank and the GEF on the one hand and the South African DEAT and the Lesotho Ministry of Tourism, Environment and Culture on the other, with input from KZN Wildlife and other agencies, such as Lesotho's National Environment Secretariat. Perhaps World Bank staff would say that this is purely technical and part of the job. But this regular access to high-ranking government personnel ensures that relations of trust can build and understanding for each other's political environment can grow. Technical negotiations become reciprocal politics as these negotiations decide how the intervention is framed and what is possible and discussable in the public sphere. And five years of cementing relationships is a long time. This does not mean that close relationships result, but at least relationships do form and parties do learn what the other is worth politically and strategically and what buttons can be pushed and how. People not involved in this process—and local communities are almost never involved—do not have the opportunity to form these relationships and networks that are so important for building alliances, creating strategic discursive space, and demanding reciprocal understanding (Blaikie 2006). Access for them is a struggle, dependent on whether they know when and how to start the engagement with intervention preparations in the first place. Much of the sociopolitical marketing during these preparations is done behind closed doors. The intervention becomes public (i.e., implemented) after the core social relations have already determined its direction, making the struggle to change it infinitely harder.

That said, the legitimation process is porous and as noted many try to gain access through lobbying. For the MDTP, however, as far as I could ascertain, there is little evidence that stakeholders tried to influence the preparation process other than when invited to do so based on "proven social science research tools" (World Bank 2001a, 72). One notable exception is a special interest group with members already strong in the networks: a mountain-conservation network that had organized itself before the 2003 World Parks Congress in Durban, South Africa, and included Trevor Sandwith.[54] Again, this came forth from a passion for mountains and was pushed mostly by whites (there were nonwhites from other countries present, but few, if any, blacks from southern Africa).[55]

Immediately before the World Parks Congress a workshop was held on mountain conservation, and a declaration was promulgated that sought, inter alia, to further the sociopolitical legitimacy for the Maloti-Drakensberg intervention, even though it had just started. "The Didima Declaration" intended to "draw attention to the continued need for co-operation among nations for the protection of globally significant biodiversity and the pursuit of peace and reconciliation among people." Moreover, and explicitly mentioning the MDTP, the writers of the declaration stated they were "aware of the value of transboundary conservation initiatives to conserve biodiversity at a landscape level, to foster peaceful co-operation among communities and societies across international boundaries, and to engender regional economic growth and integration,"[56] again triggering all the right and familiar buttons. The issue here is not so much the language used, as this falls squarely into the "mobilizing metaphors" category. The point is that "The Didima Declaration" was clearly a marketing exercise, meant to stimulate (initiatives such as) the MDTP. Marketing is a tool for accessing and influencing discursive networks that, often later, also give opportunities to influence the operationalization of discourse and policy.

Conclusion

With hindsight, it was clear that from the start of the preparation process at Giant's Castle, the MDTP was destined to materialize. Although it took a long time, the question seemed not if, but when the project would start. With the World Bank eager to join the TFCA trend, Lesotho greatly dependent on donor funding, South Africa in need of water and interested in becoming a true part of the international community, KZN Wildlife interested in biodiversity conservation of the Drakensberg Mountains, and the PPF to provide that extra push, there was a critical mass of individuals and institutions central to the donor process to guarantee the outcome. The proposal approval just seemed to take time; it could not fail. Of particular relevance here is the political strategy of consensus with its superficial emphasis on win-win solutions, all-inclusiveness, and positivist or positive-sum epistemology that succeeded in compressing the reality of the Maloti-Drakensberg area into a fundable project proposal. But while this makes for powerful and successful upward legitimation, it does not make for good orientation toward practice. As Mosse (2005) has forcefully argued, the difficulties, differences, and disjunctions concealed by the processes of technical and sociopolitical legitimation always resurface with implementation, often in unexpected ways.

Although all knew that the MDTP was going to be a complex project, it did not temper the enthusiasm of those involved with its preparation (see Sandwith 2003). To the contrary, the expectations for the project were incredibly high. Thus an interesting paradox emerged. If it took five years to gain consensus on a document that laid the groundwork for a five-year implementation phase, what was the justification for the high expectations? Why was it not assumed that if it took five years to construct consensus on a theoretical exercise, it would be infinitely harder to successfully execute an enormously complex practical exercise in the same amount of time? For one, the orientation in conservation and development is always "future positive" (see Edwards 1999; Mosse 2005). More critically, and as Quarles van Ufford, Giri, and Mosse argue, conservation and development arenas are often pervaded by an "a-historical morality" in the sense that "general criteria and rules for judging and steering interventions . . . arise irrespective of historical context" (2003, 5).[57] In turn, this ahistorical morality is usually accompanied by faith in instrumental manageability to ensure results and effectiveness (Carolan 2005b). The initial tide of fundamental critique on development (see Escobar 1995; Ferguson 1994) did not assuage this faith (Quarles van Ufford, Giri, and Mosse 2003, 8). Instead, it triggered the ever-increasing sophistication of management tools to control and manage each and every aspect of an intervention. This sophistication has arguably reached new heights with transfrontier conservation; the amount of different objectives to be linked together and managed to success are more complex than ever before. In the case of the Maloti-Drakensberg project, many issues were tabled by the preparation phase to be conjoined and managed to success. The next chapter analyzes how the project implementers faired in practice.

chapter four

DIVERGENT INTERPRETATIONS

The Maloti-Drakensberg Transfrontier Project (MDTP) officially started in early 2003. Two allegedly independent project
coordination units (PCUS), one for Lesotho and one for South
Africa, had been established some months earlier and were
busy expanding and consolidating. Coordination between the
various implementing agencies in both countries was being
established and oversight institutions started functioning. To
guide the implementation, a project implementation plan had
been developed, which together with all the other texts and
preparations aimed at providing the PCUS with "a flying start."[1]
In line with the general assumption behind Transfrontier Conservation Areas (TFCAS), cooperation and consensus between
the two PCUS was assumed: the planners "instituted the project
to lead to friendship."[2] Informed by "global best practice," the
MDTP was ready to "overcome barriers" by "minimizing differences" and "identifying and promoting common values"
(Sandwith 2003, 161–62).

How this worked out is the topic of this chapter. The experiences of, and relationship between, the two PCUS are central in
the analysis. In contrast to the plans where the PCUS were seen
to facilitate implementation by the official MDTP "implementing agencies"—national and provincial governmental departments and parastatals responsible for conservation in the
MDTP area—they turned out to be the driving forces behind the

project. The PCUS employed specialists who spent all of their time and energy on the MDTP, while staff of implementing agencies had to divide their time and attention across many different projects and activities of which, according to a staff member of the South African lead implementing agency Ezemvelo KwaZulu Natal Wildlife (KZN Wildlife), the MDTP is "only one."[3] In both countries this led to discussions on whether the lead implementing agencies were actually taking the lead and what effects this might have on the project's longer-term institutionalization. A more immediate effect was that most of the international relations within the project were defined by the relations between the PCUS, rather than staff from the implementing agencies.[4] Similarly, it was up to the PCUS to put flesh on the consensus skeleton provided by the preparation phase. By analyzing how the PCUS individually and jointly pursued this task, I show how sensitivities and difficulties related to race and sovereignty (but also institutional, personality, and conceptual issues concealed by the project preparation process) burst out of the technical and sociopolitical straitjacket that was the Project Appraisal Document.

The chapter starts by describing how the two PCUS had completely different interpretations of the proposed project, and how they struggled to "minimize differences" and "identify and promote common values." It then analyzes the main levels of engagement and tension—issues very familiar to broader political struggles in the swiftly changing southern African political economy—and how, after some time, this resulted in a peculiar type of consensus about the project. The argument that will be advanced is that this consensus and associated operationalization acquired a very particular shape and connotation in line with the increasingly progressive and seemingly enlightened mode of "rollout" neoliberalism that had started to characterize South Africa in the 2000s (Hart 2008). More precisely, I argue that along the way and during their struggles in implementing the MDTP, the PCUS discovered the value of a devolved neoliberal approach to the project and the convenience of consensus discourses as its associated mode of politics.

Divergent Approaches

Despite all the careful preparations, the South Africa and Lesotho headed off in totally different directions right from the start of the MDTP. This was mainly due to the two PCUS, which interpreted and responded to the project proposal in completely different ways.[5] In South Africa, the PCU critically challenged the Project Implementation Plan and wanted elements changed that it felt were not practical or necessary.[6] Moreover, it challenged the studies done during the preparation phases, which were intended to provide the baseline information to ensure smooth implementation.[7] According to one PCU member, these data were "anecdotal" and only accounted for roughly 10 percent of the information he thought was needed.[8] Another PCU member argued, "the idea that the World Bank had, that we could make a flying start because we had all the information that we needed, as this was gathered during the prep phase, is a flaw."[9] This led South Africa to embark on extensive data collection with the purpose of feeding the information into a bioregional planning framework, which it had extended to encompass the entire mountain bioregion, not just the MDTP area as demarcated in map 2. In taking this stance, the PCU did not want to raise too many popular and institutional expectations, but, in the words of its coordinator, "quietly trie[d] to come besides stakeholders and support their work in line with the vision of the MDTP."[10] Planning and data collection was complemented by several strategic pilot projects in the area, ranging from socioeconomic- and environmental-assessment studies to more-practical community conservation, education, and tourism projects. All in all, project dynamics in South Africa immediately differed from what was planned, and this was largely to a completely unexpected degree: the staff members that were supposed to implement the project critically engaged and reinterpreted the proposal according to their own ideas and principles.

The Lesotho PCU's approach to project implementation contrasted starkly with that of South Africa. It did not challenge the proposal, arguing that it "had been hired to implement, not redesign the project."[11] In doing so it attached great importance to outreach and first wanted to inform stakeholders and ensure their participation in project activities. To this end, the PCU erected steering committees and so-called resource management committees in the districts where the project was active: Botha-Bothe, Mokhotlong, and Qacha's Nek. To further emphasize local project presence, the PCU set up satellite offices in the three districts. According to the district coordinators, these offices focused their initial attention on raising awareness and establishing forums and committees to get buy-in from local communities.[12] But there was not a flying start in Lesotho either. As the PCU members started exploring the project area, they "discovered" that there were no representative local government structures to take up the project's objective of biodiversity conservation.[13] In response, the Lesotho PCU decided to give financial and practical support to the then-ongoing planning for the decentralization and development of local government structures, particularly focusing on developing a local planning system for natural resource management.[14] Besides outreach and local government development, important initial elements of the MDTP in Lesotho included socioeconomic, cultural, and ecological research; assisting in the planning process for the bioregion; and several practical interventions, such as the training of mountain herdboys and upgrading infrastructure (most notably in Sehlabathebe National Park).

Importantly, the disparities in how the PCUs approached the project went deeper than different interpretations of the project proposal or when and how to approach stakeholders or do outreach. I argue that there are important epistemological differences at the core of the approaches taken by the two countries about the nature of the intervention, what it should achieve, and how consensus about this should be reached. One can distinguish between what I call a "rational consensus" (South Africa) and an "accommodating commonage" approach (Lesotho). The rational-consensus approach is a combination of what John Gray (2000) argues is today's dominant form of neoliberal ideology, namely "universal rational consensus liberalism," and Robert Fletcher's (2010, 176) "neoliberal environmentality," which is "an effort to combat environmental degradation . . . through the creation of incentive structures intended to influence individuals' use of natural resources by altering the cost-benefit ratio of resource extraction so as to encourage *in situ* preservation." The South African PCU acted on these premises through a firm—latent and overt—commitment to technocratic processes based on rational planning.[15] This was coupled with a belief in "cooperative governance,"[16] which could be translated as consensus over the actions needed to achieve the MDTP planning goals and processes.

The rational-consensus approach can be illustrated by providing some detail on the bioregional planning that the South African PCU attributed great value to. Bioregional planning, as the PCU saw it, has two main components: data collection and the translation of this data into a planning model that supports conservation at the scale of the bioregion. According to the PCU's ecologist, the philosophy underpinning data collection is systematic conservation planning, which he emphasized is also the country norm set by the Department of Environmental Affairs.[17] In turn, the PCU worked to translate this data into a C-plan (conservation plan) developed earlier by KZN Wildlife. This C-plan is a spatial planning tool that for small parts of an area—grids—gives an overview of the most important conservation issues at hand. The wattled crane, a highly endangered bird, was one of the species on whose spatial distribution and conservation needs the PCU had collected data. According to the ecologist, this would be incorporated into the C-plan, which then clarified how decisions about spatial development would impact wattled crane conservation. Interestingly, while regarded as a modern conservation tool, the C-plan is reminiscent of the long history of "complex zoning systems" that Richard Schroeder argues have characterized environmental interventions in Africa since colonial times (1999, 363; see also Hughes 2001).

In turn, the data and the C-plan fed into the broader bioregional conservation planning. According to a publication I received from the PCU bioregional planner:[18]

> Conservation planning deals with space, time (in ecological and evolutionary contexts), and the choices that humans make. Consequently, it is an integrative and transdisciplinary science that should draw on many long-established disciplines in the natural and social sciences. Most progress has been made in the former disciplines. For example, great strides have been made over the past 15 years in identifying spatial priorities and ever more sophisticated and elegant approaches and techniques are being hatched. Consequently, conservation planning is making excellent progress in addressing two of its three dimensions, namely space and time. (Cowling and Pressey 2003, 6)

The article proceeds: "unfortunately, much less progress has been made with integrating the other dimension: human choice" (6). Among the reasons given is "the inability thus far of conservation planners to comprehensively and appropriately integrate implementation—or human choice for specific conservation actions—into their planning frameworks" (6–7). Interestingly, the PCU validated this argument—from the perspective of the MDTP preparation phase—with its unexpected approach to implementation. In fact, halfway through the project the PCU had effectively turned the project around from implementation to planning. One PCU member stated, "I see us in this project as planning for implementation," and the coordinator agreed "wholeheartedly with this."[19] The coordinator also mentioned that the overall project goal of the MDTP had changed from conservation of globally significant biodiversity to developing a bioregional planning strategy for the next twenty-plus years. Considering the legitimation needed to sell the project to the Global Environment Facility (GEF) and the importance of globally significant biodiversity, this was a considerable digression from earlier plans, though in line with rational-consensus liberalism and neoliberal environmentality.

Nevertheless and despite continuous criticism directed at the PCU for making this choice, the team members remained committed to the planning process throughout their tenures. Leaning heavily on technocratic planning, this was also the way the South African PCU approached Lesotho during the project. The PCU latently assumed that with a commitment to ratio and cooperative governance, the Basotho would follow its lead and consensus about implementation priorities would accrue. This was not the case, however, in large part due to Lesotho taking a fundamentally different approach to implementing the MDTP.

The accommodating-commonage approach adopted by the Lesotho PCU was based much less on rationality, technocratic processes, and neoliberalism's underlying universalism than South Africa's approach. Rather, the forming of consensus in this approach relied on constant negotiation and renegotiation in which pluralism was accepted as a given and sought accommodative structures for. Importantly, these processes of (re)negotiation seemed almost more important than actually reaching consensus. In other words, the approach was relational and more open to alternative (communal) epistemologies. In fact, when relations and "the community" are deemed sovereign, consensus does not even have to be the end goal. As the main characteristic of commonage is nonexclusivity (at least within the community), acceptance of others' right to participate might be favored over the forcing of consensus, even if this leads to detrimental (environmental) consequences. Nevertheless, as with commonage (land) tenure more generally, there are undeniable inherent tensions in the accommodating-commonage approach, especially since Lesotho also functions within a postcolonial neoliberal context that highly influenced both the state and the implementation of the MDTP. An empirical example illustrates these tensions.

A central issue in Lesotho politics in general and for the MDTP in particular is the management of the commonage rangelands on which the majority of Basotho at least partly depend for their livelihoods (see Turner 2001, 2003). Debates about access to, control over, and governance of rangelands and their resources have raged in Lesotho for decades.[20] The MDTP in Lesotho tried to influence this debate by widening its parameters from a strict focus on rangelands as supporting livestock and other productive uses to include the conservation of rangeland biodiversity. For this to succeed, it was assumed by most previous interventions and many external agents that livestock numbers had to be brought down or managed better. Underlying this assumption is the argument that commonage use of the rangelands for livestock leads to degradation and associated threats to biodiversity and mountain watersheds.[21] At a MDTP meeting in Maseru that I attended in 2005 this debate was also a topic of concern. One Mosotho member of the Lesotho PCU remarked that as an ecologist he understood that it would make sense "from a rational point of view" that livestock should be brought down and that the government would more strictly regulate access and control with regards to the rangelands. However, he also stated, "as a Mosotho, I feel that all the resources belong to all the people." The debate was not solved in the meeting, but the comment provides a typical illustration of the accommodative-commonage approach and its inherent tensions in the Lesotho context.

Levels of Engagement and Tension

How did these two approaches interact in the framework of the transfrontier project? By the time my major fieldwork started in early 2005, the MDTP was well under way and the bilateral relations had taken on a distinct dynamic and character. Of particular importance was that the South African PCU had pressured its counterpart from the start; it even "forced" its approach on the Lesotho PCU, straining relations considerably.[22] With hindsight, one could argue that this dynamic was a logical result of the South African rational-consensus perspective combined with the PCU's staff composition within the framework of the new postapartheid southern African political economy.

One of the most notable things about the South African PCU was its skewed racial balance: eleven out of eighteen staff members were white. These eleven staff members held the most-important positions in the team, including coordinator, senior bioregional planner, and the various thematic specialist positions related to (socio-)ecology, tourism, and protected area management. It was clear from my long-term engagement with the South African PCU staff members that they were all highly trained, highly motivated, and passionate for conservation. This passion was something they stressed regularly, occasionally with particular racial connotations. The PCU ecologist, for example, believed that there are "very few black biodiversity specialists," so most of the consultants they hired to do data collecting for the MDTP were white.[23] To try and change this, he promoted nonwhite implementing agency staff members to join the MDTP research teams, but found this hard due to a different "passion for nature." He mentioned that conservationists like himself usually love the outdoors, but that many of the "upcoming conservationists in the government services"—that is, non-whites—are less excited. More generally, the South African PCU found that the provincial governments neither prioritized conservation issues adequately nor had sufficient capacity to implement programs appropriately. This further increased the staff members' sense of having to fight an urgent uphill battle to preserve the region's biodiversity against developmental pressures.[24] These issues together—passion for conservation and a sense of urgency, coupled with a belief in technocratic planning—gave the South African PCU a certain conviction and determination in promoting their approach as the right one for the entire project.

Whether the South African PCU was right or wrong in its approach is not of concern here. The point is that its approach, combined with the manner in which the PCU engaged Lesotho, strongly impacted the transfrontier relationship, including what this relationship was supposed to achieve. This became especially visible in the second year of the project. After focusing mainly on their own countries' situations in the first year,[25] the divergent approaches started to become apparent, to the degree that a very strained relation developed between the PCUs, culminating in several incidents including one where, according to one South African PCU member, "the gloves almost came off."[26] What had gone wrong? How could a *peace* park project that was instituted to lead to friendship result in such severe disagreements and tension? With hindsight, several levels of strain are identifiable in the relationship between the two PCUs around the issues of general international relations, institutional embedment, race, interpersonal relations, and conceptualization of the project.

International Relations

Relations between South Africa and Lesotho have always been contentious. This tension derives from the history of the region and its resultant regional power structure, under which the economic and political viability of an independent Lesotho was seriously questioned (Ferguson 2006). Naturally, this has implications for both sides of the border, something that was stressed by informants. A senior staff member of KZN Wildlife—who had long been involved in the Maloti-Drakensberg cooperation—showed a keen awareness of the problem: "That South Africa can overshadow its neighboring poor countries is perceived as a threat to their sovereignty, as they cannot completely decide on their own future."[27]

According to him, many South Africans involved in the MDTP did not fully appreciate this and should have tempered their approach. He gave two reasons why they did not. First, there was a lack of experience in dealing with TFCAs, and while "politicians can be more diplomatic, further down the line, people don't know this." Second, the lack of appreciation of each other was borne out of frustration because "people want things to happen quickly and think they know better." He continued: "you might know better, but people have to learn themselves!" If this is not heeded, then people display what he calls a "First World mentality," which can "endanger the project, because people in developing countries feel threatened." That this is indeed the case was acknowledged by several informants from Lesotho, who described the South African PCU as "bulldozing" or "pushing" others in Lesotho *and* in South Africa, while Lesotho had to "defend" itself. In fact, the Lesotho PCU coordinator felt that his biggest task was to make sure that Lesotho's approach to the project was accepted by South Africa. When he succeeded toward the end of the project, he mentioned that "the hardest battles are fought" and his role had become less important.[28]

Institutional Embedment

The institutional embedment of the PCUs was also a source of strain. Despite the Lesotho MDTP's primary focus on three out of the country's ten districts, the PCU was housed nationally within the Ministry of Tourism, Environment and Culture. Physically, it was even located on the same floor as the offices of the minister and the principal secretary. Although officially denied, the Lesotho PCU was much closer to its national ministry than the South African PCU was to its. Various staff members, for example, were involved in other work for the ministry, work not directly related to the MDTP.[29] In contrast, the South African PCU was located on the provincial level (KwaZulu-Natal) and was formally contracted under KZN Wildlife. It had its own offices near the regional Drakensberg office. All of this gave the staff—seemingly—larger independence from the formal structures that in the end were required to take ownership of the project and carry its activities forward.

Although not inherently problematic, the institutional differences further highlighted the PCUs' divergent approaches. The Lesotho PCU strongly identified with the national state and looked at the South African PCU's relative autonomy as problematic and undesirable, especially in the context of South Africa's transformation after apartheid. The Lesotho PCU coordinator stated, "they do things without necessarily consulting with Pretoria," which he believed can create difficult situations. Instead, he felt that "the project should support government policy."[30] Indeed, as we will see in more detail in the next chapter, there were many tensions between the South African PCU and "Pretoria" (i.e., the Department of Environmental Affairs and Tourism [DEAT]) and KZN Wildlife. This not only weakened the PCU's position domestically but also vis-à-vis Lesotho, as many actors there felt that the DEAT and KZN Wildlife's critical position toward their own PCU reinforced Lesotho's approach to the project. In interviews, important members of the Lesotho MDTP's project coordination committee,[31] for example, told me that the responsible director for the MDTP in KZN Wildlife was not happy with the South African PCU.[32] The reason was that the PCU was too self-willed and convinced of its approach in the face of other opinions on how to implement the project.

As with the international relations, this level of tension was arguably exacerbated because it touches on the issue of sovereignty, both in terms of the prerogative of a, perhaps imagined, unitary and independent state (Lesotho) and the difficulty of another state (South Africa, represented by the DEAT) in dealing with different subjectivities and ideas about the governance of people and nature (see Mbembe 2001). In turn, these sovereignties were further compounded by another issue that greatly influenced transfrontier relations between the PCUs, that of race.

Race

As mentioned, the South African PCU was dominated by whites. That this was likely to draw criticism for not reflecting South Africa's demographics or contributing to redressing the injustices of South Africa's apartheid past, was already recognized by the PCU coordinator in early 2004 (MDTP 2004). Importantly, this issue must be seen in the context of South Africa's Employment Equity Act, which strongly encourages, and in some instances (such as in government) imposes, composition of staff of organizations to (better) reflect the country's demographics. According to the coordinator's position article, the PCU's composition was justified as follows: "All appointments have been subject to the World Bank's procurement procedures which clearly stipulate that where grant funding is concerned *Bank procurement policies supersede country policies.* In other words, preferential procurement is superseded by procurement of the best individual for the position through open competitive bidding" (MDTP 2004, 2; emphasis added). The article also outlines the extensive World Bank procedures followed during the filling of the positions, hoping that this would eliminate potential criticism. It concludes that "the success of the project is absolutely dependent on employing people who currently have the required capacity to immediately fulfill the project requirements. The five year term of this implementation phase does not allow time for training team members and the extreme complexities inherent within the project requires people who are fully capable of working independently on their particular discipline from the moment they join the team" (MDTP 2004, 2). Implicit here is that South Africa currently does not have enough people of disadvantaged background who are "fully capable of working independently on their particular discipline" for the PCU to fill the specialist posts.

To say that this line of argumentation was not accepted by the majority of other role players in the MDTP is an understatement. Many key informants in Lesotho *and* South Africa heavily criticized the composition of the South African PCU, accusing it of placing itself out of the South African context. Both arguments posited by the South African coordinator did not resonate well. Regarding the legalistic superseding of country policies by World Bank regulations, many pointed out that the project, despite being funded by a multilateral institution, still operates in the South (and southern) African context. Given this context, particularly as it relates to the continuing gross inequalities resulting from the apartheid past, many believe that it is not permissible to bypass national legislation that has been put there for a reason. In reply to the argument that there are not enough previously disadvantaged people with the right capacity, many respondents refuted this outright (see also Kepe 2009, 876). Several just stated that the capacity was there, with the additional remark that one perhaps "has to look better" or "search harder." A more candid position from someone in Lesotho was that because the white staff members could not speak Zulu or Sotho, the dominant languages in the MDTP area, it was they who were ill equipped for the job.[33]

Issues such as these are common in postcolonial South Africa and make for a national transformation process full of contradictory dynamics and struggles, while also strongly influencing regional relations and sovereignties. Overall, the MDTP experience corroborates a general sentiment in the literature on ethnicity and postapartheid that a "romanticized 'rainbowism' of merging colours is contradicted by the reality of heightened ethnoracial consciousness" (Moodley and Adam 2000, 55). Although it would go too far to suggest that within the MDTP international understanding and bonding occurred only between those of the same race, ethnoracial tensions did not help to further institutionalize friendship between the two PCUs. As a Lesotho PCU member stated, "In the end, we still see white people."[34]

Interpersonal Relations

Another, related, level of transfrontier tension between the two PCUs revolved around interpersonal relations. Of course, it is impossible to predict whether the various influential personalities in a project will get along. And although most would agree that interpersonal relations are tremendously important to the success of any project, it is never taken up as a variable in logical frameworks. In the case of the MDTP, staff members of both PCUs were coupled according to expertise, and it was these relationships that determined much of the international relations in the project. From my many formal interviews and informal conservations with all PCU members from both sides, it was obvious that almost no counterpart couple got along really well or had much chemistry. In South Africa, many PCU members complained that their counterparts were not meeting deadlines or even showing up to meetings. Moreover, some felt that there were big differences in technical expertise between the two PCUs and that this was problematic.[35] In Lesotho, complaints were mostly about the pressure from South Africa pushing its approach. In 2004, tensions starting running so deep that a bilateral strategic-planning workshop had to be organized to try and improve bilateral relations. The report of the workshop noted: "Interpersonal relations between key staff members on each side of the project are brittle and fragile. There is a readiness to allow relatively minor issues to fester coupled with a tendency to present a misleading façade. There is some mistrust and perceptions of self-promotion when one side initiates an action. Intentions are sometimes negatively interpreted and there is some confusion between what is real and what is expected to happen" (Matela and Fraser 2004, 27).

Critically, the two coordinators also did not get along well. One of the most telling illustrations in this respect, one that also closely hinges on the issues of race and international relations, concerned the downgrading of the performance of the MDTP in Lesotho in late 2004, early 2005. As part of the monitoring and evaluation of its projects, the World Bank regularly conducts supervision missions to review and rate progress. Basic rating is expressed in terms of "satisfactory," "unsatisfactory," or variations on these variables. Like other projects, the MDTP received supervision missions every six months (in both South Africa and Lesotho), after which the World Bank task-team leader (TTL) would assign a rating to Lesotho (as a whole) and South Africa (the PCU and implementing agencies separately). At the end of 2004 it became clear that Lesotho was behind on the original project implementation plan and subsequent implementation agreements. As a result, the South African PCU became increasingly frustrated over whether it would be able to do the conservation work it thought was urgent.

In an attempt to remedy this, the South African PCU coordinator phoned the World Bank TTL. According to the coordinator, the TTL had also noticed the problems and decided that the only way to help Lesotho deal with them was to downgrade the project-approval rate. His reasoning was that by doing so possibilities would open up for extra (technical) support. The South African PCU coordinator subsequently sent an e-mail to his staff saying that there might be a solution to the problems and mentioned what the TTL had told him.[36] The TTL, however, had not communicated this to the Lesotho PCU. Instead, staff members learned of the downgrading through a meeting between the two PCU bioregional planners where the Lesotho staff member read the e-mail, which the South African PCU member had printed and brought. The Lesotho bioregional planner subsequently informed his coordinator, who was still livid when I spoke to him on 27 April 2005, the day after the World Bank TTL had finished a supervision mission that aimed to repair the damage.

According to the Lesotho PCU coordinator, everyone in Lesotho, especially those in the Ministry of Tourism, Environment and Culture and the Ministry of Finance and Development Planning, were "unpleasantly surprised."[37] Moreover, they and many other stakeholders defended the project and some even wanted the World Bank TTL changed, preferably to somebody with a "more neutral nationality" (the TTL happened to be a white South African man). According to the coordinator, he was personally also "unpleasantly surprised" when he heard the news, since he and the TTL "were friends," and the way he heard it was not direct. In our interview, the coordinator mentioned that he suspected that the reason behind the unilateral decision by the TTL to change the project status was that the South African PCU had preconceived ideas about how the project should be run and Lesotho was not following suit. He believed that the South Africans complained about this to the TTL, who then decided to "unilaterally downgrade the project." By doing so, the Lesotho PCU coordinator felt that the TTL "abused his position," "had not been neutral," and that he was "gossiping with the South Africans over Lesotho, badmouthing the Lesotho PCU."[38] Interestingly, the South African PCU coordinator, independent of his Lesotho counterpart, had an accurate sense of how the Lesotho team reacted. He reckoned that the Lesotho PCU had said that he and the TTL "had together decided on downgrading the project in Lesotho," and that—because the World Bank TTL is a white South African—South Africa does not take Lesotho seriously and wants to play big brother, and that even racial issues had come into play.[39]

In response to the complaints from Lesotho, the World Bank TTL indicated that he would come to Lesotho to help get the project back to the satisfactory level by developing an action plan. The Lesotho PCU coordinator found this odd, as there were action and implementation plans in the original project proposals. He was even more puzzled by the fact that the TTL in his draft aide-mémoire (the name for a World Bank report after a supervision mission) had already upgraded the project back to satisfactory, when implementation of the action plan had yet to commence.[40] Both PCU coordinators advised me to talk to the TTL, but when I did, there was little response. The only thing the TTL wanted to say was that it was an "unfortunate incident" and "an unintended misunderstanding between the Lesotho government and the bank."[41] He assured me that "it has been discussed extensively, and we have restored confidence in the project and can move on now." Although this reply in itself is interesting, what is important here is that the downgrading incident greatly intensified the strained relations between the PCUs, especially between the coordinators, from late 2004 until mid-2005. Although major upsurges like this remained limited and relations improved again, it could never be said that there was real chemistry or a good working relationship between the two PCUs. Even from the outside, people could see that the relationship was not working as hoped. This disappointed Trevor Sandwith, one of the key people in the MDTP preparation phase, who stated that "the real output of such a project is building relationships, and they are not doing that."[42]

Conceptualizations

Different conceptual ideas about conservation between the PCUs are identifiable, and they are linked to the different approaches toward project implementation. One can distinguish between a conceptual approach leaning toward community-based natural resource management (CBNRM) for the Lesotho PCU and one leaning toward bioregional conservation planning (BCP) for the South African PCU. Although both are based on similar premises related to community-based conservation (CBC), there are distinct differences between them. CBNRM as conceptualized by the Lesotho PCU resembles accepted forms of CBNRM in the region, influenced—inter alia—by scholars and practitioners from the University of Zimbabwe, the University of the Western Cape,[43] Rhodes University, the (former) southern African International Union for Conservation of Nature office, and others. Although I am not doing justice to the nuances, I argue that what is distinctive about the southern African CBNRM literature is that it derives mostly from the social sciences, has a tendency toward anthropocentric arguments, and espouses a political agenda aimed at the emancipation of poor rural communities.[44] In interviews with Lesotho PCU members, this resonated unmistakably. When asked about her general view on the purpose of conservation, the socio-ecologist of the PCU mentioned that they "put the primacy on the people; they are involved in all we do." She continued, "I think we are conserving to derive benefits from it, which could promote our well-being."[45] The MDTP district conservation officer in Mokhotlong mentioned that the purpose of his work is that communities see the benefits of conservation.[46] I noted similar statements, signifying that the importance of resource conservation for the Lesotho PCU rests firstly in the use value it brings to (local) people.

The BCP approach as adopted by the South African PCU taps into quite different networks and intellectual traditions. It is associated mostly with individuals in the South Africa National Biodiversity Institute, the Botanical Society of South Africa, the botany departments of the Universities of Cape Town and Port Elizabeth, and Cape Action for People and the Environment (CAPE).[47] Conceptually, BCP derives mostly from the natural sciences, has a tendency toward biocentric arguments, and has a political agenda that emphasizes technocratic protection of biological diversity. I already noted the South African PCU members' attachment to this thinking, but another illustration related to the PCU's treasured C-plan further testifies to this. According to the grassland ecologist, the C-plan includes a map of the region's biodiversity that indicates what "has already been lost, what is most important, and what is most threatened—i.e., where are the most-irreplaceable areas requiring immediate conservation action."[48] Similarly, the ecologist mentioned that a focus on the major threats to biodiversity and their spatial dynamics should together form a good underpinning for prioritization of conservation efforts.[49] In this view—shared by most in the PCU—a constructive balance between humans and nature is derived from long-term conservation rather than direct use values for (local) people.

What made the conceptual differences between the two PCUs especially pronounced is that they were reinforced by partially overlapping but also distinctive networks. Members of the Lesotho PCU were very close to southern African CBNRM networks revolving around the above-named organizations. The majority of the South African PCU members were entrenched in BCP networks. During my fieldwork, this became clear to me when the South African PCU's bioregional planner invited me to participate in a workshop on mainstreaming biodiversity in municipalities, organized by the South Africa National Biodiversity Institute. There representatives from several bioregional programs and South African provinces explained how they were engaging "with local government through various projects aimed at integrating biodiversity priorities in land-use planning and decision-making" (the South Africa National Biodiversity Institute 2005, 2). Of the South African bioregional programs, only one was transfrontier, the MDTP. In fact, the MDTP was not even really regarded as a TFCA or peace park, but as a bioregional planning initiative, just like the others presented at the workshop.

An example of how the two networks further reinforced conceptual differences and tensions between the PCUs was the appointment of a regional planner in late 2005 or early 2006. At the MDTP midterm evaluation around mid-2005, it was noted that the two PCUs were not cooperating well and had drifted apart in their implementation strategies. The evaluators recommended that "the best way to revitalise transfrontier collaboration is by appointing one person to drive the process" (MDTP 2005b, 9). This person, so it was later decided, should be a bioregional planner, drawing together data collected by the PCUs into an overall bioregional planning framework. A call was put out for bids, and in the end, the evaluation led to two candidates scoring nearly equally high: a black Zimbabwean man and a white South African woman. These two candidates were neatly aligned with the respective networks of the PCUs. The Zimbabwean had long been involved in regional CBNRM, and was well-known to the Lesotho PCU. The South African had had a long history with BCP, through involvement with CAPE, among other organizations, and was close to the South African PCU.[50]

In the assessment, the Zimbabwean scored a tiny fraction higher than the South African. The South African PCU subsequently objected to a detail in the assessment scores and claimed that both had scored equally high. Even though the Lesotho PCU did not agree and remained convinced that the Zimbabwean was the right candidate, it succumbed to the pressure. A compromise was found by asking the two candidates to write a position paper. In the meantime, the Lesotho PCU coordinator had decided that he would hire "their candidate" no matter the outcome; if not for the overall bioregional planning, then as a consultant for Lesotho. In the end this is what happened. The South African won the bid and started her contract in March 2006, after a seven-month procurement period, while the Lesotho PCU hired the Zimbabwean somewhat earlier. This fight over the bioregional planner position again revealed the main fault lines: the Lesotho PCU favored a black person with a CBNRM background while the South African PCU opted for a white person with a BCP background. Moreover, although technically Lesotho was right that the Zimbabwean won the bid, South Africa (again) pushed through its opinion. Perhaps those involved saw this as one of many stand-alone issues or battles to be fought within the project, but the incident echoed familiar issues related to race, sovereignty, approach, and interpersonal relations.

From Implementation to Consensus

Bioregional planning, supported by research, became by far the most important activity within the MDTP. Although bioregional planning was initially unforeseen, it became so dominant under the South African PCU's pressure that a shift in thinking occurred from the MDTP as an implementation project to a planning and data-gathering project. Various PCU members, especially from South Africa but also from Lesotho, increasingly emphasized that the MDTP should be seen as a longer-term program with the current phase being a "planning phase." Accordingly, the official goal of the project changed from conservation of globally significant biodiversity to developing a bioregional planning strategy for the next twenty-plus years.[51] Moreover, during its last years, the project was reconceptualized as "MDTP phase I," to further emphasize the longer-term nature of the intervention. In the end, the project culminated in a twenty-year bioregional planning framework for the Maloti-Drakensberg area with a five-year action plan for "MDTP phase II" (2008–2012). The discussions on the planning framework that took place toward the end of the project reveal how the PCUS cooperated on the development of the framework under pressure to show results on the ground. It is in this process, I argue, that a devolved neoliberal governance approach coupled with consensus discourses as its associated politics became the logical choice for the project vis-à-vis the politics of the postcolonial neoliberal political economy.

According to an unpublished MDTP memo in 2007, the bioregional planning for the Maloti-Drakensberg bioregion is supposed to guide "all action, whether country-specific or joint, *collectively* contributing to the achievement of the project purpose (impact) and vision/overall goal."[52] In order to come to a robust framework, the collection of baseline data "about where biodiversity is located and what needs what kind of protection" was deemed crucial.[53] Data gathering in South Africa was far more extensive than in Lesotho, and the Lesotho PCU's buy-in of the overall planning process remained somewhat halfhearted throughout the project. Nevertheless, the bioregional planning process had become a reality and needed to be sold to and accepted by the wider MDTP polity. Although initially subscribing to the process, several important actors, most notably the main Lesotho implementing agencies and the South African DEAT, started doubting the extensive planning and data gathering and pressed for more implementation "on the ground".[54] In line with accepted CBNRM discourses, these actors emphasized that local communities, especially in South Africa, should be benefiting more than they were. Significantly, staff members from the DEAT and other South African actors increasingly commended the Lesotho PCU's approach of extensive community participation and collaboration as an example of how it should be in South Africa. The director of the DEAT TFCA directorate, for example, stated, "the beauty of Lesotho is that they have community conservation and that they are very good at that."[55]

What being good at community conservation entails in terms of conservation or development was usually unclear. In fact, it seemed more important to share the same discourse than ensuring that it made a difference in practice. In November 2005, the DEAT staff officer responsible for the MDTP believed that the project had not yet delivered any tangible benefits, in Lesotho or in South Africa. Yet, he remarked, "more local people in Lesotho know about the project, so Lesotho is doing better."[56] This line of thinking by South African DEAT officials was warmly welcomed by staff from Lesotho's implementing agencies, who had also gotten increasingly frustrated with the South African PCU's emphasis on planning.[57] Thus, although the practical effects of a preference for CBC remained unclear, the shared discourse and shared frustration with the emphasis on bioregional planning led to an "extremely warm relationship" between officials from national Lesotho's and South Africa's implementing agencies by the end of the project.[58] Nonetheless, some of them noted that if the end product (the bioregional strategy) is good, they will work with it.[59] According to a DEAT staff officer, the plan is that of a transfrontier project, so if the governments are committed, he reckoned that it will be used, even though he was personally "not too confident" that the bioregional planning was appropriate.[60] Overall, however, indications of this commitment in important government agencies seemed brittle. Within the South African DEAT, many staff members kept negatively referring to the MDTP as "that planning project."[61] In Lesotho, some actors from involved government agencies appeared notably hostile toward planning, while others merely noted that no matter how good the planning, "in Lesotho it will always get compromised."[62]

But this point needs to be taken further, into the context of the region's political-economic history of racial inequality and colonial fortress conservation. This, together with a neoliberal climate that stimulates positive-sum win-win conceptualizations, indicates that CBNRM and CBC are the only truly politically legitimate conservation master narratives in southern African conservation (see Benjaminsen and Svarstad 2010; Dressler and Büscher 2008). This puts enormous pressure on governments and donors to be seen as community based and making sure that "poor communities" (are believed to) benefit from conservation. Planning and data gathering do not immediately benefit poor people, and since governments and donors also know that any implementation is rife with difficulties and complications, postponing implementation is a political risk. With these pressures in mind, it seemed logical that South African and Lesotho government agencies, and later also the World Bank, started demanding more community-based implementation from the MDTP.

Evidently, it was the South African PCU that especially felt the pressure. During 2005, it was suggested that it cut its bioregional planning process short and "start implementing."[63] The PCU coordinator's reaction was that "there is no choice but to continue with the planning." He continued, "we will be hard-nosed; we are not going to compromise on our planning."[64] The goal of the planning, according to him, is institutionalization, while showing the value of the planning process to the funders. Another staff member indicated why the PCU felt it could not compromise on its strategy: "Basically, an expectation was created that our phase could just walk in and begin implementation, while the bitter truth is that the groundwork has not been done. We are now faced with producing the basic information that was supposed to be there, while delivering on implementation expectations."[65]

But the staff could not entirely ignore the pressure. Increasingly, the PCU had to repackage its approach to make it politically justifiable. The PCU did so by better spelling out the socioeconomic relevance of biodiversity conservation and its proper planning. More precisely, the South African PCU put increasingly more emphasis on marketing the services that biodiversity provides to society through the concept of "payments for environmental services" (PES). The Lesotho PCU coordinator was skeptical but indicated that in future phases Lesotho would also explore PES. His reason was straightforward: "it is a capitalist world with constant costs-benefit analyses, so if it is going to work, it is good."[66] Chapter 7 will examine how the South African PCU operationalized the governance of PES. Here, the reasons why staff members felt that PES was a viable political strategy are important.

The South African PCU had chosen an overall approach and strategy that were difficult to get accepted politically, but as the staff members remained convinced of their decision, they needed to create political legitimacy by changing the packaging of the same message. And they were highly aware of this. According to the project planner, "in conservation you feel you are playing catch-up all the time," and with respect to the planning process, he felt that they have to "tip toe through the socioeconomic agendas."[67] Moreover, the South African PCU had to do this repackaging together with the Lesotho PCU members, who were also skeptical of the planning. The suggestion to hire a bilateral bioregional planning facilitator came about to overcome this problem and coordinate the work of the PCUs.

Despite, or because of, the difficult appointment process, the consultant did not stay long with the project. A first joint PCU strategic-planning workshop organized by her and the South African PCU planner in July 2006 ended in disaster. According to the PCU planner, the idea was that the specialists would provide baseline input for the bioregional planning, and then this input could be presented and discussed in the workshop.[68] However, PCU members failed to provide this input,[69] and the objectives of the workshop had to be changed just days before it took place. The consultant and planner decided on a methodological exercise to identify root causes of conservation problems in the MDTP area and to develop causal chains that would make targeting interventions easier. This approach met with fierce resistance, both from PCU and implementing agency staff members, as most of them felt that this was going back to square one when they were already more than three years into the project. Although it seems paradoxical, this incident later helped to bring the PCUs closer together, as they now had a common adversary in the bioregional planning facilitator. This resulted in an untenable situation for her, and she resigned in October 2006. The PCUs then decided that they would work closer together, and through regular workshops they would develop the bioregional planning strategy to be offered to the outside world.

During one of these bilateral planning workshops—which I attended on 17 and 18 January 2007 in Botha-Bothe, Lesotho—it became clear that future institutionalization had a major impact on how the PCUs developed their strategy. After all, future institutionalization had become the key goal of the planning, in order to show its value to funders and stakeholders. Several observations from the workshop are worth noting. First, there was constant pressure for the incorporating and balancing of all thematic priorities. Although it was clear that several South African PCU members wanted the strategy to mainly focus on conservation, there were constant reminders from others to include social, economic, cultural, and political issues, and these requests were almost always accommodated. This led to heated debates, which the South African PCU bioregional planner tried to manage by saying, "all are saying the same things but in different wordings: they are all layers of the strategic planning." But it was obvious that not everybody was "saying the same things." The two ecologists of the South African PCU, for instance, clearly disagreed with the diluting of the conservation focus in the planning framework, but they were repeatedly and very explicitly sidelined so as not to jeopardize the thematic all-inclusiveness of the framework.

Second, the workshop encouraged a drive toward consensus and all-inclusiveness in relation to actors. The framework not only needed to cover all thematic issue areas, but it also had to incorporate the interests, ambitions, and actions of all stakeholders. This follows from the focus of the framework and action plan, which was to be on the potential for "all action" within the MDTP area to have effects on conservation. Hence, the framework speaks of "institutionalizing" the strategy into government agencies on all levels; "mainstreaming" conservation into "private production sectors"; involving the entire MDTP area (and thus all the actors involved in the area) in appropriate conservation and development "land-use planning"; enhancing "sustainable tourism" to bring local livelihoods into an appropriate conservation and development format, and so on (MDTP 2007d, 2007e).

Third, the means used to balance *all* issue areas among *all* actors could also be *any* means. In the planning framework, regulation was to be proposed to ensure conservation of priority biodiversity. This regulation, in the words of the facilitator, could have been laws, or even payments for environmental services and "mainstreaming into commercial production sectors." The South African PCU coordinator's reaction was that this regulation should not only apply to private tenure but also to commonage, to which the facilitator replied that with "private investment in a commonage structure you still have to live up to commercial laws." An article in the South African MDTP newsletter on systematic conservation planning further illustrates that "flagged areas need not become fenced nature reserves, as there are a range of 'tools' in the conservation tool box: protected areas, conservancies, stewardship agreements, incentives and education programmes can all help in achieving the targets."[70] Although several South African PCU members clearly preferred protected areas, special emphasis was laid on a wide range of devolved, self-regulatory principles (e.g., tourism, conservancies, payments for environmental services, "commercial laws") in order to not exclude any means that any of the actors in the area would be willing to employ. It was then up to the project to create the "enabling environment" (which became another strategic outcome of the overall plan) to "incentivize" stakeholders into appropriate conservation action.

All in all, the workshop was set on developing a bioregional planning framework that would be politically acceptable by being as inclusive as possible with respect to all actors and their interests and ambitions and preferred issue areas and methods of action. As such, the workshop—and the wider bioregional planning process—reinforces David Mosse's conclusion that policy models serve upward legitimation, ensure "coalitions of support," and justify "the flow of resources" (2004, 664). The workshop's conceptually vague and multi-interpretable policy discourse was *"required to conceal ideological differences, to allow compromise and the enrolment of different interests, to build coalitions, to distribute agency and to multiply criteria of success within project systems"* (Mosse 2004, 663; emphasis in original). In our personal conversations, many workshop participants would immediately agree to or complain about this, and add that they would much rather see the plan taking a hard-line conservationist or developmental approach.

The PCU members, all highly educated and experienced, were also aware of inevitable differences between policy and practice. So why did they still put so much emphasis on developing such an all-encompassing bioregional plan? After all, with respect to the MDTP project proposal, they themselves paid tribute to another conclusion by Mosse that "during the 'implementation phase' all the diverse and contradictory interests that were enrolled in the framing of an ambiguous policy model and project design, all the contests and contradictions that are embedded in policy texts, are brought to life and replayed" (2004, 664). So why did the PCUS repeat this process? In other words, if the main achievement after five years of implementing the MDTP was a document driven by the PCUS and workshopped with all stakeholders that was to be implemented in the second phase, were we not back at square one?

It is here that we have to move beyond the conclusions drawn by Mosse (2004, 2005) and seek a more structural, political-economic explanation. Despite being highly aware of the differences between policy and practice and the need to conceal differences, the PCUS still chose to continue the process, in the conviction that in the end, the right outcome would be understood, acknowledged, and acted upon by the outside (whether the outcome be the South African focus on bioregional conservation or the Lesotho focus on community-based conservation). Moreover and crucially, most PCU members were not only concerned with justifying "the flow of resources," although this was certainly important. Many were equally concerned with and even passionate about either biodiversity conservation or community development and wanted to see the project succeed as they had interpreted it. But while trying to implement the MDTP, the intensity and type of political interests that the PCUS encountered required them to employ an antipolitical consensus strategy. I will turn to the issue of the intensity of the politics and the associated necessity of reciprocal antipolitics in

more depth, but what matters here is that in their struggle over the interpretation of the MDTP proposal, the PCUs discovered through the bilateral
planning process the value of advocating a devolved governance approach
to accommodate the two competing approaches (rational consensus and
accommodating commonage) and keep official stakeholders (particularly
implementing agencies) on board. Consequently, this devolved governance approach started to be increasingly hybridized "with other institutional forms and political agendas" in the "relatively everyday sense" as
"the inextricable interweaving in practice of analytically separable policy
trends" (McCarthy 2005, 998).

Conclusion

The fragility and the appeal of consensus in the MDTP are unambiguous.
Both in the preparation and the implementation phases of the project,
consensus was far from present. Yet, at least during the preparation phase,
the appearance of consensus succeeded to a significant extent: a project
proposal for the MDTP was not only developed but also funded. Implementation, however, became a major struggle. Consensus and cooperation
between the PCUs was far from optimal and even further from what the
MDTP preparation planners had expected. However, after the major fallout
in 2005, the relationship between the PCUs improved, which had a great
deal to do with the South African PCU accepting, according to its coordinator, that it is "beautiful" that both countries could come to the same goal
through different approaches.[71] That said, the practical day-to-day cooperation continued to be difficult, which was one reason why the two countries
focused more on their own national situations rather than the transfrontier aspects of the project.[72]

This does not mean that the PCUs did not try to make the project work.
To the contrary: they undertook many initiatives to this effect. In doing so
and communicating this to the outside world, differences between the
PCUs were often downgraded or even concealed. To the outside world of
stakeholders and target populations, the idea of consensus often had to be
upheld.[73] The way to do so was found in advocating a devolved neoliberal
approach to the project and increasingly emphasizing strategies such as
payments for environmental services, tourism, mainstreaming into the
private sector, and conservation marketing, which were proactive yet non-
regulatory mechanisms to stimulate conservation in the Maloti-Drakensberg bioregion. Accordingly, a clear difference in the phrasing of con-

sensus from the preparation to the first phase of the MDTP occurred, now geared even more toward enlisting societal legitimacy. A telling example was the increasing switch from using the word water to referring to "environmental service." While seemingly a mere discursive change, this is in line with a more general, proactive rollout neoliberalism that is reshaping relations between people and nature across the southern African region and beyond.

The consensus struggle between the PCUS in the MDTP, therefore, cannot be seen outside of the wider political economy and power structures of which it is a part. If the struggle for consensus already seemed difficult between the two PCUS, the complexity increased dramatically when taking into account the wider political and governance structures and the many important actors of the region.

chapter five

PROCESSING POLITICS

Despite the minimal consensus during the implementation strategy, the Maloti-Drakensberg intervention was put into practice and it affected the regional polity. Of the many activities employed, most of the project funding was spent on consultancies, research, and planning. These had important, although perhaps indirect, effects, especially on the higher levels of scale (national and international). Money was also spent on practical interventions with more-direct effects on local or regional dynamics. This chapter analyzes how the Maloti-Drakensberg Transfrontier Project (MDTP) interacted with and affected regional and local conservation and development dynamics within the Maloti-Drakensberg area, and, vice versa, how these dynamics affected the politics of the MDTP. It is important to stress the considerable potential effects of a large intervention like the MDTP (mainly so for Lesotho) on existing power balances. After all, interventions aim to become part of a polity, thereby influencing and changing dynamics and behavior of and between actors. Any conservation and development intervention is therefore inherently political, and I will describe and analyze the political strategies used by the MDTP and the political reactions these aroused from other actors.

The most important of these other actors were the MDTP implementing agencies on the national and provincial or district level. As shown in chapter four, conservation and developments interventions have to follow many procedures in order to be seen as legitimate. One of the most important is that they are (or appear) democratic: owned by the people who have to undergo or carry out the intervention. Hence, in both Lesotho and South Africa, the MDTP was set up so that it was agreed upon by and part of democratic structures. But institutionalizing interventions is never straightforward. It is a constant struggle whereby different actors appropriate, interpret, or embrace the intervention differently. This process is the focus of the first part of the chapter. The emphasis will be on what unexpectedly became major issues in the institutionalization of the MDTP. In South Africa this was the transformation process; in Lesotho the ongoing decentralization process.

In the second part, the chapter moves from institutionalization in government agencies to engagement with local communities, as they were the other major stakeholders of the project. Given the size of the area and the number of residents, it is impossible to cover all the local dynamics in the MDTP. My snapshot of community-based conservation in the projects' commonage areas focuses on one high-profile case in each country: the 'Moteng Managed Resource Area (MRA) in the northern district of Botha-Bothe in Lesotho,[1] and Amagugu Esizwe, a MDTP pilot project in the Amazizi and AmanGwane tribal areas of northern KwaZulu-Natal province in South Africa.

Building on the previous chapter, this chapter analyzes the struggle for consensus within a larger political playing field. In this struggle, the political strategies used by the Project Coordination Units (PCUs) became antipolitical: framing issues so that they appear undebatable, that consensus is preset. In doing so, I go beyond the general way in which antipolitics has been operationalized in the literature, namely as a technical antipolitics (see Ferguson 1994; Li 2007). Instead, I employ the framework developed by Andreas Schedler (1997) around instrumental, amoral, moral, and aesthetic antipolitics. The very structure and dynamics of the MDTP make this possible in that two different interpretations of the same project led to different antipolitical strategies. In other words, the differential antipolitics of the two PCUs bring a new element to studies of interventions, as it more clearly shows the politics in antipolitics. In turn, by analyzing how these antipolitical strategies resonated with and impacted local communities, I empirically show how this dynamic reinforces structural power imbalances in a neoliberal political economy by putting both implementers and subjects under similar pressures to avoid the political realm where inequalities can be addressed.

South African Transformations

In South Africa, the main targets for institutionalization of the Maloti-Drakensberg project were the five official implementing agencies: the Department of Environmental Affairs and Tourism (DEAT) and South African National Parks on the national level, and the three relevant departments on the provincial level: the Free State Department of Tourism, Environmental and Economic Affairs; the Eastern Cape Department of Economic Affairs, Environment and Tourism; and the lead implementing agency, Ezemvelo KwaZulu Natal Wildlife (KZN Wildlife). The main strategies the PCU tried to get the MDTP objectives to become part and parcel of these organizations were interprovincial memorandums of understanding (MOUS) between and interdepartmental MOUS within provinces and integrating the MDTP into job descriptions and organizational funding cycles.[2] The PCU's view of the success or failure of the institutionalization effort differed strongly based on the implementing agency, and it is illuminating to briefly discuss the different organizations.

The Eastern Cape province's DEAT was generally seen to be performing well and doing its best to institutionalize the MDTP objectives. One of the directors within the DEAT noted that the project enjoyed high political support within the province and that local-government structures were getting involved in and even cofinancing MDTP activities. He was worried though about lack of capacity, chiefly due to reorganizations that had taken place before and during 2005, and the marriage between environmental and economic affairs in the department, which he thought did not always lead to the "hard decisions" necessary for environmental affairs.[3]

KZN Wildlife's performance was regarded with ambivalence. Compared to the other provincial implementing agencies, KZN Wildlife is generally seen as well endowed financially, technically, and administratively. As such, it was able to perform well on the scientific and planning sides of the transfrontier project. The main problems in terms of implementation and institutionalization proved less tangible: lack of political support, lack of interdepartmental coordination, and, crucially, a lack of strategic leadership, which rendered the organization unable to live up to its role as lead implementing agency.[4] Much of this has to do with KZN Wildlife's complex institutional structure and history.[5]

The third provincial implementing body, the Free State Department of Tourism, Economic Affairs and Environment, was generally considered to be performing poorly. Its staff members often missed meetings without apologies, did not take part in most activities, and showed a general lack of interest in the project. According to the director of scientific services, "real involvement is difficult because we are understaffed and have budget constraints."[6] He further emphasized the lack of political support from higher levels and noted that some managers in the department felt that only KwaZulu-Natal would benefit from the MDTP, not the Free State province. These issues led the South African PCU coordinator in late 2005 to avow that the Free State may be "a bit of a lost cause." He later qualified this by stating that despite continued disinterest from higher political levels, on-the-ground cooperation is fine.[7] These conclusions were echoed in March 2007 by the then newly appointed director in the department. He noted that there is "very little, if any" institutionalization of the MDTP in the Free State.[8]

Of the national agencies, South African National Parks (SANParks) was generally regarded as performing well.[9] Although managing only a small portion of the Maloti-Drakensberg area—the Golden Gate Highlands National Parks in the Free State—SANParks is, according to its TFCA coordinator, "very serious in the MDTP."[10] The Golden Gate park manager agreed and added that although SANParks is formally only responsible for what happens inside its parks, it has been under increasing pressure to deal with wider (social, political, economic) environments. This has led to increased activities outside protected areas and therefore more need to coordinate with other institutions.[11]

The fifth official implementing agency was the DEAT, although its role was supervision rather than actual implementation. On behalf of the South African government, the DEAT received the funding from the World Bank, after which it transferred the funds to KZN Wildlife. Transfrontier conservation enjoys strong political support in the department and has its own directorate. In an interview, the head of this directorate mentioned that the diplomatic Joint Bilateral Committee between South Africa and Lesotho considers the MDTP a priority activity, again emphasizing political support.[12] The degree of support, however, has been contentious. Some disgruntlement arose within the PCU about non-MDTP related work that the specially appointed MDTP officer within the DEAT was doing. Although the officer admitted this was true, he (and his boss) denied that this impacted political support.

This is of course a mere snapshot of MDTP institutionalization in South Africa. There were also major issues that affected the relationship between the project and the implementing agencies that demonstrate the political complexities that the PCU had to mediate. Based on interviews and participatory observation, three issues stand out: capacity, interdepartmental and interprovincial cooperation, and leadership and authority. In turn, these issues were influenced by one major underlying dynamic: South Africa's ongoing transformation process from apartheid to postapartheid. A key aim of transformation in South Africa is to redress racial imbalances in both public and private spheres. Obviously, this has been an enormously complex and difficult process, characterized by resistance, personal hardships, legal battles, and so forth. A common problem was that organizations were transformed for the public eye but whites still held power by occupying strategic positions. This also characterized KZN Wildlife's transformation process.[13] In 2001, a black CEO was appointed, but of the eight executive directors below him, six were white and still held de facto power. This led to many internal struggles, which eventually culminated in the retrenchment of all directors in October 2004 "as part of a restructuring process."[14] In their place came three new executive directors (for biodiversity conservation, commercial operations, and support services). These had to be black, and it so happened that the then regional manager for the uKhahlamba region received a rapid promotion to the new post of executive director of biodiversity conservation.

In an interview, one of the previous directors—the one responsible for hiring the South African PCU coordinator—mentioned that the MDTP was having a hard time with implementation. He attributed this mostly to a lack of leadership and capacity in KZN Wildlife and to the PCU being too far from reality with its focus on planning. Regarding the former, my interview notes are worth quoting at some length:

Mr. Ethan Peters argues that a lot has changed that was not foreseen when the MDTP was conceptualized. According to him, KZN Wildlife used to be a very efficient and highly capacitated organization, where institutionalization and rolling out of a project such as the MDTP would have been very smooth. That has changed now, says Mr. Peters, and he points for example to the current lack of top level leadership experience in people like the new executive director biodiversity conservation. Related to the remark by a PCU member that this new director has been promoted too fast for him and the organization, Mr. Peters completely agrees. He also thinks the director is a motivated and competent man, but needed more time to grow into his previous position, let alone taking up his present position replacing two or three directors. Thus, says Mr. Peters, falls all the leadership responsibility in the MDTP on the South African PCU coordinator, and although Mr. Peters believes the coordinator is doing an "excellent job," he also needs someone to strategically support him from time to time, and this is not what he gets now. Mr. Peters also relates the lack of implementation to the current lack of capacity in KZN Wildlife. He agrees that this has to do with the whole transformation process, and also that it is a curve and that the capacity level of the organization will go up again, but it will take a long time, and in the meantime, "the MDTP is suffering."[15]

The former executive director was not the only one to lament the loss of leadership experience and general capacity in KZN Wildlife that resulted from the transformation. The South African PCU coordinator repeatedly mentioned that he felt that he received little leadership support from KZN Wildlife.[16] Like the director, he attributed this to "the institutional changes in KZN Wildlife and not to the abilities of the individuals concerned."[17] There were, however, initial tensions between the South African PCU coordinator and the new director. This was noted by several informants in both South Africa and Lesotho and recognized by the individuals concerned. The new executive director stated that one knows how things can go in the beginnings of marriages but that they "now understand each other."[18] Interestingly, while he and other staff admitted that KZN Wildlife does not have the capacity to absorb a project of the MDTP's magnitude and that "as the lead, [they] can't make available what is expected," they did not attribute this to transformation-induced reorganizations. Rather, they noted that they just do not have the time to be involved more because they are "generalists" for whom the MDTP is one of many tasks, whereas the PCU staff members are full-time "specialists."[19]

KZN Wildlife, in and outside South Africa, is regarded as an organization with a tremendous budget and capacity. One can therefore imagine the turmoil that often accompanies the transformation process in other organizations. And although transformation can impact institutional capacity,[20] the reactions to this in my research were markedly different per racial group. Whereas Marxist academics note that the African National Congress—instead of taking the neoliberal path—should have instigated a much deeper transformation process in South Africa in order to redress the inequalities of the past (see Alexander 2002; Bond 2000), many whites involved in the MDTP already took the soft-transformation process negatively and personally. During my talks with white, usually male, conservation professionals, I repeatedly noted statements of personal worry, especially in terms of job security, and not feeling appreciated in the "new South Africa." One stated, "there is a strong antiwhite feeling in government, which cannot be denied."[21] Again, white men also especially noted their worries about what the transformation was doing to the capacity of government institutions. One white male, at an MDTP stakeholder workshop in March 2007, cynically remarked that the "erosion of the human-resource base goes faster than the biodiversity base." In contrast, many blacks viewed the transformation process as positive and necessary. A typical illustration was given by the director for conservation and ecotourism in the Free State. He acknowledged that whites feel that they are losing out and thus see the transformation as turmoil, but he thinks it is good to see more nonwhite faces in the department. He added that nonwhite people "in these jobs" are still a small minority; most black people are very poor and feel that they have been sold out after apartheid.[22]

Clearly, then, race played an important role in the politics of institutionalizing the MDTP. The fact that the South African PCU was overwhelmingly white further added to the intensity of these dynamics. One black South African PCU member in fact stated, "the basis of the project's problem is that we are not in the transformation process."[23] Most likely, this—at least partly—explains why political support for the MDTP in the Free State was lacking. According to a Free State DEAT staff member, the whole scientific-services division of the department is white, "because the last person was appointed in 1993."[24] But despite the problems at the department, some of his coworkers were still participating in the MDTP, mostly on the technical level—for instance in a study on mammals. The technical, scientific level is also where the PCU felt most comfortable, and the wedge between the technical cooperation among whites in the DEAT and the MDTP and the lack of (black) political support must then partly be explained by the issue of race.[25]

In the Eastern Cape the situation was quite different, as the people there seemed to have avoided the political turmoil that characterized provinces such as the Free State. According to the responsible staff member for the MDTP, "We have been fortunate in the Eastern Cape because transformation was a smooth process. There were no mass retrenchments of white males as happened in other provinces. Even the appointment of new personnel has been largely a fair process where competent people have been appointed."[26] His biggest practical constraint is the lack of personnel and getting personnel involved in the MDTP. According to him, the Eastern Cape has trained many people who then leave to make more money in other government sectors. He stressed that a "phenomenal amount" of people left because the province cannot pay them more. In short, and also corroborated by the South African PCU, the Eastern Cape's involvement in the MDTP was hampered more by practical human-resource constraints than issues of race or political support.

SANParks seemed to have even fewer transformation issues within the MDTP. This is not to say that SANParks had a smooth transformation; it just did not really affect the MDTP due to the organization's limited role in the project. The opposite is true for the DEAT, albeit this did not have much to do with internal transformation issues. Rather, of all implementing agencies, the DEAT took most offense to the South African PCU being overwhelmingly white. Like others, the DEAT's director of TFCAs wondered whether the South African PCU coordinator lacked understanding of the South African context or whether he did not search well enough. He stated, "if I were in that position I would have gone for diversity." Although he said he knew about the argument that there are few qualified blacks, he maintained that the project coordinator should then have gone out and found them. He added that "they didn't go that extra step," and actually suspected that "maybe they thus didn't want to find" black people.[27] Although these issues are not often spoken about openly, it is clear from my observations in the DEAT that the directors' views were supported by prominent staff officers. On top of the race issue, the DEAT was not very content with the PCU's emphasis on planning and the resultant small amount of work "on the ground."[28] All in all, this resulted in a fickle and sometimes antagonistic relationship. In sum, the institutionalization of the MDTP in South Africa was complex and all but smooth.

Lesotho's Decentralization

Lesotho's institutionalization picture was wholly different from South Africa's. This stemmed in part from the fact that Lesotho is much smaller in size and population than any of South Africa's three MDTP provinces, thus radically increasing the intervention's relative impact. As a result, the MDTP in Lesotho, despite strong presence in and focus on the districts, had a distinctly national character, exemplified by the fact that the project's implementing agencies were all national ministries. Also, Lesotho's capacity to absorb projects like the MDTP is much smaller than South Africa's, giving them even more weight. Like many postcolonial African countries, Lesotho is heavily dependent on donor funding to finance government services (Matlosa 1999). Instead of being an add-on to ongoing programs and policies—like in South Africa—donor projects often provide services that otherwise would not have been possible due to lack of funding or capacity. This gave the institutionalization of the MDTP in Lesotho a completely different character and dynamic.

Due to the Lesotho PCU's emphasis on managed resource areas and local buy-in, the most important implementing agencies were the Ministry of Tourism, Environment and Culture (MTEC), the Range Management Resources Division, and the Ministry of Local Government.[29] The MTEC, in particular, was quite active in the MDTP, but this was partly due to the PCU being embedded in that ministry and because the project enjoyed strong political support. This was clear from early on; in November 2003 the minister thanked remote local communities for participating in an MDTP study on rangeland conditions. The minister's support never wavered, and with backing from the prime minister she even successfully challenged the World Bank in early 2005 after it had downgraded the project's rating. Nevertheless, the institutionalization in MTEC and other Lesotho agencies was fragile at least partly for reasons other than failing to meet the project objectives. It was fragile because the majority of the work on the project was done by the PCU, which even took over regular government functions.

The Lesotho PCU ecologist told me an example related to clearing alien and invasive species in Sehlabathebe National Park.[30] He mentioned that in the "olden days" local communities would form *matsema* (communal work parties; the singular is *letsema*), and a village chief would call a meeting and all the villagers would go out and eradicate all known invasive alien plants. According to the ecologist, over the years this practice has been replaced by an incentive-based practice;[31] villagers would demand payment from the government, in this case the MTEC Department of Parks. In turn, the department requested funds from the MDTP for transport, lodging, and meals. The ecologist remarked, "What should happen is that the

MDTP should support the Department of Parks with expertise and payments for communities, not for Department of Parks personnel." Despite knowing that this would create further donor dependency, the PCU often gave in to such requests, which reinforced the way the MDTP was viewed. In the ecologist's words: "It is a challenge to bring all the ministries on board and make them see the success of the project as their success and not see it as a separate entity."[32]

With respect to the MTEC, it is crucial that institutionalization was at least partially done for reasons other than achieving the MDTP's objectives. This is best captured in my interview with the National Environment Secretariat director who said, "It is good for us to do our best, because it will open new doors for us. . . . If we do well, we will get benefits." He implied that this success is mostly achieved by the PCU by emphasizing how well the team was doing and how hard the members worked and noting, "the MDTP is our flagship."[33] What makes this and other similar remarks interesting is that they are often stated without knowing whether the project is actually achieving its objectives. It thus confirms that images of project success or failure often function at least party to guarantee the flow of resources on which ministries like the MTEC largely depend (Mosse 2005).

When asked about the performance of the implementing agencies, the Lesotho PCU coordinator stated in 2005 that the Range Management Division had been very active.[34] This was not further qualified, and it appeared in my own research that the Range Management Division is a prime example of Lesotho's donor dependency and the subsequent challenges for the type of institutionalization sought by the MDTP. From its inception in 1979, the Range Management Division was strongly influenced by donor projects. Its very existence, according to its director, was motivated by the early stages of the USAID-funded Land Conservation and Range Development project, which also initiated the predecessors of the managed resource areas, namely the resource management areas.[35] Thereafter, different projects by the same and other donors kept the activities of the division— managing Lesotho's range areas—afloat, especially by providing transport.

Donor projects had always provided vehicles for range managers to travel to districts in order to liaise with local and traditional authorities about the management of grazing areas. According to a range management officer at the division, in 1996, due to various projects, the Range Management Division had seventeen vehicles, including several in the districts.[36] After the mid-1990s, donor funding for the division decreased, ultimately drying up completely. The consequence was that the number of vehicles at the division went down to two, one for Maseru and one to service the districts.[37] As a result, range management staff members in the districts were "stuck,"[38] while those in Maseru started relying on lifts from people working on projects outside the division. One range officer remarked that when the United Nations Development Programme–funded Conserving Mountain Biodiversity in Southern Lesotho project started in 1999, he and his colleagues then "put a lot of emphasis on the south because of the project."[39] This project was "relieved" by a World Bank project in the same districts, after which came the MDTP.

The range officer added, "[The MDTP] is talking our language. . . . [T]he MDTP have provided a lot of support for our staff."[40] This was particularly the case in boosting range management in previously neglected districts. Although the division is responsible for the entire country, the range officer made it clear that he focused on the three easternmost districts because the MDTP is active there. This same issue led the director of the division to state: "I am worried about the one-sided attention for the MDTP area. Other areas are not getting serviced." Still, she believed that "it is better than sitting in the office."[41] After my question what happens after the project is gone, both the director and range officer answered similarly. According to the director, "We can't do much with two vehicles, so we have to intensely train the communities so they can do it."[42] The officer stated, "Possibly we need to decentralize more." After the project there should be a shift in responsibility to local government, "so it is not [the Range Management Division] anymore."[43] These remarks about a shift in responsibility from national to local government occurred with some frequency during my research from 2005 to 2007. And perhaps logically so, because since 1997 Lesotho had been working on establishing a local-government system, which received a major boost when, after much delay, local community councilors were elected on 30 April 2005 and sworn in on 17 June 2005.

Lesotho's current local-government system is based on the Local Government Act of 1997, which provides for 128 community councils as the lowest level of government, district councils for each of the ten districts, and one municipal council for Maseru. Community councils usually comprise nine to fifteen electoral divisions (villages) and are sector-wide government bodies, mandated by the local population through elections. As such, they function next to, and sometimes compete with, traditional authorities. The possibility of friction between these authorities therefore looms large, especially in the areas of range management and natural resources as these used to be the exclusive domain of chiefs. However, in the Lesotho PCU's drive to institutionalize the MDTP locally, it discovered that although the establishment of the local-government system was progressing, it was only focused on service delivery in a very ad hoc and unstructured manner, and natural resource management was absent altogether.[44] In response to this discovery, one of the main activities of the MDTP in Lesotho became assisting in establishing the natural-resources-management part of the local-government system.

The PCU first helped the Ministry of Local Government develop a concept note on natural resources management in the new local-government settings into a "proper framework document," which by April 2005 was almost ready to be submitted to the cabinet for approval (MDTP 2005c).[45] The document suggested that under each community council there would be a standing committee on natural resource management, which in turn would oversee and guide the then yet-to-be-established managed resource committees (MRCs). These would be responsible for overseeing the newly established managed resource areas, which were basically—and confusingly—the old resource management areas, but with enlarged mandates to include biodiversity conservation and natural resource management in addition to grazing issues. The PCU saw that its role was to assist in the capacity building of the community councils, the MRCs, and the local communities around the managed resource areas so that it could take up the MDTP's objective of "securing globally important biodiversity."[46] Again this is evidence that the MDTP in Lesotho not merely aided the government to function but also performed government functions, and even helped in establishing government where it found none. Hence, it is clear that James Ferguson's "instrument-effects" of development interventions, which perform, "almost unnoticed, [their] own pre-eminently political operation of expanding bureaucratic state power," remain an inherent part of the antipolitics machine in Lesotho (1994, xv).

Setting up local institutions and making them work are two different things though. Beside a general lack of financial and human resources, several issues appeared to be major obstacles for institutions in 2005. Among these were the finalization of the MRC terms of reference, the role of community councils and MRCs vis-à-vis traditional authorities, and the issue of boundaries: several managed resource areas did not fit neatly in one community council and thus had to clarify their relationships with several (Turner 2005). Later, in 2007, these issues still appeared as strong as before, although the terms of references had been finalized. The MDTP was busy turning these into local bylaws, to be signed by the national minister of local government, giving MRCs a legal mandate. The PCU ecologist stated that he believed that with this legal framework in place, offenses to grazing plans could now be enforced.[47] For reasons related to the other issues, and especially financial and human resources, the PCU coordinator believed that the local-government structures would not be fully functional by the end of the MDTP IN 2008. In 2005 he therefore recommended that the project be extended for another five years and that the central government continue to give support to local government. Later he again acknowledged that institutionalization is a problem, specifically mentioning that the implementing ministries have few resources, such as cars. He therefore wanted to do an institutional analysis of the implementing ministries to see if they could sustain their parts of the project, adding, "this is also why we target the local level; to build capacity so that they can continue with minimal resources."[48]

Antipolitics as Political Strategy I

Clearly, institutionalization dynamics in the two countries were totally different. In South Africa the MDTP was a relatively small extra for the various implementing agencies, while in Lesotho the MDTP provided vital support to implementing agencies, to the extent that activities would otherwise not have been possible.[49] Another important difference relates to political legitimacy within the two polities. Due to the historical differentiation of sovereignties and related different administrative, political, social, and economic trajectories, transfrontier interventions that try to act as bridges are inherently split. It means having to simultaneously take into account the different sensitivities that grant the intervention political legitimacy in particular polities. In South Africa this was chiefly the transformation process. In Lesotho this was the ongoing expansion of state power through decentralization. In both countries the MDTP implementers struggled to find a balance between their own ideas about the project and the sensitivities that granted it legitimacy.

This kind of thinking reinforces the need to change the way interventions are habitually conceptualized. "Institutionalization" connotes images of formal alignment and rational order—images actively promoted by the World Bank and later taken up by the PCUs (see Goldman 2005). In the various phases of the MDTP, it was assumed that if memorandums of understanding were in place, if MDTP objectives were taken up in job descriptions and organizational processes, and if implementing agencies would understand those objectives, then the intervention would become an integral part of public institutions and continue into the future.[50] In contrast, the MDTP is better conceptualized as a set of complex formal and informal activities, assumptions, desires, and ambitions (loaded with donor money) entering an even more complex set of social, political, economic, and institutional settings and dynamics. This triggered all kinds of reactions by actors while assuming specific outcomes. Hence, rather than formal alignment and rational order, an intervention should be conceptualized as one set of political strategies entering a pool of ever changing social, economic, and political dynamics, in turn eliciting a variety of opposing political strategies. Obviously, this entering should not be taken too literally: to varying degrees most interventions already have roots in their target polities—in terms of expectations, vested interests, and relationships with those behind the intervention—which further puts pressure on framing strategies and counterstrategies.

Through all this, the question for the PCUs remained how to manage all the conflicting interests and dynamics in such a way that they could promote the intervention as they had conceptualized it. This is where antipolitics becomes a vital political strategy. Simply put, the argument comes down to "the more intense the politics, the more intense the antipolitics." Interventions such as the MDTP are enormously complex endeavors in which every possible implementation move can lead to criticism or resistance. The real and perceived political intensity around the implementation of the MDTP—related to the transformation and decentralization processes in particular—was immense and heavily impacted the PCUs. Many PCU members expressed feelings of huge personal and professional strain. Some stated that had they known this before, they might not have taken their jobs; several others "could not wait for their contracts to end." Added to this in South Africa was the fact that most of the PCU staff members were white, which is considered politically inappropriate in postapartheid South Africa. In Lesotho, an added strain was the co-opting of the project by numerous actors who all wanted a piece of the pie.

All of this meant that making any decision regarding the project was extremely difficult, and reaching any consensus among all the stakeholders around the project's objectives was even more so. The PCUs responded by amplifying their consensus strategies to such an extent that they became antipolitical—a nonnegotiable high ground. In doing so, the two PCUs employed different antipolitical tactics: the South African PCU resorted to instrumental antipolitics, while the Lesotho PCU relied on moral antipolitics. The South African PCU interpreted the MDTP in a technical sense by especially focusing on rational planning, supported by "hard" scientific data. Its assumption was that if decision makers were presented with up-to-date information about where, what, and how biodiversity should to be conserved, they would rationally make the logical and right decision. Not making the logical decision would be irrational, so consensus had to ensue. This is the core of the South African PCU's antipolitics. The Lesotho PCU primarily interpreted the MDTP in a moral way, focusing on community buy-in through extensive local participation. The assumption underlying the Lesotho strategy was that if communities would understand and be convinced by the importance of biodiversity conservation, they would take it into their own hands and better care for their natural environment. The Lesotho PCU chose the moral high ground, whereby the "right" behavior would ensue after sensitization and incentives, and seemingly naturally develop from the bottom up. Not granting this process legitimacy would be unthinkable, and so consensus had to ensue. This is the core of the Lesotho PCU's antipolitics.

These antipolitical dynamics made for a frustrating experience during the initial stages of my research, because the two different interpretations both seemed to make sense. When talking to South African PCU members, I could see the merits in their approach. Despite being very different, I had the same feeling when conversing with members of the Lesotho PCU about their approach to the project. Later I realized that this is inherent in antipolitics: it makes one feel as if the thing you are being told is completely logical and that to think otherwise would be unreasonable or mistaken. Such is the power of a coherent discourse based on a certain high ground. But in the MDTP these high grounds were not the same; they led to very different operationalizations of what appeared to be similar discourses. This explains why the PCUs clashed so strongly and so frequently and why institutionalizing the MDTP took on such specific characteristics. This is also why the project ultimately ended up being a hybrid of the instrumental and the moral high grounds. About three years into the project, both PCUs had concluded that their objectives could be reached by employing two different strategies: rational-consensus bioregional conservation planning *and* accommodating-commonage community-based conservation. And, because the PCUS *had* to work together they had to—at least on the surface—give each other's approach some consideration. The bioregional plan, therefore, became a hybrid antipolitical document with great emphasis on mechanisms of neoliberal devolved governance, seemingly to defuse the intense political dynamics in the implementation and institutionalization of the project.

But the act of antipolitics is inherently political, and I noted that different actors assign different values to what seemed like a consensus. Hence, the South African PCU put primacy on instrumental rationale in places where many important project stakeholders did not see this as the project's overarching value. For them, moral values, operationalized as community-based conservation, were paramount. Through this shared concern, the Lesotho PCU, the MTEC and the South African implementing agencies DEAT and KZN Wildlife strengthened their ties, which in turn marginalized the South African PCU.[51] This, however, is not to say that the South African PCU or its political strategy became powerless. Even though it was not given emphasis in many stakeholders' political rhetoric, instrumental rationalism remained prominent in the MDTP. Like most donor projects, the MDTP comes with Western-oriented conditions and instrumentalities based on rationalism (see Dressler 2009; Schroeder 1999). Furthermore, despite not seeing rational planning and scientific research as its ultimate priority, the South African project-coordination committee members almost always approved of the MDTP workload as proposed by the PCU. Thus, they bought into and were partly receptive to the logic of rational reductionism, which is no surprise for those studying bureaucratic institutions (Quarles van Ufford 1988).

This uncertain and paradoxical situation had several consequences. The PCUS, despite threats to cut it short, could continue the bioregional planning they had already invested so much in. Because of this, the institutionalization of the bioregional plan became an even bigger imperative, further increasing the plan's susceptibility to antipolitical dynamics of both the instrumental and moral kinds. All this led to an uncomfortable state of affairs in the context of the fundamental shift in momentum that favored community-based "on-the-ground" implementation. Despite being able to continue the planning, the success of the MDTP was increasingly judged by whether it could make "an impact on the ground" and provide opportunities for "communities."

Lesotho: The 'Moteng Managed Resource Area

With all the planning and research, how did the MDTP try to institutionalize its objectives at the local level, and has this led to the "on-the-ground" community benefits that stakeholders desired? This and the next section discuss and analyze the experiences of two villages, one in each country. In Lesotho, the village is Nyakoaneng in the 'Moteng MRA. In South Africa, the village is Obonjaneni in the MDTP-funded Supporting Community-Led Initiatives in Natural and Cultural Resource Management in the Upper uThukela Region project. I will argue that the inhabitants of both villages employed a similar response to the Maloti-Drakensberg project, namely the disguising of their own political agendas in order to use the MDTP to expand livelihood options. This type of antipolitics does not neatly fit into Schedler's typology. I therefore call the hiding of one's political interests for opportunistic reasons of practical gain "pragmatic antipolitics." This antipolitical response to antipolitical strategies is highly significant, as it leads both implementers and subjects to avoid the political realm where inequalities can be addressed.

Unlike South Africa, Lesotho does not have a tradition of protected areas and wildlife management. Instead, the country's conservation governance has long centered on concerns about land and rangeland degradation and soil erosion, and the related issue of overgrazing (see Showers 1989; Turner 2003). When traveling through the rugged eastern highlands, it is easy to concur that these are serious problems. Many mountain slopes look totally barren, and giant erosion gullies (dongas) cut everywhere through the landscape. Local people shared stories with me about how growing food and rearing livestock in these conditions is difficult, and now further compounded by irregular rainfall due to climate change. Yet the very real environmental problems that Lesotho faces need to be treated with caution and analyzed in their historical and political-economic contexts, something many conservation and development interventions in the country have neglected (see Ferguson 1994; Showers 1989).

In order to address these concerns, resource management areas were set up in the 1980s, which the MDTP transformed into MRAS, redesigned to account for grasslands *and* biodiversity (MDTP 2005a). Three out of Lesotho's twelve resource management areas were chosen for conversion: 'Moteng in Botha-Bothe, Mokhotlong-Sanqebethu in Mokhotlong, and Khomo-Phatšoa in Qacha's Nek. Importantly, MRAS were not conceptualized to resemble

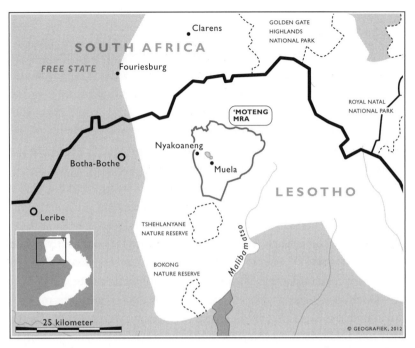

MAP 3 The 'Moteng MRA in Lesotho. Nyakoaneng is west of Muela © GEOGRAFIEK, 2012.

protected areas. Commonage culture runs deep in Lesotho, so exclusion from land in official policies remains anathema (Turner 2006). Accordingly, the MRA concept was "founded on the principles of Community Based Natural Resource Management (CBNRM) which aims at empowering the local community to manage all natural resources within their jurisdiction in a sustainable manner" (MDTP 2005a, 27). In practice, this was mainly operationalized by developing institutions and management plans, linking them with the new local-government structure, and ensuring their legal backing through bylaws.[52] Responsibilities for biodiversity conservation were slowly deferred to the local level and local communities. This move can be seen from the perspective of villagers living in the 'Moteng MRA. The 'Moteng MRA (see map 3) is located in the northern part of the Botha-Bothe district of Lesotho, alongside the Caledon River, which forms the international border with South Africa. The MRA consists of seven grazing areas, totaling almost 6,385 hectares (see table 5.1). The area is home to about seventeen villages, one of which is the village of Nyakoaneng, which has been the focus of my research on the MRA. Nyakoaneng has approximately 150 households of up to six or even ten individuals. As in many

TABLE 5.1 Grazing areas in 'Moteng MRA.

GRAZING AREA	AREA (HECTARES)
Solane	1172.0
Lekhoakhoeng	450.0
Masapong/Letlapeng	402.5
Ha Moloi	970.0
Ha Mapulutsoana	852.5
'Moteng	1330.0
Molikaliko	1207.5

Source: MDTP 2007c, 3.

other African cultures, households in Lesotho are flexible and ever changing. Social, economic, and political dynamics are shifting quickly in the
village, and pressures on livelihoods in Nyakoaneng are acute.

In line with a survey done on livelihoods in Lesotho by Stephen Turner
(2001), several issues seem to be especially pressing: HIV/AIDS; crime,
especially livestock theft; and increasing pressure on the land.[53] Concerning the pressure on the land, villagers in Nyakoaneng offered many reasons why this was happening, among them drought caused by climate
change, population pressure, and retrenchments from South African
mines. Of these, the retrenchment issue is especially salient. The majority
of households that Julia Wittmayer and I visited demonstrated that men
have come back to the village in substantial numbers, often after many
years or even decades in the mines (Wittmayer 2007). One villager esti-
mated that while 90 percent of the men used to work in the mines a decade
ago, this figure dropped to 10 or 20 percent. This obviously caused adjustment problems for both the men and the households they returned to (see,
e.g., Turner 2001, 25). Several people also cited this dynamic as a reason
for the rise in crime in recent years.

Most inhabitants of Nyakoaneng work the land, either part time or full
time. At the same time, the attachment to the land in Nyakoaneng, as in the
rest of Lesotho, should not be overestimated (Boehm 2003). Broader processes of changing rural conditions in Africa have also affected Lesotho,
and Deborah Bryceson's notion of "multiplex livelihoods"—"the complex
multidimensional interplay of social, political, cultural and economic dynamics that are recasting the terms and conditions of rural work"—fits well
in this context (2002, 2). Retrenchment from mines is one of the major

dynamics in this recasting, while the MDTP aimed to be another. During our first round of interviews, one of the villagers, Ntate Morobe, told us how the project fared in practice.[54] He worked in the mines in Johannesburg from 1977 to 2005. Now, he "uses the soil to make ends meet, nothing else." Morobe knows a little about the MDTP because he attended *pitsos* (public gatherings). He said that the MDTP had been trying to set up new grazing plans for the 'Moteng area and that the project had instigated various capacity-building exercises to reduce the pressure on the land and stimulate development, such as range-management training for herd boys and training in handicraft production. To the question of whether he has benefited from the MDTP, Morobe answered that there have been environmental benefits because the pastures were now well conserved. He knew this because his animals were "right up the mountains where conservation is taking place."

Interestingly, many people whom I asked in January 2007 about the impact of the MDTP on the land gave a similar answer: now that the MDTP is here, the grasslands are well conserved. Letsie Nkopane was one of the herd boys who received range-management training.[55] He said, "we were taken to grazing fields and taught how to protect wild animals and plants." He considered the training to have brought major change: "Before, some lands were bad, but now they are better." After the training he tried to tell others this had happened, but "not all others understand and changed." In the future, Nkopane said they need more training and seeds for trees for wood. 'M'e Ts'ehlo is one of the richer villagers.[56] She has a big homestead consisting of two rectangular houses and one rondavel and owns fields and livestock, which earn her a living. Ts'ehlo says that she knows of the MDTP through pitsos. According to her, the MDTP sensitizes people about the grazing lands and how to take care of them. Upon asking whether this has effects on villagers' behavior, she answered, "The damage is going down, so they must understand." Ts'ehlo believed that fewer animals had been killed, which she knew because "the people who hunt say they have reduced their killing."

After several days of interviews and participatory observation in the village, I noticed we were only visiting people who had actually been involved in the MDTP. Our guide, one of three brothers running the local Mamohase bed and breakfast, thought this was what we wanted. Upon returning to Nyakoaneng in May 2007, I decided to concentrate on villagers who had not been involved in the project. When asked about the

MDTP, many said that they had heard of it, but none could say what it was about. Many said they had "forgotten." With respect to the 'Moteng area, where most people graze their cattle in summer, they seemed to not know about the newly instituted MRA and its rules for grazing and range use. Most people assumed that the area was still under the rotational transhumance system. When I later shared these findings with the guide, he said that people knew about the MDTP plans, but that they were waiting to get money out of it. If that does not happen, "they tend to forget." Later observations and casual chats corroborated his view. Villagers stated that they either did not know about the new rules or made it clear that these were not to be taken very seriously. The son of the headman stated that although people chase away and kill less wildlife, many still did not adhere to the new rules and regulations and continued grazing as before. Later visits to Nyakoaneng, in July 2007 and March 2008, led to similar observations.

These latter testimonies seemed to be more in accordance with an interview I conducted in January 2007 with the area chief.[57] She stated that the project thus far had been very good, and that the MDTP held pitsos over natural resources to create more environmental awareness. She maintained, however, that the attitudes of the people were not changing: "It is very difficult to change the mindsets." She added that, "There is a grazing system, but at night they go grazing wherever they want." These contradictory views on the impact of the MDTP on the environmental quality of the 'Moteng MRA beg two questions: Has the condition of the range indeed improved due to the MDTP intervention? Why are there such differences of local opinion?

The answer to the first question is inconclusive. First, it is incredibly hard, if not impossible, to measure the impact of MDTP activities around capacity building and institutional development, or even establish a causal link between them and rangeland condition. Second, opinions on improvement or degradation differ and are to a great degree socially constructed (Quinlan 1995). The MDTP developed a grazing plan for 'Moteng, for which it measured the condition of the vegetation in the MRA. The plan concludes that of the seven grazing areas, three have experienced "insignificant grade of deterioration," one has experienced "minimal grade of soil erosion," two have experienced moderate soil erosion, and one has "generally degraded" (MDTP 2007c, 6–7). Although this does not mean that things have worsened, the range in the 'Moteng MRA has not improved either. Out of the seven, at least four areas have experienced erosion to one degree or another. Some biologists might argue that livestock grazing should therefore be better regulated in order to curb this trend. Livestock owners, in contrast, might argue that only one area has generally degraded while others have retained fairly good grass cover. They could therefore maintain the area's suitability for livestock. This echoes what Tim Quinlan already concluded: "Although the RMA [resource management area] programme addresses the bio-physical problems of live-stock rearing, it ignores the rationale and political implications of stock-owners' consideration of these problems" (1995, 505).

The environmental condition of the 'Moteng MRA is thus at least partly in the eye of the beholder (see, e.g., Fairhead and Leach 1996; West and Brockington 2006). This conclusion seems to hold for villagers too. The difference in how people view the impact of the MDTP on the land comes down to the argument that those who profited from the project do not bite the hand that feeds them. Many involved in the MDTP hoped that the project would come back or stay longer. Those not involved did not have a real opinion about a return of the MDTP, although some hoped for an extension with an eye at their own inclusion and benefit. Meanwhile, it seemed that life went on as normal and that villagers in Nyakoaneng followed the same cycles with respect to land, agriculture, and grazing that they have done for long (Wittmayer 2007). An intervention like the MDTP, despite its fair overall size, remained a mere superficial intrusion into the lives of so-called ordinary people and seemed to be an add-on to villagers' livelihood options rather than fundamentally changing (or challenging) their way of life (Wittmayer and Büscher 2010).[58]

South Africa: The Amagugu Esizwe project

The South African PCU operationalized community development very differently from Lesotho. This, we saw, led to frictions between it and the Lesotho PCU and some South African implementing agencies. In my first interview with the South African PCU socio-ecologist in May 2005, she mentioned that there are 1.5 million people living in the South African MDTP area, which is too large to get everyone involved.[59] Thus, rather than creating extensive participation processes and setting up local structures like in Lesotho, the South African PCU instigated pilot projects to institutionalize the MDTP's objectives on the local level. Not all of these engaged local communities. The projects ranged from ecological, socioeconomic, and land-use assessments to tourism and community conservation proj-

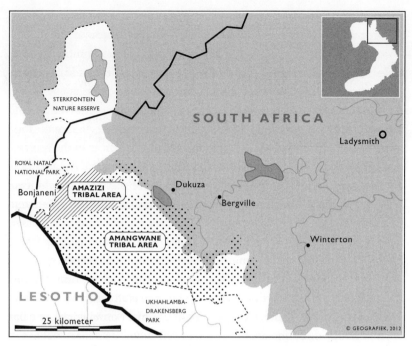

MAP 4 Map of uThukela District Municipality. Far left are Royal Natal National Park and the Amazizi Tribal Area © GEOGRAFIEK, 2012.

ects. The main pilot project aimed at community development was called Supporting Community-Led Initiatives in Natural and Cultural Resource Management in the Upper uThukela Region; it was later baptized Amagugu Esizwe, which is Zulu for "treasure of the nation."

Amagugu Esizwe was active in the Amazizi and AmanGwane tribal areas in northern KwaZulu-Natal, two sizable areas wedged in between national parks to the north and south and the massive Drakensberg ridge to the west (see map 4). Three villages in each tribal area were selected to participate in the project: Manzana, Mabhuleseni, and Isandlwana in AmanGwane (also together known as Mnweni) and Ebusingatha, Obonjaneni, and Okhombe in Amazizi. My research is mostly based on interviews and participatory observation in Obonjaneni village, but I visited Ebusingatha and Okhombe for comparative voices. The project was implemented by a consortium of two NGOs and a university department,[60] and it lasted from September 2004 to December 2006. According to the MDTP socio-ecologist and project implementers, this short time period was unfortunate and due to a difficult and elongated procurement process that lasted almost two years: one year conceptualizing and eleven months for the World Bank to give its mandatory "no objection" approval.[61]

A project brief that was sent to the participating communities in 2004 stated: "The MDTP vision is that by the end of 2007 all major stakeholders (local community structures, municipalities, conservation agencies and government departments—environment, agriculture, conservation, and tourism) will be actively involved in coordinated efforts to ensure the long term sustainability of conservation, and land use practices in the region." Amagugu Esizwe was supposed to fulfill this vision for the AmanGwane and Amazizi areas. Eight formal outcomes were planned, but the core activities within the project were capacity building and the establishment or strengthening of committees around issues such as land care, wilderness, guiding, livestock, handicrafts, tourism, and fire and grazing (MDTP 2007a, 24). In Obonjaneni, four committees were established or strengthened: the Siyaphambili committee on land care and tourism, a donga, and a livestock committee, and the Thandanani Mazizi craft group.[62]

Obonjaneni lies on the border of the Royal Natal National Park and has approximately three thousand inhabitants. The village shares many features with Nyakoaneng: households are flexible; people depend largely on agriculture, livestock, remittances, or jobs elsewhere; and HIV/AIDS and crime are real problems. There are also distinct differences. Besides cultural differences—Obonjaneni is Zulu and Nyakoaneng is Sotho—because Obonjaneni is part of South Africa, there are opportunities in terms of government support and social security grants. In general, people in Obonjaneni seem to be somewhat better off than people in Nyakoaneng. Houses are larger and often better furnished, transport is more regular, and services such as schooling, medical facilities, supermarkets, and post offices are better and closer by, although not in reach for everyone. Besides, Obonjaneni's strategic location next to Royal Natal National Park brings opportunities from tourism and provides people with resources, both legally (jobs, grass for weaving, selling handicrafts, and so on) and illegally (livestock grazing, grass for weaving outside the permitted season, and so on).[63] Lastly, it seems that political struggles in Obonjaneni are fiercer, which relates to the intense and historically violent rivalry between the Zulu Inkhata Freedom Party and the African National Congress in the province (see Sisitka 2007, 18).

In Obonjaneni in March 2007, as in Nyakoaneng, a local guide (one trained by Amagugu Esizwe) accompanied me through the village and first brought me to people actually involved in the project. Francis Kaleni,[64] a builder and bricklayer, was in charge of donga rehabilitation and thought the project went "alright." He believed that the trainings, especially those related to donga rehabilitation, were good things. What worried him was that there was only one training in conservation management, but according to him the project promised the community certificates, which they could use in job applications, which never came.[65] Kaleni explained the main problem: "In the beginning they always ask what we want, but during the course of the project, they always push their own things and then it is no longer what we want." Despite this, he believed that the project should have stayed longer, and he hopes that it will come back in the future. A similar story comes from Robert Silongo,[66] who was also part of the donga rehabilitation project. Although he initially told me that the project was not a success, he later stated that in terms of tourism the project made a big difference. He pointed to the training of guides, who can now "put bread on the table." Silongo received English literacy training, and he feels that his English has improved. But when I asked him why the project was not a success, he replied, "They were only giving the highlights and then they left." He also hoped that the project will return.

Later, in May 2007, I interviewed the local headman of Obonjaneni,[67] who believed that Amagugu Eziswe was doing well and that it was the first time he had this opinion of a project. He specifically mentioned Heritage Day on 24 September and that the project helped with the celebrations and bought a cow so that the people in the community did not have to pay. He added that donga rehabilitation also helped a lot because the water from the mountains no longer flows directly into the village. The headman said that people still continued with the donga work because they hoped the project would come back and that they would then be appointed leaders of the new project. I asked him whether there is a realistic chance of this, and he replied that he is more than hopeful. He added that Siyaphambili, the tourism and land committee, kept saying to people that they must hope the project will come back.

I noted similar accounts, but other people were more pessimistic. In the neighboring Ebusingatha, several people were outright critical. Charlotte Shabangu, for instance, said that she learned a lot from the project about donga rehabilitation and got paid for her work on dongas.[68] Still, she felt that nothing came of the project "except for a T-shirt and a signpost."

Related to the Donga project, she mentioned that at first they received thirty rand every second day for their work, and then ten rand, and then it stopped. She stated that they have been continuing the work in hopes that the project will come back and pay them again. Shabangu's other complaint is around certificates for trainings, which according to her were promised but never came. She mentioned that one NGO staff member had said that the project was over and that the local people could stop working on the dongas, but they were still continuing, hoping for the certificates and payments. Rebecca Dlamini agreed and told me that they received no money and no certificates to help them look for a job: "They have been wasting our time."[69]

These issues (not receiving certificates and not being paid anymore for work on donga rehabilitation) bothered more people. Nomcebo Hlanganani from Obonjaneni was still working (allegedly voluntarily) on the dongas around May 2007.[70] She said that she has been "somewhat crossed" with the project because of discontinued payments and the lack of certificates, and she was hoping that the project would come back. With certificates people could go to hotels to get jobs. Now, Hlanganani told me, child grants—grants to support raising children—are "where her hopes are," and that due to the end of the project she lost income, which made life worse. Mia Mabuza, like Hlanganani, was also still hoping for certificates. She, however, did not work on the donga project during the Amagugu Esizwe project; she joined the donga workers in February 2007, after the project had stopped, hoping for a certificate and for the project to come back.

I found more examples of this mindset, but the overall sentiment remained the same. Many community members who were involved in the project were disgruntled about its short timeframe, the fact that they lost income after it stopped, and not receiving certificates for their work or training. Consequently, they kept on working on the dongas, wishing that the project would return, hand out certificates, and resume payments. These issues were acknowledged and put into context in the Amagugu Esizwe final project report:

> Other setbacks involved . . . the implementation by Rand Water [a private company] of an 18 month poverty relief project in Mnweni involving community members in rehabilitation work, similar to that being carried out by the project, but on the basis of payment rather than as volunteers. Exacerbating the situation was the fact that Rand Water did

not appear keen to consult or collaborate with the project team about their activities and their potential impact on the project's work. There remained some tension, as many community members involved in the Amagugu Esizwe project, including the whole of the donga committee, were employed by Rand Water, and had little time for their project work, or even to attend meetings. People employed in the poverty relief project were not allowed to take time off to attend training or other activities under Amagugu Esizwe. Rand Water has been described as "harsh" by community members. As the Rand Water intervention was taking place only in the AmanGwane tribal area, community members in the Amazizi area did not have access to this work and were concerned that they were "losing out." The project then decided to offer some small "compensation" payments to the Amazizi rehabilitation volunteers of R30 [thirty rand] for each second day worked. Although this was accepted by the communities there is a strong feeling among many that this was not nearly enough, particularly as people were only active for relatively short periods of time (3 months). (MDTP 2007a, 10–11)

The excerpt shows that another, similar intervention changed the dynamics in Amagugu Esizwe completely. While payments were not an issue before—the project was about capacity building (MDTP 2007a)—they became an issue because Rand Water paid local people during its intervention in Mnweni, something the people preferred. Consequently, local people, both in Mnweni and Amazizi, started looking at Amagugu Esizwe less favorably and became less enthusiastic about participating. In Amazizi, however, they could not get involved in the Rand Water project and thus demanded payments from Amagugu Esizwe, and the implementers eventually agreed. When people in Mnweni learned that people in Amazizi were getting paid for donga work, they wanted the Amagugu Esizwe project to pay them also, even though most of them were already paid by the other project (Sisitka 2007, 16).

The emphasis on training and capacity building in the Amagugu Esizwe project made it hard to establish the project's impact on the land. This was acknowledged by the MDTP's final report: "Overall, the training programme . . . has been very well received, and is almost universally considered the greatest benefit of the project. In particular the training in committee skills and financial management were singled out for particular praise, although these were less directly concerned with land-use management!" (MDTP

2007a, 15). This is then qualified: "There is no doubt that there is, however, a much heightened sense of 'environment' and 'conservation,' certainly among those who have received training in these areas, and also among others in the communities. The idea of 'wilderness' has also been internalised very strongly, with quite poetic descriptions of how people feel about this and its effect on people's lives" (15). Further on, the report notes that "in terms of the short lifespan of this project by itself, therefore, it is unrealistic to expect much sign of change" (28). Yet, the implementers still felt compelled to convince the reader of the value of the intervention within the framework of the MDTP:

> The most important feature of these activities, however, may not be in their actual, direct impact on the land (which in the case of the donga rehabilitation is inevitably on a small scale within the vastness of this landscape), but in illustrating the possibilities for change and improvement in land management, and in demonstrating people's own agency in effecting such change. This is a very potent impact, which can be seen in the pride people take in showing visitors the work they have done, and their enthusiasm to continue to do such work, even on a voluntary basis. (MDTP 2007a, 29)

From my interviews and observations, as well as those by Inge Droog (2008), however, it is clear that the continuation of the work on a voluntary basis is not solely out of enthusiasm, but rather in the hope that the project will come back, resume payments, and hand out certificates. The certificates were especially sought after, which was later explained to me by a hostel owner close to Amazizi. She mentioned that she receives local people on a daily basis, asking for jobs and using their certificates to prove that they are worthy of employment. According to her, the "certificate fetishism" had taken on grand proportions with people believing that a certificate would increase their chances for employment at one of the nearby hotels. This dynamic had been encouraged by hotels, who could receive subsidies from the government if they hire local people, build their capacity, and give them a certificate. The effect was that hotels were keen to take on local people, but only for the minimum time necessary, while for local people certificates became synonymous with jobs. Looking at the trainings provided by Amagugu Esizwe from this perspective, I would argue that villagers did not just see the trainings' value in terms of how they helped in effecting change but also as a practical stepping-stone for employment with the hotels in the area.

Antipolitics as Political Strategy II

The two local cases are quite different. What surfaced from the Lesotho discussion are the significantly different views held by local people involved and not involved in the MDTP. Many villagers involved in the intervention seemed to have used it to further complement their livelihoods. Especially when MDTP staff members are around, they are very positive about the project and hail its results on the land. Whether or not this is actually true is a different story, but one could ask why local villagers in Nyakoaneng would not be positive about the MDTP. This is what the MDTP implementers and funders wanted to hear and many people would probably not want to jeopardize potential future benefits. Local people not involved in the MDTP expressed more indifference with the project and were less positive about its impact on the land. In sum, although this is not necessarily all there is to this case, the villagers' stance toward the MDTP can be interpreted as a political strategy, revolving around their needs to secure and diversify their livelihoods (see, e.g., Wittmayer and Büscher 2010).

Two issues stand out in the Lesotho case though. The intervention dynamic necessitated superficiality, and it was fragile. The intervention only touched the surface of the livelihoods of the people in Nyakoaneng, so actual behavior change was highly uncertain and unlikely (see, e.g., Wittmayer 2007, 12). This superficiality, however, lets both parties (the MDTP and the villagers) interpret the intervention in different ways and construct political benefits from it. The deeper and more thorough the intervention, the harder this would be.[71] At the same time, the intervention is fragile: because of the superficiality it is uncertain and unlikely that anything in terms of conservation and the land has really changed. Fragility thus lies in the (inherent) paradox between the representation and actual environmental reality of the 'Moteng mountain range. This guarantees that the intervention can be interpreted by various sides the way they see fit.[72] How this bodes for the reinvigorated MRAS remains to be seen, but neither communities nor project implementers seemed eager to critically assess the impact. This would lead to political debate, something that both parties tried to avoid because this can be exploited in their favor, especially for the local villagers, in order to extract livelihoods benefits. In sum, the local villagers in Nyakoaneng opted for a political strategy of pragmatic antipolitics.

In South Africa, the case was more complex. Local people in Amazizi were more openly critical about Amagugu Esizwe, although their critique was not reported in the project's final report. The report does note disturbances and setbacks, leading to recommendations so that the management of the next intervention can be refined. This is an instrumental way of dealing with local dynamics that allows feedback into the mechanics of the conservation and development bureaucracy. I would like to give a different, more political interpretation, namely that the politics of the intervention was inherently different from the politics of the community. First, the project's political agenda, which had been preset by the World Bank and on which it was to be evaluated, was "effective conservation management" (World Bank 2001a, 42). This clashed with the political agenda of the communities, which was mainly to get jobs. So although the communities kept working on the dongas, they did so for other reasons than the project implementers and the MDTP would have wanted. Of course, this is an open secret: both implementing partners and the MDTP were well aware that one of people's highest priorities is to get jobs.[73]

But as the former director of one of the implementing NGOS pointed out, they were not in favor of job creation where people get paid a daily rate, because this raises expectations and kills any volunteer effort.[74] This logic was shared by the MDTP, and Amagugu Esizwe was therefore focused on capacity building.[75] While in principle this seems justifiable, in practice it often forecloses political debate. The point is that the political goal behind capacity building is predefined, and once it has been established it has to be "managed" and "capacitated" into reality. Consequently, in Amagugu Esizwe it had been established that capacity building was to lead to effective conservation management, and the project implementers went to great lengths in the final report to establish this link, no matter how fragile it was. The vision workshops at the start of the project did not make a difference either,[76] because the logistical framework and outcomes were already determined. To repeat the statement by one of the villagers: "In the beginning they [the project implementers] always ask what we want, but during the course of the project, they always push their own things and then it is no longer what we want."

It seemed paradoxical that many people wanted the project to return, even though it was not in line with what they wanted. I argue that the reason for this resembles Taylor's argument with respect to spatial-development initiatives in southern Africa in that they are "not only driven by state elites, who have their own agenda, but by communities and peoples who utilize the micro-region for a heterogeneous set of reasons and motives" (2003, 325). In Lesotho and South Africa, local people have their reasons for pursuing linkages with outside agencies, such as development projects or the state; this is an important way for them to augment their livelihoods. Although this seems to be the case in many developing societies, it has taken on a whole new dimension in South Africa, where expectations of the postapartheid state have been especially high (partly fueled by the state and the African National Congress). In this vein, Michael Neocosmos argues that

> In South Africa . . . , state fetishism is so pervasive within the hegemonic political discourse that debate is structured by the apparently evident "common sense" notion that the post-apartheid state can "deliver" everything from jobs to empowerment, from development to human rights, from peace in Africa to a cure for HIV-AIDS. As a result not only is the state deified, but social debate is foreclosed from the start; the idea simply becomes one of assessing policy or capacity. In other words the focus is on management not on politics. (2003, 343)

Even if the project implementers or the MDTP had wanted to acknowledge and deal with their clash of political agendas with the local communities, they could not do so, because political debate was closed beforehand. It was capacity for conservation that needed to be managed into reality, not capacity for jobs. As a result, the project implementers were fated to the roles of broker and translator between local dynamic realities and the conservation and development bureaucracy that they—consciously or unconsciously and despite often honest commitment to ownership and participation—helped to further expand and fortify (see Mosse and Lewis 2006). But if the implementers could not change the intervention's political agenda, then neither could the villagers. As a result, local villagers hid their political agenda from the implementers and went along with what was presented in order to extract benefits to their livelihoods. Thus, even though villagers in Obonjaneni did not commend as readily as those in Nyakoaneng the emperor's clothes (Bending 2003), they ultimately resorted to the same political strategy of pragmatic antipolitics.

Conclusion

The chapter examined how the MDTP tried to become part of the Maloti-Drakensberg polity. In this process, both PCUs used antipolitical strategies —albeit of a different character—to get the MDTP objectives accepted by important stakeholders. The South African PCU employed instrumental antipolitics that emphasized technical and scientific rationalism, while the Lesotho PCU employed moral antipolitics based on the primacy of (local) people's right to access, use, and manage natural resources. Both PCUs resorted to a certain high ground that to them was the logical way of operationalizing the MDTP and thus not up for discussion. These political strategies elicited opposing political strategies, which were remarkably different per country. In South Africa, several implementing agencies challenged their PCU, while in Lesotho they acquiesced and co-opted what the project had to offer. In South Africa, the result was a lot of friction and the political marginalization of the PCU. In Lesotho, there was little friction between the PCU and implementing agencies, but this was due to the latter employing a pragmatic strategy that used the intervention to support duties they could otherwise not pursue. The project's international relations further complicated these dynamics. In Lesotho, the implementing agencies aligned themselves with the PCU, but in South Africa the most-important implementing agencies (the DEAT and KZN Wildlife) challenged their PCU and started supporting Lesotho's moral antipolitical strategy. The more-abstract effects of the MDTP on the Maloti-Drakensberg polity were present in the struggles over the political legitimacy of the two main ways to pursue consensus among stakeholders. And although the community-based-conservation paradigm resonated more than the bioregional planning paradigm, the end result—the bioregional strategy—was a mix of both.

How then did the intervention affect power relations within the MDTP polity? Although I said that the potential effects of a large intervention such as the MDTP are considerable, it must be concluded that the actual effects of the MDTP (in South Africa and Lesotho) on existing power balances were negligible. This became especially clear from the analysis on the local level: because neither implementers nor local communities can fundamentally change preset intervention objectives and rationales, they both resort to tactics that let them get as much out of the intervention as they can. For the local villagers, this is a political strategy of pragmatic antipolitics: going along with what is presented in order to extract livelihood benefits. This finding supports the notion that within a framework where the conservation and development discourse is hegemonic, it remains crucial to appreciate the nuanced multidirectionality in conservation and development—or the agency of both the implementers and subjects of interventions (see, e.g., Bending 2003; Mosse 2004).

But whereas actor-oriented aidnography would emphasize "the political contests, the feigned compliance, the compromises and contingencies involved in the accomplishment of rule" (Mosse 2004, 645; see also Li 2007), I argue for a more structural view, based on the more abstract dominance of neoliberalism and its propensity to maintain and increase inequality (Harvey 2005). In the two PCUs' struggle to institutionalize the project, they increasingly resorted to devolved governance mechanisms or strategies of regulation that are distinctly neoliberal. This is a move that strengthens particular structures of political power, as argued by Nikolas Rose: "The strategies of regulation that have made up our modern experience of 'power' are thus assembled into complexes that connect up forces and institutions deemed 'political' with apparatuses that shape and manage individual and collective conduct in relation to norms and objectives but yet are constituted as 'non-political'" (1996, 37).

The strategy of antipolitics reinforces general tendencies in a neoliberal political economy by putting both conservation and development implementers and subjects under similar pressures to avoid the realm where inequality can be addressed. This is the messy realm of politics, characterized by gray zones, winners and losers, and trade-offs rather than win-win ideals of all-inclusiveness. Antipolitics ensures a focus on the realm of discourse, the only realm in which consensus can (seemingly) be attained and maintained. As a consequence, this increases the importance of discursive power over other sources of power, such as regulatory or decisional powers (see Arts and van Tatenhove 2004). Hence, to understand power in conservation and development governance we must further analyze the discursive side of the MDTP in relation to the intervention's material effects.

chapter six

IMAGES OF AN INTERVENTION

The last two chapters identified and analyzed two modes of political conduct in the Maloti-Drakensberg Transfrontier Project (MDTP): consensus and antipolitics. These were corollary and continuous struggles. The need for a politics of consensus was bolstered during a shift from (colonial) government to (postcolonial) governance, combined with an ideology that claims to value individualism and the participation and accountability of stakeholders. As a result, constituency building and political legitimacy become increasingly difficult and fragile. We saw this in the necessary superficiality of the MDTP proposal and in the way the Project Coordination Units (PCUS) tried to institutionalize the project's objectives, which led them to rely on antipolitics and conceptually vague mobilizing metaphors in the bioregional plan. The fragility of consensus became evident from how the PCUS operationalized and interpreted the MDTP proposal and the stakeholders' subsequent reactions to the intervention. The dynamics of these political struggles developed through a dialectic of practice and discourse, whereby discourse offered greater possibilities for consensus. Hence, discourse has become an important retreat (and new type of practice) for those able to make a living out of abstraction (papers, plans, maps, and so on). This is where the last mode of neoliberal politics comes in: marketing, or the struggle to gain competitive advantage through the manipulation of abstraction.

In essence, the marketing struggle in conservation and development is the result of the paradox between increasingly complex realities and the inability to accept or communicate this in order to sell a project or enact behavioral change. Rather than try to critically understand this paradox, many actors construct and promote images and discourses that exploit the potential competitive advantage that can be gained from the spaces and incongruities left in its wake. Crucially, the MDTP is only one of many actors trying to market ideas about conservation and development. The MDTP has to compete or align with many alternative images, some of which are backed up by powerful actors. The argument in this chapter is that dominant images about conservation and development in the Maloti-Drakensberg work to reconstitute the area in neoliberal terms, thereby disciplining actors' behavior and positions within the new setup.[1] It follows that this can only succeed in conjunction with neoliberal modes of devolved governance. These, in fact, became central to how the MDTP operationalized its planning framework practically, namely through payments for environmental services and tourism. Politically, this was convenient: devolved governance mechanisms (seemingly) further defuse political sensitivities by stimulating economic equalization and market prioritization of political and social values, while they help to align the project with powerful neoliberal actors. The next chapter will deal with these practical strategies in depth. This chapter analyzes the images presented by powerful actors involved in or impacting the MDTP intervention to make these strategies legible and logical.

In a complex project such as the MDTP, many powerful actors espouse ideas and images that influence conservation and development in the region, so I had to decide which to include. Several arguments guided my selection. First, not all actors have equal access to the spaces or processes where marketing matters and particular operationalizations of the project can have an impact. We saw this with respect to the Peace Parks Foundation and regional transfrontier conservation. Likewise with the MDTP, certain actors are more central to the intervention than others because of their networks, resources, or institutional positions. Second, the MDTP was not particularly focused on local "on-the-ground" implementation, which meant that there were few extensive local struggles that markedly influenced the direction of the intervention. Third, the history and setup of the intervention strongly influenced which actors would be central to the MDTP implementation process.

These arguments show the problematic nature of the focus of the MDTP bioregional strategy "on all action (whether country specific or joint) *collectively* contributing to the achievement of the MDTFCA [Maloti-Drakensberg Transfrontier Conservation Area] Purpose" (MDTP 2007d, 63; emphasis in original). Both during the preparation and during the implementation phase, some actors were closer to the intervention than others and had more power over its operationalization. Based on this and my fieldwork observations, I argue that the donor's, the private sector's, and consultants' ideas of the MDTP or conservation and development dynamics in the Maloti-Drakensberg mattered most in reframing the area in neoliberal terms. These actors instilled, fortified, compromised, or monitored the neoliberal tendencies already present in the PCUS and implementing agencies. However, my focus on these actors does not mean that other images are not important. To augment the analysis and cater for bias, I juxtapose the images by the above actors with images of and by local communities and through a discussion of an issue crucial to any conservation and development project: the politics of success and failure.

Donor Discipline

By the donor I mean the World Bank, even though the MDTP was funded by the Global Environment Facility (GEF). The World Bank was the official GEF implementing agency for the MDTP, and therefore its rules and strictures applied to the project. From the side of the World Bank, a task-team leader (TTL) was appointed for the MDTP. A TTL is a project's first contact with the institution. The post was first occupied by a white South African man (until 2006) and thereafter by a black Ghanaian man. This is important, as it gives an indication of how different personalities influence the course of a project.

Several general issues were important in the World Bank's engagement with and influence over the MDTP. To begin with, the MDTP case reinforces Harrison's argument about the World Bank's "exceptional outside influence over African states" and the limited self-understanding of its power (2005b, 253–54). In our interview, the first TTL mentioned that projects like the MDTP are designed by the countries, "so, they are responsible." According to him, the World Bank merely supports the countries.[2] In another interview, the TTL stated that he had a "technical approach" to cooperation between South Africa and Lesotho, which means that one should "only discuss the things that are international in character; you should not discuss things that are national in character."[3] While these realms were not neatly separable in the MDTP, this technical approach was also reflected in World Bank documents on the MDTP (e.g., in supervision mission reports). The World Bank's assumption about its recipients still hinges on the idea of governmentality pointed out by James Ferguson (1994, 72), namely that there is a rational, reasonably effective government in place that can be assisted through neutral outside help. This assistance is seen as instrumental and apolitical, in line with what governments (should) want (see Demmers, Fernández Jilberto, Hogenboom 2004; Goldman 2005).

This point can be further illustrated by images of the World Bank from those involved in the MDTP. An important issue for many informants was the World Bank's procurement rules, which were described to me as "cumbersome," "difficult," "too long," and so forth. A member of the Lesotho project-coordination committee even believed that the procurement rules were harmful to the project, while a South African PCU staff member mentioned that the procurement rules "impede heavily on the project."[4] She pointed out that the first two procurements took eleven and seven months, respectively. According to her, this is risk-avoiding behavior, which suits a bank, but does not suit work in real life: "Of course, you can demand deliverables, but you have to take some risks in reality as well."[5]

Although admitting that the procedures can take a long time, both TTLs brushed aside the complaints and viewed the procurement rules as regular technical processes that cannot be problematized. The first TTL mentioned that all the procedures are available in two small booklets and that their cumbersomeness just depends on how familiar one is with them.[6] He added that the World Bank provides training and that the board of directors endorses the procedures—again implying that the member countries that make up the board are responsible. The second TTL defended the procurement procedures by noting that unlike South Africa, Lesotho had no problems.[7] Yet the PCUs could not hide their irritation with the procedures and wrote the following in an early draft of the bioregional strategy:

> While this phase has been made possible by GEF funding through the World Bank, the bureaucratic requirements of this institution have impacted significantly on efficient implementation. While these requirements are understandable in that they ensure that financial and pro-

curement management follow the necessary processes required to prevent the misappropriation of funds, they have caused very serious delays in the procurement of key services which could impact on the ability of the PCUS to meet their Project Development Objectives. Many serious errors have been made by World Bank staff with no recourse for the countries and one is left with the impression that the Bank is untouchable and that project managers must take this into account when undertaking a risk analysis on implementation planning. (MDTP 2007d, 14)

In a later draft, however, this section was rewritten so as not to endanger relations between the countries and the World Bank, showing the felt need to suppress political sensitivities.

MDTP staff predominately saw the World Bank as a large, cumbersome, technocratic bureaucracy. But informants also saw the World Bank in other ways. The World Bank is a powerful global institute, so it was also presented an opportunity for networking, future funding, and potential jobs, especially in Lesotho. Thus, despite finding the procedures cumbersome, the director of the Lesotho National Environment Secretariat said, "It is good for us to do our best, because it will open new doors."[8] Although less explicitly so, this belief also played a role in South Africa. According to a Department of Environmental Affairs and Tourism (DEAT) MDTP staff member, the image of the World Bank as both evaluator and opportunity led to fierce competition between the countries: "Each PCU wants to do better than the other and this is exacerbated by the World Bank."[9] According to him, this issue could only be solved by strong leadership, for instance by the governments. However, he added that developing countries often hesitate: "We feel if we state our authority, we don't get the money."[10]

This delicate and interdependent relationship between donor and recipient further fueled the antipolitical dynamics in the project described in the previous chapter. The World Bank needs continuous endorsement from countries for its existence and actions, while many governments that depend on donor aid cannot easily ignore a player with the size and influence of the World Bank. It is therefore logical for both sides to view the other instrumentally and to (publicly) avoid issues that can be construed as political. Moreover, according to the DEAT MDTP staff member, this is a reason for the World Bank's focus on strict, bureaucratic planning procedures, as its employees are then "protecting themselves more than if they would be doing things on the ground."[11]

It is important to add that this mutual instrumentalization between the World Bank and governments is a process-oriented dynamic that can become more important than the purpose of their cooperation. At the very least, it often constrains and partly predetermines action in specific institutional contexts. This does not mean that all action is predetermined or that outcomes of processes do not matter. The opposite is true, albeit in a different way than often perceived: when (enough powerful) people believe that outcomes are successful, it often means more for the legitimacy of interventions than actual success or failure (however measured). Although never absolute, this logic compels actors to market themselves in a positive light and to increasingly concern themselves with their brand. For an actor as politically significant and contested as the World Bank, this is especially true given, for example, the caution with which it approaches those who could potentially (negatively) influence its image (see fig. 6.1).

The World Bank had a strong structuralizing effect on the MDTP. Besides the procedural effects due to cumbersome bureaucracy, the World Bank also had strong instrumentalizing effects, trying to "render technical" the intervention to such an extent that even transfrontier relations should reflect the logic of procedural reductionism (see Li 2007, 230). But the World Bank is even more (in)famous for its economic reductionism. Michael Goldman argues: "In prodding state agencies to become more environmental and neoliberal, the World Bank prompts them to make a country's natural assets accountable in two senses: first, in being counted and thereby made visible locally and transnationally, and second, in reference to new environmental, economic, and cultural norms and responsibilities" (2005, 189–90). Some early discussions between the South African PCU and the World Bank about the twenty-year transfrontier strategy corroborate these arguments. According to the first World Bank TTL in a mission report: "The mission provided guidance on improving the preliminary table of contents for the transfrontier strategy. . . . It also suggested the need for the strategy to be underpinned by a sound economic and land use understanding in support of South Africa's development priorities (i.e. towards a 'conservation economy')" (World Bank 2005, 7). Later in the same document, the TTL urges the PCUs to take responsibility for the neoliberal constitution of the Maloti-Drakensberg: "The mission, as indicated earlier, discussed the concept of a conservation economy based on the region's comparative advantage in natural resources and cultural heritage. It is therefore *important that this bigger picture view of the role of the project in*

Researcher Agreement on Special Access

I, _____Bмм Büschek_____, acknowledge that I have been given Special Access to *Guidelines to Staff on Project Supervision* under the provisions of paragraph 80 of The World Bank Policy on Disclosure of Information. I understand that I may not publish or otherwise disclose the information obtained during my research without the express permission of the World Bank. I further understand that any information relating to a country may be made available only after the World Bank has obtained the consent of the country concerned.

1. Prior to publication I will submit to the World Bank any manuscript or portion thereof that uses information gained through my research in *Guidelines to Staff on Project Supervision.* I understand that until permission is received from the World Bank I may not publish such information.

2. Prior to an oral presentation that uses information gained through my research in *Guidelines to Staff on Project Supervision* I will submit to the World Bank a text or synopsis of the proposed presentation. I understand that until permission is received from the World Bank I may not use such information in an oral presentation.

3. If I have obtained copies of documents during my research, I will not share them with other persons nor will I deposit them in another repository.

4. I understand that failure to abide by the research rules may result in the suspension of research privileges.

Name: _____Bмм Büschek_____

Date: ___02 -01 - 2007___

FIGURE 6.1 World Bank "Researcher Agreement on Special Access." In December 2006 I tried to contact the World Bank to get more information, but before it was granted, I had to sign a "Researcher Agreement on Special Access." The information I requested was, to me, of no profile or high significance. I wanted to know the criteria the World Bank uses to rate projects during supervision missions. However, in order to get the bank's *Guidelines to Staff on Project Supervision*, I had to agree to "submit to the World Bank any manuscript or portion thereof that uses information through my research" in the guidelines document. The same applied to "oral presentations." Also, I was not allowed to "share the document with other persons." Finally, I had to "*understand*" that "failure to abide by *the research rules* may result in the suspension of research privileges" (emphasis added). Unfortunately, after I received the document it did not contain anything I did not already know (and hence, I am not obliged to ask "permission from the World Bank" to publish this book). The whole issue illustrates how cautious the World Bank is in protecting its image. After all, resorting to legal means is a rather far-reaching way of trying to control the information flows that affect one's image. But then again, in a neoliberal world whereby an increasing amount of actors "sell" themselves by the power of their image, this is not only to be expected, but simply a necessity in increasingly competitive environments.

developing the conservation economy of the region is correctly conceptualized to inform the preparation and implementation of the 20 year transfrontier conservation strategy" (12–13; emphasis added).

A cornerstone in this "correct conceptualization" of the Maloti-Drakensberg as a conservation economy is the concept of payments for environmental services, discussed in the next chapter. Important here is that the World Bank continued to support and provide donor legitimacy to neoliberal models of conservation within the MDTP. However, two important caveats are in order. First, the two TTL's differed on this point. It was the first TTL who was especially pressing for neoliberal conservation models on behalf of the World Bank. The second TTL, a Ghanaian national, was much less enthusiastic and put more emphasis on community conservation as practiced by the Lesotho PCU,[12] thereby illustrating that neoliberal ideas are unevenly promoted (or resisted), even in the World Bank. Second, South African PCU members did not accept the idea of a conservation economy and decided not to pursue it in the transfrontier strategy. Although the staff members embraced payments for environmental services, they were more cautious about economic models in general than the first World Bank TTL, as exemplified by the latest version of the transfrontier strategy (MDTP 2007c), which cautions against unsustainable market forces and unlimited growth.[13] They were equally concerned about the impact and influence of the private sector on the Maloti-Drakensberg ecosystem, and with good reason.

Private Interests

In contemporary (neoliberal) conservation and development circles, it has become a truism to strive for close cooperation between public and private actors (Tsing 2005). The idea is to draw the private sector into public objectives (public-private partnerships) or concerns (corporate responsibility). Regarding the MDTP, the World Bank also believed that the private sector was to bring "managerial know-how," "marketing skills," and "capital" to the table (2001a, 14). Yet, even if it is seen as desirable, public-private cooperation often proves elusive. We saw how the private company Rand Water interfered in the Amagugu Esizwe project, changing its dynamics considerably. Despite many attempts, it proved impossible to get Rand Water to partner with Amagugu Esizwe (MDTP 2007a). Rand Water's reasons for not cooperating are not important here. The company simply did its own thing and as such presented the MDTP with challenges.[14] Nonetheless, many private-sector actors and conservation and development inter-ventions have started using similar rhetoric and increasingly need each other for the marketing of their public legitimacy.

An especially telling illustration of problematic public-private engage-ment under similar rhetoric in the MDTP is the proposed Royal Maluti golf estate in between the towns of Clarens and Fouriesburg in the South Afri-can Free State. At a public consultation meeting about the environmental-impact assessment of the proposed golf estate on 19 January 2007 in Clarens, it was clear that the private sector was not the least bit interested in the objectives of the MDTP. The meeting was attended by some two hundred people, mostly black people from the Clarens township of Kgubetswana. They could write their names on a register if they were interested in poten-tial jobs at the golf estate. This was the reason why so many people attended the meeting, as the presentation of the environmental-impact assessment was so technical that almost certainly none of the township residents pres-ent understood it, even though everything was translated into Sesotho. Moreover, the discussion after the presentation almost solely dealt with social issues, such as jobs and the overstretching of Clarens's limited ser-vices due to the large number of people that the golf estate was aiming to accommodate.

It was clear from the beginning of the meeting that the Royal Maluti representative had come to push through his own agenda.[15] Undeterred, the South African MDTP bioregional planner asked whether Royal Maluti, in the spirit of regional initiatives such as the New Partnership for Africa's Development (NEPAD), the Southern African Development Community, SADC, and the MDTP, would consider granting some employment to the communities on the other side of the border in Lesotho—simply because they are much closer to the (proposed) golf estate than either the Clarens or Fouriesburg townships. The Royal Maluti representative answered that his allegiance is with South Africa and that (potential) jobs will thus go to Clarens and Fouriesburg. This was legalistically correct, and he was awarded with applause by the township residents. The representative then insisted: "We want a profitable business that benefits you and our shareholders to the benefit of all." He asked the communities to join Royal Maluti "hand in hand for sustainable development."

This anecdote not only illustrates that public-private partnerships are difficult but also shows the private sector's bottom line. And even though Royal Maluti did not appear keen to cooperate with the MDTP, it used similar rhetoric about sustainable development to market the project. The company advertises itself as "the rare exception" and boasts of possessing "a place of untouched beauty . . . where the mountains meet the sky. A place where you can live, breathe and relax, where freedom and security come together."[16] But, of course, Royal Maluti's interpretation of sustainable development was quite different from the MDTP, especially in the light of the company's aim to irrigate the golf course with water from the Lesotho Highlands Water Project tunnel, which goes directly under the proposed golf estate. In a dry region that is set to have major water problems in the near future (Solomon and Turton 2000), and considering the fact that the Basotho communities living immediately next to the proposed estate often have no access to clean water, one realizes the Janus-faced connotation to Royal Maluti's commitment to sustainable development (Büscher 2009).

Other problematic aspects of public-private partnerships relate to democratic accountability (as we saw in chapter 2) and the further fueling of neoliberal antipolitical tendencies in the public sector and in conservation and development interventions. Together, these are having major effects on conservation and development realities in the Maloti-Drakensberg and on how these realities are framed. Indeed, because the private interest in the (South African) Drakensberg is enormous, the issues related to the Royal Maluti case will likely be compounded in the future. According to one participant from KZN Wildlife at an MDTP stakeholder workshop in March 2007, the Drakensberg area is flooded with development applications. He expressed his deep worry and said that developers want the area to be like the South African South Coast with "wall-to-wall development." This statement can be substantiated by paying attention to private-sector marketing in the economic heart of South Africa: the Gauteng province.

One example is the private company Nondela, a massive golfing and residential estate in the northern Drakensberg. Nondela advertised on South African television (seen in June 2007) saying that investors can now enjoy and make a profit out of the "unspoilt" Drakensberg World Heritage Site. According to its website, "Nondela Drakensberg Mountain Estate is a once-in-a-lifetime opportunity to invest in rejuvenation and to bank on increasingly sought-after land, a project blessed by tribal elders and founded on the community-mindedness that is 'Abalengani'—the Zulu for friend or partner."[17] In the estate, you can "become one with nature" and "escape, relax, rejuvenate." Another example was presented in the Brooklyn shopping mall in Pretoria on 1 August 2007, where a big display by the company Dunblane marketed stands in its Golf, Trout and Game Mountain Estate.[18] The Dunblane slogan is "complete yourself," which one can do in its "massive estate, comprising a total of 3,000 hectares of pristine ecology in the Northern Drakensberg Mountains, with 15 kms of 2,000 foot high escarpment face running through its centre." Here again capitalist development goes hand in hand with the marketing of Africa's Garden of Eden. Thus, Dunblane advertises "five star," "unprecedented convenience" in luxury real estate with the "latest" ICT technologies for security and leisure, while at the same time "the idea is to return the natural beauty and life to what it would have looked like some 200 years ago."

The power of marketing is obvious here. These private companies deliberately combine colonial Garden of Eden images with unrivaled luxury to attract investors. They see the Drakensberg area as an investment opportunity where capitalist development, luxurious elite lifestyles, and nature conservation go hand in hand without any conflict. Moreover, Nondela boasted that its "4.5 Billion [rand] capital injection" would enhance "one of the most economically challenged areas of KwaZulu Natal" by bringing "thousands of employment opportunities and training in the hospitality industry."[19] Like Royal Maluti, these estates see themselves as the ultimate promoters of win-win solutions that benefit shareholders, investors, communities, the environment, and tourists (see, e.g., Igoe and Brockington 2007). This is the image they are keen to portray, and it is clear from television commercials, billboards, advertising stands in shopping malls, and flashy websites that they have the networks and resources to forcefully do so. Yet the gap between these images and those put forth by marginal actors is enormous (see, e.g., Li 2007).[20] Indeed, these private initiatives entrench social inequalities by further enclosing natural areas and fortifying class boundaries between white owners of tourism companies and black dependents (see, e.g., Rogerson 2004). It is sheer financial power that enables these private companies to buy themselves into the Maloti-Drakensberg polity and so drastically change conservation and development configurations, while simultaneously being able to influence public interpretation by the power of their marketing. And while the MDTP did not automatically endorse all these private interests, it is clear that the private images about the Maloti-Drakensberg area, albeit more lyrically, share more than just cursory resemblance to the increasingly neoliberal way in which the MDTP portrayed the region's environmental services.

Fluid Consultancies

Very different types of private actors are consultants. Although fully part of the private sector, consultants in the conservation and development field usually make a living by providing services to the public sector and often espouse accordant visions of sustainable development, community conservation, poverty alleviation, and so on. Consultants act as "brokers and translators" (Mosse and Lewis 2006), and they often stimulate the (further) neoliberalization of nonbusiness institutions (Van der Pijl 1998). Like in other Transfrontier Conservation Areas, consultants played a very important role in the MDTP. In Lesotho and South Africa, approximately half of the budget was dedicated to the consultant-services category.[21] This included two basic types of consultants: the PCU members and staff deployed at other (implementing) agencies and external consultants for shorter-term assignments. Although my research did not explicitly focus on external consultants, several more general remarks can be made based on my long-term engagement with the project.

The short-term and flexible nature of consultancies made them a very fluid presence in the MDTP. Besides being the main reason why my interaction with consultants was limited, this reality had implications for the project. One implication was a further strengthening of the focus on the abstract, on discourse. Consultants are often fixated on "manipulating abstract concepts" (Van der Pijl 1998, 160), in that they are often concerned with the abstract, strategic management levels of organizational action. The outcome of consultancy products—for example, strategies, recommendations, and models—are then supposed to streamline organizational or management processes, increase accountability structures or financial visibility, and so on. A KZN Wildlife employee at the park level mentioned that he is very critical about the huge gap between the various levels in the organization, with the practical level being more and more financially squeezed, while at "head office they hire all these fancy consultants, who earn a lot of money and give all kinds of advice (usually finance or management), while often knowing nothing about the core business: conservation and ecotourism." He added that he is also critical about the financial support staff who have become so powerful that they seem to "rule rather than support." All this was making his job and participation in the MDTP harder.[22]

An illustration of the fluidness of consultants comes from the local

MDTP office in the Botha-Bothe district of Lesotho in January 2007. After an informal discussion about job opportunities, one of the MDTP community facilitators started complaining about the many white consultants coming and going throughout the project. She had few positive things to say about most consultants, stating that they just "have another community meeting" that the facilitators have to organize and then they leave, "write a report," and "get the money." The local office, especially the community facilitators (the lowest-ranking officials in the MDTP Lesotho PCU), never sees the reports. According to her, one consultant was so bad that she thought he did not know what he was doing, which to her surprise he actually admitted. But this "did not inhibit him to write a report and get the money," she added. Coming back to the issue of jobs, she noted that the job market is much better for white people and that I should become a consultant, come back to Lesotho, and employ her.

This example leads to a second remark, namely consultants' role in the project's racial dynamics. The MDTP hired many consultants with specific ecological expertise to fill in data gaps, especially in South Africa. Most of these consultants were white as there were "very few black biodiversity specialists."[23] In response, a member of the Lesotho project-coordination committee noted that South Africa does have black specialists and that he is "worried that the brunt of the money goes to consultants that are friends of the PCU."[24] Who is right here is not the point. The issue of the expertise that was needed, together with the white consultants who supplied this expertise, again fueled racial tensions within the project. On the Lesotho side, many of the consultants were also white and a "fluid" presence in the project. Of course there were notable exceptions, but the general complaints from the Botha-Bothe office resonated on other occasions as well. When I returned to the village of Malefiloane in May 2007 (I had last been there in January of the same year), the members of the local handicraft group that was supported by the MDTP told me they were very surprised to see me because "white people" (i.e., consultants) normally never return.

A related point deals with the knowledge that consultants bring to the table along with their familiarity of the project area. This was particularly poignant in Lesotho, as a meeting at Lesotho Northern Park on 30 January 2007 in Botha-Bothe shows. On this day, four white South African consultants, assigned to do the bioregional planning and zoning by the Lesotho PCU, were interviewing a staff member. Two things in the meeting stood out. First, the staff member of Lesotho Northern Parks started the meeting by complaining that he had "seen so many researchers and consultants come by and no reports." He said that it cost him a lot of time to attend to all the consultancy "missions" while no information filtered through to him. One consultant said that they have "lots of maps" and that they will send them to the national ministry so that he can get them there. The staff member replied, "They often stay there and we get nothing." He had tried to access reports from the Ministry of Tourism, Environment and Culture several times, but this rarely succeeded. He again asked the consultants to send him documents directly, which they said they can do. Then the meeting officially started. I noted how little the consultants knew about local realities in the project area. For all of them it was their first journey to Lesotho, which they did in what they called a "rush trip" "to see what is happening in the districts."[25] I was wondering how much one could see in a "rush trip," but the consultants seemed happy. One noted, "We have been pouring over maps for one and a half years," so it was great "to finally hear what was happening on the ground."

From these examples, it cannot be generalized that consultants had a major negative or positive impact on the project. What can be concluded is that consultants as a group play an important part in the governance of conservation and development,[26] and that the outcome of consultants' work is usually targeted at the abstract or discursive level. Consequently, many battles over strategies, management structures, and policy directions are fought with, over, and between consultancies, and they are almost never public.

An example from the MDTP was between two consultancies done in 2005 in Lesotho. Both dealt broadly with the issue of how to integrate the MDTP in the ongoing decentralization process and ensure the project's impact on the local level. The first consultancy recommended the establishment of community trusts: "umbrella bod[ies] of the community representing all sections of the community" that "will need to become a legal entity since it will enter into contractual agreements with the private sector" (Khanya 2005, 3, 4). Although the unfinished report was not clear on what level of community this should take place, it seemed to recommend the district, community council, and ward or village level (Khanya 2005, 9). Another consultancy report, coming out later in 2005, noted in response: "Given the level of community empowerment and capacity that currently exists in rural Lesotho and the number of other institutional innovations currently occurring there, these are ambitious proposals. A more feasible arrangement might be to focus on Community Councils as the legal entities that might represent community interests in PA [protected area] management generally and in ecotourism enterprises within PAS specifically" (Turner 2005, 5). In the end, the latter recommendation was more or less followed. This example implies that—because so much implementation happens on the abstract, discursive level—one should have access in order to influence the direction of the intervention. Communities are often said not to have this access, and therefore we now turn to them.

The Idea of Community

Community-based conservation is the dominant paradigm and images of local communities therefore abound in conservation rhetoric and marketing (see Agrawal and Gibson 1999; Blaikie 2006; Brosius, Tsing, and Zerner 2005; Mavhunga and Dressler 2007; Mosimane and Aribeb 2005; Songorwa 1999).[27] In a review of the literature, Jim Igoe and Crystal Fortwangler argue that images around and of communities are historically constituted in relation to other actors and interventions, within "networks of governance" and, increasingly, within a "neoliberal perspective of privatization, marketization, deregulation and 'reregulation'" (2007, 66). I build on these points by showing the differences between the MDTP's images of communities and local images of the project. These differences matter, as they say much about the way unequal actors position themselves within the marketing struggle and try to gain competitive advantage through the manipulation of abstraction.

In MDTP documentation, the idea of communities is important. A good example is the newsletters produced by the project, which are littered with grandstanding statements about communities.[28] In one MDTP newsletter from Lesotho, the project coordinator writes, "The progress made so far is attributed to the commitment and support of all stakeholders, including the implementing departments and local communities. We see the Project Coordination Unit's role as facilitation rather than implementation. Local communities are the legitimate project implementers and should be continuously supported by relevant Government Departments, Parastatals and NGO's."[29]

The first joint MDTP newsletter from September 2005 carried an article titled "Friends in High Places: Caretaker Communities at Senqu Sources." The article introduces various local MDTP initiatives (like the Amagugu

Esizwe project and Lesotho's managed resource areas) and states that "these community structures will help to ensure that local communities are able to manage their natural resources in a sustainable manner," and that "while rural people are contributing to their own long-term sustainability, they are also being asked to invest their resources for the benefit of the wider Southern African community." The article proceeds: "The MDTP is proposing a concept of 'payment for environmental services.' The ability of the environment to provide a service (e.g. that of water catchment) depends on its integrity being restored and maintained. Those who maintain it should derive part of the revenues generated from those who use the service. In future this may provide another source of income to the rural communities charged with protecting the region's water supply."[30]

More examples can be found, but an analysis of available documentation suggests that the MDTP employed two types of community images. The first is that of the responsible community. Documents produced by the MDTP, especially in Lesotho, constantly purvey the feeling that local people are ultimately both responsible for and crucial in the conservation of the MDTP bioregion: crucial because local people could—intentionally or unintentionally—destroy the biodiversity and so, as a corollary, they are responsible for making sure that this does not happen. The project's role is then to "unlock" this responsibility through awareness raising, capacity building, and sensitization: "The MDTP has embarked on a comprehensive awareness raising strategy to raise awareness, educate and empower the community to develop necessary skills, facilitate informed decision making in order to address challenges, change attitudes and foster responsibility in conservation programmes."[31] The other image is that of the community as manager. This image portrays local people as natural and intrinsic parts of the wider state-led system of government and bureaucratic management wherein each actor has a clear role. Here one is reminded of Fletcher's (2010) discussion of "neoliberal environmentality" as communities can now be charged or delegated with the management of their surrounding biodiversity.

These were obviously not the only images that the MDTP implementers had of communities. In fact, many PCU staff members had quite nuanced ideas about the flexibility and fluidity of rural life and issues of local politics and struggles.[32] However, these more complicated and nuanced views could not be communicated. In order to maintain legitimacy and keep avenues for practical action open, the project had to portray communities as responsible and as managers. In this sense, the responsibility image serves to emphasize communities' agency, which is necessary to maintain the policy ideals of ownership and participation, and possibly stimulate them in practice. The manager image, especially when put into the context of payment for environmental services, serves to stimulate consensus by ascribing communities a role in the wider (neoliberal) governmental system and vis-à-vis other actors, such as the state, private sector, and NGOS (see Brosius, Tsing, and Zerner 2005). In this way, the communities' values become the project's values and a shared roadmap for the future becomes possible. The problem is that this consensus is only at the level of abstraction and is developed by those who implement the project. In the face of unpredictable and disjointed local realities—compounded by social pathologies such as HIV/AIDS—it became increasingly difficult for the MDTP implementers to translate this reality and make it fit within the logical frameworks and policy models (see, e.g., Lewis and Mosse 2006).[33] I base this on two observations. The first links in with the pragmatic antipolitics argument, namely that local people also often portray things optimistically to market their inclusion into the flow of resources generated by the project. The second—to be discussed in the next section—is the (slightly) positive modification or interpretation of realities to swing the construction of the intervention toward success rather than failure.

As argued in the previous chapter, those undergoing the intervention—the local communities—had different political agendas from, and a different image of, the project, sometimes even actively resisting the images they were molded into. For most people in Obonjaneni and Nyakoaneng, however, the MDTP was a mere superficial intrusion in their lives, providing some modest livelihood benefits, depending on their abilities to appropriate the project. A strategy of pragmatic antipolitics was essential: the hiding of particular interests and praising the intervention so as not to risk possible future gains. Earlier in 2005, I had found similar images of the MDTP when I traveled with a consultant through the Lesotho MDTP project area. In Malefiloane, in the Mokhotlong district, I spoke to Ntate Maseela, a community council member, and Ntate Ralekhetla after a meeting of the newly formed Environmental Resource Management Association.[34] Maseela told me that the MDTP "will help make the people feel healthy by finding good meat, good pastures and natural resource management and the combating of soil erosion." Both men stated that they think that the project will make a positive impact on people's lives. Following a question on the link with South Africa, they said that the link is very important: "We can sell resources [mohair and wool] that they don't have, and we can buy from them resources that we don't have, like certain animal breeds."

After the same meeting, I asked similar questions to a group of women. They believed that the MDTP is "about improving the lives of the people through tourism." When I ask how, they said mostly through "the building of traditional huts that tourists like." They added that they wanted to weave traditional items to sell to tourists. When I prompted them again on the goal of the project, they responded that it is about biodiversity and protecting wild animals. Which wild animals they were not sure. All the women believed they would benefit from the MDTP, especially because "they do most of the weaving and cooking for tourists." Several days later, in Qacha's Nek district, I held a short interview with 'M'e Mthimkhulu who believed that the MDTP "made Lesotho more important," and hence there are "more resources for communities." The main goal of the MDTP according to her is to protect natural resources and have communities benefit from this. When I asked how this works out, she replied, "by making people produce things from natural resources," like from fodder grass, and sell them to tourists. These tourists are "from South Africa and from far away." They would want to come to Lesotho to "to see what the people here have, to see what is most important in Lesotho." The MDTP will help in this, according to her. And although she had never been to South Africa, she remarked, "Lesotho is poor, South Africa is richer, so we can become rich if we do exactly what they tell us to do." Surprised by this statement, I asked her to elaborate. Toning it down somewhat, she maintained that South Africa "will need to tell us what they have done" so that Lesotho can do the same.

During my travels in June 2005 in Lesotho, and later in September 2005 in the area around Matatiele in the South African Eastern Cape part of the MDTP area, I picked up more local statements in a similar vein. The image that many local people seemed to have of an intervention is that of an opportunity to augment their livelihoods. At the same time, many did not expect too much because they knew they were not in the position to direct the flow of resources. Hence, they tried to go with the flow for the short time they can, hoping for some benefits. In doing so, they marketed both themselves and the project, thereby reinforcing the status quo in terms of power relations between them and other actors. This was also apparent in the discussion about consultants; local people did not expect consultants to return to their villages, and local MDTP project staff envy them for being able to make better use of the project's flow of resources.

Not all local people were so appeasing, and pragmatic antipolitics sometimes made way for very explicit politics. As we saw, many people in Obonjaneni and Ebusingatha were outright negative about the project, while others also articulated criticism. An example is the owner of the local Mamohase Bed and Breakfast in Nyakoaneng, Lesotho. In an interview he mentioned that the MDTP staff wanted to pursue their own agenda in the face of existing arrangements. In particular, "they wanted people to start B&BS instead of investing in Mamohase." And in general, "they formed many associations that had no use, like a tourism association, which even already existed." The bed and breakfast owner said that "at the end of the day, there is nothing," adding, "[the MDTP] could have helped us with signposts, a road, like they helped Liphofung [nearby attraction], but nothing for us, no brochures, no management plan, so the MDTP are fumbling." His explanation for this was that "they just involve us to fill their records," referring specifically to the planning meeting that he and his brother went to that afternoon. He continued: "They are very open with planning and facilitating, but not with implementation, and if they implement, they still do it their way."[35] Yet, despite this and similar critiques from others, few openly confronted the MDTP. The bed and breakfast owner and his brother also fulfilled contradictory roles: they were arguably the most involved in the MDTP (the bed and breakfast owner was the chairman of the Botha-Bothe district steering committee) and benefited much more than other community members, but they were also most critical, at least when talking to a researcher. This apparent paradox is not wholly illogical, as the brothers' exposure to the MDTP probably made them understand the workings of the project better than others who usually did not have access to the policy networks that determine project implementation and success and failure. It is again this basic inequality that is little recognized and addressed in conservation and development interventions. In fact, this inequality in access is necessary in order to construct an intervention as a success.

Images of Success and Failure

Blaikie's conclusion that the success of community-based natural resource management (CBNRM) is reproduced within interpretative networks and "defined in ways that will allow it to be found" needs to be augmented to include the neoliberal hybridization of CBNRM over the last decades and the idea that CBNRM might no longer be as hegemonic as portrayed, when taking into account the popularity of Transfrontier Conservation Areas (2006, 1954). Yet this should not detract from his basic point, which echoes Mosse's conclusion that "'success' and 'failure' are policy-oriented judgments that obscure project effects" (2004, 662). I fortify and expand on this conclusion by arguing that the interpretative coalitions that determine success or failure depend on the marketing capabilities of those who are primarily responsible for implementation as well as those who are in some way linked to or dependent on the success of an intervention (e.g., states and donors, but also communities). Marketing in this sense means that in every step of the interpretation of reality, a promotional spin is put on the project to legitimate and sell it through the bureaucratic chains of power and so reinforce—or at least not damage—the brand of the various actors.

Let me illustrate this practically. In the case of the Amagugu Esizwe project in South Africa, the formal project-accountability structure starts with communities, then leads to the contracted implementing organizations, to the MDTP, to the World Bank, and finally to member countries' governments. This bureaucratic chain ensures that reality is negotiated several times over and allows for what I call "interpretative translation." The start of the chain is what happened in the communities in Mnweni and Amazizi during the project period. I argued that there was a clash of political agendas that in the end reified the status quo and had some, mostly unintended, positive and negative outcomes. In the project evaluation, these are mentioned, but the emphasis is on the construction of success from the implementing organizations to the MDTP, which is obvious from the following passages of the evaluation report and the final report:

> It is therefore clear that many community members, if not whole communities, are in a better position now, at the end of Amagugu Esizwe, to take the management of their resources and therefore their lives into their own hands than they were at the beginning. (Sisitka 2007, 1–2)

> The most important feature of these [project] activities, however, may not be in their actual, direct impact on the land . . . , but in illustrating the possibilities for change and improvement in land management, and in demonstrating people's own agency in effecting such change. This is a very potent impact, which can be seen in the pride people take in

showing visitors the work they have done, and their enthusiasm to continue to do such work, even on a voluntary basis. (MDTP 2007a, 29)

With regards to livelihood changes, these are less easy to detect, except for the obvious direct benefits to people employed in the project, the community facilitators, and the compensation paid for voluntary work. There is no doubt that the capacity being built in various skills has the potential for improving people's livelihoods, and this may manifest in the longer term. (MDTP 2007a, 29)

Both reports are quite detailed and still fairly accurate, although it is clear that the overall conclusion can be debated. For these types of reports, filtering the grounded realities during project implementation and trying to tip the balance toward success is difficult, but still attempted.[36] Thus we have the first step with positive spin. The next step in the interpretation chain is from the MDTP to the World Bank. Besides interpretation, translation is in order, as is clear from an interview with the South African PCU socio-ecologist, who claimed, "As managers we translate and are in between log frames and indicators on the one hand and communities on the other."[37] She added that each MDTP subproject has to contribute to the 13.59 percent of the area that needed to be "under conservation management" at the end of the GEF funding: "We are playing with numbers, so that the World Bank can tick." In all of this, the socio-ecologist maintains that she is learning about being outcome oriented, "because the heat is on the project now."[38]

This "heat on the project" around mid-2005 especially came from the DEAT and the World Bank, who wanted to ensure that the projected outcomes of the MDTP were met. These outcomes were supposed to be measured by concrete, specific, and measurable indicators. In fact, during the preparation phase of the MDTP, earlier versions of the Project Appraisal Document (PAD) had received criticism from the GEF secretariat because "the logframe is very general, and the indicators are very aggregate." In response, a cover letter from the World Bank GEF executive coordinator to the GEF CEO noted,

The PAD now contains eight outcome indicators, and no less than forty-four (44) different output indicators. No component has less than three indicators. The output indicators are usually quite specific: "Recruitment of 1 social ecologist/country." They are often easy to measure in quantitative terms: "Number of kilometres of hiking trails established." They are time-bound in several cases: "At least 100 community entrepreneurs and 10 civil servants trained each year starting in year 2." Other indicators are by nature more general: "Completed biodiversity surveys in priority areas" is one example. Greater precision in such cases can only be provided by sound expert judgment pertaining to the complexities of a particular output.[39]

The letter continues: "No indicators can replace the need or a sensible, holistic interpretation of project implementation. The institutional structure that has been designed, enhanced by the Bank's supervision, is meant to ensure a transparent and accountable system where lessons from implementation are continuously interpreted and incorporated in the execution of the project." Despite this disclaimer, the World Bank, like many donors, remained fixated on technical and measurable outputs, for instance on the 13.59 percent of the area that needed to be under some form of conservation management at the end of the MDTP.[40] In turn, the PCUs tried hard to live up to these indicator outputs, but again the socio-ecologist of the South African PCU noted that unintended external influences always occur; something "you cannot say to funders." Hence, the gap between proposals and reports and reality is often big, as reality is often "sugarcoated."[41]

The next step is from the World Bank and the GEF to those funding those institutions or the funds: the member governments. With many projects going on, there is little space for detail, and thus in the World Bank's "Status of Projects in Execution" report, the success or failure (phrased as "Progress toward achieving development objective[s]") of the MDTP comes down to the following five sentences for fiscal year 2005:

> The project is making progress towards achieving its development objectives. Trans-frontier cooperation and development is taking place with Lesotho to identify threats to biodiversity and to support planning for the area. In South Africa, protected area planning is advancing well and community based natural resource management is taking place. On the ground, investment is taking place in rehabilitation of degraded areas. A Geographical Information System capability has been established to support the project and good linkages have been forged with all implementing agencies concerned.[42]

The following three sentences were noted for fiscal year 2006:

The project is on the track towards achieving its development objective, despite slow implementation and disbursements. Work has primarily focused on assessing how best to address trans-frontier cooperation and development with South Africa including preparation of a trans-frontier plan, addressing transfrontier issues, conserving biodiversity and supporting district plans, the conservation of protected areas, tourism strategy development and support to range management. Capacity building has taken place for officials from the government and tourism parastatal entities.[43]

Lastly, the fiscal year 2007 saw one sentence for Lesotho: "After initial implementation delays, the following critical milestones have been achieved: a 20-year transfrontier conservation strategy with a 5-year action plans; and improved conservation of 136,000 ha of off-reserve land."[44] And two sentences for South Africa: "The 20-year transfrontier development strategy and the associated 5-year action plan has been completed. The tourism strategy and tourism book highlighting the tourists attractions and activities in the region have also been completed."[45]

These paragraphs do not say much because detail has been shed, but they are undeniably exaggerated in several respects. For example, to say that CBNRM is taking place in 2005 is exaggerated because there was little happening on the ground in 2005, while to say that good linkages had been forged with all implementing agencies is simply untrue: the South African linkages with the Free State were very poor and were often difficult with the DEAT, while the linkages between the Lesotho PCU and its implementing agencies could just as well be termed "dependent." For fiscal year 2006, the report is somewhat more careful and notes that implementation and disbursements have been slow—the latter of which seems to be a typical concern of the World Bank. But the report continues with more positive-sounding, general sentences that aim to leave the reader feeling good about the project being on track. Finally, the report for fiscal year 2007 just tries to give the very basic facts in terms of completed milestones, of which the twenty-year strategy and the tourism book arguably were the biggest outcomes. Yet, to state that there has been "improved conservation of 136,000 ha of off-reserve land" is astonishing because no consensus exists on how to measure improved conservation in common-age settings, and a detailed measurement had not been performed under the MDTP. Moreover, this has to be seen in context of the overall argument put forward in this book that such a (quantitative) consensus on something so politically contested as improved conservation is posited for reasons of political legitimation rather than whether or not this holds in reality.

These critical comments notwithstanding, in the end the dominant interpretation of the MDTP by the GEF, built up through several chains of interpretation, was that the project was successful. This last piece of the puzzle became clear to me on 27 July 2007, when I gave a presentation on my research findings to the South African PCU. My presentation was attended by a government official from Sweden, who was sent by the Swedish government to personally assess the effectiveness of the GEF portfolio, to which the Swedish government contributes substantially. During my introduction to the Swedish officer, I was told that members of the GEF secretariat had recommended that the Swedish government study the MDPT because they regarded it an example of a successful project. Interestingly, the official had never been to southern Africa before and had to assess an immensely complex project in a very short time span, which did not appear problematic to him.

Different levels of accountability provide space for sugarcoated interpretations of the project, and details, different values, or alternative views are often gradually filtered out in the paper/policy trail.[46] But interpretations of success and failure are a constant struggle in every conservation and development intervention. The downgraded rating of the MDTP in Lesotho is a good illustration of a severe challenge to and successful defense of the then-dominant consensus that the MDTP was successful among the Lesotho interpretative coalition. The downgrading highlighted many issues within the project, among them the difficult working relationship between the PCUs, the sensitivity of race in southern Africa, and the World Bank's fear for its brand. With respect to success and failure, it confirms that these are indeed value judgments that are (at least partly) decided by interpretative coalitions rather than reality. In this case, the Lesotho government had the complete opposite interpretation of the MDTP than the World Bank and the South African PCU. This is not to say that reality does not count. It is multi-interpretable and gets translated and sugarcoated along the conservation and development chain.

Although they could not talk about it in public, many PCU members were highly aware of the situation. The South African PCU bioregional planner mentioned that sometimes he felt that it would be better if those involved in conservation use more-severe presentations, "more doom-

and-gloom messages so that people will listen."[47] Yet it is clear from the MDTP's external communication—especially newsletters but also project reports—that doom-and-gloom messages were not acceptable. And from a conservation and development marketing perspective this makes sense, because failure usually does not sell. Hence, success or failure in conservation and development is increasingly determined by a focus on demand (what kind of reality do interpretative coalitions want to buy into) rather than supply (what is actually going on). In short, I argue that there is a neoliberal alignment of images, which explains the seeming cacophony on the surface in conservation and development discourse by pointing out the underlying neoliberal convergence on types of action, behavior, and ideas. It is at this point that neoliberal modes of political conduct and devolved governance become most concrete in an intervention that occurred mostly within the discursive (mesa and macro) realms. As such, the next task is to delve into these devolved governance strategies.

Conclusion

Among dominant and influential actors there seemed to be a converging image of what conservation and development should like in the Maloti-Drakensberg. This picture conforms to neoliberal win-win ideals around nature, development, and markets, often with rather explicit (post)colonial connotations. Within this converging image there is a lot of space for actors to try and create competitive advantage. This is the politics of marketing: through the manipulation of abstraction, actors try to turn the operationalization of antipolitical consensus discourses in their favor. As a consequence, the level of discourse truly becomes a distinct type of reality where the construction of success through marketing *becomes* success, as long as one can muster sufficient buy-in from a relevant interpretative community. The construction of success is not only a policy judgment but also a necessity to engage in political debate. Within our postmodern world it is generally accepted that knowledge is constructed, so marketing becomes a political strategy, all the while further separating image from reality and aligning social norms in neoliberal terms. Barrie Axford and Richard Huggins call this a "mediatized politics," which they argue "is expressed increasingly through the forms and discourses of a postmodern populism and that what ensues is not symptomatic of democracy in crisis, but part of a radical transformation of politics and political identities" (1998, 182).

Even though the politics of conservation has been undergoing a radical transformation, not everyone has access to these battles of abstraction. The marketing struggle is a porous system where everybody can take part in principle, but the dominant voices are those in positions of access (such as influential institutions and consultants) or those with the resources to market themselves or put their ideas into material practice (especially elite golf estates). The point of marketing then is usually not just to mold the image to fit one's specific needs or interests. After all, despite the cacophony of different images, there is a tendency toward using the same rhetoric, whether it is the public or private sector, or even communities. The image is not just important in itself, even though many actors still maintain a firm belief in the transformative potential of the latest policy developments. Rather, the importance of adding to, buying into, or developing conservation and development images lies in creating potential for gaining competitive advantage and legitimacy in the underlying currents of the conservation and development discourse: the narrowing discursive and material spaces of neoliberal devolved governance.

At the same time, there are limits to and contradictions within the converging image of a neoliberal Maloti-Drakensberg polity. Not all actors accepted neoliberal discourses; sometimes acceptance was highly contradictory, like the South African PCU's critique of economic growth yet enthusiastic embrace of payments for environmental services, and sometimes acceptance was dependent on different personalities, like with the different World Bank task-team leaders. Moreover, marginal actors, such as local communities, can also be critical of the images put forward by other actors, especially images about them. Yet, despite these reservations and contradictions, there was no real resistance to the MDTP or the way in which it and other actors constituted the area in neoliberal terms. But for this political constitution to work, it needs to reinforce, and be reinforced by, other, more practical (and material) markers of that same process.

chapter seven

NEOLIBERAL ALIGNMENTS

While the Project Coordination Unit (PCUS) were trying to come to terms with each other's interpretation of the Maloti-Drakensberg Transfrontier Project (MDTP) and were engaged in a political struggle with the wider polity on how to move forward, the ecological problems that (officially) triggered the intervention continued apace. The many studies conducted by MDTP consultants indicated that biodiversity richness and eco-systems are at risk, that rangelands and associated water quality and quantity are under threat, and that human pressures play an important role in both. The "Payments for Environmental Services Baseline Study" that was commissioned by the South African PCU writes: "The demand for environmental goods and services supplied by the Maloti Drakensberg Bio-region is already significant, and will continue to increase into the future. However, the ability of the area to continue to supply abundant, high quality environmental goods and services is declining, while demand for these is increasing as a result of growing population and development pressures" (Diederichs and Mander 2004, 4). Living up to Nigel Thrift's comment that it is "increasingly difficult to conceive of the world in any terms except those of a calculus of supply and demand" (2005, 4), the report served to align the MDTP with the rapidly popularizing international "payments for environmental services" para-digm (see Muradian et al. 2010; Sullivan 2009). Moreover, it fit the overall drive of the MDTP implementers to tackle the area's problems in line with the dominant political economy. Transfrontier conservation had become neoliberal conservation.

This obviously is not how the MDTP implementers characterized their strategy. They were concerned with making an impact and employed the political strategies that they felt aided them in doing so, even though this led the project to focus mostly on abstract planning. At the same time, the PCUs understood that they could not solely rely on abstract activities to bring their vision for the MDTP into being. These had to be constituted by and steeped in strategies about influencing conservation and development dynamics in practical realities. That gets us to the heart of neoliberal conservation in the MDTP: the way the project worked to open up neoliberal frontiers through economic reductionism and the concomitant alignment of rules, regulations, and systems of governance.

Payments for environmental services (PES) and tourism are neoliberal conservation's currently preferred strategies—in the MDTP, southern Africa, and across the globe (see Brockington, Duffy, and Igoe 2008; Büscher 2011; Duffy 2006a; Fletcher 2009; Sullivan 2009; West and Carrier 2004). This chapter shows how they function as the practical tools that allow the three modes of politics to open up new frontiers of neoliberal conservation by exploiting the tensions between contradictory realities and reified representations.[1] In doing so, it presents definitive evidence of how neoliberal conservation produces and favors discourses seemingly free of contradictions, while contradictions saturate its practices. One of the most poignant contradictions is the drive toward discourse and the abstract as a favored mode of practical implementation. Intriguingly, this is also the case for practical strategies such as payments for environmental services and especially tourism, leading to what I call the "bubble of neoliberal conservation." This bubble resembles Guy Debord's (1967, 19) "Spectacle" as idealized images dressed up as the epitome of reality. But again, some realities are coarser than others, which, in the second half of the chapter, brings the analysis back to the political ecology of it all: the material consequences and contradictions, particularly with respect to local people in the Maloti-Drakensberg area.

Payments for Environmental Services

In the MDTP, payments for environmental services was most enthusiastically embraced by the South African PCU. It offered a seemingly attractive way to deal with all the ecological, political, and economic pressures the team was facing, and for many PCU members it made good intuitive sense. The South African coordinator, for example, said that many environmental elements in the MDTP area, especially water and biodiversity, are not sufficiently acknowledged for providing vital services to people, and that they need to start carrying a price tag so that people can see their value. The Lesotho coordinator also deemed PES "a brilliant concept," but specified that it should be implemented in later phases of the project.[2] To explore the potential of PES for the Maloti-Drakensberg bioregion, the South African PCU commissioned a baseline study in 2004. The report from this study explains what PES should be about:

> Payment for environmental services provides an incentive for directing landowners towards environment management actions that address priority environmental services, such as water security. As a payment system directly links buyers and producers of environmental services, it build relationships between people who are economically linked and allows market based transactions to take place, reducing the need for further state regulation. Furthermore it focuses on measurable deliverables and consequently sharpens the performance of conservation actors (public, private or communal). (Diederichs and Mander 2004, 5)

Clearly this short paragraph aims to open a new neoliberal frontier: it reduces relations between the main MDTP stakeholders to their roles in an environmental-services market chain and realigns rules, regulations, and governance norms accordingly. The opening of this frontier was in turn wholeheartedly embraced by the PCUs and further stimulated: "An initial baseline study determined the initial feasibility of establishing a trade system around the water production and use patterns associated with the Maloti Drakensberg region. In effect, it suggested that there was scope for investigating and piloting this trade system. In this regard, a consultancy was appointed in 2006 to do just this" (MDTP 2007e, 38).

In effect, the baseline study functioned to make PES a priority for the long-term planning of the MDTP bioregion:

> Both countries recognise the vital role that environmental economics tools play in (i) placing a monetary value on ecosystem goods and services (where their lack of monetary value in the past has meant they are treated as "free resources" often resulting in overutilisation), and (ii) in

defining how such values can assist decision-makers in mainstreaming ecosystem goods and services into accounting and other business practices. The tools are vital to determine the value of biodiversity to the economy and to people's lives. (MDTP 2007e, 106)

In this reconstitution of the Maloti-Drakensberg polity in neoliberal terms, the MDTP was not alone. The baseline study mentions that the South African government promotes PES, while the World Bank was equally eager to "sell nature to save it" (McAfee 1999). According to the first MDTP task-team leader, there is a "need for conservationists to show the economic value of nature," and "if the global community or South African government want nature to be preserved, they should be willing to pay for it."[3] Noticeably, these or other assumptions underlying PES were little discussed, let alone problematized in any of the MDTP outlets.[4] The problems and paradoxes in the reference to a "global community" and the ascribing of roles to actors in a system of devolved governance that professes to value individual choice; the mistrust of commonage systems to conserve nature and the tendency toward privatization; the potential for conflict between actors and values in markets; the placing of monetary over intrinsic values and the reduction of the myriad of human-environment interactions to economic and methodological management were all swept aside to accommodate the latest trend.[5]

But problematizing what was regarded as a potential magic bullet was not on the radar of the MDTP or its consultants. To them it provided a way to deal with the pressures they were under, while the rationalizing and reductionist properties of a PES system also allowed for good marketing opportunities. "We must stop being scared of placing proper value on biodiversity, [because] if we can't put a value on it, we can't convince people," said a KZN Wildlife staff member during a strategic-planning workshop in March 2007 in South Africa.[6] A perverse aspect of the neoliberalization of the Maloti-Drakensberg polity was that the commodification of nature was deemed necessary to place conservation on the political agenda and show its importance. As such, Nicci Diederichs and Myles Mander advised the MDTP to "package the message appropriately": "Biodiversity conservation has little appeal to decision makers in South Africa. Biodiversity conservation has to be shown to be a human development tool, where investing in the natural asset enables humans to benefit as directly as possible. Package the message appropriately and gain the support of the politicians" (2004, 47).

Accordingly, the MDTP went ahead and asked the same consultants and their companies to set up a bigger PES pilot project, which resulted in an Ecosystem-Services Trading Model for the Mnweni/Cathedral Peak and Eastern Cape Drakensberg Areas. Interestingly, and while the baseline study had developed up to twelve different potential ecosystem services in the MDTP area, the subsequent report argues, "As this feasibility study was initiated it became clear that the market was only ready for water and carbon sequestration services" (Mander 2007, 4). Under the "ecosystem service" label, the importance of water for the MDTP was reemphasized, whereas before it had been downplayed to deemphasize the origins of the MDTP in the Lesotho Highlands Water Project and its role in conserving the apartheid political economy. But the postcolonial neoliberal political economy—which is even "thirstier" than colonial apartheid—also depends on the Lesotho Highlands Water Project, and, not without some controversy, continued to support the project after 1994. Payments for environmental services enabled the MDTP to reinterpret and legitimate earlier concerns for water and biodiversity in line with broader community-development and postapartheid transformation objectives.

The report, however, resorts to some tricky maneuvering to construct the link between PES and community development. To do so, it needed to construct communities as the perpetrators of the old "unsustainable" system *and* the beneficiaries of the new, "sustainable" PES system. The report argues that the vegetation and land-use practices that impact vegetation types greatly influence the regulation of the water supply and that upstream users in particular influence the catchments being studied.[7] In the old, unsustainable scenario: "The application of regulations relating to fire management and stocking rates has been largely unsuccessful, with large areas of landscape becoming seriously degraded. In addition, previously well managed areas are coming under increasing pressure from arson, excessive grazing and land use transformation" (Mander 2007, 95). And while this land-use transformation could be instigated by any actor, the report is clear about who should supply the services: "Due to the high value of the water resource supplied from the Maloti Drakensberg, and the growing scarcity of water in South Africa, there is an emerging need to incentivise mountain catchment management *by paying mountain communities to supply ecosystem services*, and in particular, water related services" (Mander 2007, 95; emphasis added).

The report does not mention golf courses and their owners as potential culprits, for example Royal Maluti, which directly taps into the Lesotho High-lands Water Project tunnel. Instead, communities that have historically been confined to these areas under apartheid and their "traditional" lifestyles around livestock and grazing are blamed and targeted for "incentivization" to make them better "managers" in the state-led Maloti-Drakensberg aqua economy. PES in the MDTP thus gave a practical impetus to broader neoliberal governance structures that seek "to create external incentive structures within which individuals, understood as self-interested rational actors, can be motivated to exhibit appropriate behaviours through manipulation of incentives" (Fletcher 2010, 173).

The report is steeped in the political strategies of consensus, antipolitics, and marketing, and after reducing all relations in the Maloti-Drakensberg bioregion to a positivist, positive-sum vision of neoliberal governance, it states, "A payment for water and carbon services is ecologically, hydro-logically, economically and institutionally feasible. It is also desirable from a development and social equity perspective, rewarding those who main-tain a water supply engine but who are spatially and economically margin-alised." The conclusion is therefore obvious: "The eco-hydrological/eco-nomic assessment has shown conclusively that it is feasible and indeed economically desirable for a payment for ecosystem services system to be established in the Maloti Drakensberg" (Mander 2007, 98). Only one ques-tion remained, according to the report: "What is the institutional system required to establish and implement such a trade system?" (98).

The answer given further corroborates Jamie Peck and Adam Tickell's (2002, 384) "roll-out neoliberalism" and Robert Fletcher's (2010) "neo-liberal environmentality" by emphasizing the role of the state:

> The feasibility assessment shows that consumers could pay for man-agement, but the income from water is generally not sufficient to pay for restoration actions. This implies that the state should use state funds to implement restoration of state lands, and then it becomes feasible to charge the ensuing service users for the upkeep of those lands. The results of the assessment shows that there is a need for a combination of both market based trade in ecosystem services and state funded natural capital restoration programmes. (Mander 2007, 97)

But this does not mean that the ambivalence toward the state is gone. While providing for a role for the state, the report also argues, "The whole area of building/facilitating a market for trading ecosystem services is one that lends itself to more of a private sector input. It has even been suggested that some sort of public-private partnership should be explored" (Mander 2007, 93). The report perceives the public sector as just another player in the PES market, thereby de facto subjecting democratic legitimacy to the legitimacy of the market and facilitating a devolved governance system that deepens and strengthens neoliberalism across society (see, e.g., McDonald and Ruiters 2005).

It follows—but this is evidently left out of the report—that introducing PES in the Maloti-Drakensberg brings the region's ecology and its people further into the capitalist mode of production. And it is clear from large bodies of work, particularly in the Marxist tradition, that this mode of production contains deep-seated social and ecological contradictions (see Burkett 2005; Foster 2000; Kovel 2002; Moore 2010). While I am not able to go into this literature in depth, I concur with Burkett that "Marx's analysis contains a powerful ecological indictment of capitalism's valuation of natural wealth" (2005, 54). Hence, when the MDTP states that it "recognise[s] the vital role that environmental economics tools play in placing a monetary value on ecosystem goods and services" (2007e, 106), it is critical to juxtapose this to Burkett's reminder that Marx's analysis "emphasises the tensions between value's monetary forms on the one hand, and the natural environment on the other. Money is homogenous, divisible, mobile, and quantitatively unlimited, by contrast with the qualitative variegation, interconnection, locational uniqueness, and quantitative limits of natural and ecological wealth" (2005, 54).

By ignoring these problematic issues, the MDTP and its PES consultants attempted "to explain away the contradictions of the capitalist process of production by dissolving the relations between persons engaged in that process of production into the simple relations arising out of the circulation of commodities" (Marx 1976, 209). But, crucially, the MDTP and its consultants did not just ignore many problematic assumptions; they amplified the supposed benefits associated with PES to grand proportions and were indeed excited about bringing new commodities into capitalist circulation. Through payments for environmental services, they became part of a new capitalist frontier. Let us here recall Joel Kovel's explanation of how capitalism needs frontiers:

> It constantly seeks to go beyond the limits that it itself has imposed, and so can neither rest nor find equilibrium: it is irremediably self-contradictory.

Every quantitative increase becomes a new boundary, which is immediately transformed into a new barrier. The boundary/barrier ensemble
then becomes the site of new value and the potential for new capital
formation which then becomes another boundary/barrier, and so forth
and on into infinity—at least in the logical schemata of capital. (Kovel
2002, 41–42)

Clearly, with PES, the MDTP entered an exciting and uncertain frontier.
This is most clearly articulated when the MDTP's report discusses carbon
and biodiversity trading: "Carbon trading is still an emerging market with
significant uncertainly. Biodiversity trading is even less developed but
clearly an area that has great potential considering the international biodiversity importance of the area as a whole, and the emerging global markets in biodiversity offsets" (Mander 2007, 93), The report continues:
"This is such a new area that there may be a range of other innovative
mechanisms and options that can be considered for implementation." It
adds that "the big attraction of course is that the more funding that can be
generated, the more will be available for rehabilitation and for payments to
poor rural communities." This closes the discursive loop: PES brings in
more money, with which more environmental and social benefits can be
generated, which brings in more money. That these are tenuous expectations does not deter the report from portraying payments for environmental services as the new frontier; a frontier untainted by politics, inclusive of
all stakeholders, and with plenty of opportunities for marketing.

Tourism: A Kind of Magic?

Whereas payments for environmental services was conceptualized for implementation in future phases of the MDTP, tourism was actually implemented in the first phase. Tourism was often regarded as the project's
magic bullet, connecting conservation and development in the bioregion.[8]
This not only made the jobs of the tourism specialists in the PCUS extremely demanding, but they also had to continuously temper high expectations.[9] Nonetheless, while careful not to push tourism as *the* panacea for
the area's problems, the specialists were keen to use tourism as a devolved
governance strategy to constitute the area in neoliberal terms.

In a revealing interview, the Lesotho tourism specialist told me that
tourism was barely recognized in Lesotho and that the objective of the
project was to change this. When asked whether tourism is the only way to

connect conservation and development, he referred to payments for eco-logical services. According to him, this is not an "open shop" but a pay-ment to the collective, which—in Lesotho—is the management unit of a particular resource. When I asked how the management unit determines the price of the ecological service when people, for instance, also value cattle for what it represents culturally (Ferguson 1994), the tourism spe-cialist answered that the "people will have to learn then." According to him, people have to learn that when they "sing for pleasure, they could also be singing for money, and if they dance for pleasure, they could also dance for money." To press the point, he elaborated, "cultures are changing and we can't get stuck in the sixteenth century. We have to go for the spirit of the time."[10]

And this spirit is neoliberal indeed. The specialist explained that gener-ally in tourism, it does not matter how similar the product is, it is how you market it. According to him, the key trademark or symbol of the Basotho is "primitivism." More specifically, he mentioned that it is invariably cold in Lesotho and that people therefore walk with blankets, which is a sign of primitivism. What tourism must then work on the "romanticization of primitivism"; a trip to Lesotho must become a "nostalgia trip." He believed that many people feel alienated from the West and that tourism can cater for a longing for a rediscovery of the past. Intrigued, I asked if this creates a false picture of reality. The tourism specialist replied that it is a "staged reality"; people still express their culture without tourism in the sense that they still "dance as a longing for the past," but a Western tourist needs to have a picture that shows he or she has been to Africa. This picture cannot be made in downtown "Joburg"; tourists have to go to rural areas and game parks for a picture with lions or traditional dancers. He concluded: "In tourism you don't cater for reality, you cater for perceptions."[11]

The South African tourism specialist did not agree with her Lesotho counterpart on everything, but she did agree that one should "cater for per-ceptions" by looking at what the market wants and "play[ing] into that." For instance: "People want authentic—culture, nature—and if one doesn't ac-cept this, your marketing will not be as successful."[12] Accordingly, her main priority in the project was the overall marketing of the Maloti-Drak-ensberg region under a common single brand. In fact, she believed that without a single brand, the tourism component of the project would fail.[13] This became the main tourism activity within the MDTP—another activity focused on the abstract discursive level. After much debate it was decided in a "historic agreement" between the agencies responsible for tourism in the MDTP area in May 2006 that the single brand would be the "Maloti-Drakensberg Route."[14] In order to market the brand, the MDTP published a book in 2007 titled *The Maloti Drakensberg Experience: Exploring the Maloti Drakensberg Route* (MDTP 2007b). The route to the brand and the book, however, was not without challenges.

In the 2001 MDTP project proposal, the World Bank had mentioned with respect to tourism in the Maloti-Drakensberg region: "The area is attracting a considerable number of visitors; around 300,000 registered visits per year on the South African side, while the Lesotho side remains rather inaccessible and underappreciated. Therefore, its economic potential is not realized, and the local population remains in poverty" (World Bank 2001b, 49).

After the 2005 midterm review, the World Bank noted:

> Discussions have taken place with Lesotho on how best to develop a transfrontier tourism strategy, including possible tourism routes and a single brand for the bioregion. Discussions were held . . . with the tourism sector to propose introducing a single marketing brand for the project area. This activity is important to both South Africa and Lesotho as current bed occupancy in the South African portion of the MDTP stands below 40% *i.e.* there is current surplus capacity which prevents further growth. The outcome of the single brand workshop was that a single brand will be developed to coincide with DEAT's [Department of Environmental Affairs and Tourism's] strategy to market TFCA's [Transfrontier Conservation Areas] in order to benefit from the 2010 Soccer World Cup. (2005, 12)

Leaving aside the preoccupation with the 2010 World Cup and the unsubstantiated remark about the economic potential of tourism to alleviate poverty, these statements show that the World Bank also saw a strong role for tourism in connecting conservation and development, especially in Lesotho. The Lesotho PCU, however, was not particularly happy with the single brand. The tourism specialist complained that "you need to brand a product and Lesotho does not have a product."[15] Because of this, they were "going to spend no money on branding."[16] Later, the Lesotho coordinator mentioned that the joint marketing strategy with South Africa was not the right thing for Lesotho, because the country was "marketing nothing."[17] He only agreed to it because "it stimulates transfrontier cooperation." In turn, the PCU engaged the Peace Parks Foundation to identify tourism nodes, such as Sani Top and Sehlabathebe National Park, to stimulate tourism exchanges with South Africa, especially in relation to the World Cup. Most of this was on the strategic level, which the coordinator believed is the level one needs to start from, after which it will "trickle down."[18]

Both PCUS focused the tourism component mostly on the macro, abstract level, but it was supposed to be a practical strategy linking biodiversity conservation and poverty reduction. Yet this is not as contradictory as it seems, since the reconstitution of an area in neoliberal terms is usually an imposed, even violent process, especially in a postcolonial context (Mbembe 2001, 56–57). In this case, the "refashioning of cultures," according to the "spirit of the time," through ecotourism is a more subtle, disciplinary process whereby marketing works to stimulate demand from clients (tourists) in response to which local people have to start behaving like entrepreneurs, to live up to this demand, for instance by providing so-called authenticity (see, e.g., West and Carrier 2004). This process is filled with struggles and contradictions. For one, in Lesotho, the Mokhotlong district officer for the Ministry of Tourism, Environment and Culture noted that Lesotho is not benefiting from tourism because tourists "don't leave a penny" in Lesotho.[19] PCU members also informally complained about the fact that South Africa's industry is much stronger and that it takes tourists in and out of Lesotho while leaving little for Lesotho's poor. Yet in South Africa the inequality between those who do and do not benefit from tourism is equally big (Rogerson 2004). In this respect, a local farmer from Ebusingatha in northern KwaZulu-Natal noted that there are many tourists going to the Cavern (a hotel nearby), but none come to his village. He blamed the "fact" that the community is not developed and therefore "cannot market itself."[20]

Despite these contradictions, the MDTP bioregional plan placed great importance on tourism. At a South African stakeholder workshop in March 2007 it was mentioned that scenic beauty and cultural heritage are "key resources" that are not yet "capitalized" on enough and should be marketed because they are a "goldmine." Moreover, someone pointed out that with the World Cup around the corner, "the time is right" and there might be more political will and political buy-in for issues around conservation and development if it is economically connected to tourism. Despite this emphasis, the bioregional plan does show a more nuanced awareness of the contradictions in tourism in the region than earlier MDTP documentation. It lays out these contradictions and concludes: "The general picture is then one of an underdeveloped tourism industry in Lesotho and certain portions in SA [South Africa] (including Free State and Eastern Cape) and an over development of the same kind of products in certain areas/nodes of South Africa. In addition, there is a lack of diversification of products in both countries" (MDTP 2007e, 65). However, the plan later returns to seamlessly repeat the earlier preoccupations:

> There are three key areas that need to be addressed for tourism to become entrenched as a viable additional livelihood option within the MDTFCA [Maloti-Drakensberg Transfrontier Conversation Area]. These key areas are directly linked to (i) the need for a single, effective, consolidated marketing brand and associated strategy for the Maloti Drakensberg Route, (ii) the need for a diverse set of tourism products in the region in order to access the diverse set of experiences associated with the region—including the development of the road and bulk infrastructure network within the Maloti Drakensberg Route and MDTFCA, and (iii) the need for a coordinated and effective investment strategy to encourage private sector investment in tourism in general, and more effective community-public-private partnerships to ensure viable community-based tourism enterprises. (MDTP 2007e, 69)

It seems then that interventions such as the MDTP are better aware of the contradictions and struggles inherent in tourism than they are with PES (possibly because of tourism's longer history). For example, the bioregional planner of the South African PCU had accepted that tourism is usually an add-on to diverse livelihoods "palettes" of local people rather than a complete alternative, recognizing the importance of land-based economies where many other tourism projects often "drag people off the land" and into the service sector (Dressler and Büscher 2008). Yet, in all, tourism has not benefited local people in the MDTP region much and this was acknowledged by the project. Two final points can therefore be noted about tourism. First, the focus on marketing and branding stimulates the further constitution of the Maloti-Drakensberg area in neoliberal terms. Second, tourism makes the importance of marketing in a project such as the MDTP more concrete than any other issue. However, this is accompanied by the openly accepted wisdom that image is more important than reality, which leads us to the bubble of neoliberal conservation.

The Bubble of Neoliberal Conservation

Like with the Boundless Southern Africa branding, this narrative on tourism in the MDTP explicates how neoliberal governance mechanisms for stimulating conservation and development linkages led to "derivative nature." Understanding the ways in which people and ecosystems interact in the Maloti-Drakensberg area became secondary; what mattered more was what tourists want (to see or to experience). The images longed for by the market determine the construction and value of the Maloti-Drakensberg area and the behavior of the people, not vice versa. Hence derivative nature: the investment of capital is focused on creating value out of meaning and images that nature and poverty ideally represent, rather than their contradictory realities. Tourism, operationalized as branding in the project, used natural scenery and poverty (i.e., primitiveness) as the "underlying assets" to generate value in the contemporary neoliberal political economy. Akin to the global financial market where the value of derivatives now far supersedes the value of their underlying assets, the discussion of tourism in the MDTP showed that the value of branding and creating infrastructure and regulatory frameworks for its market-based management were thought to provide greater value than the contradictory realities of its underlying assets. Tourism in the project, after all, "catered to perceptions, not reality."

Crucially, this catering to perceptions should be seen against the observation that tourism, or the project in general, had not benefited local people in the MDTP region much or made a big impact on the environment. This is where derivative nature leads to the bubble of neoliberal conservation. The investment in derivatives leads to the building of harmonious constructions of nature and poverty that become increasingly alienated from the natural environments and peoples they are derived from. Processes of virtualization and speculation set in, in order to attract investors (tourists and buyers of environmental services) and create and re-create value, with nature and communities as the collateral (see Carrier and West 2009). As a result, localized realities of nature and poverty are allowed to be alienated and forgotten as complex and contradictory spaces that deserve long-term engagement, human interaction, and critical understanding.

This is not to say that the realities of environmental degradation and social inequality fall off the neoliberal capitalist radar. The constructed and the real remain closely tied and highly interdependent. The importance attached to PES in the project testifies to this. According to Kovel (2002), capitalism has to be thoroughly realistic on one level, but it can only deal with this in terms of what is valued in market terms. Thus, on the one hand, the MDTP payments for environmental services report went to great lengths to present the intricate and complex technicalities of the water ecology of two catchment areas as a basis for a PES system in the Maloti-Drakensberg. On the other hand, it was an instrumental, positive-sum exercise that needed to leave out tricky questions that could problematize its findings, recommendations, and the associated political agenda of the authors whose career paths depended on this new trend (Li 2007). But the report did more. It opened new frontiers for capital:

> The land owners or users are essentially becoming the sellers of a range of products that have value to a diverse range of buyers. Those keen on receiving the additional baseflow might be the Department of Water Affairs and Forestry and/or large water users and utilities. The water could either be used to augment the ecological reserve, be sold as additional registered water use to a third party, or be bought by a third party to offset an increase in water use or streamflow reduction activity elsewhere. Both carbon and biodiversity have an international appeal, but in and through different markets. A multiple number of market permutations are therefore possible. (Mander 2007, 46–47)

The frontier is seen as an exciting development that allows economic value to flow through multiple "market permutations" (Mander 2007, 42, 49, 68). What is left out is that these market permutations and especially the "third-party" purchases could lead to very narrow (profit) pressures, rendering PES susceptible to speculation (Redford and Adams 2009). As with derivative markets internationally, market representations of the "ecosystem goods and services" by third parties could come under pressure from equity firms and investment brokers to exaggerate the value of the service in order to make a profit,[21] leading to the classic problems of overaccumulation and devaluation or destruction of capital (which evidently is what the MDTP would want the bioregion's environment *not* to be subjected to). But this is inherent to capitalism: to exploit the inherent tensions between reality and representation rather than appreciating and understanding uncomfortable complexities and contradictions. The sheer complexity of ecosystems and related social interaction exacerbates this tendency: "Since no one in fact can predict the outcome of the ecological crisis, or any of its constituent ecosystemic threads, the way is left open for optimistic denial, in short, minimization of the dangers, and inadequate responses taken for opportunistic motives rather than from a real appreciation of the problem" (Kovel 2002, 81).

In response, one might wonder why the bubble of neoliberal conservation does not burst, especially when James Carrier and Donald Macleod conceptualize this bursting by showing how it does not "accord with its goal of respecting and supporting local people," and it is clear that the MDTP brought few tangible social and environmental improvements to the Maloti-Drakensberg bioregion (2005, 319). The problem with Carrier and Macleod's otherwise incisive argument is that it gives epistemological primacy to the bubble, whereas the bubble and other, more contradictory realities are in fact mutually constituted in the global capitalist political economy. To explain this we need to recall the nature of contemporary capitalism and Porter's associated "two characteristic features" of the global knowledge structure: first, "there is an increasing tendency to negotiate or rework the fabric of understandings that constitute our notion of what is real," and second, "this reworking becomes effective not through centralized controls and directives but through its acceptance and reproduction at the micro-level" (1999, 138).

Building on the first feature, it becomes possible to purposefully use the tension between reality and image to espouse interpretations that are in favor of the bubble, even though it bursts all the time. This is why the bubble of neoliberal conservation is inherently antipolitical; it becomes a way to at least discursively adhere to contradictions (the bursts) in practice. In turn and as we shall see below, those who command the resources to create the bubble are also the most active in creating legitimacy and buy-in for it. At the same time, I have argued that a neoliberal alignment of interests takes place, and this brings us to the second feature. The constitution of the Maloti-Drakensberg polity in neoliberal terms is possible exactly because of the local microproduction and diffusion of tourism and PES assumptions and images. As Peck and Tickell argue, "one of the fundamental features of neoliberalism is its pervasiveness as a system of *diffused power*" (2002, 400; emphasis in original). In turn, there are systemic features in the politics of this diffusion. A politics around consensus, antipolitics, and marketing enables and facilitates the diffusion and local micro-reproduction of neoliberal conservation through devolved governance mechanisms.

The neoliberal modes of political conduct and devolved governance employed in the Maloti-Drakensberg intervention seem to suggest that the implementers deliberately invested in derivatives to avoid the risks of local struggles and all the contradictions associated with modern-day human-nature interactions. This, like with financial derivatives, would allow capitalism to become increasingly self-referential and create value out of itself, further fueling the bubble of neoliberal conservation. But this reasoning only holds so far. Explaining the bubble does not render the material consequences of the MDTP less important, even if the intervention was mostly focused on the abstract.

Material Consequences

The MDTP seemed to be a peculiar kind of intervention, particularly for its focus on the abstract, on discourse, and on the enabling environment through research, planning, and even practical devolved governance strategies. In the wider conservation and development arena, however, many interventions nowadays focus on the abstract and discursive through empowerment, capacity building, benchmarking, and especially policy advice (Mosse 2005). This general focus on the abstract makes it all the more important to emphasize material consequences. In fact, it necessitates a different idea of what is meant by "material" to include resources, either monetary or other, that enable actors to pursue particular political agendas and influence social relations (see Neves 2010). Commanding resources can make a major difference in pursuing political agendas, as the example of the Peace Parks Foundation showed. Another example was the golf estates, which have very particular ideas about the Maloti-Drakensberg and command resources to alter material realities accordingly. Theirs was a specific notion of the landscape where pristine nature goes hand in hand with luxury residences, golf courses, and conspicuous modes of consumption that cause further direct and indirect material consequences.[22]

Needless to say, few of the local people surrounding the golf courses in the Maloti-Drakensberg command the resources to access and enjoy these estates. If they are "lucky," they could get some employment, but otherwise the estates mean a further privatization of land and diminished access to natural resources. This was certainly clear from the Royal Maluti golf estate on the border with Lesotho. Though the land was in private hands before Royal Maluti took over, local Basotho did have de facto access to the land, and thus to some modest (natural) resources. With the transfer of the land, they will lose this access, as the estate representative made it clear that the area would be fenced off so as to provide guests with optimal "security." Security and access to material resources (and land) for some means loss of resources and access to land for others. With the developmental pressure on the Maloti-Drakensberg area set to continue, these struggles will inevitably become more pronounced.

Commanding resources can also help in gaining a competitive edge in the discursive, abstract realm in which the MDTP pursued most of its intervention. In the case of the MDTP, a substantial sum that flowed into the area through the intervention was geared toward constructing neoliberal discourses that give some groups a material advantage over others and further strengthen particular political agendas and related subjectivities and disciplinary tactics created to control and direct people (Mbembe 2000, 2001). Interestingly, the PES baseline study makes the same argument:

> The Maloti Drakensberg Transfrontier Conservation and Development Programme offers a window of opportunity to implement . . . a payment system. The mountain ecosystem has the capability to make a significant impact on mountain communities' well-being and on distant urban residents well-being if resources are managed appropriately and strategically. *The resources available to this project (MDTCDP [Maloti-Drakensberg Transfrontier Conservation and Development Project]), both internally and externally (by means of partners), and the willingness of the MDTCDP to use economics for conservation action, generates a practical opportunity to initiate a market development process in the next three years.* (Diederichs and Mander 2004, 46; emphasis added)

Hence, the MDTP consultants are very much aware that material resources matter. In the case of the MDTP, these resources were put to use in a very specific way, namely to strengthen and deepen the neoliberalization of the Maloti-Drakensberg polity.

On an even more practical level, the material consequences of the PES study can be illustrated by pointing out that the MDTP paid a group of consultants from Pietermaritzburg, South Africa, a substantial sum of money to do the baseline study. One of the recommendations of this study was the bigger pilot project, which the MDTP eagerly followed up on. It then paid 1,174,493 rand for the new project to a group of consultants; several of whom were also involved in the baseline study. In turn, we saw how this project actively worked to further construct the MDTP area in neoliberal terms. Ironically, then, instead of spending this money on more community-oriented practical work, it was spent on strengthening the very political economy in which local communities so far have been marginal.

But the material consequences go further. Included in the commanding of resources I also regard the resources needed to engage in the politics of neoliberal conservation, most especially the marketing struggle. The story as told in this book is obviously a marginal interpretation to the arenas and networks where PES, tourism, and neoliberal conservation are trendy, where it is necessary to stay on top of the latest developments and market their success. It is interestingly therefore that the marketing of the MDTP PES endeavors has been quickly making the rounds. One example from the policy world is a report by the NGO Swedish Water House (Forslund et al. 2009). According to the document, "the report is a joint collaboration between member organizations of The Global Environmental Flows Net-work," which includes such influential organizations as the International Union for Conservation of Nature, World Wildlife Fund, the United Nations Environment Programme, and UNESCO. Remarkably, since the PES project had not yet been implemented, the report concludes:

> PES has proven to be a viable option to enhance supply in the catchments of the Maloti Drakensberg Mountains on the border between Lesotho and South Africa. Land use in the surrounding grassland has reduced stream flow in the dry season and intensified flow in wet season. This has resulted in seasonal water shortage, reduced water quality, soil erosion, reduced productivity and increased water vulnerability. The Maloti Drakensberg Transfrontier Project showed that implementing a PES system . . . would be an economically and institutionally feasible way to incorporate ecosystem services into water management. There are significant benefits to be gained by both local ecosystem services producers (the mountain communities) and by the broader user or catchment community: less water vulnerability, more jobs in the region, and improved land quality that can stimulate the development of other economic options, such as tourism, game farming, improved grazing and natural products harvesting. The Transfrontier Project also showed that such a system is desirable from a rural development and

social equity perspective, rewarding those who maintain a water supply engine but who are spatially and economically marginalised. (Forslund et al. 2009, 31)

Not only does the report insinuate that the results of the PES project have already been ascertained but some of the language is exactly the same as that of the MDTP report, providing ample evidence of the power of networks that take the message of the MDTP consultants at face value.

An example from the academic world is an article by Jane Turpie, Christo Marais, and James Blignaut (2008) in *Ecological Economics*. It includes some of the same authors as the MDTP PES reports.[23] While the article deals with another South African environmental program, it is clear that it aims to advance PES in general, which its subtitle makes clear: "Evolution of a Payments for Ecosystem Services Mechanism That Addresses Both Poverty and Ecosystem Service Delivery in South Africa." The article approvingly refers to the MDTP as a one of the "conservation initiatives" where "conservation planners in South Africa are currently looking to PES as potentially playing a major role" (796). Interestingly, it then cites the MDTP baseline study (Diederichs and Mander 2004). Another example is an article in the popular science magazine *Environmental Scientist*, coauthored again by one of the same consultants hired by the MDTP (Mander and Everard 2008). It argues,

South Africa's innovative water laws, which enshrine the principles of equity, sustainability and efficiency, have enabled the development of some of the most advanced approaches to PES in the world. The Maloti Drakensberg Transfrontier Project [PES report, *sic*], published in 2007, explored hydrological and economic linkages between uplands that "produce" water and the consumption of water lower down in selected river catchments, progressing this into the design of market mechanisms for payment from consumers for the protection, restoration and management of upper catchment areas critical for dependable run-off of clean water. (33)

In sum, the actors that benefitted materially from the MDTP are in a position to command resources to actively try and control the interpretation of their own work around PES. Needless to say, similar examples of local community voices and interpretations are not publicized as widely, at least not in the places (such as the institutions around the Global Environmental Flows Network) that matter when it comes to deciding how public resources around conservation and development issues are spent. In sum, it is crucial not to lose sight of the material realities behind the bubble of neoliberal conservation, as in many ways they shape the structures that create and sustain social inequalities and environmental degradation.

Marketing the Local

What, then, about the local (material) realities in the Maloti-Drakensberg region, particularly the mountain communities that were said to benefit significantly from PES, tourism, and other MDTP activities? Or how to characterize the MDTP's "actually existing neoliberalism" (Brenner and Theodore 2002)? The argument here extends that of the last section in that those with the initiative and the resources often also instigate the disciplining necessary to create acceptance and neoliberal alignment at the micro-level (Porter 1999). It is important in this respect to make explicit something that has been implicit throughout the book, namely that conservation and development interventions are increasingly like marketplaces where commodities are traded (Mosse 2005; Olivier de Sardan 2005). These commodities are not merely ordinary goods and services. They also (and predominantly) include expertise, knowledge, legitimacy, branding, and so forth. Actors in the conservation and development market are highly aware of these special features. Legitimacy in particular is seen as a valuable and scarce good which actors go to great lengths to acquire (see Li 2007; Underhill 2003). Chapter three showed how this quest led to superficial legitimacy in the MDTP proposal, while throughout the project references to communities, especially, were used to legitimate the intervention. The Lesotho PCU and some South African stakeholders honestly believed that this was crucial for project success, while the more skeptical South African PCU used similar references to support its approach. Important here is that, despite their differences, both PCUs had the resources to create buy-in and —arguably superficial—legitimacy at the local level.

Whether they succeeded in creating local buy-in is doubtful, but it was clear that there was plenty of pressure on the PCUs to do so. One example of this pressure came from discussions during a South African stakeholder workshop on the bioregional strategic plan in March 2007. Despite extensive consultation, many in the audience commented that the bioregional plan was still supply driven. It was suggested that the PCU "make it demand driven." One participant even advised that they "put a spin doctor on it" and to add a "seventh outcome on marketing" to get the plan "accepted by everybody." Almost everyone seemed to agree with this comment, and it became a major issue throughout the workshop. The point for most participants was not whether the plan *was* demand driven. It had to be *made* demand driven through marketing. Legitimacy in conservation and development is something increasingly sought through the production of buy-in and the political conduct of marketing.

How does this relate to the targets of this production of buy-in? Because the project was mainly focused on planning and discourse, few community benefits were realized through the MDTP. Even where local community activities were instigated, as we saw in chapter 5, the project only made a marginal and superficial impact on the lives of local people (although some received certain benefits from the project). Despite this, the discourses and reports produced by the project remained littered with references to "communities" and the myriad of benefits they will come to receive in the future.

The MDTP PES program provides a good example. In the various reports discussed, there is continuous reference to the benefits, jobs, and additional income that the upstream or mountain communities will receive. The PES pilot project focused on two catchment areas (the Mnweni/Cathedral Peak and Eastern Cape Drakensberg areas), so it assumed that it is then apparent who the appropriate communities are. From my own research in the same areas, however, this is far from clear. For one, the PES reports make no distinction between what Alfons Mosimane and Karl Aribeb (2005) refer to as "communities of use" and "communities of place." The upstream users of the catchment areas are seen as communities of place, whereas the wider community that uses these areas is much larger. This was evident in a community meeting organized by the MDTP in Lesotho, just over the border from the Mnweni/Cathedral Peak catchment area, in an area known as Liqobong. Liqobong is the catchment area for the Caledon River, and the MDTP had proposed a protected area to protect the catchment. This led to intense resistance from local communities, who feared loss of access to this land. Upon closer inspection, however, these local communities did not appear to be very local. They included people from the entire surrounding area, including from the South African Mnweni/Cathedral Peak area, who all had a stake in the area (Wittmayer and Büscher 2010).

It became clear during my further research that the same applied to the whole Maloti-Drakensberg mountain area: people are very mobile and travel across the border regularly to collect resources. Who then is the PES project going to compensate? Again, this question was conveniently left out and replaced with reassuring-sounding sentences about how communities and tribal authorities are interested in an extra income stream, which is presented as proof that PES is feasible and desirable. But local realities are of course much more complex. Much of the area, for example, suffers from various types of criminal activities. People do not only cross the border to collect natural resources; many also cross the border to steal livestock and illegally trade cannabis. On both sides of the border, people complained bitterly about the "people on the other side" stealing their cattle and taking what was not theirs. This reality imposed itself on the MDTP to such an extent that the intervention felt compelled to initiate an unforeseen security component. The MDTP midterm review says, "The issue of security for visitors and management personnel in the transfrontier area was not addressed specifically in the Project Appraisal Document. Nor is it mentioned as a risk factor in the original or modified logframes. Yet it is widely appreciated that tourism, on which both countries are pinning their hopes for economic prosperity in general, and sustainable revenue generation for conservation in particular, is critically dependent on national and international perceptions of safety in the destination areas" (MDTP 2005b, 14). Hence, even though the MDTP felt it had to react to this inconvenient reality (that was not addressed in the project proposal, or mentioned as a risk), it rarely touches on this issue in publications such as the PES report, but it is clear that this reality will influence PES if implemented.

One last example is in order, namely the material realities of the Balala lihloliloeng me o phele Malefiloane (we conserve to live out of what we conserved), the local handicraft group established by the MDTP I mentioned in the introduction. This example made abundantly clear that the material realities of local communities are radically different from the discursive and planning realities of project implementers. And while the members of Balala lihloliloeng me o phele wanted to market their wares, they did not have the resources or skills to do so. The MDTP organized one trip to take them to the nearby South African town of Clarens—a local art center—but what came out of this trip was very little in the way of added income for the group. As such, it does make sense that the project aimed to help build capacity, but local reality again proved much coarser than is stated in the many documents. Capacity building was seen as a package to be given to the locals, while the community facilitator made it clear that it was a process fraught with difficulties and struggle. Local violence, disputes, and competition often made it hard to hold meetings, which, according to the community facilitator, the MDTP still used to "tick off" an item on the work plan. Some of these difficulties and struggles are mentioned in reports, but most of these stay internal and do not reach a broader public. In the more-public pieces that needed to set up the MDTP area as an environmental-services market or an attractive tourist attraction around the FIFA World Cup and beyond, these issues quickly disappeared. Neoliberal conservation becomes neoliberal business, which Jan Nederveen Pieterse notes "is characterized by an inverse relationship between marketing and product, with more effort and quality going into marketing than the product. Customers are supposed to buy the marketing rather than the product and salespersons often begin to believe their own story" (2004, 129). This is both a discursive and material reality clearly corroborated by the MDTP experience. The project is all about the local and benefits for local people, but actual local, material realities and the messiness of local life are habitually left out of sight, particularly in the marketing pieces that have to convince donors about the future projects and benefits that are always around the corner.

Conclusion

Analyzing the practical devolved governance strategies of the MDTP reaffirms the project's drive toward the abstract level of discourse. While previous chapters already noted that the pressures toward consensus and antipolitics led important actors in the MDTP to focus on the realm of discourse and the politics of marketing, it is the practical devolved governance strategies of PES and tourism that truly provide evidence for the argument that discourse is the preferred level of engagement and even implementation. Discourse becomes the new reality, making the increasing gap between rhetoric and reality of less concern to implementers and planners. It is the level of discourse one must master and survive in within conservation and development, not the grounded struggles and complexities that dominate rhetoric. This explains why there was surprisingly little debate within the MDTP on the actual impact of the intervention on the environment and poverty levels in the Maloti-Drakensberg area.[24] Impact remained a preoccupation that was shrouded in the future positive, to be realized by proper planning and the further reconstitution of the area in neoliberal terms.

Yet, following the logic of derivative nature, why would one want to find out whether something works in practice or whether some explanations hold a greater truth value when legitimacy is calculated in quantitative monetary terms rather than critical understanding or the intrinsic quality of an explanation or product? Not surprisingly, this tendency is also reflected in the wider conservation community, which, like the MDTP, is equally enchanted by superficially seductive neoliberal conservation rhetoric (see Büscher 2008; Dresser 2009). Like development more generally, the bubble of neoliberal conservation becomes immune to criticism and "devoid of reference to questions [it] cannot address, or that might cast doubt upon the completeness of [its] diagnoses or the feasibility of [its] solutions" (Li 2007, 11). This, however, is also not new. Kent Redford and William Adams argue: "Conservation has a history of placing great faith in new ideas and approaches that appear to offer dramatic solutions to humanity's chronic disregard for nature (e.g., sustainable development, community conservation, sustainable use, wilderness), only to become disillusioned with them a few years later. The payment for ecosystem services framework fits this model disturbingly well" (2009, 785).

As the chapter has shown though, this new trend and other neoliberal activities, such as the tourism strategy, do have material consequences. The resources of the project are appropriated mostly by people who further the constitution of the MDTP area in neoliberal terms, while they also have the resources and networks to market the so-called appropriate way of interpreting these events within the narrow spaces of the international neoliberal conservation and development arena. All the while, local realities in the Maloti-Drakensberg area remain alienated from these concerns, and inequality is further cemented into the fabric of society where those who command resources also actively produce the buy-in and construct the "success" necessary to feign legitimacy. Needless to say, this practice of fueling the bubble of neoliberal conservation could have dire consequences if degradation of biodiversity or the inequalities between people are still realities, irrespective of intricate constructions and reified representations. It is this epistemological tension between reality and representation that is at the heart of the major environmental struggles of our time.

conclusion

The relation between representation and reality under

capitalism has always been problematic.

David Harvey, *The Enigma of Capital and the Crises of Capitalism*

The frontiers of conservation are ever changing; its parameters
shift and vary constantly. This keeps many actors on their toes
as they try to keep up with new trends and developments,
adjusting and reinventing themselves and institutions accordingly. Above all, they work hard to keep conservation legitimate
in and functional to a global political economy that is alienated
from ecological and developmental realities. The result is neoliberal conservation, and one of its latest vehicles is transfrontier conservation. Under the "peace parks" banner, conservation agents have been able to reach out to new audiences and
form new partnerships. These new alliances cut across public,
private, and community domains, (re)aligning old divides on
new foundations. The possibilities in this process seem infinite, yet the new frontiers tightly align with a long history of
contradiction-riddled capitalist development. This, however,
has spurred on many actors even more. Frontiers *need* to be
transformed; they *must* be overcome, so it seems. Conservation has no choice, I was told on many occasions; it has to
realign itself to the powers that be. That is the practical way
forward. The result is an awkward situation in which neoliberal conservation, especially in its transfrontier incarnation,

produces ever-grander discourses seemingly free of contradictions, while these saturate its practices.

The book aimed to build a critical analytical framework to study transfrontier conservation areas as contemporary manifestations of the neoliberal governance of conservation and development in Southern Africa. The crucial building block in this framework is the distinction between neoliberalism as a mode of political conduct and a mode of devolved governance. While these two "sides" of neoliberalism hybridize in practice, they present two analytically separate realms that enable the constitution of a system loaded with contradictions. Neoliberal modes of devolved governance have become the general (self-)regulatory, structural principles for (rational, economic) behavior in conservation, particularly through tourism and payments for environmental services.[1] The book showed how proponents of transfrontier conservation were quick to align with and give new impetus to these modes of governance, both on the regional level and in the Maloti-Drakensberg intervention. In turn, these mechanisms worked to reinforce a focus on the abstract through branding, marketing, and the building of an "enabling environment" to discipline people and nature into correct market behavior. The result is a broad conservation frontier characterized by increasingly complex epistemological maneuvering with due consequences for the politics of conservation.

Peace parks were a way to obtain a more in-depth understanding of neoliberalism's contemporary modes of political conduct in the conservation and development arena, and to better take "account of the ways in which ideologies of neoliberalism are themselves produced and reproduced through institutional forms and political action" (Peck and Tickell 2002, 383). Three modes of politics are essential in this (re)production: consensus, antipolitics, and marketing. All three mutually reinforce each other to constitute neoliberal devolved governance practices within transfrontier governance structures and intervention strategies that link conservation and development in southern Africa. This concluding chapter reviews the main tenets of these politics of neoliberal conservation, and the central contradictions it stimulates and masks. By doing so, a final objective of the book emerges, namely to assess the potential for progressive possibilities in the frontier struggles over what constitute reality and representation in human-nature relationships.

The Politics of Neoliberal Conservation

The contemporary politics of neoliberal conservation arose from the hybridization of postcolonial demands for socially inclusive conservation and an increasingly hegemonic neoliberalism (see Dressler 2009; McCarthy 2005; Sullivan 2006; West 2006). This increasingly forced conservation and development interventions to speak using rhetoric of consensus to capture as broad a buy-in as possible and retain legitimacy. This process is not new. Colonial interventions often employed similar rhetoric to make it seem as though "native" and colonial interests were compatible. However, this could not hide the fact that they were treated inherently unequally. The colonial agenda led to the steady rise and intensification of racial capitalism over the centuries in southern Africa, which affected the regional political economy in penetrating and lasting ways, particularly with respect to the marginalization of local or native interests (see Mamdani 1996; Mbembe 2001). Conservation was central in these developments, which was exemplified by early concerns over overstocking, the cutting of trees, and competition for natural resources in colonial frontiers. Although conservation was later overshadowed by the capitalist subjecting of the region's peoples to the emergent commodity production of gold, diamond, and mineral resources, it remained crucial through the rise and fall of apartheid and the further development of the capitalist political economy.

Conservation in southern Africa cannot be seen outside of the political economy in which it developed, and one of my aims has been to clarify this link. How different, then, are contemporary conservation interventions, which, while further cementing conservation into the current political economy, purge all historical awareness and effects of this same political economy from their discourses. Instead, interventions work hard to accommodate the pressures of the historical demands for socially inclusive conservation and hegemonic neoliberalism into a consensus framework that increases the amount of wins desired (Igoe and Brockington 2007). The peace park discourse appears as the epitome of this trend. Not only does it cater to biodiversity and local communities but it also claims to stimulate international cooperation between states, increase business opportunities, provide prospects for nongovernmental organizations and much more. On the regional level, dominant actors such as the Department of Environmental Affairs and Tourism (DEAT) and the Peace Parks Foundation stated that transfrontier conservation could cater for nearly all different stakeholders. The case study of the Maloti-Drakensberg Trans-frontier Project (MDTP) showed how the preparation phases and the intervention itself also went to great lengths to try and capture "all actors," "all themes," and "all activities" under the proposal and the bioregional planning framework.

But retaining the image of all-inclusiveness and consensus in the face of growing numbers of actors capable of critically scrutinizing and resisting a political agenda requires a second mode of political conduct: antipolitics, or the political act of doing away with politics. Based on neoliberalism's universalist ambitions and the associated drive toward consensus, the book showed that the competing interests that determine social or public outcomes are managed by suppressing political debate through political strategies of antipolitics. On the regional level, it was the Peace Parks Foundation above all that aimed to do so by amplifying the peace parks discourse to huge proportions and presenting it as the telos of conservation—a model of meaning to which people should attach their hope and fortunes. Other spectacles, such as the 2010 World Cup, boosted these dynamics, further increasing the value of Transfrontier Conservation Areas (TFCAS). On the case-study level, however, the real political intricacies of the antipolitics strategy were revealed. The study of a transfrontier project with two different Project Coordination Units (PCUs) allowed for a more refined understanding of antipolitics that goes beyond the standard interpretation of the concept as technical or instrumental (see Ferguson 1994; Li 2007).

Based on work by Andreas Schedler (1997), I distinguish between the moral and instrumental antipolitical strategies employed by the PCUs to make something happen in, and get something out of, the intensely politicized environments they were working in. The Lesotho PCU chose the moral high ground and argued from a position of seemingly undebatable moral tenets of community-based conservation. The South African PCU employed instrumental antipolitics that emphasized a rational, technical high ground. Ultimately the MDTP became a hybrid of both, although influential regional actors clearly favored Lesotho's approach, thereby politically marginalizing the South African PCU. But antipolitical dynamics were not solely the purview of those at the helm of the intervention. In explaining how local communities pragmatically forfeited their own political agenda to obtain livelihood benefits, I tried to present a nuanced multidirectionality in conservation and development interventions that does not solely acknowledge marginal actors in terms of their domination by others.

Taken together, the political strategies of consensus and antipolitics reified the status quo and stimulated a focus on discourse through planning and research: the realm where—ostensibly—contradictions can be avoided. Ostensibly, because contradictions abounded: the vast inequality in resources and access to key political and business figures between the Peace Parks Foundation and marginal actors; the irony of the South African PCU's challenge of the consensus of the MDTP proposal while eventually facing the same challenge of obtaining consensus for its twenty-year plan and its implied implementation; and the expectations of those planning the MDTP that cooperation and friendship would develop when the actual intervention was characterized by tensions rather than friendship. These are just some of the empirical dynamics applicable here. In order then to manage these contradictions and retain legitimacy for a concept such as peace parks or an intervention such as the MDTP, constant discursive grooming and spin are necessary. Nonconformity regarding consensus and antipolitics is countered, or rendered less visible, by the disciplining force of the third political strategy: marketing.

The political strategy of marketing involves the manipulation of abstraction in order to gain competitive advantage in the conservation and development marketplace. This works out in two main ways. First, we saw that especially the Peace Parks Foundation used modern marketing tools to sell the peace parks discourse so that consensus about its importance and global applicability is not imposed, but comes from actors themselves. This is marketing in the way the commercial sector works: the instilling of a desire or need so that the purchase of a specific product becomes the embodied choice (see Arvidsson 2005; Kovel 2002).[2] But there is also a second, more refined, type of marketing, namely the manipulation of abstraction on an everyday basis. Based on the analysis of the Maloti-Drakensberg intervention, I conclude that within highly competitive environments such as conservation and development marketplaces, actors such as the World Bank, businesses and consultants, but also communities and the state, increasingly use every opportunity to gain competitive advantage over others to strengthen their brands. This deeper penetration of marketing into the lifeworlds of actors signifies the neoliberal ambition of becoming the global social order. However, not all actors have equal access to the marketing struggle. Those with more resources are better able to access and influence public images in their favor.

Overall, the three modes present an exceptionally strong and resilient set of political practices that maintains legitimation for interventions as well as masks the "uneasy contradictions" inherent in present-day conservation and development.[3] However, by themselves these are not able to constitute transfrontier conservation and development in southern Africa in neoliberal terms. Modes of political conduct stimulate and thrive on neoliberal modes of devolved governance—especially those revolving around competition and commodification. It is these mechanisms that truly allow the politics of neoliberal conservation to be summed up as contradictory realities and reified representations.

Constructing Contradictory Realities

Development schemes, as Tania Li (2007) has pointed out, always leave contradictions in their wake. I have argued and empirically shown that the politics of neoliberal conservation lead to a very particular, far-reaching contradiction: between the (often passionate) struggle to accept and do something about the reality of degrading biodiversity and worsening poverty and doing so through means that place representation over reality and fuel the exploitation of the construction of nature. My point here relates to the argument that neoliberal modes of political conduct should be seen within an "emergent abstract knowledge structure" that is based on the "increasing tendency to negotiate or rework the fabric of understandings that constitute our notion of what is real" (Porter 1999, 138). Practical modes of devolved governance, such as tourism and payments for environmental services, are constructed along these lines and thus contribute to the same contradiction.

The results included a regional TFCA route—where it is advertised that one can visit nine countries in five days—and the Maloti-Drakensberg route, which were, in PFF founder Anton Rupert's words, supposed to alleviate stress for the "affluent Western man" while providing "alternatives to subsistence living" for "poverty-stricken" Africans (Peace Parks Foundation 2000, 2). The results also included resettlements in the Great Limpopo and the overall poor offerings to local people other than being "enabled" and "incentivized" to start selling "environmental services." Noting these same contradictions, Paige West and Daniel Brockington argue that "it is ironic that African transboundary conservation areas, which can require displacement and fuel ethnic tensions, have sought popular support as 'peace parks'" (2006, 613). Based on my framework around the politics of neoliberal conservation, these contradictory realities are not just explained but in fact exploited in order to gain competitive advantage. That is an even greater irony. In the logic of derivative nature, the images and technocratic representations around people and environmental services were deemed more important than the contradictory realities they engendered or were to address. Neoliberal conservation does not cater for reality; it caters for perceptions.

Representation and reality find themselves in an awkward relationship in neoliberal conservation. But, as pointed out by Harvey in the opening quote of this chapter, it builds on a long tradition in capitalism. In Joel Kovel's words:

> The capitalist has to be thoroughly realistic on one level, but insofar as he is immersed in commodity exchange, he is also subject to a high degree of wishful thinking. Success in the imponderable market depends a great deal upon instilling confidence and assurance that such and such will really sell, for whether such and such actually sells depends in part upon whether people believe in it. This attitude, so essential to huckstering and 'hustling customers,' is normally balanced by shrewdness of one kind or another. However, where, as with the ecological crisis, the shrewdness is misplaced because the situation is incomprehensible, then the all-too-human traits of denying reality and resorting to wishful thinking come to the fore. Since no one in fact can predict the outcome of the ecological crisis, or any of its constituent ecosystemic threads, the way is left open for optimistic denial, in short, minimization of the dangers, and inadequate responses taken for opportunistic motives rather than from a real appreciation of the problem. (Kovel 2002, 81)

Hence, within a political economy subject(ed) to the legitimacy of the market, it actually makes good sense to emphasize discourse over practice: this is the realm where consensus can be achieved, and where reality can be sugarcoated or constructed so that it leads to competitive advantage. The discursive level becomes a distinct type of reality; something that I have termed the "bubble of neoliberal conservation." Evidence on both the regional and the MDTP level showed that many in conservation and development make a living out of abstraction, out of paper and policy, and they often even prefer to engage implementation on this level (such as with tourism in the MDTP). From a critical perspective, one could even conclude that the retreat into this bubble offers greater levels of security than do complex struggles on the ground (see, e.g., Büscher and Dressler 2007). Or, stated differently, value in neoliberal conservation shifts from the contradictory, mundane realities of nature and communities to their derivatives or ideal (spectacular) representations (see Büscher 2010b; Igoe 2010).

The epistemological reality-representation struggle in conservation and development has become one of the major struggles of our time (witness the debates around climate change). What is at stake is the way we see, experience, and understand reality and whether it indeed continues to be increasingly pervaded by neoliberal logics of economic reductionism. For now this epistemological contradiction continues to be fed, amounting to a bubble that is bound to burst sooner or later. At the same time, there are cracks in the bubble. More precisely, the political strategies of consensus, antipolitics, and marketing are risky and enmeshed in intensifying struggles—exactly because they fashion the further separation between representation and reality. With neoliberal expansion continuing unabated in transfrontier conservation, political strategies that (ex ante) rely on image rather than grounded realities—even if these are always constructed—risk losing "real appreciation" of conservation and development problems, thereby opening them up for predatory interpretation that is focused on competitive gain rather than critical understanding (see, e.g., Quarles van Ufford, Giri, and Mosse 2003). Nils Peterson, Markus Peterson, and Tarla Peterson phrase this succinctly: "The shift towards consensus in conservation planning will have deleterious environmental consequences if continued at its current rate. If social dominance alone constitutes reality, powerful conservation metaphors such as sustainable development will be colonized by proponents of the most powerful social construction of reality, and the conservation community will be rendered powerless to challenge the dominant economic growth and efficiency paradigm for decision making" (2005, 766).

While these arguments lead me to conclude that the chances for peace parks to contribute to just, humane and, diverse conservation and development constructions or broader nature-society relations are rather slim (see W. Adams and Jeanrenauld 2008), this does not mean that nothing constructive happened in the research sites I studied. It is, for example, important to note that strong bonds between various people and institutions in

Lesotho and South Africa have been established. Even if the PCUs did not get along well, the very fact that they were confronted with each other meant that they had to reflect on these experiences, and learn about each other's political strategies and sensitivities. Many staff members from South Africa noted that they had never been to Lesotho or even thought about visiting the country. Hence, new engagements can create opportunities for critical understanding and mutual appreciation, just as they can trigger conflict (Quarles van Ufford, Giri, and Mosse 2003). Whether these engagements become meaningful in a conservation and development context depends on how actors deal with the differences and contradictions that invariably emerge.

Importantly, neoliberal models and contradictions are resisted and have their limits. On the regional level we saw that several organizations do not agree with the peace parks discourse as put forth by the Peace Parks Foundation, including staff members from the DEAT. In the MDTP case, we saw communities criticizing the intervention, and the second World Bank task-team leader taking a more critical stance toward payments for environmental services. Active resistance to neoliberal conservation brought in by the peace parks discourse or the Maloti-Drakensberg intervention was minimal though.[4] Whereas criticism was plenty during interviews and behind closed doors, actual resistance was limited and only indirectly focused on some of the implementers or the World Bank. This is perhaps explained by the fact that the MDTP was not primarily focused on "on-the-ground" local implementation, but even on the regional level there was limited active resistance against the establishment of TFCAS.[5] Not even the expelling of people from Mozambique's Limpopo National Park created the controversies that could have been expected considering the scale of the issue. As of yet, it appears that the neoliberal constitution of southern African transfrontier conservation is able to manage the contradictions it stimulates, but this of course might change in the (near) future. With the further implementation of transfrontier conservation in southern Africa, it remains to be seen exactly how challenges to neoliberal modes of political conduct and devolved governance will be dealt with. Quite likely, coercion and discipline will have to move beyond the politics of marketing and become more direct or even violent in order to safeguard further neoliberal expansion.

Progressive Possibilities

But is it not possible to go beyond mere neoliberal expansion? Or does this entail an obligatory engagement in the described modes of politics, rendering more-progressive possibilities futile? I argue to the contrary. Consensus, antipolitics, and marketing are not inherently neoliberal. While they fit the neoliberal political economy extremely well, they could lead to different ends. And this is the crux: they are means for structuring and legitimating particular ends, not ends in themselves. These modes of politics currently work to further a particular postcolonial political economy grounded in a capitalist mode of production and focused on creating capitalist sovereignties, as in the subjectivities and disciplinary tactics that control and direct people (see Mbembe 2000, 2001). This should be explicated at all times. In turn, it must be made clear that, in Sian Sullivan's words, "the proliferating freedoms and futures espoused by free-market environmentalism simultaneously close off possibilities for other freedoms and futures in how relationships between human and non-human worlds are practiced and expressed" (2009, 24). At the very least, then, the task for critical research is to open up these possibilities and to ensure that they remain wide open. What seems to be a closed framework of neoliberal modes of political conduct can and must be (re)opened. In fact, this has been one of the main reasons for the book: the critical understanding of the politics that further entrench the status quo can help to make explicit the more structural ends of political conduct and to bring back into view what continues to be constructed out of sight.[6]

Progressive possibilities in the (scholarly) arena of human-nature relations should be firmly embedded in and build on the work done in political ecology over the last decades,[7] with an emphasis on the political. In line with the argument of the book, the suggestions I make relate mostly to the debate around the construction of nature, about which Aletta Biersack notes:

> The constructionist position has fuelled a debate, ontological and epistemological, about whether (first) nature actually exists (the realist position) or is only construction (the constructionist position), and, if it does exist, whether it can be known as such or whether every attempt to know it necessarily results in another subjective construction rather than in objective facts. I dare to say that the argument that there is no

nature, only "nature," a construction, has little appeal for most political ecologists, for whom the stakes must be real and material if they are to be fully political. (Biersack 2006, 27)

It should be clear that I agree with this statement, especially because my research shows that the "real" and "material" as discursive and nondiscursive categories are becoming increasingly foreign to conservation and development interventions yet continue to haunt and affect them intimately. However, "to be fully political" can be taken further still.

If indeed the reality and representation struggle in conservation and development has become one of the major struggles of our time, then this should be tackled head-on. *How* will not be easy. As more and more people become accustomed to the fast-changing imagery of the realities around them, they also get more accustomed to regarding information, knowledge and truth-statements as mere constructions. This dramatically complicates any politics, let alone those based on ideas about fundamental truth-statements (Harvey, 1996). Less dramatically, it also means that we all contribute to the modes of political conduct I have distinguished in this book: we all play the games of consensus, antipolitics, and marketing to some degree. The challenge then becomes how to mediate these modes of politics while challenging the underlying currents of continuously increasing neoliberalism as devolved governance in all aspects of society including our own lifeworlds (Kovel 2002). This is where the findings of the book can add to the "political" in "political ecology."

First, it is necessary to continue the infusion of anthropology- and geography-dominated political ecology with influences from political science, especially international relations. Above all, this involves more clearly defining and conceptualizing politics, power, governance, and so forth (see, e.g., Paulson, Gezon, Watts 2003), and, crucially, linking the ethnographic to the abstract debates surrounding these concepts (Ferguson 2006). It is the latter especially where I feel that political ecology could find fruitful new avenues in research and writing. By presenting a multilevel analysis, I have aimed to do exactly that: to be sensitive to ethnographic details while making explicit how these connect to larger debates, drawing for instance on political science interpretations of such a well-known but little-developed concept in political ecology as antipolitics.

Second, political ecology also has to go beyond "specifying" the political (Paulson, Gezon, and Watts 2003, 209), and indeed *be* more political: to accept that science is inherently political and to make a constructive political stance, especially toward the many perverse effects of neoliberal conservation and to make these concrete. Here, political ecology could consider taking inspiration from recent aidnography that emphasizes critical engagement with conservation and development practioners (see, e.g., Lewis et al. 2003; Mosse 2004, 2005; Quarles van Ufford, Giri, and Mosse 2003) and take this into new (social, political) terrains.[8] In the light of pressures toward different kinds of antipolitics, also within the arena of academia that itself is increasingly subjected to economic reductionism, this seems to be an issue of the utmost pertinence. However, it is crucially important that this should be done without falling into the trap of letting science be driven by politics. We need to heed the methodological implications of Bruno Latour's work, and in particular his argument that "the mistake is not in trying to do two things at once—every science is also a political project—the mistake is to interrupt the former because of the urgency of the latter" (2005, 259–60).

A third point relates to the intricacies of measuring legitimacy in terms of what the market wants, and its implications for the politics of democratic conservation. This argument must be seen in light of the hybridizing of public and private spheres where not only the penetration of the private sphere into the public sphere was stimulated, but also the opposite: public into private through the mainstreaming of conservation in production sectors. This has complicated traditional public structures for democratic accountability, leading to further emphasis on market legitimacy and associated neoliberal governance strategies such as competition and commodification. Further research should concentrate on this complication, focusing especially on issues of all-inclusiveness, consensus struggles, and so forth.

The final point is a call to considerably broaden the postmodern frontier, especially the reality and representation debates, beyond the academic realm. So far, the very nature of the debate has hindered this from taking place as even its participants get confused by the many levels of possible meta-analysis. With this in mind, it seems almost impossible to relate to the mediatized, "twittered" world of sound bites where knowledge seems to become irrelevant and old news minutes after it appears.[9] Yet it still needs to be tried, time and again, as the stakes are too high to become cynical. One fruitful avenue is to juxtapose neoliberal epistemologies with other ways of seeing the world, for example so-called indigenous epistemologies (see, e.g., West 2006; Sullivan, 2009). Offering and supporting radically different ways of seeing the world—especially in the face of seemingly all-encompassing and colonizing epistemologies—directly impacts our ability to make space for progressive possibilities.

Critical Realities

As neoliberal conservation is set to trigger new and even greater contradictions for the foreseeable future, it is crucial to keep emphasizing that conservation and development practitioners and indeed all of us have a choice. We do not have to overcome every frontier set for us by the capitalist political economy. Instead we need to engage this political economy in a way that does justice to critical realities. "Critical realities" harbor two different meanings of "critical." The first is that realities matter. Massive environmental degradation and growing inequalities are "real" and need to be engaged as such, especially in face of images and simplistic silver-bullet solutions that seem to suggest otherwise or that suggest easy or win-win ways out. Those critical of capitalism likely agree on this, yet they take it up in different ways. Hence, the second meaning of "critical" focuses on overcoming and confronting the trend to use the tension between reality and construction in a cynical way for competitive gain. Instead, this use of "critical" focuses on dealing with these tensions in a positive way to lead to what Philip Quarles van Ufford, Ananta Kumar Giri, and David Mosse call "critical understanding" (2003).

Critical understanding means that just because reality is always at least partially constructed does not mean that we cannot find better explanations for it, and also better ways of living with each other and the biodiversity around us. For many this then begs the questions, "what is to be done?" Or "what are the practical actions we must follow in order to solve "the" problem?" When faced with a global ideological system that is this dominant, perverse, and seductive, it is perhaps easy to succumb to the idea that putting alternatives on the table solely to provide people with a sense that the problem is being addressed is too simple and is contrary to how historical change unfolds. However, alternative, critical ways of thinking and social spaces are charted and embraced by an increasing number of actors, while simultaneously—in dialectical conjunction—associated processes of action, institutions, relations, and engagements are continuously invented, changed, and (re)ignited (see Dyer-Witheford 1999; Kovel 2002; Quarles van Ufford, Giri, and Mosse 2003). At the basis of these is some form of critical understanding as the only way to get beyond the major pitfall of the bubble of neoliberal conservation: the danger of not needing or wanting to find out whether anything works in practice, whether some explanations hold a greater truth value than others, or whether some compositions are better constructed because legitimacy and validity are calculated in quantitative monetary terms rather than the intrinsic quality of an explanation, product, or possibility.

When thinking along these lines, it becomes easier to chart critical ways forward. These should principally target some of the most-prominent frontier and frontier-producing elements of contemporary neoliberal capitalism and their associated consensuses, (anti)politics, and marketing, most notably the need for economic growth, continuous (reliance on) consumption, ever-increasing circulation of goods and services, intensification of labor time, and the omnipresence of commercial advertising.[10] Questioning the automaticity with which these issues are often accepted and promoted by governments, donors, companies, and others might give interventions such as the MDTP space to start engaging with the material and discursive struggles necessary to truly address power imbalances and social inequities, as well as to start promoting ways of living that reduce rather than stimulate the extraction of resources and degradation of biologically diverse areas. In the current climate, however, these are all so generally accepted that calling them into question is often seen as radical. And this is exactly the point. Radical means getting to the roots of things, to tackle their source.[11] It seems that if we actually care about issues of conservation and development, then tackling radical issues is not something extreme or impractical but the opposite: logical, practical, highly necessary, and long overdue. Tackling and targeting radical roots allows us to imagine that not every frontier set for us by the neoliberal political economy has to be overcome. It allows us to start thinking of a different transformation toward a more hopeful, just, and sustainable future.

notes

Preface

1. The quotes by Latour in the preface are not meant to imply that this book is an actor-network theory account. I am inspired more by the methodological implications of Latour's work than his ontology of actors, networks, and connections.

2. I follow Escobar (1995) and Bending (2003) that the "radical critique of development . . . can be extended to this sphere of environmental governance" (Bending 2003, 9), especially because with the advent of the concept of "sustainable development" in the 1980s the two are often intertwined in theory and practice.

Introduction

1. Nelson Mandela, speech at the ceremony for the translocation of elephants from Kruger Park into Mozambique, 4 October 2001, Great Limpopo National Park, South Africa. See www.peaceparks.org.

2. There is a large and important body of literature on postcolonialism in Africa, including major works by Jean-François Bayart (2009 [1989]), Patrick Chabal and Jean-Pascal Daloz (1999), Mahmood Mamdani (1996), Achilles Mbembe (2000, 2001), and Valentin Y. Mudimbe (1988), and more-recent works by Ferguson (2006) and the intriguing collection of essays by Adesanmi (2011), among others. I engage this work, but only insofar as it relates to and impacts the prime concerns around the politics of neoliberal conservation interventions such as peace parks.

3. The degree to which this is true varies wildly across the African continent. See, for example, the literature of voluntary resettlement, which is about displacement from conservation areas (e.g., Brockington and Igoe 2006; Cernea and Schmidt-Soltau 2006; Schmidt-Soltau and Brockington 2007).

4. I refer to interventions broadly to signify (mostly) donor- or state-driven, or funded projects and programs that aim to change social, economic, environmental, and other dynamics in a particular area.

5. Several major recent studies, such as Dressler 2009, Ferguson 2006, Hughes 2006, Li 2007, and West 2006, productively fuse ethnography with political economy but lack an in-depth engagement with the concept of neoliberalism.

6. This is true even if, or perhaps because, the uses of neoliberalism are not always spelled out by those who wield the term (Ferguson 2010).

7. There is a fast-growing body of literature on this topic, which I build on and aim to contribute to. Some of the more-recent contributions include Brockington 2008, 2009; Brockington, Duffy, and Igoe 2008; Brondo and Brown 2011; Büscher 2008, 2010a, 2010b, 2010c; Büscher et al. 2012; Dressler 2011; Dressler and Büscher 2008; Fay 2013; Fletcher 2010, 2011; Igoe 2010; Igoe and Brockington 2007; and Sullivan 2006, 2009, 2010. See also Arsel and Büscher 2012, Brockington and Duffy 2010, and Roth and Dressler 2012 and the articles of the special journal issues introduced by these pieces.

8. This takes the book beyond aidnography, whose engagement with political economy has been limited. David Mosse, for example, argues that the populist community-participation discourse "fabricate its separation from political economy and that it becomes isolated from the local or vernacular to which it is nonetheless materially connected" (2005, 238). Accordingly, his study of a British aid project in India details how this "produces ignorance of project effects." While Mosse is correct in arguing that ethnographic research is needed to bring these effects back into the open, his analysis stops short of showing how both acts of fabrication and project effects are connected to the wider political economy.

9. *MDTP News*, 1 (4): 6.

10. There are obvious parallels to poststructuralist work on changing relations of governance here, particularly Michel Foucault's (1995) work on discipline, biopower, and governmentality, as both (post-) Marxist and poststructuralist literatures indicate tensions among the (felt) need for coherence, some form of direction in systems of rule, and the relocation, de- and recentralization of authority between actors. A focus on poststructuralist pluralism, however, ultimately misjudges the nature of structural power in a neoliberal political economy—a critique often applicable more to those who are inspired by Foucault than to Foucault himself (Nealon 2008). I believe that some poststructuralist work, especially work (inspired) by Foucault, forms a good antidote against an overt reliance on the structural features of neoliberal governance and usefully stresses the micro- and biopolitics at work in the execution of rule. See the work by Robert Fletcher (2010), who usefully distinguishes between various forms of governmentality in relation to conservation. He argues that neoliberal governmentality entails "an effort to combat environmental degradation . . . through the creation of incentive structures intended to influence individuals' use of natural resources by altering the cost-benefit ratio of resource extraction so as to encourage *in situ* preservation" (176). However, I use the broader term "governance" to denote the regulation of public affairs, and I

only refer to the concept of governmentality when making specific points that aim to draw attention to the fruitful linkages that can be made between post-Marxist and poststructuralist modes of analysis.

11. I want to distance myself from Barnett's rejection of the possibility of fruitfully combining Foucauldian poststructuralist theories with (post)Marxist theories of neoliberalism. Barnett rightly criticizes some literature on neoliberalism for not being able to make the link between differences in individual life-words and neoliberalism's structural, homogenizing tendencies. He fails, in my view, to show that this is a problem inherent to neoliberalism, rather than the scholars trying to understand neoliberal processes. Hence, the scholarly task is to show in detail how the neoliberal abstract is linked to ethnographic realities. By agreeing to this, Barnett seems to defuse his own critique (2005, 11).

12. David McDonald and Greg Ruiters argue that "although all things have a 'use value'—the qualitatively defined characteristics that differentiate something from other goods or services and may differentiate it from itself across time and space—this use value is transformed to 'exchange value' in the exchange process, a strictly quantitative measurement that differentiates goods by the monetary worth alone, as determined by the market" (2005, 21).

13. The term "universalism" signifies an ambition rather than an end state as such (see Peck and Tickell 2002, 383).

14. What this means in practical terms is explained by McDonald and Ruiters, who show that "private sector operating principles and mechanisms," such as profit maximization, cost recovery, competitive bidding, cost-benefit analyses, performance targeted salaries, ring-fenced decision making, and demand-driven investments, are swiftly replacing "traditional public sector operating principles," such as integrated planning, (cross)subsidization, supply-driven decision making, equity orientation, within public organizations (e.g., state institutions on various levels) (2005, 17). Obviously, one needs to be careful here and heed those who would rightly criticize this statement and point toward patron-client relations and the state as a resource rather than an instrument of service to characterize the African postcolonial state (see, e.g., Bayart 2009; Migdal 1988; Tordoff 2002). While maintaining that neoliberal restructuring has also influenced African states, especially the South African state that plays a key role in southern African transfrontier conservation, it is crucial to point to the partial and wildly diverging nature of this process across the African continent.

15. For example, the UN Global Compact with the private sector consists of "ten principles in the areas of human rights, labour, the environment and anti-corruption," and "enjoys universal consensus" (UN Global Compact, "The Ten Principles," http://www.unglobalcompact.org/AboutTheGC/TheTenPrinciples/index.html; accessed 18 January 2010).

16. The (post) Washington Consensus comes to mind.

17. A relevant illustration of this belief is the UN's Millennium Development

Goals (MDGS): "The adoption of the Millennium Declaration by the United Nations General Assembly in September 2000, and the reformulation of the International Development Targets (IDTS) into the MDGS, can be seen as part of a broader consensus with an extraordinarily diverse buy-in" (Cornwall and Brock 2005, 1049).

18. A notable exception is a volume edited by Philip Quarles van Ufford and Ananta Kumar Giri (2003) that tries to develop a moral critique of development.

19. This is not to say that politics is only constituted by language, communication, and deliberation. As mentioned, force, domination, and violence are also part of politics (see, e.g., Mbembe 2001).

20. Andrew Barry, Thomas Osborne, and Nikolas Rose (1996) argue for accepting rationality's and technocracy's limitations and studying the eclectic ways that politics and the technical mutually constitute each other.

21. Ferguson, however, did not link his analysis to wider discussions on the political economy. I have argued elsewhere that much development literature that insists on the importance of reconstituting poverty within the political domain has done little to further investigate the nature of politics, which is demonstrated by how few scholars have elaborated on the antipolitics concept (Büscher 2010a).

22. This is not to suggest that the visual cannot be political. The visual and the symbolic have always been part and parcel of political practice. Aesthetic antipolitics relates to the point that images are used to avoid or misrepresent political issues (see Debord 1967).

23. I am grateful to James Ferguson for pointing out this distinction to me.

24. See the "Goede Doelen" page of the website of the Nationale Postcode Loterij, http://www.postcodeloterij.nl, for an overview of the funds donated to the PPF (accessed 29 August 2012).

25. In the field of conservation, this means that the product of environmentally sound behavior should out compete environmentally unfriendly behavior in the marketplace of possible behaviors vis-à-vis the environment, as several conservation biologists argue: "Pragmatic solutions are required to overcome the inertia in engendering pro-nature behaviors of individuals and organizations that are required for mainstreaming. Social marketing is very promising in this respect: rather than attempting to understand the complex causes of behavior, it takes existing behaviors as a given and then seeks to identify the barriers to behavior change and to design specific incentive based programs to overcome these barriers" (Cowling et al. 2008, 9486).

26. But see, among others, the work published in the *Journal of Consumer Culture* over the last few years.

1. Forging (Trans)frontier Spaces

1. Also see the video "Peace Parks Foundation," narrated by the actor Morgan Freeman, where the same message is repeated. See http://www.peaceparks .org/, http://www.youtube.com/watch?v=R-Yozh22S_M&feature=player_e mbedded#!, accessed on 29 August 2012.

2. For a historical comparison of the frontier in both regions, see Lamar and Thompson 1981.

3. Howard Lamar and Leonard Thompson regard a "frontier not as a boundary or line, but as a territory or zone of interpenetration between two previously distinct societies" (1981, 7). Contrary to Lamar and Thompson, I agree with David Hughes (2006, 4) that frontiers do not close once political authority is established by a single party.

4. This also happened in other parts of the world; see, e.g., Peluso 1992, 44–78.

5. Citizens of Lesotho and others of Sotho origin are called Basotho (Mosotho is the singular). The culture is described as Sesotho.

6. But note that this was of course tremendously uneven, with different forms and intensities of resistance and possibilities for Africans to continue forms of so-called traditional livelihoods and land management. See, e.g., Cousins 2007, 296–302; Mamdani 1996.

7. In relation to this, Patrick Bond concludes that "these economic phenomena reflect as severe a case of uneven socio-economic development as exists any-where on earth, and along with apartheid policies help explain why the top 5 per cent of South Africa's population consume more than the bottom 85 per-cent, resulting in a Gini coefficient (the main measure of income disparity) of 0.61, matching Brazil and Nigeria as major countries with the worst levels of inequality" (2000, 18–19). Following Bond, however, I want to emphasize that capitalism and apartheid should not be equated, or that there were no class differences within racial groups, as there certainly were.

8. South African "capitalist agriculture" was generalized in the period from 1920 to 1950 (Bernstein 1998, 2). Bernstein argues that this generalization was characterized by three central elements: massive dispossession, the institution of a "variety of coercive labour regimes," and the organization of agricultural markets through subsidies, price agreements, guaranteed sales, and so on. In turn, this "'organised agriculture' was key to the political bloc of 1948 and grand apartheid" until the late 1970s (2).

9. See Dressler 2009, Slater 2002, and West 2006 for similar experiences in the Philippines, Brazil, and Papua New Guinea.

10. See various chapters in Hulme and Murphree 2001 for discussions of these programs.

11. World Bank, press release, 6 June 1998. See http://www.e-tools.co.za/news brief/1998/news0606, accessed 7 December 2012.

12. I use "community-based conservation" and "community-based natural re-

source management" interchangeably, even though there are some nuanced differences between them.

13. Around the time, this concerned in particular an active group of scholars associated with the IUCN Southern Africa office, the University of Zimbabwe, and the University of Western Cape.

14. A powerful example is the increasing number of wealthy "green barons" intervening in developing countries to save nature through fortress means yet cloaked in "community-based" language (see Chudy 2006; Nelson 2003). According to Jolanta Chudy, there is "a growing trend of western philanthropists who use their personal fortunes to buy enormous tracts of land in countries where they feel that governments are failing to safeguard their natural heritage" (2006, 45). See also Ramutsindela, Spierenburg, and Wels 2011 for a broader exposition of this trend.

15. This also goes for the neoprotectionist criticism of CBC (for critiques, see Büscher and Dressler 2007; Hutton, Adams, and Murombedzi 2005). The contradictory nature of the neoprotectionist argument vis-à-vis the neoliberal political economy is well illustrated by Flora Lu Holt, who argues that local people become "caught in a conservation Catch-22" (2005, 209). She shows that neoprotectionists see capitalist Western culture both as a problem and a solution, leaving non-Westerners caught in the middle; neoprotectionists prefer that local people not develop, but they would need to develop in order to be instilled by the same conservation ethic that (apparently) pervades civilized Westerners. Holt's conclusion reverts back to the CBC ideal that it is morally correct to include local people in conservation. She does not draw another implication of the double standards proposed by neoprotectionists, namely that they effectively endorse and reinforce the status quo of the global neoliberal political economy.

16. These ideas, obviously, were conceptualized differently by the parties involved. It helped the black majority think about an Africa before the corrupting influences of colonization and apartheid, while the same images of Africa resonated well with whites and international audiences due to their Garden of Eden appeal (see Adams and McShane 1996; Nelson 2003).

17. According to Malcolm Draper, Marja Spierenburg, and Harry Wels, Hanks was crucial to the PPF's early development thanks to his "formidable lobbying and fund-raising capacities" (2004, 342).

18. Although the same document states that poverty reduction in Mozambique has the highest priority, Wolmer (2003) sees the quote as a rationalization for the World Bank to extend its mandate to include conservation and try to mend its negative environmental image (see also Ramutsindela 2007). The World Bank did the same for the Maloti-Drakensberg project with the objective to jump on the fashionable TFCA bandwagon (Magome and Murombedzi 2003).

19. See the Kavango Zambezi Transfrontier Conservation Area website, http://www.kavangozambezi.org/.

20. To sum up, these included the founding of the PPF; the personal interest in TFCAS by key politicians (including the former South African presidents Nelson Mandela and Thabo Mbeki and the former environment minister Valli Moosa); South Africa's emerging environmental image due to its hosting of the 2002 World Summit on Sustainable Development and the 2003 World Parks Congress; the search, particularly by donors, for alternatives to community conservation interventions; and the increasing importance of (nature-based) tourism for the South (and southern) African economy.

21. The name Kgalagadi comes from the San language and is normally translated as "place of thirst."

22. All this is not to say that everything was smooth and there were no problems related to the transfrontier park. As Thondhlana, Shackleton, and Muchapondwa (2011) and Ellis (2011) show, the Kgalagadi continues to suffer from many of the same issues around lack of community participation, unequal access to resources, and wrought interpretations and representations of historical dispossessions as other TFCAS.

23. The transfrontier park encompasses 35,000 square kilometers, while the larger transfrontier conservation area, which includes the Banhine and Zinave National Parks; the Massingir, Corumana, and interlinking areas in Mozambique; and several private and state-owned conservation estates in South Africa and Zimbabwe, comes to a massive 100,000 square kilometers.

24. Interview with independent consultant, Johannesburg, 16 November 2003; interview with marketing manager, TFCA 2010 Development Unit, Department of Environmental Affairs and Tourism, South Africa, 13 August 2007.

25. The main problems include land invasions and wildlife poaching in Gonarezhou National Park, the general lack of participation in the organizational development of the transfrontier park, and the still-unresolved issue of the Sengwe corridor that has to link Gonarezhou to the rest of the GLTP (Van Amerom and Büscher 2005; also see the *Zimbabwe Independent,* 11 May 2005, "Zim lags behind on Transfrontier National Park Project by Ray Matikinye. See http://www.theindependent.co.zw/2005/03/11/zim-lags-behind-on-tran frontier-national-park-project/, and the *Zimbabwe Independent,* 13 May 2005, "Poaching Threatens Megapark" by Munyaradzi Wasosa at http://www.thein dependent.co.zw/2005/05/13/poaching-threatens-megapark-project/, accessed on 30 August 2012.

2. Neoliberal Amplifications

1. Interview with staff member, Transfrontier Conservation Areas Directorate, DEAT, South Africa, 22 August 2006.

2. Http://www.ppf.org.za/story.php?mid=10&pid=6, accessed 21 December 2009. The idea that tourism is the magic bullet to connect conservation and development is obviously a global trend. In turn, it is generally recognized in the literature that "tourism and ecotourism are underpinned by a market ori-

ented strategy that neatly fits with the outlook of neo-liberalism" (Duffy 2006a, 131).

3. Http://www.peaceparks.org/xMedia/PDF/News/News%20Stories/10yr_re view.pdf and http://www.ppf.org.za/news.php?pid=15&mid=632, accessed 21 December 2009. Also see the Leadership for Conservation in Africa website, http://lcafrica.org/index.php, accessed 21 December 2009.

4. See PPF, 2007, 22; 2008, 16.

5. Interview with staff member, Transfrontier Conservation Areas Directorate, DEAT, South Africa, 17 November 2003.

6. See, among others, Büscher 2010b; Büscher and Dressler 2007; Draper, Spierenburg, and Wels 2004; Duffy 2006b; Munthali and Soto 2001; Van Amerom 2005; Wolmer 2003, 2006.

7. Which was later reflected in the PPF's policy on crosscutting programs.

8. Interview with independent consultant, 16 November 2003; interview with former coordinator for the Great Limpopo Transfrontier Park, 15 November 2003.

9. Interview with independent consultant, 16 November 2003.

10. See Government Communication and Information System, Decision on Kruger National Park Land claims, 28 January 2009, http://www.gcis.gov.za/ content/newsroom/media-releases/media-statements/decision-kruger-nati onal-park-land-claims, accessed 31 August 2012.

11. See Robins and van der Waal 2011 for a critical discussion about the construction of the Makuleke case as "successful" in relation to enduring local tensions and unresolved issues.

12. "Kruger Land Claimants Furious," *Mail and Guardian* (South Africa), 8 February 2009, http://mg.co.za/article/2009–02–08-kruger-land-claimants-furious.

13. Also see the literature on voluntary resettlement, for example Brockington and Igoe 2006; Cernea and Schmidt-Soltau 2006; and Schmidt-Soltau and Brockington 2007.

14. See also Itai Mabasa, "Land Invasions, Poaching Threaten Trans-frontier Tourism," *Zimbabwean*, 20 September 2011, http://www.thezimbabwean.co.uk/ travel/52920/land-invasions-poaching-threaten-trans.html.

15. See "Futi Corridor Now a Protected Area," Peace Parks Foundation, 24 June 2011, http://www.peaceparks.org/news.php?pid=1098&mid=1118, accessed 20 October 2011.

16. "SA, Namibia cross-border park," SouthAfrica.info, http://www.southafrica .info/about/sustainable/sanamibia-park.htm, accessed 31 August 2012. See also http://www.brandsouthafrica.com/.

17. "Less favourable" is an understatement with respect to Zimbabwe, where the infrastructure problem is dwarfed by the country's political and economic crisis (see Van Amerom 2005; Wolmer 2003).

18. This argument is inspired by Joel Kovel's argument that "capital" is more than

eager to allow environmental movements a seat at the table for the purposes of legitimation of the capitalist system, control of popular dissent, and as a rationalization strategy to protect the system from its worst contradictions (2002, 154).

19. Interview with director, Transfrontier Conservation, Conservation International, 11 August 2006; interview with former staff member, Natal Parks Board, 22 December 2005.

20. Interview with director, Transfrontier Conservation, Conservation International, 11 August 2006.

21. This is something I also regularly noticed: many times, during interviews or regular chats, I was shown designs for a new tourism infrastructure in TFCAS and asked what I thought about the designs.

22. More-recent research (July 2009) on TFCAS in Zambia illustrates the point: in interviews it became clear that Zambian policy officers at the Zambian Wildlife Authority, which is responsible for the Kavango-Zambezi TFCA, are all funded through the PPF and were highly constrained. They could not criticize their funder even though they admitted that there were major problems with local communities resisting the PPF's plans for an "elephant corridor" from Botswana's delta to Zambia's Kafue floodplains.

23. Incidentally, the same project also sought to "help establish an enabling environment in which the private sector can play an enhanced role within the TFCAS and in Mozambique generally" (World Bank, 1996, 83).

24. Many documents from the World Bank, UN, or other donors bear the following or a similar notice: "This document has a restricted distribution and may be used by recipients only in the performance of their official duties. Its contents may not otherwise be disclosed without World Bank authorization" (World Bank 2004, 1).

25. Transfrontier conservation thus neatly links in with the "preoccupation among development agencies and researchers with getting policy right; with exerting influence over policy, linking research to policy, and of course with implementing policy around the world" (Mosse 2004, 639).

26. See the discussion on consensus in the introduction.

27. Although see Fletcher 2010 for nuance to this reasoning based on Foucault's (2008) "Birth of Biopolitics" lectures that the entire point of neoliberalism was to change state and other governmentalities to provide the enabling environment for intensified capital circulation (see also Peck 2010).

28. This setup resembles the market as the typical institution that is characterized on a surface level by little consensus, but functions according to underlying principles such as competition and commodification.

29. Again, research on the Great Limpopo shows that the reverse is also often the case, namely that transfrontier conservation fuels conflict (Van Amerom 2005). Tensions seem to be especially "reflected in struggles over the sharing of benefits between South Africa and neighbouring countries and over land

harmonisation policies" (Van Amerom and Büscher 2005, 170; see also Büscher and Schoon 2009, 45–54).

30. Personal communication with a PPF staff member, 10–12 April 2005.

31. In possession of the author; no date available.

32. Such as: "He who covets all will lose all. Only through sharing will mankind preserve itself from harm. Self-interest does not necessarily mean selfishness" and "Confidence begets confidence. It certainly is a risk to trust, but mistrust is an even greater risk that can lead to disaster. If you don't trust others, you probably can't trust yourself!"

33. To quote but one example, the South African *Sunday Times* from 22 January 2006 titled its piece "The Benevolent Tycoon" and added that, according to Chris Barron, "the good doctor" "Anton Rupert channelled his desire to be a doctor into using his wealth to benefit others."

34. For general expositions about celebrity, philanthropy, and conservation, see Brockington 2009; Holmes 2012; and Ramutsindela, Spierenburg, and Wels 2011.

35. While a quarterly, this informal magazine of the Peace Parks Foundation only saw several issues being published during the starting years of the foundation. Copy in possession of the author.

36. This is not to say that all whites saw their fortunes change for the better with the end of apartheid. To the contrary: as with neoliberalism more generally, the white community after the end of apartheid saw a steep rise in inequality, with white poverty levels rising as quickly as levels of affluence.

37. Robert Nelson argues that "the advocates of exclusion of people were driven by the familiar myths of a "wild Africa" that must be maintained in its "original wilderness" condition. The emotional power of these images for European and American audiences is not in doubt; nor is their usefulness for fundraising purposes" (2003, 80). Note that this is not to say that black South African marketers do not use the same themes and myths; they often do as many of them know that these themes appeal to their target audiences.

38. Further evidence for this argument can found in several-high quality brochures produced by SAFRI (Southern Africa Initiative of German Business) and DaimlerChrysler about peace parks. Both are lyrical about peace parks and anxious to showcase their good relations with Rupert and Mandela. Both also see "tourism as a key to development and investment incentives" and are eager to outline its attraction for business (M. Pabst, Transfrontier Peace Parks in Southern Africa: Unspoiled Ecosystems; Magnets for Tourism; Creating Employment," Southern Africa Initiative of German Business—SAFRI, 40).

39. Or rather the 2010 FIFA World Cup South Africa™. In true neoliberal style, the event became a patented trademark. See the official website at http://www.fifa.com/worldcup/archive/southafrica2010/index.html, accessed 17 June 2011.

40. See the Revolutionary Conservation Area on Track page on the PPF website,

http://www.peaceparks.org/news.php?mid=612&pid=1093&year=2011&lid= 1004, accessed 1 September 2012. Interestingly, there are only eight countries mentioned, Swaziland is missing in this list.

41. Interview with marketing manager, TFCA 2010 Development Unit, DEAT, South Africa, 13 August 2007.

42. This quote was repeated on many websites and brochures, including Bound lessinvest.com; Kingsley Holgate's Boundless Southern Africa Expedition website, http://www.imagineering.co.za/boundlesssa/; and the "South Africa Alive!" complementary guide, Johannesburg: wwwadvertising, June 2009, 44.

43. Rejoice Mabudafhasi, "Speech delivered by the Honourable Deputy Minister of Environmental Affairs and Tourism, Ms Rejoice Mabudafhasi, at the Launch of the Strategic Branding of Transfrontier Conservation Areas (TFCAS) at Tourism Indaba," Department of Environmental Affairs and Tourism, 10 May 2008, available at the South African Government Information website, http://www.info.gov.za/speeches/2008/08051213451001.htm, accessed 14 December 2009.

44. Open spaces, unlimited beauty, infinite possibilities. Investment Opportunities October 2008, 11. Available at http://www.boundlessa.com/en/packs/bo undless_br.pdf, accessed 14 December 2009.

45. Ibid.

46. Rejoice Mabudafhasi, "Speech delivered by the Honourable Deputy Minister of Environmental Affairs and Tourism, Ms Rejoice Mabudafhasi, at the Launch of the Strategic Branding of Transfrontier Conservation Areas (TFCAS) at Tourism Indaba," Department of Environmental Affairs and Tourism, 10 May 2008, available at the South African Government Information website, http://www.info.gov.za/speeches/2008/08051213451001.htm, accessed 14 December 2009.

47. M. Pabst, Transfrontier Peace Parks in Southern Africa: Unspoiled Ecosystems; Magnets for Tourism; Creating Employment," Southern Africa Initiative of German Business—SAFRI, 9.

48. Which it is not, because to enter some new countries (such as Mozambique) a new visa is still required and has to be received at the border post inside the transfrontier park.

49. The contradictions obviously refer to the "aboriginal state" of peace parks, "free of borders and bureaucracy," and showing only "minimal traces of human intervention."

50. Hughes refers to this "rezoning for business" as the "new colonization" whereby "a business ethic, rather than racial solidarity, gives these colonisers their unity of purpose" (2001, 593).

3. Compressing Reality

1. In brief, the PPF helped Lesotho mainly by assisting in the attainment of the conditions set for the World Bank and GEF grant that funded the Maloti-Drakensberg Transfrontier Project and with several other issues, such as tourism development in Sehlabathebe National Park.

2. This is despite the hiccup in 1998 of the invasion of Lesotho by South African and Botswana forces under the Southern African Development Community flag, supposedly to restore rule and order and prevent a coup d'état after contested elections that ended up causing prolonged riots.

3. An example of this line of argumentation comes from Nüsser and Grab: "A primary objective for the planned Transfrontier Park development would thus be to ensure ecological and hydrological functioning of the alpine wetlands, which are crucial to the local stockholders and a precondition for water supply for much of southern Africa" (2002, 307). The extent of the degradation, however, is heavily debated.

4. As mentioned in the preface, the names of this and other informants have been changed to guarantee anonymity, unless they gave permission to use their real name.

5. Interview with retired independent consultant, 1 August 2005; interview with independent consultant, 28 April 2005; interview with staff member, KZN Wildlife, 10 May 2005; interview with independent consultant, 29 July 2005; interview with former staff member, Natal Parks Board, 10 August 2005.

6. Interview with retired independent consultant, 1 August 2005.

7. Interview with independent consultant, 28 April 2005.

8. Interview with independent consultant, 28 April 2005.

9. A point that was not mentioned by any interviewee, but no doubt also played a role in the growing attention for the Maloti-Drakensberg TFCA, is the symbolic significance of a peace park in a province that had long been mired in political violence between the Inkatha Freedom Party and the African National Congress (see Jeffery 1997 for an extensive review of this history).

10. The MDTP preproject amounted to US$4.7 million and was funded by the GEF and the Japanese Policy and Human Resources Development Fund, which was established in 1990 as a partnership between the government of Japan and the World Bank.

11. The DMMCP studies were concluded with nine thick reports and many more intermediary outputs, collated into Bainbridge, Motsamai, and Weaver (1991); the European Union project also produced a deluge of reports (literally several meters of reports can be found on various shelves at the National Environmental Secretariat in Maseru, Lesotho), while the MDTP preproject again hired many consultants to provide the baseline information that was needed to develop the final Project Appraisal Document upon which the MDTP is based.

12. Ian Player is a world-renowned conservationist and founder of the Wild Foun-

dation (www.wild.org). He is known for his leading role in the Natal Parks Board's Operation Rhino, which in the 1960s is said to have saved the white rhino from extinction.

13. Interview with retired independent consultant, 1 August 2005.
14. Interview with independent consultant, 28 April 2005.
15. Interview with staff member, Ministry of Agriculture and Food Security, 20 October 2005.
16. Interview with retired independent consultant, 1 August 2005; interview with staff member, Ministry of Agriculture and Food Security, 20 October 2005; interview with independent consultant, 28 April 2005; interview with staff member, Transfrontier Conservation Areas Directorate, DEAT, South Africa, 22 April 2005.
17. Another example is on page 9: "It can be stated with confidence that the Study Area is a key water source area for the Lesotho Highlands Water Project. Unsympathetic land uses in the sensitive Alpine Zone could destabilise current stable stream flow patterns, reduce water quality, and increase siltation rates (resulting in depleted storage capacity of the dams) and water borne diseases." And page 40: "The long-term success of the entire LHWP is dependent on the conservation of the catchments."
18. See also the Lesotho Highlands Water Project website, www.lhwp.org.ls.
19. Interview with retired independent consultant, 1 August 2005.
20. Interview with independent consultant, 28 April 2005.
21. Interview with former staff member, Natal Parks Board, 22 December 2005. Sandwith also mentioned that his first permit for the Drakensberg was signed by Williams.
22. The International Union for Conservation of Nature /WCPA Parks for Peace Conference was held in Somerset West, South Africa, 16–18 September 1997.
23. It must be stated that several key players in the Maloti-Drakensberg scheme also actively tried to persuade the World Bank to get involved. Sandwith in this respect mentioned that they "teased the World Bank into the MDTP" (interview with former staff member Natal Parks Board, 10 August 2005), and hence the interest to join hands was mutual.
24. Interview with retired independent consultant, 1 August 2005; interview with former staff member, Natal Parks Board, 22 December 2005.
25. This is based on interviews and conversations with MDTP role players as well as personal experience in my former capacity as project manager at the Centre for International Cooperation of the VU University Amsterdam. There we were involved in developing a medium-sized GEF project (up to US$1 million) under the UNEP. Medium-sized projects were created to expedite the approval process, but the acquisition process nonetheless took more than seven years before the project was approved.
26. After restructuring in 1994, the GEF is formally governed by the GEF assembly and the GEF council. The GEF assembly is a gathering where its members—now

182 states, termed "participants"—review progress made after three or four year periods. The GEF council oversees the day-to-day GEF operations and is modeled on the World Bank power structure with permanent seats for some countries (including the United States, Germany, the United Kingdom, France, Germany, Canada, and Japan) and the rest for "constituencies," and shared seats for the remaining participants. The assembly and council are supported by a GEF secretariat. See the GEF's website, www.gefweb.org, for an overview of participants and constituencies and the general structure of the GEF.

27. This was acknowledged by the first independent review of the GEF in 1994 (United Nations Development Programme, United Nations Environment Programme, and World Bank 1994, 137): "The competition in the GEF has been about power, control, and money. The World Bank is accustomed to having an abundance of these, and with encouragement from the founding donors, designed the GEF in such a way that the World Bank would control the global initiative, receive the lion's share of its resources, and in the process, help mitigate criticism alleging World Bank insensitivity to environmental concerns."

28. Class-based and poststructuralist theories on the African state contrast starkly with the World Bank's view (see, for example, Gill 1995). Class-based theories stress the African state as colonial intervention and argue that no original bourgeoisie existed in African societies but that there now exists a "state-class": those who occupy the state institutions and use it as a resource rather than an instrument to implement development programs (Harrison 2005b, 251). Poststructuralists emphasize the indigenous and historical in relation to the state. They identify the functionality of processes and see the state as a complex network of clientelism and social-ethnic networks. The state and its occupants in this perspective are not "isolationist and utilitarian," but are part of "ethnically-defined networks of power and mutual support" from where they derive their subjectivities (Harrison 2005b, 253).

29. See the GEF website, www.gefweb.org, for more information about these two principles.

30. http://documents.worldbank.org/curated/en/2008/05/10547057/japan-policy-human-resources-development-fund-annual-report-2008, accessed 1 September 2012.

31. Interview with staff member, Ministry of Agriculture and Food Security, Lesotho, 20 October 2005.

32. Ibid. The eight project components were: (a) project management and transfrontier cooperation, (b) conservation planning, (c) protected area planning, (d) conservation management in protected areas, (e) conservation management in community conservation areas, (f) community involvement, (g) sustainable livelihoods and (h) institutional development.

33. The report continues: "In the field . . . participatory rural appraisals, participatory stakeholder workshops, participatory land-use planning, and institutional

surveys were carried out to elicit the relevant information as well as engage the stakeholders in the assessment of the issues" (World Bank 2001a, 72).

34. Interview with staff member, National Environment Secretariat, Lesotho, 1 June 2005.

35. In another article, Harrison refers to this epistemology as a "foundational belief in the nature of societies," which expounds "that there is an immanent free-market-like essence to all societies" (2005a, 1307).

36. Interview with South African MDTP PCU specialist, 3 May 2005.

37. But these also remain inherently political.

38. It would arguably be more apt to refer to this type of legitimation as inherently biased or even nepotistic as this referral to documents and processes that have their origins in the same narrow global consensus discourses around neoliberalism and sustainable development seem to merely reinforce the same dogmatic thinking that pervades most international treaties and national policies.

39. On the whole, when one looks at the legacies of several important interventions, it seems that they were more negative than positive. One project positively referred to in the PAD, for example, was the UNDP-funded Conserving Mountain Biodiversity in Southern Lesotho project, which lasted from 1999 to 2005 and was generally regarded as a major failure (interview with staff member, UNDP, 20 October 2005; Timberlake and Mateka 2004). According to the final report, many things were wrong with the project—personnel problems, slow implementation, insufficient oversight, bad financial planning, etc.—but arguably the main factor influencing the MDTP was that "there is a perceived legacy of 'unfulfilled promises,' with communities believing that the project has not delivered the developments they had come to expect" (Timberlake and Mateka 2004, 4). Although the report and the responsible UNDP program officer downplayed the impact of this legacy in an interview, my later interaction with MDTP staff in Lesotho revealed that the MDTP could not really work in the area where this previous intervention had been active. In fact, staff of the range-management unit informally mentioned that communities even started throwing stones at their vehicles when they entered the area.

40. Interview with South African MDTP PCU specialist, 22 July 2005; interview with Lesotho MDTP PCU specialist, 27 April 2005.

41. This is spelled out in the Employment Equity Act (nr. 55 of 1998); see www.labour.co.za.

42. See section 15 (1) of the Employment Equity Act (nr. 55 of 1998).

43. This is arguably less the case in business, as many white men still dominate the South African economy and many have actually gained economically from the end of apartheid (see Alexander 2002).

44. Interview with independent consultant, 29 July 2005. See also Sandwith 2003.

45. Ibid.

46. Ibid.

47. MDTP Lesotho PCU staff member who asked to remain anonymous.

48. Interview with staff member, National Environment Secretariat Lesotho, 1 June 2005.
49. Memo in possession of the author.
50. Interview with staff member, National Environment Secretariat Lesotho, 1 June 2005.
51. Interview with staff member, PPF, 26 April 2005.
52. This might be a coincidence as the World Bank employs men and women from all over the world.
53. According to the PAD, there were at least nineteen staff from the World Bank involved in the MDTP to check whether the project conformed to all the requirements both of the GEF and the World Bank and to provide crosschecks and other tasks (World Bank 2001a, 64). How these people were selected is not clear.
54. The World Parks Congress is a centennial conference organized by the International Union for Conservation of Nature—World Conservation Union to promote protected areas.
55. See workshop photos posted by the Mountain Protected Areas Network on its website: http://protectmountains.org/images/mountains-network-drakensb erg-workshop-2003-south-africa/, accessed 4 April 2012.
56. "The Didma Declaration," Mountain Protected Areas Network, 6 September 2003, http://mountains.squarespace.com/statements/.
57. Indeed, Sandwith talks about "setting aside the past" in the Maloti-Drakensberg, in order to "obtain and maintain the support of decision-makers" (Sandwith 2003, 162).

4. Divergent Interpretations

1. Interview with South African MDTP PCU specialist, 3 May 2005.
2. Interview with former staff member, Natal Parks Board, 22 December 2005. This is not to say that everyone in the project agreed with and relied on this assumption. For example, the World Bank MDTP task team leader, at the time, did not. He stated, "I have a more technical approach: you identify the issues where transfrontier cooperation is required and you work on those issues" (telephone interview with staff member, World Bank, 25 April 2005).
3. Interview with staff member, KZN Wildlife, 26 July 2005.
4. One staff member of an MDTP implementing agency in South Africa even stated that for him the MDTP is a "transprovincial" project rather than a transboundary project, since he felt that he spent more time with staff from other South African implementing agencies than from Lesotho (interview with staff member, Eastern Cape Department of Economic Affairs, Environment and Tourism, 17 September 2005).
5. The MDTP midterm review understated the differences between the PCUs as follows: "Lesotho followed the logframe in implementation, but South Africa chose to use an adaptive management approach" (MDTP 2005b, 5).
6. Interview with South African MDTP PCU specialist, 22 July 2005.

7. Interview with staff member, Lesotho Ministry of Agriculture and Food Security, 20 October 2005.
8. Interview with South African MDTP PCU specialist, 20 September 2005.
9. Interview with South African MDTP PCU specialist, 3 May 2005.
10. Interview with South African MDTP PCU specialist, 22 July 2005.
11. Interview with Lesotho MDTP PCU specialist, 27 April 2005.
12. Interview with Lesotho MDTP PCU specialist, 3 June 2005; interview with Lesotho MDTP PCU specialist, 8 June 2005; interview with Lesotho MDTP PCU specialist, 14 June 2005.
13. Interview with Lesotho MDTP PCU specialist, 27 April 2005.
14. Despite the fact that the current local-government system in Lesotho originates from the Local Government Act of 1997, it was not in place when the MDTP started in 2003.
15. Interview with South African MDTP PCU specialist, 22 July 2005; interview with South African MDTP PCU specialist, 20 September 2005. In many interviews with conservationists there was, I believe, an honest relief not to be embroiled too much in politics, which was seen as something not very positive. A South African MDTP PCU specialist for instance stated that he was "glad to be a technocrat" (interview with South African MDTP PCU specialist, 20 September 2005).
16. Interview with South African MDTP PCU specialist, 22 July 2005.
17. Interview with South African MDTP PCU specialist, 20 September 2005.
18. Interview with South African MDTP PCU specialist, 23 September 2005.
19. Interview with South African MDTP PCU specialist, 3 May 2005; interview with South African MDTP PCU specialist, 22 July 2005.
20. See Turner 2003 for an overview of the debate.
21. For instance the MDTP Project Appraisal Document says: "It is generally noted that areas under common property regimes are subjected to high levels of resource degradation," and later, "the local perception that rangeland can be exploited for free, challenges concepts of conserving biodiversity that is of global significance" (World Bank 2001a, 70, 72).
22. Interview with South African MDTP PCU specialist, 22 July 2005; interview with Lesotho MDTP PCU specialist, 27 April 2005; interview with staff member, KZN Wildlife, 10 May 2005.
23. Interview with South African MDTP PCU specialist, 20 September 2005. See also Kepe 2009.
24. Among others, interview with South African MDTP PCU specialist, 23 September 2005.
25. In particular: establishing and expanding their teams through the hiring of specialists, planning and organizing work schedules, liaising with domestic implementing agencies, doing stakeholder analyses, and so on.
26. Interview with South African MDTP PCU specialist, 23 September 2005.
27. Interview with staff member, KZN Wildlife, 10 May 2005. Similar arguments

have been made with respect to other TFCAS; see Büscher and Schoon 2009; Van Amerom 2005; Van Amerom and Büscher 2005.

28. Personal communication with Lesotho PCU coordinator, May 2007.

29. The project coordinator was, for instance, assigned with reediting an important report on the state of Lesotho's environment.

30. Interview with Lesotho MDTP PCU specialist, 26 October 2005.

31. The project coordination committee, consisting of staff of relevant government agencies, was established in both countries to oversee the work of the PCUS.

32. Interview with staff member National Environment Secretariat, Ministry of Tourism, Environment and Culture of Lesotho, 21 October 2005.

33. Interview with member of the Lesotho project coordination committee, 21 October 2005.

34. Ibid.

35. Interview with South African MDTP PCU specialist, 20 September 2005.

36. Interview with South African MDTP PCU specialist, 22 July 2005.

37. Interview with Lesotho MDTP PCU specialist, 27 April 2005.

38. Ibid.

39. Interview with South African MDTP PCU specialist, 22 July 2005.

40. Interview with Lesotho MDTP PCU specialist, 27 April 2005.

41. Telephone interview with staff member, World Bank, 25 April 2005.

42. Interview with former staff member, Natal Parks Board, 22 December 2005.

43. Together these organizations have implemented two consecutive CBNRM regional research programs, while some of the most well-known CBNRM researchers in the region, such as Marshall Murphree, Vupenyu Dzingirai, Ben Cousins, and James Murombedzi, are or have been associated with them. Moreover, CASS Centre of Applied Social Sciences and PLAAS researchers have been very close to the development and analysis of one of the most well-known CBNRM experiments, the Zimbabwean CAMPFIRE (Community Areas Management Programme for Indigenous Resources) program.

44. See, for instance, Fabricius and Koch 2004; Hulme and Murphree 2001; Shackleton and Shackleton 2004.

45. Interview with Lesotho MDTP PCU specialist, 19 October 2005.

46. Interview with Lesotho MDTP PCU specialist, 8 June 2005.

47. According its website, http://www.capeaction.org.za/index.php?C=about, "Cape Action for People and the Environment (C.A.P.E.) is a partnership of government and civil society aimed at conserving and restoring the biodiversity of the Cape Floristic Region and the adjacent marine environment, while delivering significant benefits to the people of the region," accessed 2 September 2012.

48. Interview with South African MDTP PCU specialist, 29 July 2005. This specialist has a Ph.D. from the Botany Department of the University of Cape Town.

49. Interview with South African MDTP PCU specialist, 20 September 2005.

50. In fact, before the issue of a joint bioregional planner had come up, the South African PCU bioregional planner had referred me to her as someone who could make useful comparisons between the MDTP and CAPE. Interview with South African MDTP PCU specialist, 9 May 2005.

51. Interview with South African MDTP PCU specialist, 22 July 2005.

52. Memo in possession of the author; emphasis in original.

53. Interview with South African MDTP PCU specialist, 29 July 2005.

54. Interview with staff member, Transfrontier Conservation Areas Directorate, DEAT, South Africa, 20 May 2005; interview with staff member, Transfrontier Conservation Areas Directorate, DEAT, South Africa, 9 February 2007; interview with staff member, National Environment Secretariat, Ministry of Tourism, Environment and Culture of Lesotho, 21 October 2005.

55. Interview with staff member, Transfrontier Conservation Areas Directorate, DEAT, South Africa, 10 October 2005.

56. Interview with staff member, Transfrontier Conservation Areas Directorate, DEAT, South Africa, 22 November 2005.

57. Interview with staff member, National Environment Secretariat, Ministry of Tourism, Environment and Culture of Lesotho, 21 October 2005; interview with staff member, National Environment Secretariat, Lesotho, 1 June 2005.

58. Interview with staff member, Transfrontier Conservation Areas Directorate, DEAT, South Africa, 20 February 2007.

59. Interview with staff member, Transfrontier Conservation Areas Directorate, DEAT, South Africa, 20 February 2007; interview with staff member, Transfrontier Conservation Areas Directorate, DEAT, South Africa, 9 February 2007; interview with staff member, KZN Wildlife, 28 February 2007.

60. Interview with staff member, Transfrontier Conservation Areas Directorate, DEAT, South Africa, 9 February 2007.

61. This became increasingly clear from many observations and informal talks in the DEAT during 2005 and 2007 and applies to officers on all levels from the biodiversity-conservation branch of the department.

62. Interview with staff member, National Environment Secretariat, Ministry of Tourism, Environment and Culture of Lesotho, 21 October 2005; personal communication, staff member of the Lesotho Ministry of Local Government, Maseru, 1 June 2005.

63. Interview with South African MDTP PCU specialist, 21 September 2005.

64. Interview with South African MDTP PCU specialist, 23 September 2005.

65. Interview with South African MDTP PCU specialist, 29 July 2005.

66. Interview with Lesotho MDTP PCU specialist, 26 October 2005.

67. Interview with South African MDTP PCU specialist, 23 September 2005.

68. Interview with South African MDTP PCU specialist, 11 September 2006.

69. Most PCU members indicated that they did not understand what kind of data were needed and in what format.

70. *MDTP News* 1 (4): 6. From its third year onward, the MDTP staff published

regular newsletters. However, due to their different opinions about the project, the two PCUs each published their own newsletters for their own countries, occasionally complemented by a joint newsletter.

71. Interview with South African MDTP PCU specialist, 23 September 2005.

72. Among others: interview with South African MDTP PCU specialist, 21 September 2005; interview with Lesotho MDTP PCU specialist, 19 October 2005.

73. As visible from MDTP newsletters and the MDTP website (www.maloti.org), among others.

5. Processing Politics

1. Managed resource areas were implemented in Botha-Bothe, Mokhotlong, and Qacha's Nek districts. The one in Botha-Bothe became my prime focus due to its interesting transfrontier dynamics and the fact that I had opportunities to stay in a village in the 'Moteng area.

2. Interview with South African MDTP PCU specialist, 3 May 2005; interview with South African MDTP PCU specialist, 22 July 2005.

3. Interview with staff member, Eastern Cape Department of Economic Affairs, Environment and Tourism, South Africa, 2 August 2005.

4. Interview with South African MDTP PCU specialist, 22 July 2005; interview with staff member, KZN Wildlife, 26 July 2005; interview with staff member, KZN Wildlife, 28 February 2007.

5. The parastatal KZN Wildlife falls under the Department of Agriculture and Environment Affairs, but it has a self-standing mandate for conservation throughout the province in and outside protected areas. Historically, the Natal province used to have two conservation entities: the Natal Parks Board (now KZN Wildlife) for the main parks and typically white settlement areas and the Bureau of Natural Resources for other parks and the black settlement areas (now mainly the Department of Environmental Affairs). These components, as well as agriculture, did not talk to each other or coordinate their actions for a long time and there are still tensions between them.

6. Interview with staff member, Free State Department of Tourism, Economic Affairs and Environment, South Africa, 30 May 2005.

7. Interview with South African MDTP PCU specialist, 23 September 2005; interview with South African MDTP PCU specialist, 1 March 2007.

8. Interview with staff member, Free State Department of Tourism, Economic Affairs and Environment, South Africa, 15 March 2007.

9. Interview with South African MDTP PCU specialist, 23 September 2005; interview with South African MDTP PCU specialist, 1 March 2007.

10. Interview with staff member, South African National Parks, 20 May 2005.

11. Interview with staff member, South African National Parks, 31 May 2007.

12. Interview with staff member, Transfrontier Conservation Areas Directorate, DEAT, South Africa, 10 October 2005; interview with staff member, Transfrontier Conservation Areas Directorate, DEAT, South Africa, 20 February 2007.

13. Interview with staff member, KZN Wildlife, 10 May 2005.

14. Ibid.

15. Interview with independent consultant, 29 July 2005.

16. Interview with South African MDTP PCU specialist, 22 July 2005; interview with South African MDTP PCU specialist, 23 September 2005; interview with South African MDTP PCU specialist, 11 September 2006.

17. Interview with South African MDTP PCU specialist, 23 September 2005.

18. Interview with staff member, KZN Wildlife, 28 February 2007.

19. Interview staff member, KZN Wildlife, 26 July 2005; interview with staff member, KZN Wildlife, 28 February 2007.

20. I have seen this repeatedly through observations at the DEAT in Pretoria, where, for example, many black staff members who do not perform their functions still often get promoted or hired when they apply for higher posts.

21. Anonymous, September 2005.

22. Interview with staff member, Free State Department of Tourism, Economic Affairs and Environment, South Africa, 15 March 2007.

23. Interview with MDTP South Africa PCU specialist, 19 September 2005.

24. Interview with staff member, Free State Department of Tourism, Economic Affairs and Environment, South Africa, 30 May 2005.

25. The same staff member also noted that the lack of political support had to do with provincialism, and, like in the Eastern Cape, the fact that environmental and economic affairs are in the same department.

26. Interview with staff member, Eastern Cape Department of Economic Affairs, Environment and Tourism, South Africa, 17 September 2005.

27. Interview with staff member, Transfrontier Conservation Areas Directorate, DEAT, South Africa, 10 October 2005.

28. Interview with staff member, Transfrontier Conservation Areas Directorate, DEAT, South Africa, 01 September 2005; interview with staff member, Transfrontier Conservation Areas Directorate, DEAT, South Africa, 22 November 2005; interview with staff member, Transfrontier Conservation Areas Directorate, DEAT, South Africa, 9 February 2007.

29. Interview with Lesotho MDTP PCU specialist, 26 October 2005. The main Lesotho implementing agencies were the MTEC as lead agency; the Ministries of Foreign Affairs, Local Government, and Finance and Development Planning; the Range Management Resources Division of the Ministry of Forestry and Land Reclamation; the Department of Livestock of the Ministry of Agriculture and Food Security; and the Lesotho Mounted Police.

30. Interview with Lesotho MDTP PCU specialist, 24 May 2007.

31. Incentive-based practice is itself an interesting shift that indicates increased dependency by local people on the state and increased opportunities for state control (see Scott 1998).

32. Interview with Lesotho MDTP PCU specialist, 24 May 2007.

33. Interview with staff member, National Environment Secretariat, Ministry of Tourism, Environment and Culture of Lesotho, 21 October 2005.

34. Interview with Lesotho MDTP PCU specialist, 26 October 2005.
35. Interview with staff member, Ministry of Forestry and Land Reclamation, Lesotho, 25 October 2005.
36. Interview with staff member, Ministry of Forestry and Land Reclamation, Lesotho, 14 June 2005.
37. Ibid.; interview with staff member, Ministry of Forestry and Land Reclamation, Lesotho, 25 October 2005.
38. Ibid.
39. Interview with staff member, Ministry of Forestry and Land Reclamation, Lesotho, 14 June 2005.
40. Ibid.
41. Ibid.
42. Interview with staff member, Ministry of Forestry and Land Reclamation, Lesotho, 25 October 2005.
43. Interview with staff member, Ministry of Forestry and Land Reclamation, Lesotho, 14 June 2005.
44. Interview with Lesotho MDTP PCU specialist, 26 October 2005.
45. Ibid.
46. Interview with Lesotho MDTP PCU specialist, 27 April 2005; interview with Lesotho MDTP PCU specialist, 19 October 2005.
47. Interview with Lesotho MDTP PCU specialist, 24 May 2007.
48. Interview with Lesotho MDTP PCU specialist, 26 October 2005; interview with Lesotho MDTP PCU specialist, 26 January 2007.
49. One could argue that to a degree this is also true for South Africa. For example, the South African PCU provided the extra manpower needed to update management plans for some protected areas. Nonetheless, the dependency on interventions in South Africa is minor compared to Lesotho.
50. Interview with South African MDTP PCU specialist, 23 September 2005; interview with Lesotho MDTP PCU specialist, 24 May 2007.
51. This was something that several PCU members noted they increasingly felt during the course of the project.
52. Interview with Lesotho MDTP PCU specialist, 24 May 2007.
53. Note that both this survey, as well as that of Sechaba Consultants (2000) indicates that poverty is worst in the high mountains of Lesotho, whereas Nyakoaneng lies in the so-called foothills.
54. Interviewed on 23 January 2007, Nyakoaneng, Lesotho. "Ntate" means "sir or "Mr." in Sesotho.
55. Interviewed on 24 January 2007, Nyakoaneng, Lesotho.
56. Interviewed on 23 January 2007, Nyakoaneng, Lesotho. " 'M'e" is "madam" or "Mrs." in Sesotho.
57. Interviewed on 22 January 2007, Ha Malopo, Lesotho.
58. This is at least true for the vast majority of the village.
59. Interview with South African MDTP PCU specialist, 3 May 2005.

60. These had been working together for long and for them Amagugu Esizwe was in fact a follow-up to several other interventions that they had undertaken in AmanGwane and Amazizi. Interview with staff member, Farmer Support Group, 4 May 2005.
61. Interview with South African MDTP PCU specialist, 3 May 2005; interview with staff member, Centre for Environment, Agriculture and Development, University of KwaZulu-Natal, South Africa, 5 March 2007.
62. Sarah Milne and William Adams (2012, 145) note that the "practice of 'committee-making' is widespread in participatory development, because it makes community-based interventions possible."
63. It must be said that villagers sometimes also experience hardship from proximity to the park, especially when baboons raid their crops.
64. Interviewed on 8 March 2007, Obonjaneni, South Africa.
65. According to project implementers, certificates were never promised.
66. Interviewed on 8 March 2007, Obonjaneni, South Africa.
67. Interviewed on 22 May 2007, Obonjaneni, South Africa.
68. Interviewed on 8 March 2007, Ebusingatha, South Africa
69. Interviewed on 8 March 2007, Ebusingatha, South Africa
70. Interviewed on 22 May 2007, Obonjaneni, South Africa.
71. One could then expect other clashes and problems, most notably with the very different mindsets and cultural backgrounds that need to be accommodated in one developmental model, which often leads to the marginalization of the less powerful (Lewis et al. 2003).
72. For instance, the World Bank and the MDTP can claim that the 'Moteng area has been placed under appropriate conservation management, while the local villagers in Nyakoaneng can claim that the MDTP was a success with the hope that it will continue providing a source of livelihood.
73. Interview with staff member, Centre for Environment, Agriculture and Development, University of KwaZulu-Natal, South Africa, 5 March 2007.
74. Ibid.
75. Obviously, this is in line with a broader trend in contemporary development that focuses on building people's capacity rather than giving handouts, which in turn fits a political economy focused on devolved neoliberal governance.
76. For Obonjaneni, this workshop took place 11–13 May 2005, which I was able to attend.

6. Images of an Intervention

1. The gist of the argumentation is similar to Robert Cox's (1992) concept of *nébuleuse*, the global realignment of thinking toward the world economy, and Arturo Escobar's capitalist nature regime, which emphasizes "new ways of seeing, rationality, governmentality, and the commodification of nature linked to capitalist modernity" in the "articulation of nature" (1999, 5). Building on this work, I emphasize the importance of marketing, which, I argue, is first

and foremost a tool for, as well as a specific effect of, global neoliberal expansion of the disciplinary type, as explained by Stephen Gill: "Neoliberal forms of discipline are not necessarily universal nor consistent, but they are bureaucratised and institutionalised, and they operate with different degrees of intensity across a range of 'public' and 'private' spheres" (1995, 411–12).

2. Interview with staff member, World Bank, 19 January 2006.

3. Telephone interview with staff member, World Bank, 27 September 2005.

4. Interview with staff member, National Environment Secretariat, Ministry of Tourism, Environment and Culture of Lesotho, 21 October 2005; interview with South African MDTP PCU specialist, 3 May 2005.

5. Interview with South African MDTP PCU specialist, 3 May 2005.

6. Interview with staff member, World Bank, 19 January 2006.

7. Interview with staff member, World Bank, 24 May 2007.

8. Interview with staff member, National Environment Secretariat, Ministry of Tourism, Environment and Culture of Lesotho, 21 October 2005.

9. Interview with staff member, Transfrontier Conservation Areas Directorate, DEAT, South Africa, 1 September 2005.

10. Ibid.

11. Ibid.

12. Interview with staff member, World Bank, 24 May 2007.

13. The strategy notes, "We have an economic system that prioritises short-term profit and unlimited economic growth over long-term cumulative impacts of unsustainable economic activities on people, their livelihoods and on the natural resources. In addition, it is an economic system that continues to see poverty exist among many in the region. These market forces result in a lack of benefit-sharing and access to benefits. This is not being addressed by the policy- and decision-makers. Economic value of ecosystem services remains largely unaccounted for in resource use and allocation" (MDTP 2007e, 19). Interestingly, the strategy does not see a problem with problematizing an "economic system that prioritises short-term profit" and in the same paragraph subjecting the Maloti-Drakensberg ecosystem to that same economic system.

14. Lawrence Sisitka, the author of the Amagugu Esizwe final report, writes, "The bigger question here is the seeming reluctance of Rand Water, certainly at a senior level, to make any undertakings to protect the interests of the Amagugu Esizwe project, although great efforts were made by the project team to come to agreement with Rand Water concerning issues such as attendance at MDTP training sessions or the types of activities to be undertaken in certain areas. In such circumstances projects such as Amagugu Esizwe can be relatively powerless in the face of strong, commercially and technically driven agendas" (2007, 16).

15. For example, some local people asked critical questions about Royal Maluti keeping their promises with respect to jobs, because another golf estate around Clarens had made the same promises and did not live up to them. The Royal

Maluti representative then replied that the community should hold the company accountable, adding that if the communities would allow the process to stall for months and years, it will go somewhere else and the Clarens area will lose the investment and employment opportunities.

16. "The Rare Exception," Royal Maluti Golf and Country Club, http://www.royal maluti.com, accessed 23 October 2011.

17. Nondela, www.nondela.com, accessed 18 March 2011.

18. See the Dunblane website, www.dunblane.co.za, accessed 16 November 2007. More info about the golf estate can now be found on: http://www.golflinx .co.za/courses/about.php?cid=477, accessed 6 December 2012. Obviously, it is no coincidence that these marketing exercises are directed at the Gauteng province, as this is where most of the potential, wealthy (and white) customers reside and work. From their websites, as well as that of Royal Maluti, it is clear that these initiatives are overwhelmingly owned and pushed by whites.

19. Nondela, www.nondela.com, accessed 18 March 2011.

20. One would, for example, never find the Obonjaneni community advertising its Thandanani handicraft store in one of the many shopping malls in Pretoria, or find its advertisements on TV.

21. The budget was 2,550,000 of 6,000,000 "Special Drawing Rights" (US $7,920,000) for South Africa, and 2,350,000 of 5,600,000 "Special Drawing Rights" (US$7,320,000) for Lesotho World Bank, 2001a; 2001b.

22. Interview with staff member, KZN Wildlife, 7 March 2007.

23. Interview with South African MDTP PCU specialist, 20 September 2005.

24. Interview with member of Lesotho project coordination committee, 21 October 2005.

25. The itinerary was as follows: first day from Maseru to Tse'shlanyane (overnight), second day from Botha-Bothe to Oxbow (overnight), third day from Mokhotlong to Sehlabathebe (overnight), and back to Maseru on the fourth day.

26. Also see a report by Actionaid International that concludes that "nowhere is the challenge of increasing real aid as a share of overall aid greater than in the case of technical assistance. At least one quarter of donor budgets—some $19 billion in 2004—is spent in this way: on consultants, research and training" (2006, 3).

27. According to Christian Lund, "certain policies and actions are justified and legitimated with reference to the local; not necessarily always out of a considered strategy, but often with a taken-for-granted naturalness" (2006, 694).

28. Due to their differences in outlook to the project, three different newsletters were produced: one from South Africa, one from Lesotho, and one from both countries.

29. "New Year Greetings!," Lesotho MDTP Quarterly 2, 1 (2006): 2.

30. "Friend in High Places: Caretaker Communities at Senqu Sources," MDTP Quarterly, first joint edition 2, 1 (2005): 4–5.

31. "Fostering Concern and Responsibility for Conservation," Lesotho MDTP Quarterly 2, 1 (2006): 3.

32. Interview with South African MDTP PCU specialist, 3 May 2005.

33. Interview with South African MDTP PCU specialist, 20 September 2005.

34. This is the former name for the Managed Resource Committee.

35. Interview with bed and breakfast owner, Lesotho, 23 July 2007.

36. Inge Droog (2008, 69–72) mentions that outside of the formal accountability structure, the three agencies and the MDTP did try to positively influence the picture of the project by actively influencing a project video they had asked a community member from Ebusingatha to produce. The agencies wanted some critical commentaries replaced by "perfect promo-talk" (70).

37. Interview with South African MDTP PCU specialist, 20 September 2005.

38. Ibid.

39. The GEF has an online repository of documents from the projects. See The World Bank/IFC/M.I.G.A, "Office Memorandum," from Lars Vidaeus to Mohamed El-Ashry, April 11, 2000, http://www.thegef.org/gef/sites/thegef.org/files/repository/Regional_Maloti.pdf (the memorandum is on pages 2–4).

40. It must be said that the MDTP laid equal emphasis on the technical outcomes in its assessment of the Amagugu Esizwe project.

41. Interview with South African MDTP PCU specialist, 20 September 2005

42. World Bank, "Status of Projects in Execution—FY 05 SOPE," Operations Policy and Country Services, September 23, 2005, 370, http://www1.worldbank.org/operations/disclosure/SOPE/FY05/SOPEreportFY05-Final.pdf.

43. World Bank, "Status of Projects in Execution—FY 06 SOPE: Region: Africa," Operations Policy and Country Services, September 19, 2006, 288, http://www1.worldbank.org/operations/disclosure/SOPE/FY06/AFRSOPEreport FY06.pdf.

44. World Bank, "Status of Projects in Execution—FY 07 SOPE," Operations Policy and Country Services, October 10, 2007, 298, http://www1.worldbank .org/operations/disclosure/SOPE/FY07/SOPE_FY07_FINAL.pdf.

45. Ibid., 564.

46. As Piers Blaikie (2006) states, communities and critical researchers are usually not part of interpretative coalitions, and when they are it can seriously disrupt relations and the interpretative business as usual (Mosse 2006).

47. Interview with South African MDTP PCU specialist, 23 September 2005.

7. Neoliberal Alignments

1. This does not mean that these were the only practical governance strategies pursued under the MDTP. Among others, they also instigated an environmental education program that provided another incentive for people to learn about the value of nature and conservation.

2. Interview with South African MDTP PCU specialist, 22 July 2005; interview with Lesotho MDTP PCU specialist, 26 October 2005.

3. Telephone interview with staff member, World Bank, 25 April 2005.

4. Kent Redford and William Adams (2009) argue that this is a more general tendency in PES.

5. While PES is indeed trendy at the moment, these assumptions are nothing new. Paul Burkett argues that ecological economists have long been making the same assumptions, as have eighteenth- and nineteenth-century "physiocrats." He explains: "As with the physiocrats, this lack of attention to the connections between the system's internal economic relations and the way the system values nature leads to an identification of nature's value with its use-value, an acceptance of exchange-value and money as natural ways of valuing nature, and a one-sidedly quantitative perspective on nature's value" (Burkett 2005, 37).

6. It must be noted that not everyone at the workshop agreed with this statement, although most participants did. One participant explicitly noted that biodiversity should not have to pay for itself or create livelihoods: "There can be spin-offs but it mustn't be the primary motive." Again, this shows that neoliberal conservation is also resisted.

7. To quote from the report: "A robust basal cover, together will a dense canopy, promotes greater infiltration and reduced storm flow, and increased soil water storage. Such improved water retention capacity allows for the slow release of such retained water over time. Improved land use management will reduce stormflow reduce soil erosion—and hence siltation. An additional benefit is that there would be a higher carbon sequestration capacity of the area under management" (Mander 2007, 40). It should be noted that reducing the water quality of the area to "a robust basal cover" is also quite problematic, especially in light of the uncertainties over climate change.

8. See, for example, World Bank 2001a, 6, 89, and Sisitka 2007, 31.

9. Interview with Lesotho MDTP PCU specialist, 19 October 2005; interview with South African MDTP PCU specialist, 26 July 2005; interview with marketing manager, TFCA 2010 Development Unit, Department of Environmental Affairs and Tourism, South Africa, 13 August 2007.

10. Interview with Lesotho MDTP Project Coordination Unit specialist, 19 October 2005.

11. Ibid.

12. Interview with marketing manager, TFCA 2010 Development Unit, Department of Environmental Affairs and Tourism, South Africa, 13 August 2007. Interview with Lesotho MDTP Project Coordination Unit specialist, 19 October 2005.

13. Interview with South African MDTP PCU specialist, 26 July 2005; interview with marketing manager, TFCA 2010 Development Unit, DEAT, South Africa, 13 August 2007. Interview with Lesotho MDTP PCU specialist, 19 October 2005.

14. Interview with marketing manager, TFCA 2010 Development Unit, DEAT, South Africa, 13 August 2007. The agencies are the Eastern Cape Tourism Board, Ezemvelo KZN Wildlife, Free State Tourism Authority, Lesotho Tourism Development Corporation, South African National Parks, and Tourism KwaZulu-Natal (MDTP 2007e). See also the website http://www.malotidrakensbergroute

.com/. Interestingly, the Eastern Free State section of the website features a photograph of a lion, perhaps to signify that this is also "real Africa," even though lions do not live in the area.

15. This was mostly seen in terms of tourism infrastructure, such as hotels, lodges, bed and breakfasts, and tourism operators. Paul Wellings and Jonathan Crush (1983) argue that Lesotho's tourism industry used to be focused solely on providing the casino opportunities that South Africans were denied at home. While more-diversified tourism infrastructure has been developed since the early 1980s, it remains very limited, as illustrated by travel guides such as the Lonely Planet or specials on Lesotho in the April 2007 issue of *Go! Magazine* (www.gomag.co.za) and the April 2008 issue of *Getaway* magazine (www.get away.co.za).

16. Interview with Lesotho MDTP PCU specialist, 19 October 2005.

17. Interview with Lesotho MDTP PCU specialist, 24 May 2007.

18. Ibid.

19. Meeting, 9 June 2005, Mokhotlong, Lesotho.

20. Meeting, 8 March 2007, Ebusingatha, South Africa.

21. This, of course, has long been a reality in Africa (Bracking 2012).

22. This links in with recent debates about golf in tourism and sport studies more generally, which note that impacts on landscapes and environments due to golf courses have created increased international resistance and commotion (see Wheeler and Nauright 2006).

23. In general, many of the authors of these reports and studies are part of what I refer to as the "bioregional conservation planning" network.

24. To be sure: I am not arguing here for more impact assessment, and certainly not according to the current trends that are exemplary illustrations of methodological and economic reductionism.

Conclusion

1. However, clearly many more neoliberal conservation mechanisms exist and are gaining ground (see Sullivan 2010).

2. Hence, contrary to Saleem Ali (2007), I argue that the term "peace park" is part and parcel of the politics of neoliberal conservation that is supposed to bring TFCAs' political legitimation and is therefore not the same as the term "transfrontier conservation area."

3. I borrowed the term "uneasy contradictions" from photographer Edward Burtynsky. See his website, http://www.edwardburtynsky.com.

4. There was one instance in the Amagugu Esizwe project whereby traditional authorities actively resisted the project, which put it on hold for three months. However, it did not become clear whether the exact reasons for this resistance had much to do with the intervention as such or more with local politics (interview with South African MDTP PCU specialist, 20 September 2005).

5. It is interesting to note Pete Brosius's argument here in that "acts of resis-

tance" should simultaneously also be seen as attempts at engagement (2006, 283). While big resistance seemed to be lacking, local actors did try to engage the MDTP, albeit mostly on the MDTP's terms.

6. There is of course a wide body of academic and nonacademic literature and other art forms that have done this and continue doing so—too extensive to reference in detail here but important to acknowledge.

7. Political ecology broadly conceived, including its anthropological, geography, sociology, and political science incarnations.

8. Some have already been doing this, especially in recent event ethnographies (see Brosius and Campbell 2010 and the articles of the special issue of *Conservation and Society*). See also King 2009.

9. Although Thomas Eriksen does not link his analysis of the information age with the political economy that stimulates it, his warning is nonetheless worth repeating and keeping in mind: "The unhindered and massive flow of information in our time is about to fill all the gaps, leading as a consequence to a situation where everything threatens to become a hysterical series of saturated moments, without a 'before' and 'after,' a 'here' and 'there' to separate them. Indeed, even the 'here and now' is threatened since the next moment comes so quickly that it becomes difficult to live in the present. . . . The consequences of this extreme hurriedness are overwhelming; both the past and the future as mental categories are threatened by the tyranny of the moment" (2001, 2–3).

10. I am building on and contributing to the many experiences, institutions, and relations that already address these, and have done so for a long time. See, for an interesting discussion of these in the age of high-technology capitalism, Dyer-Witheford 1999 (especially chapter 7).

11. I am grateful to Jim Igoe for pointing this out to me.

references

Actionaid International. 2006. *Real Aid 2: Making Technical Assistance Work*. Johannesburg: Actionaid International.

Adams, J. S., and T. O. McShane. 1996. *The Myth of Wild Africa: Conservation without Illusion*. Berkeley: University of California Press.

Adams, W. 2004. *Against Extinction: The Story of Conservation*. London: Earthscan.

Adams, W., and D. Hulme. 2001. "Conservation and Community: Changing Narratives, Policies and Practices in African Conservation." In *African Wildlife and Livelihoods: The Promise and Performance of Community Conservation*, ed. D. Hulme and M. Murphree, 9–23. Oxford: James Currey.

Adams, W., and J. Hutton. 2007. "People, Parks and Poverty: Political Ecology and Biodiversity Conservation." *Conservation and Society* 5 (2): 147–83.

Adams, W., and S. Jeanrenaud. 2008. *Transition to Sustainability: Towards a Humane and Diverse World*. Gland, Switzerland: IUCN.

Adesanmi, P. 2011. *You're Not a Country, Africa: A Personal History of the African Present*. Johannesburg: Penguin.

Agrawal, A., and C. Gibson. 1999. "Enchantment and Disenchantment: The Role of Community in Natural Resource Conservation." *World Development* 27 (4): 629–49.

Alexander, N. 2002. *An Ordinary Country: Issues in the Transition from Apartheid to Democracy in South Africa*. Pietermaritzburg, South Africa: University of Natal Press.

Ali, S. H. 2007. *Peace Parks: Conservation and Conflict Resolution*. Cambridge: MIT Press.

Anders, G. 2003. "Good Governance as Technology: Towards an Ethnography of the Bretton Woods Institutions." In *The Aid Effect: Giving and Governing in International Development*, ed. D. Mosse and D. Lewis, 37–60. London: Pluto Press.

Arsel, M., and B. Büscher. 2012. "Nature™ Inc.: Changes and Continuities in Neoliberal Conservation and Environmental Markets." *Development and Change* 43 (1): 53–78.

Arts, B., and J. van Tatenhove. 2004. "Policy and Power: A Conceptual Framework between the 'Old' and 'New' Policy Idioms." *Policy Sciences* 37: 339–56.

Arvidsson, A. 2005. "Brands: A Critical Perspective." *Journal of Consumer Culture* 5 (2): 235–58.

Axford, B., and R. Huggins. 1998. "Anti-politics or the Triumph of Postmodern Populism in Promotional Cultures?" *Telematics and Informatics* 15: 181–202.

Ayers, A. J. 2006. "Demystifying Democratisation: The Global Constitution of (Neo)Liberal Polities in Africa." *Third World Quarterly* 27 (2): 321–38.

Bainbridge, W. R., B. Motsamai, and L. C. Weaver. 1991. *Report of the Drakensberg/Maluti Conservation Programme*. Pietermaritzburg, South Africa: Natal Parks Board.

Barber, B. 1995. *Jihad vs. McWorld*. New York: Times Books.

Barnett, C. 2005. "The Consolations of 'Neoliberalism.'" *Geoforum* 36 (1): 7–12.

Barret, C. B., and P. Arcese. 1995. "Are Integrated Conservation-Development Projects (ICDPs) Sustainable? On the Conservation of Large Mammals in Sub-Saharan Africa." *World Development* 23 (6): 1073–84.

Barrow, E., and M. Murphree. 2001. "Community Conservation: From Concept to Practice." In *African Wildlife and Livelihoods: The Promise and Performance of Community Conservation*, ed. D. Hulme and M. Murphree, 24–37. Oxford: James Currey.

Barry, A., T. Osborne, and N. Rose. 1996. "Introduction." In *Foucault and Political Reason: Liberalism, Neo-liberalism and Rationalities of Government*, ed. A. Barry, T. Osborne, and N. Rose, 1–17. London: University College London Press.

Bayart, J. 2009. *The State in Africa. The Politics of the Belly. Second Edition*. Cambridge: Polity.

Baudrillard, J. 1994. *Simulacra and Simulation*. Ann Arbor: University of Michigan Press.

Bebbington, A. 2005. "Donor-NGO Relations and Representations of Livelihood in Nongovermental Aid Chains." *World Development* 33 (6): 937–50.

Beinart, W. 2003. *The Rise of Conservation in South Africa: Settlers, Livestock, and the Environment 1770–1950*. Oxford: Oxford University Press.

Bending, T. 2003. "The Emperor's New Clothes: Rethinking the Mechanics of the 'Anti-politics Machine.'" Paper presented at "Order and Disjuncture: The Organisation of Aid and Development," EIDOS workshop, London, 26–28 September.

Benjaminsen, T. A., and H. Svarstad. 2010. "The Death of an Elephant: Conservation Discourses versus Practices in Africa." *Forum for Development Studies* 37 (3): 385–408.

Berman, M. 1988. *All That Is Solid Melts Into Air. The Experience of Modernity*. New York: Penguin.

Bernstein, H. 1998. "Social Change in the South African Countryside? Land and Production, Poverty and Power." *Journal of Peasant Studies* 25 (4): 1–32.

Biersack, A. 2006. "Reimagining Political Ecology: Culture/Power/History/Nature." In *Reimagining Political Ecology*, ed. A. Biersack and J. B. Greenberg, 3–42. Durham: Duke University Press.

Blaikie, P. 2006. "Is Small Really Beautiful? Community-Based Natural Resource Management in Malawi and Botswana." *World Development* 34 (11): 1942–57.

Bleiker, R. 2000. "The 'End of Modernity'?" In *Contending Images of World Politics*, ed. G. Fry and J. O'Hagan, 227–41. London: Macmillan Press.

Boehm, C. 2003. "The Social Life of Fields: Labour Markets and Agrarian Change in Lesotho." *Paideusis—Journal for Interdisciplinary and Cross-Cultural Studies* 3: 1–20.

Bond, P. 2000. *Elite Transition: From Apartheid to Neoliberalism in South Africa.* Pietermaritzburg, South Africa: University of Natal Press.

Borrini-Feyerabend, G., M. Pimbert, M. Farvar, A. Kothari, and Y. Renard. 2004. *Sharing Power: A Global Guide to Collaborative Management of Natural Resources.* London: Earthscan.

Bracking, S. 2012. "How Do Investors Value Environmental Harm/Care? Private Equity Funds, Development Finance Institutions and the Partial Financialization of Nature-Based Industries." *Development and Change* 43 (1): 271–93.

Brenner, N., J. Peck, and N. Theodore. 2010. "After Neoliberalization?" *Globalizations* 7 (3): 327–45.

Brenner, N., and N. Theodore. 2002. "Cities and the Geographies of 'Actually Existing Neoliberalism.'" *Antipode* 34 (3): 356–86.

Brockington, D. 2002. *Fortress Conservation: The Preservation of the Mkomazi Game Reserve, Tanzania.* Oxford: James Currey.

Brockington, D. 2008. "Powerful Environmentalisms: Conservation, Celebrity and Capitalism." *Media Culture Society* 30 (4): 551–68.

——. 2009. *Celebrity and the Environment: Fame, Wealth and Power in Conservation.* London: Zed Books.

Brockington, D., R. Duffy, and J. Igoe. 2008. *Nature Unbound: Conservation, Capitalism and the Future of Protected Areas.* Earthscan: London.

Brockington, D., and R. Duffy. 2010. "Capitalism and Conservation: The Production and Reproduction of Biodiversity Conservation." *Antipode* 42 (3): 469–84.

Brockington, D., and J. Igoe. 2006. "Eviction for Conservation: A Global Overview." *Conservation and Society* 4 (3): 424–70.

Brondo, K. V., and N. Brown. 2011. "Neoliberal Conservation, Garifuna Territorial Rights and Resource Management in the Cayos Cochinos Marine Protected Area." *Conservation and Society* 9 (2): 91–105.

Brosius, J. P. 2006. "Between Politics and Poetics: Narratives of Dispossession in Sarawak, East Malaysia." In *Reimagining Political Ecology*, ed. A. Biersack and J. B. Greenberg, 281–322. Durham: Duke University Press.

Brosius, J. P., and L. M. Campbell. 2010. "Collaborative Event Ethnography: Conservation and Development Trade-offs at the Fourth World Conservation Congress." *Conservation and Society* 8 (4): 245–55.

Brosius, J. P., A. Tsing, and C. Zerner. 2005. *Communities and Conservation: Histories and Politics of Community-Based Natural Resource Management.* Lanham, Md.: AltaMira.

Bryceson, D. 2002. "Multiplex Livelihoods in Rural Africa: Recasting the Terms and Conditions of Gainful Employment." *Journal of Modern African Studies* 40 (1): 1–28.

Burkett, P. 2005. *Marxism and Ecological Economics: Toward a Red and Green Political Economy.* Leiden, the Netherlands: Brill.

Büscher, B. E. 2008. "Conservation, Neoliberalism and Social Science: A Critical Reflection on the SCB 2007 Annual Meeting, South Africa." *Conservation Biology* 22 (2): 229–31.

———. 2009. "Letters of Gold: Enabling Primitive Accumulation through Neoliberal Conservation." *Human Geography* 2 (3): 91–94.

———. 2010a. "Anti-politics as Political Strategy: Neoliberalism and Transfrontier Conservation and Development in Southern Africa." *Development and Change* 41 (1): 29–51.

———. 2010b. "Derivative Nature: Interrogating the Value of Conservation in 'Boundless Southern Africa.'" *Third World Quarterly* 31 (2): 259–76.

———. 2010c. "Seeking Telos in the 'Transfrontier': Neoliberalism and the Transcending of Community Conservation in Southern Africa." *Environment and Planning A* 42 (3): 644–60.

———. 2011. "The Neoliberalisation of Nature in Africa." In *New Topographies of Power? Africa Negotiating an Emerging Multi-polar World*, ed. T. Dietz, K. Havnevik, M. Kaag, and T. Ostigard, 84–109. Leiden: Brill.

Büscher, B. E., and T. Dietz. 2005. "Conjunctions of Governance: The State and the Conservation-Development Nexus in Southern Africa." *Journal of Transdisciplinary Environmental Studies* 4 (2): 1–15.

Büscher, B. E., and W. Dressler. 2007. "Linking Neoprotectionism and Environmental Governance: On the Rapidly Increasing Tensions between Actors in the Environment-Development Nexus." *Conservation and Society* 5 (4): 586–611.

———. 2012. "Commodity Conservation: The Restructuring of Community Conservation in South Africa and the Philippines." *Geoforum* 43 (3): 367–76.

Büscher, B. E., and T. Mutimukuru. 2007. "Buzzing Too Far? The Ideological Echo of the Global Governance Agenda on the Local Level: The Case of the Mafungautsi Forest in Zimbabwe." *Development Southern Africa* 24 (5): 649–64.

Büscher, B. E., and M. L. Schoon. 2009. "Competition over Conservation: Collective Action and Negotiating Transfrontier Conservation in Southern Africa." *Journal of International Wildlife Law and Policy* 12 (1–2): 33–59.

Büscher, B., S. Sullivan, K. Neves, J. Igoe, and D. Brockington. 2012. "Towards a Synthesized Critique of Neoliberal Biodiversity Conservation." *Capitalism, Nature Socialism* 23 (2): 4–30.

Büscher, B. E., and W. Wolmer. 2007. "Introduction: The Politics of Engagement between Biodiversity Conservation and the Social Sciences." *Conservation and Society* 5 (1): 1–21.

Buzzard, C. H. 2001. *Policy Environment Governing the Great Limpopo Transfrontier Park and Conservation Area: A Review of Relevant International Agreements, SADC*

Protocols, and National Policies. Nelspruit, South Africa: Development Alternatives.

Cammack, P. 2003. "The Governance of Global Capitalism: A New Materialist
Perspective." *Historical Materialism* 11 (2): 37–59.

Carolan, M. S. 2005a. "Disciplining Nature: The Homogenising and Constraining
Forces of Anti-markets on the Food System." *Environmental Values* 14: 363–87.

———. 2005b. "Society, Biology, and Ecology: Bringing Nature Back into Sociology's
Disciplinary Narrative through Critical Realism." *Organization and Environment*
18 (4): 393–421.

———. 2006. "Scientific Knowledge and Environmental Policy: Why Science Needs
Values." *Environmental Sciences* 3 (4): 229–37.

Carrier, J. G., and D. V. L. Macleod. 2005. "Bursting the Bubble: The Socio-cultural
Context of Ecotourism." *Journal of the Royal Anthropological Institute* 11: 315–34.

Carrier, J., and P. West. 2009. *Virtualism, Governance and Practice: Vision and Execution in Enviornmental Conservation.* New York: Berghahn.

Carruthers, J. 1995. *The Kruger National Park: A Social and Political History.* Pietermaritzburg, South Africa: University of Natal Press.

Castells, M. 1996. *The Rise of the Network Society.* Oxford: Blackwell Publishers.

Castree, N., and B. Braun. 1998. "The Construction of Nature and the Nature of
Construction: Analytical and Political Tools for Building Survivable Futures." In
Remaking Reality: Nature at the Millenium, ed. B. Braun and N. Castree, 3–42.
London: Routledge.

Castree, N. 2008a. "Neoliberalising Nature: Processes, Effects, and Evaluations."
Environment and Planning A 40 (1): 153–73.

———. 2008b. "Neoliberalising Nature: The Logics of Deregulation and Reregulation." *Environment and Planning A* 40 (1): 131–52.

———. 2010. "Neoliberalism and the Biophysical Environment: A Synthesis and
Evaluation of the Research." *Environment and Society: Advances in Research* 1 (1):
5–45.

Cernea, M., and K. Schmidt-Soltau. 2006. "Poverty Risks and National Parks:
Policy Issues in Conservation and Resettlement." *World Development* 34 (10):
1808–30.

Chabal, P., and J. P. Daloz. 1999. *Africa Works: Disorder as Political Instrument.*
Oxford: James Currey.

Chambers, R. 1983. *Rural Development: Putting the Last First.* Longman: Harlow.

Chudy, J. 2006. "Green Barons." *Portfolio* (August/September): 45–46.

Clarke, J. 2004. "Dissolving the Public Realm? The Logics and Limits of Neoliberalism." *Journal of Social Policy* 33 (1): 27–48.

Cooke, B., and U. Kothari. 2001. "The Case for Participation as Tyranny." In *Participation: The New Tyranny?,* ed. B. Cooke and U. Kothari, 1–15. London: Zed
Books.

Coplan, D. B. 2001. "A River Runs through It: The Meaning of the Lesotho-Free
State Border." *African Affairs* 100: 81–116.

Cornwall, A., and K. Brock. 2005. "What Do Buzzwords Do for Development Policy? A Critical Look at 'Participation,' 'Empowerment,' and 'Poverty Reduction.'" *Third World Quarterly* 26 (7): 1043–60.

Corson, C. 2011. "Territorialization, Enclosure and Neoliberalism: Non-state Influence in Struggles over Madagascar's Forests." *Journal of Peasant Studies* 38 (4): 703–26.

Cousins, B. 2007. "More Than Socially Embedded: The Distinctive Character of 'Communal Tenure' Regimes in South Africa and Its Implications for Land Policy." *Journal of Agrarian Change* 7 (3): 281–315.

Cowling, R. M., B. Egoh, A. T. Knight, P. O'Farrel, B. Reyers, M. Rouget, D. Roux, A. Welz, and A. Wilhelm-Rechman. 2008. "An Operational Model for Mainstreaming Ecosystem Services for Implementation." *Proceedings of the National Academy of Sciences* 105 (28): 9483–88.

Cowling, R. M., and R. L. Pressey. 2003. "Introduction to Systematic Conservation Planning in the Cape Floristic Region." *Biological Conservation* 112: 1–13.

Cox, R. W. 1981. "Social Forces, States and World Orders: Beyond International Relations Theory." *Millennium: Journal of International Studies* 10 (2): 126–55.

——. 1992. "Global Perestroika." In *New World Order? The Socialist Register*, ed. R. Miliband and L. Panitch, 26–43. London: Merlin.

Critchley, W. R. S. 2000. "Inquiry, Initiative and Inventiveness: Farmer Innovators in East Africa." *Physics and Chemistry of the Earth* 25 (3): 285–88.

Death, C. 2010. *Governing Sustainable Development: Partnerships, Protests and Power at the World Summit*. London: Routledge.

——. 2011. "Leading by Example: South African Foreign Policy and Global Environmental Politics." *International Relations* 25 (4): 455–78.

Debord, G. 1967. *Society of the Spectacle*. London: Rebel Press.

De Jonge Schuermans, A. M., J. Helbing, and R. Fedosseev. 2004. *Evaluation of Success and Failure in the International Water Management*. Zurich: ETH Zurich.

Demmers, J., A. E. Fernández Jilberto, and B. Hogenboom. 2004. "Good Governance and Democracy in a World of Neoliberal Regimes." In *Good Governance in the Era of Global Neoliberalism: Conflict and Depolitisation in Latin America, Eastern Europe, Asia and Africa*, ed. J. Demmers, A. E. Fernández Jilberto, and B. Hogenboom, 1–37. London: Routledge.

DeMotts, R. 2009. "Of Football and Zebras: Imagining 2010 in the Southern African Wilderness." Paper presented at the Annual Meeting of the International Studies Association, New York, 15–18 February.

Department of Environmental Affairs and Tourism. 2005. "Positioning the Transfrontier Parks (TFPS) and Transfrontier Conservation Areas (TFCAS) as Southern Africa's Premiere International Tourism Destination: A Strategy Paper Phase One—2005–2010." Draft discussion document, Pretoria, South Africa.

Diederichs, N., and M. Mander. 2004. "Payments for Environmental Services Baseline Study." Final report to the Maloti Drakensberg Transfrontier Project, Everton, Futureworks!

Dietz, T. 1996. *Entitlements to Natural Resources: Contours of Political Environmental Geography*. Utrecht, the Netherlands: International Books.

Dowie, M. 2009. *Conservation Refugees: The Hundred-Year Conflict between Global Conservation and Native Peoples*. Cambridge: MIT Press.

Drainville, A. C. 1994. "International Political Economy in the Age of Open Marxism." *Review of International Political Economy* 1 (1): 105–32.

Draper, M., M. Spierenburg, and H. Wels. 2004. "African Dreams of Cohesion: Elite Pacting and Community Development in Transfrontier Conservation Areas in Southern Africa." *Culture and Organization* 10 (4): 341–53.

Dressler, W. 2009. *Old Thoughts in New Ideas: State Conservation Measures, Development and Livelihood on Palawan Island*. Manila: Ateneo de Manila University Press.

——. 2011. "First to Third Nature: The Rise of Capitalist Conservation on Palawan Island, the Philippines." *Journal of Peasant Studies* 38 (3): 533–57.

Dressler, W., and B. E. Büscher. 2008. "Market Triumphalism and the So-Called CBNRM 'Crisis' at the South African Section of the Great Limpopo Transfrontier Park." *Geoforum* 39 (1): 452–65.

Dressler, W., B. E. Büscher, M. Schoon, D. Brockington, T. Hayes, C. Kull, J. McCarthy, and K. Streshta. 2010. "From Hope to Crisis and Back? A Critical History of the Global CBNRM Narrative." *Environmental Conservation* 37 (1): 5–15

Droog, I. 2008. "The Show Must Go On: The Violation of Trust and the Continuation of Cooperation in the Amagugu Esizwe Project, South Africa." Master's thesis, VU University Amsterdam.

Duffy, R. 1997. "The Environmental Challenge to the Nation-State: Superparks and National Parks Policy in Zimbabwe." *Journal of Southern African Studies* 23 (3): 441–51.

——. 2002. *A Trip Too Far: Ecotourism, Politics, and Exploitation*. London: Earthscan.

——. 2006a. "Global Environmental Governance and the Politics of Ecotourism in Madagascar." *Journal of Ecotourism* 5: 128–44.

——. 2006b. "The Potential and Pitfalls of Global Environmental Governance: The Politics of Transfrontier Conservation Areas in Southern Africa." *Political Geography* 25: 89–112.

——. 2010. *Nature Crime: How We're Getting Conservation Wrong*. New Haven: Yale University Press.

Dyer-Witheford, N. 1999. *Cyber-Marx: Cycles and Circuits of Struggle in High-Technology Capitalism*. Urbana: University of Illinois Press.

Edwards, M. 1999. *Future Positive: International Cooperation in the 21st Century*. London: Routledge.

Ellis, W. 2011. "The ≠Khomani San Land Claim against the Kalahari Gemsbok National Park: Requiring and Acquiring Authenticity." In *Land Memory, Reconstruction, and Justice: Perspectives on Land Claims in South Africa*, ed. C. Walker, A. Bohlin, R. Hall, and T. Kepe, 181–97. Pietermaritzburg, South Africa: University of KwaZulu-Natal Press.

Eriksen, T. H. 2001. *Tyranny of the Moment: Fast and Slow Time in the Information Age*. London: Pluto Press.

Escobar, A. 1995. *Encountering Development: The Making and Unmaking of the Third World*. Princeton: Princeton University Press.

———. 1999. "After Nature: Steps Towards an Antiessentialist Political Ecology." *Current Anthropology* 40 (1): 1–30.

European Union and Kingdom of Lesotho. 2002. "Joint Annual Report on Co-operation between the European Union and the Kingdom of Lesotho." Delegation of the European Commission in the Kingdom of Lesotho and the National Authorising Officer of the Lesotho Ministry of Finance and Development Planning, Maseru, Lesotho. ec.europa.eu/development/icenter/repository/jar07_ls_en.pdf.

Fabricius, C., and E. Koch. 2004. *Rights Resources and Rural Development: Community-Based Natural Resource Management in Southern Africa*. Edited with H. Magome and S. Turner. London: Earthscan.

Fairhead, J., and M. Leach. 1996. *Misreading the African Landscape: Society and Ecology in a Forest-Savanna Mosaic*. Cambridge: Cambridge University Press.

Fay, D. 2013. "Neoliberal Conservation and Lawfare: New Legal Entities and the Political Ecology of Litigation at Dwesa-Cwebe, South Africa." *Geoforum* 44 (1): 170–81.

Fay, D., and D. James. 2009. *The Rights and Wrongs of Land Restitution: Restoring What Was Ours*. London: Routledge.

Ferguson, J. 1994. *The Anti-politics Machine: "Development," Depoliticization, and Bureaucratic Power in Lesotho*. Minneapolis: University of Minnesota Press.

———. 2006. *Global Shadows: Africa in the Neoliberal World Order*. Durham: Duke University Press.

———. 2010. "The Uses of Neoliberalism." *Antipode* 41 (1): 166–84.

Fine, B., and Z. Rustomjee. 1996. *The Political Economy of South Africa: From Minerals-Energy Complex to Industrialisation*. Boulder, Colo.: Westview Press.

Fletcher, R. 2009. "Ecotourism Discourse: Challenging the Stakeholders Theory." *Journal of Ecotourism* 8 (3): 269–85.

———. 2010. "Neoliberal Environmentality: Towards a Poststructural Political Ecology of the Conservation Debate." *Conservation and Society* 8 (3): 171–81.

———. 2011. "Sustaining Tourism, Sustaining Capitalism? The Tourism Industry's Role in Global Capitalist Expansion." *Tourism Geographies* 13 (3): 443–61.

Ford, L. 2003. "Challenging Global Environmental Governance: Social Movement Agency and Global Civil Society." *Global Environmental Politics* 3 (2): 120–34.

Forslund, A., et al. 2009. "Securing Water for Ecosystems and Human Well-Being: The Importance of Environmental Flows." Swedish Water House Report 24, Stockholm International Water Institute.

Foster, J. B. 2000. *Marx's Ecology: Materialism and Nature*. New York: Monthly Review Press.

Foucault, M. 1995. *Discipline and Punish: The Birth of the Prison*. New York: Vintage Books.

Foucault, M. 2008. *The Birth of Biopolitics. Lectures at the College de France 1978–1979.* Translated by Graham Burchell. Basingstoke: Palgrave MacMillan.

Galvin, M., and T. Haller. 2008. *People, Protected Areas and Global Change.* Bern: NCCR North-South, Swiss National Centre of Competence in Research North-South, University of Bern.

Garland, E. 2008. "The Elephant in the Room: Confronting the Colonial Character of Wildlife Conservation in Africa." *African Studies Review* 51 (3): 51–74.

Gibson, C. C. 1999. *Politicians and Poachers: The Political Economy of Wildlife Policy in Africa.* Cambridge: Cambridge University Press.

Gibson, C. C., and S. A. Marks. 1995. "Turning Hunters into Conservationists: An Assessment of Community-Based Wildlife Programs in Africa." *World Development* 23 (6): 941–57.

Gill, S. 1993. "A Short History of Lesotho." In *Lesotho, Kingdom in the Sky,* ed. J. A. M. Giessen, 9–167. Berg en Dal, the Netherlands: Afrika Museum.

——. 1995. "Globalisation, Market Civilisation, and Disciplinary Neoliberalism." *Millennium: Journal of International Studies* 24 (3): 399–423.

Goldman, M. 2005. *Imperial Nature: The World Bank and Struggles for Social Justice in the Age of Globalization.* New Haven: Yale University Press.

Gray, J. 2000. *Two Faces of Liberalism.* Cambridge, U.K.: Polity Press.

Griffin, J., D. Cumming, S. Metcalfe, M. t'Sas-Rolfes, J. Singh, E. Chonguiça, M. Rowen, and J. Oglethorpe. 1999. *Study on the Development of Transboundary Natural Resource Management Areas in Southern Africa.* Washington, D.C.: Biodiversity Support Program.

Grove, R. 1989. "Scottish Missionaries, Evangelical Discourses and the Origins of Conservation Thinking in Southern Africa 1820–1900." *Journal of Southern African Studies* 15 (2): 163–87.

Hanks, J. 2000. *The Origin and Objectives of the Peace Parks Foundation.* Stellenbosch, South Africa: Peace Parks Foundation.

——. 2003. "Transfrontier Conservation Areas (TFCAS) in Southern Africa." *Journal of Sustainable Forestry* 17 (1–2): 127–48.

Haraway, D. J. 1997. *Modest_Witness@second_Millennium.FemaleMan©_Meets_OncoMouse™: Feminism and Technoscience.* New York: Routledge.

Harrison, G. 2005a. "Economic Faith, Social Project and a Misreading of African Society: The Travails of Neoliberalism in Africa." *Third World Quarterly* 26 (8): 1303–20.

——. 2005b. "The World Bank, Governance and Theories of Political Action in Africa." *British Journal of Politics and International Relations* 7: 240–60.

Hart, G. 2002. *Disabling Globalization: Places of Power in Post-Apartheid South Africa.* Berkeley: University of California Press.

——. 2008. "The Provocations of Neoliberalism: Contesting the Nation and Liberation after Apartheid." *Antipode* 40 (4): 678–705.

Hartwick, E., and R. Peet. 2003. "Neoliberalism and Nature: The Case of the WTO." *The Annals of the American Academy of Political and Social Science* 590 (1): 188–211.

Harvey, D. 1996. *Justice, Nature and the Geography of Difference*. Malden: Blackwell.

———. 2005. *A Brief History of Neoliberalism*. Oxford: Oxford University Press.

———. 2006. *Spaces of Global Capitalism: A Theory of Uneven Geographical Development*. London: Verso.

———. 2010. *The Enigma of Capital and the Crises of Capitalism*. Oxford: Oxford University Press.

Heynen, N., S. Prudham, J. McCarthy, and P. Robbins. 2007. *Neoliberal Environments: False Promises and Unnatural Consequences*. London: Routledge.

Holmes, G. 2012. "Biodiversity for Billionaires: Capitalism, Conservation and the Role of Philanthropy in Saving/Selling Nature." *Development and Change* 43 (1): 185–203.

Holt, F. L. 2005. "The Catch-22 of Conservation: Indigenous Peoples, Biologists, and Cultural Change." *Human Ecology* 33 (2): 199–215.

Horta, K. 1995. "The Mountain Kingdom's White Oil: The Lesotho Highlands Water Project." *Ecologist* 25: 227–31.

Horta, K., R. Round, and Z. Young. 2002. *The Global Environment Facility: The First Ten Years—Growing Pains or Inherent Flaws*. Halifax, Canada: Halifax Initiative and Environmental Defense.

Huggins, G., E. Barendse, A. Fischer, and J. Sitoi. 2003. "Limpopo National Park: Resettlement Policy Framework." Washington, D.C.; Maputo: World Bank; Limpopo National Park.

Hughes, D. M. 2001. "'Rezoned for Business': How Ecotourism Unlocked Black Farmland in Eastern Zimbabwe." *Journal of Agrarian Change* 1 (4): 575–99.

———. 2005. "Third Nature: Making Space and Time in the Great Limpopo Conservation Area." *Cultural Anthropology* 20 (2): 157–84.

———. 2006. *From Enslavement to Environmentalism: Politics on a Southern African Frontier*. Seattle: University of Washington Press.

———. 2010. *Whiteness in Zimbabwe: Race, Landscape, and the Problem of Belonging*. New York: Palgrave MacMillan.

Hulme, D., and M. Murphree. 2001. *African Wildlife and Livelihoods: The Promise and Performance of Community Conservation*. Oxford: James Currey.

Hutton, J., W., M. Adams, and J. C. Murombedzi. 2005. "Back to the Barriers? Changing Narratives in Biodiversity Conservation." *Forum for Development Studies* 2: 341–70.

Igoe, J. 2004. *Conservation and Globalization: A Study of National Parks and Indigenous Communities from East Africa to South Dakota*. Belmont, Calif.: Wadsworth.

———. 2010. "The Spectacle of Nature in the Global Economy of Appearances: Anthropological Engagements with the Images of Transnational Conservation." *Critique of Anthropology* 30 (4): 375–97.

Igoe, J., and D. Brockington. 2007. "Neoliberal Conservation: A Brief Introduction." *Conservation and Society* 5 (4): 432–49.

Igoe, J., and C. Fortwangler. 2007. "Introduction: Whither Communities and Conservation?" *International Journal of Biodiversity Science and Management* 3: 65–76.

Igoe, J., K. Neves, and D. Brockington. 2010. "A Spectacular Eco-tour around the Historic Bloc: Theorising the Convergence of Biodiversity Conservation and Capitalist Expansion." *Antipode* 42 (3): 486–512.

International Union for Conservation of Nature. 1994. *Guidelines for Protected Area Management Categories.* Gland, Switzerland: IUCN Commission on National Parks and Protected Areas, with the World Conservation Monitoring Centre.

Jeffery, A. J. 1997. *The Natal Story: Sixteen Years of Conflict.* Johannesburg: South African Institute of Race Relations.

Jones, J. L. 2005. "Transboundary Conservation: Development Implications for Communities in KwaZulu-Natal, South Africa." *The International Journal of Sustainable Development and World Ecology* 12 (3): 266–78.

Kepe, T. 2009. "Shaped by Race: Why 'Race' Still Matters in the Challenges Facing Biodiversity Conservation in Africa." *Local Environment* 14: 871–78.

Khanya. 2005. "Community-Based Management of Eco-tourism in Lesotho." Partial draft report. Bloemfontein: Khanya—Managing Rural Change cc.

King, B. 2009. "Commercializing Conservation in South Africa." *Environment and Planning A* 41 (2): 407–24.

Konrád, G. 1984. *Anti-politics.* London: Quartet.

Kovel, J. 2002. *The Enemy of Nature, the End of Capitalism or the End of the World?* London: Zed Books.

Kusters, K., R. Achdiawan, B. Belcher, and M. Ruiz Perez. 2006. "Balancing Development and Conservation? An Assessment of Livelihood and Environmental Outcomes of Nontimber Forest Product Trade in Asia, Africa, and Latin America." *Ecology and Society* 11 (2): 20.

Lamar, H., and L. Thompson 1981. *The Frontier in History: North America and Southern Africa Compared.* New Haven: Yale University Press.

Latour, B. 2005. *Reassembling the Social: An Introduction to Actor-Network-Theory.* Oxford: Oxford University Press.

Lefebvre, H. 1991. *The Production of Space.* Oxford: Blackwell.

Lewis, D., A. J. Bebbington, S. P. J. Batterbury, A. Shah, E. Olson, M. Shameem Siddiqi, and S. Duvall. 2003. "Practice, Power and Meaning: Frameworks for Studying Organizational Culture in Multi-agency Rural Development Projects." *Journal of International Development* 15: 541–57.

Lewis, D., and D. Mosse. 2006. *Development Brokers and Translators: The Ethnography of Aid Agencies.* Bloomfield, Conn.: Kumarian Press.

Li, T. M. 2007. *The Will to Improve: Governmentality, Development, and the Practice of Politics.* Durham: Duke University Press.

Lugard, F. 1965. *The Dual Mandate in British Tropical Africa.* London: Routledge.

Lund, C. 2006. "Twilight Institutions: Public Authority and Local Politics in Africa." *Development and Change* 37 (4): 685–705.

MacDonald, K. 2010. "The Devil Is in the (Bio)diversity: Private Sector 'Engagement' and the Restructuring of Biodiversity Conservation." *Antipode* 42 (3): 513–50.

Magome, H., and J. C. Murombedzi. 2003. "Sharing South African National Parks:

Community Land and Conservation in a Democratic South Africa." In *Decolonising Nature: Strategies for Conservation in a Post-colonial Era*, ed. W. M. Adams and M. Mulligan, 108–43. London: Earthscan.

Mamdani, M. 1996. *Citizen and Subject: Contemporary Africa and the Legacy of Late Colonialism*. Princeton: Princeton University Press.

Mander, M., et al. 2007. "Payment for Ecosystem Services: Developing an Ecosystem Services Trading Model for the Mnweni/Cathedral Peak and Eastern Cape Drakensberg Areas." Institute of Natural Resources Report IR281, Institute of Natural Resources, Development Bank of Southern Africa, Department of Water Affairs and Forestry, Department of Environment Affairs and Tourism, Ezemvelo KZN Wildlife, Pietermaritzburg, South Africa.

Mander, M., and M. Everard. 2008. "The Socio-economics of River Management." *Environmental Scientist* 17 (3): 31–34.

Mansfield, B. 2004. "Neoliberalism in the Oceans: 'Rationalization,' Property Rights and the Commons Question." *Geoforum* 35: 313–26.

Marden, P. 2003. *The Decline of Politics: Governance, Globalisation and the Public Sphere*. Aldershot, U.K.: Ashgate.

Marx, K. 1976. *Capital: Volume I*. London: Penguin Books.

Matela, L. S., and D. Fraser. 2004. MDTP *Bi-lateral Strategic Planning Workshop*. Proceedings recorded at Didima Hutted Camp, Lesotho, 25–28 July, by the Maloti-Drakensberg Transfrontier Project.

Matlosa, K. 1999. "Aid, Development and Democracy in Lesotho, 1966–1996." Paper presented at the "Aid, Development and Democracy in Southern Africa" workshop organized by the Centre for Southern African Studies, University of the Western Cape, Cape Town, South Africa, 21–22 November.

Mavhunga, C., and W. Dressler. 2007. "On the Local Community: The Language of Disengagement?" *Conservation and Society* 5 (1): 44–59.

Mbembe, A. 2000. "At the Edge of the World: Boundaries, Territoriality, and Sovereignty in Africa." *Public Culture* 12 (1): 259–84.

———. 2001. *On the Postcolony*. Berkeley: University of California Press.

McAfee, K. 1999. "Selling Nature to Save It? Biodiversity and Green Developmentalism." *Society and Space* 17 (2): 203–19.

McCarthy, J. 2005. "Devolution in the Woods: Community Forestry as Hybrid Neoliberalism." *Environment and Planning A* 37: 995–1014.

McCarthy, J., and S. Prudham. 2004. "Neoliberal Nature and the Nature of Neoliberalism." *Geoforum* 35: 275–83.

McDonald, D. A., and G. Ruiters. 2005. "Theorizing Water Privatization in Southern Africa." In *The Age of Commodity: Water Privatization in Southern Africa*, ed. D. A. McDonald and G. Ruiters, 13–42. London: Earthscan.

Maloti-Drakensberg Transfrontier Project. 2004. "Position Article: Employment Equity within the Maloti-Drakensberg Transfrontier Project Coordinating Unit —South Africa." Howick, South Africa.

———. 2005a. "Environmental Resources Management Areas (ERMAS): Concept Development and Implementation Strategy." Unpublished concept note.

———. 2005b. "Mid Term Review of the Maloti-Drakensberg Transfrontier Conservation and Development Project June–July 2005." Howick, South Africa: Maloti-Drakensberg Transfrontier Project.

———. 2005c. "System of Integrated Community and District Planning for Lesotho." Unpublished document, Maseru, Lesotho.

———. 2007a. "Amagugu Esizwe MDTP Project, Supporting Community-Led Initiatives in Natural and Cultural Resource Management in the Upper uThukela Region." Unpublished final project report by Farmer Support Group, Bergwatch, and Grassland Science, University of KwaZulu-Natal, Howick, South Africa.

———. 2007b. *The Maloti Drakensberg Experience: Exploring the Maloti Drakensberg Route*. Howick, South Africa: Maloti-Drakensberg Transfrontier Project.

———. 2007c. "Moteng Vegetation Report and Grazing Management Plan." Unpublished report, Botha-Bothe, Lesotho.

———. 2007d. "20-year (2008–2028) Conservation and Development Strategy for the Maloti Drakensberg Transfrontier Conservation Area: Natural and Cultural Heritage and Sustainable Livelihoods in the Maloti Drakensberg Mountains." Draft version 6, 10 May, Howick, South Africa, and Maseru, Lesotho.

———. 2007e. "20-year (2008–2028) Conservation and Development Strategy for the Maloti Drakensberg Transfrontier Conservation Area: Natural and Cultural Heritage and Sustainable Livelihoods in the Maloti Drakensberg Mountains." Final draft. Howick, South Africa, and Maseru, Lesotho, 30 July.

Migdal, J. 1988. *Strong Societies and Weak States. State-Society Relations and Stace Capabilities in the Third World*. Princeton: Princeton University Press.

Milgroom, J., and M. Spierenburg. 2008. "Induced Volition: Resettlement from the Limpopo National Park, Mozambique." *Journal of Contemporary African Studies* 26 (4): 435–48.

Milne, S., and W. A. Adams. 2012. "Market Masquerades: The Politics of Community-Level Payments for Environmental Services in Cambodia." *Development and Change* 43 (1): 133–58.

Mittermeier, R. A., C. F. Kormos, C. G. Mittermeier, P. Robles Gil, T. Sandwith, and C. Besançon. 2005. *Transboundary Conservation: A New Vision for Protected Areas*. Mexico City: CEMEX, Agrupación Sierra Madre, and Conservation International.

Mittermeier, R. A., C. F. Kormos, C. G. Mittermeier, T. Sandwith, C. Besançon, D. C. Zbicz, P. Robles Gil, J. Hanks, L. Braack, M. Hoffmann, et al. 2005. "An Introduction to Transboundary Conservation." In *Transboundary Conservation: A New Vision for Protected Areas*, ed. R. A. Mittermeier, C. F. Kormos, C. G. Mittermeier, P. Robles Gil, T. Sandwith and C. Besançon, 27–66. Mexico City: CEMEX, Agrupación Sierra Madre, Conservation International.

Moodley, K., and H. Adam. 2000. "Race and Nation in Post-apartheid South Africa." *Current Sociology* 48 (3): 51–69.

Moore, D. 1999. "'Sail on, O Ship of State': Neo-liberalism, Globalisation and the Governance of Africa." *Journal of Peasant Studies* 27 (1): 61–96.

Moore, D. S. 2005. *Suffering for Territory: Race, Place, and Power in Zimbabwe*. Durham: Duke University Press.

———. 2008. "Sovereignty, Spatiality and Spectres of Race." *Singapore Journal of Tropical Geography* 29: 254–61.

Moore, J. W. 2010. "The End of the Road? Agricultural Revolutions in the Capitalist World-Ecology, 1450–2010." *Journal of Agrarian Change* 10 (3): 389–413.

Moosa, M. V. 2002. "Truly the Greatest Animal Kingdom." *Bojanala* 1 (1): 11–12.

Mosimane, A. W., and K. M. Aribeb. 2005. "Exclusion through Defined Membership in People-Centred Natural Resources Management: Who Defines?" Commons Southern Africa Occasional Paper Series, no. 14, Centre for Applied Social Sciences and Programme for Land and Agrarian Studies, Harare, Zimbabwe, and Cape Town.

Mosse, D. 2004. "Is Good Policy Unimplementable? Reflections on the Ethnography of Aid Policy and Practice." *Development and Change* 35 (4): 639–71.

———. 2005. *Cultivating Development: An Ethnography of Aid Policy and Practice*. London: Pluto Press.

———. 2006. "Anti-social Anthropology? Objectivity, Objection and the Ethnography of Public Policy and Professional Communities." *Journal of the Royal Anthropological Institute* 12: 935–56.

Mosse, D., and D. Lewis 2006. "Theoretical Approaches to Brokerage and Translation in Development." In *Development Brokers and Translators: The Ethnography of Aid and Agencies*, ed. D. Lewis and D. Mosse, 1–26. Bloomfield, Conn.: Kumarian Press.

Mudimbe, V. Y. 1988. *The Invention of Africa: Gnosis, Philosophy, and the Order of Knowledge*. Bloomington: Indiana University Press.

Mulgan, G. J. 1994. *Politics in an Antipolitical Age*. Cambridge, U.K.: Polity Press.

Munthali, S. M., and B. Soto. 2001. *Overt and Latent Conflicts Associated with the Establishment, Development and Management of the Great Limpopo Transfrontier Park*. Maputo, Mozambique: Transfrontier Conservation Areas Secretariat.

Muradian, R., E. Corbera, U. Pascual, N. Kosoy, and P. H. May. 2010. "Reconciling Theory and Practice: An Alternative Conceptual Framework for Understanding Payments for Environmental Services." *Ecological Economics* 69 (6): 1202–8.

Mwangi, O. 2007. "Hydropolitics, Ecocide and Human Security in Lesotho: A Case Study of the Highlands Water Project." *Journal of Southern African Studies* 33 (1): 3–17.

Myburgh, W. 2005. "Fostering Tourism in Southern Africa through Transfrontier Conservation." Presentation at the Third International Institute for Peace through Tourism African Conference, Lusaka, Zambia, 6–11 February.

Nealon, J. T. 2008. *Foucault beyond Foucault: Power and Its Intensification since 1984*. Stanford: Stanford University Press.

Nederveen Pieterse, J. 2004. "Neoliberal Empire." *Theory, Culture and Society* 21 (3): 119–40.

Nelson, R. H. 2003. "Environmental Colonialism: 'Saving Africa from Africans.'" *The Independent Review* 8 (1): 65–86.

Neocosmos, M. 2003. "Neo-liberalism versus State Nationalism: Beyond State Thinking in Southern Africa." *Journal of Contemporary African Studies* 21 (2): 341–57.

Neumann, R. P. 1998. *Imposing Wilderness: Struggles over Livelihoods and Nature Preservation in Africa.* Berkeley: University of California Press.

———. 2004. "Moral and Discursive Geographies in the War for Biodiversity in Africa." *Political Geography* 23: 813–37.

———. 2005. *Making Political Ecology.* London: Hodder Arnold.

Neves, K. 2010. "Cashing in on Cetourism: A Critical Ecological Engagement with Dominant E-NGO Discourses on Whaling, Cetacean Conservation, and Whale Watching." *Antipode* 42: 719–41.

Nüsser, M., and S. Grab. 2002. "Land Degradation and Soil Erosion in the Eastern Highlands of Lesotho, Southern Africa." *Die Erde: Beitrag zur Physischen Geographie* 133: 291–311.

Nustad, K. G. 2001. "Development: The Devil We Know?" *Third World Quarterly* 22 (4): 479–98.

Oates, J. F. 1999. *Myth and Reality in the Rain Forest: How Conservation Strategies Are Failing in West Africa.* Berkeley: University of California Press.

Olivier de Sardan, J. P. 2005. *Anthropology and Development: Understanding Contemporary Social Change.* London: Zed Books.

Ong, A. 2006. *Neoliberalism as Exception: Mutations in Citizenship and Sovereignty.* Durham: Duke University Press.

Overbeek, H. 1999. "Globalisation and Britain's Decline." In *Rethinking Decline: Britain Towards 2000,* ed. R. English and M. Kenny, 231–56. London: Macmillan.

———. 2005. "Global Governance, Class, Hegemony: A Historical Materialist Perspective." In *Contending Perspectives on Global Governance: Coherence, Contestation and World Order,* ed. A. D. Ba and M. J. Hoffman, 39–56. London: Routledge.

Paulson, S., L. L. Gezon, and M. Watts. 2003. "Locating the Political in Political Ecology: An Introduction." *Human Organization* 62 (3): 205–17.

Peace Parks Foundation. 2000. *Annual Review 1999.* Stellenbosch, South Africa: Peace Parks Foundation.

Peace Parks Foundation. 2002. *Annual Review 2001.* Stellenbosch, South Africa: Peace Parks Foundation.

———. 2002. *Funding Application in Support of a TFCA Technical Advisor: Department of Wildlife and National Parks, Botswana.* Stellenbosch, South Africa: Peace Parks Foundation.

———. 2007. *Review 1997–2006.* Stellenbosch: Peace Parks Foundation.

———. 2008. *Annual Report 2007.* Stellenbosch, South Africa: Peace Parks Foundation.

Peck, J. 2010. *Constructions of Neoliberal Reason.* Oxford: Oxford University Press.

Peck, J., and A. Tickell. 2002. "Neoliberalizing Space." *Antipode* 34 (3): 380–404.

Peluso, N. L. 1992. *Rich Forests, Poor People: Resource Control and Resistance in Java.* Berkeley: University of California Press.

———. 1993. "Coercing Conservation? The Politics of State Resource Control." *Global Environmental Change* 3 (2): 199–218.

Peterson, M. N., M. J. Peterson, and T. R. Peterson. 2005. "Conservation and the Myth of Consensus." *Conservation Biology* 19 (3): 762–67.

Polanyi, K. 2001 [1944]. The *Great Transformation: The Political and Economic Origins of Our Time.* Boston: Beacon Press.

Pomela, E. M. 1998. "Maloti-Drakensberg Transfrontier Conservation and Development Project." Unpublished paper, Ministry of Environment, Gender and Youth Affairs, Maseru, Lesotho.

Porter, T. 1999. "The Late-Modern Knowledge Structure and World Politics." In *Approaches to Global Governance Theory,* ed. M. Hewson and T. J. Sinclair, 137–56. Albany: State University of New York Press.

Pottier, J. 1993. "The Role of Ethnography in Project Appraisal." In *Practicing Development: Social Science Perspectives,* ed. J. Pottier, 13–33. London: Routledge.

Prudham, W. S. 2005. *Knock on Wood: Nature as Commodity in Douglas-Fir Country.* New York: Routledge.

Quarles van Ufford, P. 1988. "The Hidden Crisis in Development: Development Bureaucracies in between Intentions and Outcomes." In *The Hidden Crisis in Development: Development Bureaucracies,* ed. P. Quarles van Ufford, D. Kruijt, and T. Downing, 9–38. Amsterdam: VU University Press.

Quarles van Ufford, P., and A. K. Giri, eds. 2003. *A Moral Critique of Development: In Search of Global Responsibilities.* London: Routledge.

Quarles van Ufford, P., A. K. Giri, and D. Mosse. 2003. "Interventions in Development: Towards a New Moral Understanding of Our Experiences and an Agenda for the Future." In *A Moral Critique of Development: In Search of Global Responsibilities,* ed. P. Quarles van Ufford and A. K. Giri, 3–43. London: Routledge.

Quinlan, T. 1995. "Grassland Degradation and Livestock Rearing in Lesotho." *Journal of Southern African Studies* 21 (3): 491–507.

Quinlan, T., and C. D. Morris. 1994. "Implications of Changes to the Transhumance System for Conservation of the Mountain Catchments in Eastern Lesotho." *African Journal of Range and Forage Science* 11 (3): 76–81.

Ramutsindela, M. 2007. *Transfrontier Conservation in Africa: At the Confluence of Capital, Politics and Nature.* Wallingford, U.K.: CABI.

Ramutsindela, M., M. Spierenburg, and H. Wels. 2011. *Environmental Philanthropy.* London: Routledge.

Redford, K., and W. M. Adams. 2009. "Payment for Ecosystem Services and the Challenge of Saving Nature." *Conservation Biology* 23 (4): 785–87.

Refugee Research Programme. 2002. "A Park for the People? Great Limpopo Transfrontier Park—Community Consultation in Coutada 16, Mozambique." Johannesburg: University of the Witswatersrand.

Richardson, J. L. 2001. *Contending Liberalisms in World Politics: Ideology and Power.* Boulder, Colo.: Lynne Rienner Publishers.

Robins, S., and K. van der Waal. 2011. "'Model Tribes' and Iconic Conservationists?

Tracking the Makuleke Restitution Case in Kruger National Park." In *Land Memory, Reconstruction, and Justice: Perspectives on Land Claims in South Africa*, ed. C. Walker, A. Bohlin, R. Hall, and T. Kepe, 163–80. Pietermaritzburg, South Africa: University of KwaZulu-Natal Press.

Rogerson, C. M. 2004. "Transforming the South African Tourism Industry: The Emerging Black-Owned Bed and Breakfast Economy." *Geojournal* 60: 273–81.

Rohde, R. F., N. M. Moleele, M. Mphale, N. Allsopp, R. Chanda, M. T. Hoffman, L. Magole, and E. Young. 2006. "Dynamics of Grazing Policy and Practice: Environmental and Social Impacts in Three Communal Areas of Southern Africa." *Environmental Science and Policy* 9: 302–16.

Rose, N. 1996. "Governing 'Advanced' Liberal Democracies." In *Foucault and Political Reason: Liberalism, Neo-liberalism and Rationalities of Government*, ed. A. Barry, T. Osborne, and N. Rose, 37–64. London: University College London Press.

Rosenau, J. N. 1997. *Along the Domestic-Foreign Frontier: Exploring Governance in a Turbulent World*. Cambridge: Cambridge University Press.

Rosenau, J. N., and E-O. Czempiel. 1992. *Governance without Government: Order and Change in World Politics*. Cambridge: Cambridge University Press.

Ross, R. 1981. "Capitalism, Expansion, and the Incorporation on the Southern African Frontier." In *The Frontier in History: North America and Southern Africa Compared*, ed. H. Lamar and L. Thomson, 209–33. New Haven: Yale University Press.

Ros-Tonen, M. A. F., and T. Dietz. 2005. *African Forests between Nature and Livelihood Resource: Interdisciplinary Studies in Conservation and Forest Management*. New York: Edwin Mellen Press.

Roth, R., and W. Dressler. 2012. "Market-Oriented Conservation Governance: The Particularities of Place." *Geoforum* 43 (3): 363–66.

Sandwith, T. 1997a. "Drakensberg-Maloti Transfrontier Conservation and Development Area." Planning Division Document 1997/1. Notes recorded at a project-development workshop convened by Natal Parks Board, South Africa, and the National Environment Secretariat of Lesotho at Giant's Castle in the Natal Drakensberg Park, 12–13 September.

——. 1997b. "The Drakensberg-Maloti Transfrontier Conservation Area: Experience and Lessons Learned." In IUCN World Commission on Protected Areas, *Parks for Peace: Conference Proceedings, International Conference on Transboundary Protected Areas as a Vehicle for International Co-operation, 16–18 September 1997, Somerset West, near Cape Town, South Africa*. Gland, Switzerland: IUCN.

——. 2003. "Overcoming Barriers: Conservation and Development in the Maloti-Drakensberg Mountains of Southern Africa." *Journal of Sustainable Forestry* 17 (1–2): 149–69.

Sandwith, T., C. Shine, L. Hamilton, and D. Sheppard. 2001. *Transboundary Protected Areas for Peace and Co-operation*. Gland, Switzerland: IUCN.

Schedler, A. 1997. "Introduction." In *The End of Politics? Explorations into Modern Anti-politics*, ed. A. Schedler, 1–20. New York: Macmillan.

Schmidt-Soltau, K., and D. Brockington. 2007. "Protected Areas and Resettlement: What Scope for Voluntary Relocation?" *World Development* 35 (12): 2182–202.

Schmitz, T. T. 1992. "The Lesotho Highlands Water Project: A Systematic Narrowing of Benefits." Occasional paper 31, Third World Centre, Catholic University of Nijmegen, the Netherlands.

Schoon, M. L. 2009. "Building Robustness to Disturbance: Governance in Southern African Peace Parks." Ph.D. dissertation, Indiana University.

Schroeder, R. A. 1999. "Geographies of Environmental Intervention in Africa." *Progress in Human Geography* 23 (3): 359–78.

Scott, J. 1985. *Weapons of the Weak: Everyday Forms of Peasant Resistance.* New Haven: Yale University Press.

Scott, J. 1998. *Seeing Like a State. How Certain Schemes to Improve the Human Condition Have Failed.* New Haven: Yale University Press.

Sechaba Consultants. 2000. *Poverty and Livelihoods in Lesotho, 2000: More Than a Mapping Exercise.* Maseru, Lesotho: Sechaba Consultants.

Secretariat of the Convention on Biological Diversity. 2010. *Global Biodiversity Outlook 3.* Montreal: Secretariat of Convention on Biological Diversity.

Shackleton S., and C. Shackleton. 2004. "Everyday Resources Are Valuable Enough for Community-Based Natural Resources Management Programme Support: Evidence from South Africa." In *Rights, Resources and Rural Development,* ed. C. Fabricius, E. Kock, H. Magone, and S. Turner, 134–46. London: Earthscan.

Showers, K. B. 1989. "Soil Erosion in the Kingdom of Lesotho: Origins and Colonial Response, 1830s–1950s." *Journal of Southern African Studies* 15 (2): 263–86.

Singh, J., and H. van Houtum. 2002. "Post-colonial Nature Conservation in Southern Africa: Same Emperors, New Clothes?" *Geojournal* 58: 253–63.

Sisitka, L. 2007. "Amagugu Esizwe: End of Term Evaluation; Final Report." Unpublished report, FSG, Pietermaritzburg, South Africa.

Slater, C. 2002. *Entangled Edens: Visions of the Amazon.* Berkeley: University of California Press.

Solomon, H., and A. Turton. 2000. *Water Wars: Enduring Myth or Impending Reality.* Durban, South Africa: ACCORD.

Songorwa, A. N. 1999. "Community-Based Wildlife Management (CWM) in Tanzania: Are the Communities Interested?" *World Development* 27 (12): 2061–79.

South Africa National Biodiversity Institute. 2005. *Mainstreaming Biodiversity in Municipalities.* Unpublished proceedings of a workshop, 4–5 October, Biodiversity Centre, SANBI National Botanical Garden, Pretoria.

Spenceley, A. 2005. *Tourism Investment in the Great Limpopo Transfrontier Conservation Area. Scoping Report.* Johannesburg: Transboundary Protected Areas Research Initiative.

Spierenburg, M., C. Steenkamp, and H. Wels. 2006. "Resistance of Local Communities against Marginalization in the Great Limpopo Transfrontier Park." *Focaal* 47: 18–31.

Spierenburg, M., and H. Wels. 2010. "Conservative Philanthropists, Royalty and Business Elites in Nature Conservation in Southern Africa." *Antipode* 42 (3): 647–70.

Strange, S. 1970. "International Economics and International Relations: A Case of Mutual Neglect." *International Affairs* 46 (2): 304–15.

Sullivan, S. 2006. "The Elephant in the Room? Problematising 'New' (Neoliberal) Biodiversity Conservation." *Forum for Development Studies* 12 (1): 105–35.

———. 2009. "Green Capitalism, and the Cultural Poverty of Constructing Nature as Service Provider." *Radical Anthropology* 3: 18–27.

———. 2010. "The Environmentality of 'Earth Incorporated': On Contemporary Primitive Accumulation and the Financialisation of Environmental Conservation." Paper presented at the "An Environmental History of Neoliberalism" conference, Lund University, Lund, Sweden, 6–8 May.

Tanner, R. J. 2003. "Transfrontier Conservation Areas of Southern Africa and Community Involvement in the Context of International Law." Master's thesis, University of Montana.

Taylor, I. 2003. "Globalization and Regionalization in Africa: Reactions to Attempts at Neo-liberal Regionalism." *Review of International Political Economy* 10 (2): 310–30.

Terborgh, J. 1999. *Requiem for Nature.* Washington, D.C.: Island Press.

Thabane, M. 2000. "Shifts from Old to New Social and Ecological Environments in the Lesotho Highlands Water Scheme: Relocating Residents of the Mohale Dam Area." *Journal of Southern African Studies* 26 (4): 633–54.

———. 2002. "Aspects of Colonial Economy and Society, 1868–1966." In *Essays on Aspects of the Political Economy of Lesotho 1500–2000,* ed. N. W. Pule and M. Thabane, 103–30. Roma: National University of Lesotho.

Thompson, L. 2001. *A History of South Africa.* New Haven: Yale University Press.

Thondhlana, G., S. Shackleton, and E. Muchapondwa. 2011. "Kgalagadi Transfrontier Park and Its Land Claimants: A Pre- and Post-land Claim Conservation and Development History." *Environmental Research Letters* 6 (2): 1–12.

Thrift, N. 2005. *Knowing Capitalism.* London: Sage Publications.

Timberlake, J., and B. Mateka. 2004. "Conserving Mountain Biodiversity in Southern Lesotho." Final Report, Project Number LES/97/G31/B/IG/99, United Nations Development Programme, Maseru, Lesotho.

Tordoff, W. 2002. *Government and Politics in Africa. Fourth Edition.* Bloomington: Indiana University Press.

Tsing, A. 2005. *Friction: An Ethnography of Global Connection.* Princeton: Princeton University Press.

Turner, S. D. 2001. *Livelihoods in Lesotho.* Maseru: CARE Lesotho.

———. 2003. "Rangelands in Lesotho: Can Common Property Resources Succeed in the 21st Century?" Paper presented at the International Rangelands Conference, Durban, South Africa, 26 July–1 August.

———. 2005. *Natural Resource Management and Local Government in the Maloti.* Maseru, Lesotho: Maloti-Drakensberg Transfrontier Project.

———. 2006. "The State, Legal Reform and Decentralisation: Consequences for the Commons in Lesotho." Paper presented at "Survival of the Commons: Mounting Challenges and New Realities," 11th biannual conference of the International Association for the Study of Common Property, Bali, Indonesia, 19–23 June.

Turpie, J. K., C. Marais, and J. Blignaut. 2008. "The Working for Water Programme: Evolution of a Payments for Ecosystem Services Mechanism Addresses Both Poverty and Ecosystem Service Delivery in South Africa." *Ecological Economics* 65: 788–98.

Turton, A. R. 2000. "Precipitation, People, Pipelines and Power in Southern Africa." In *Political Ecology: Science, Myth and Power*, P. Stott and S. Sullivan, 132–56. London: Arnold.

Underhill, G. R. D. 2003. "States, Markets and Governance for Emerging Market Economies: Private Interests, the Public Good and the Legitimacy of the Development Process." *International Affairs* 79 (4): 755–81.

United Nations Development Programme, United Nations Environment Programme, and World Bank. 1994. *Global Environment Facility: Independent Evaluation of the Pilot Phase*. Washington, D.C.: World Bank.

Van Amerom, M. 2005. "On the Road to Peace? Cooperation and Conflict in Southern Africa's Peace Parks." Ph.D. thesis, University of Durham, United Kingdom.

Van Amerom, M., and B. E. Büscher. 2005. "Peace Parks in Southern Africa: Bringers of an African Renaissance?" *Journal of Modern African Studies* 43 (2): 159–82.

Van der Pijl, K. 1998. *Transnational Classes and International Relations*. London: Routledge.

Van der Westhuizen, J. 2005. "Plugging into Circuits of Consumption: Marketing the South African State through Sports Events and Celebrity Celebrations." Paper presented at the Globalization Studies Network, Second International Conference, Dakar, Senegal, 29–31 August.

Venema, B, and H. van den Breemer. 1999. *Towards Negotiated Co-management of Natural Resources in Africa*. Munich: Lit Verlag.

Walker, C., A. Bohlin, R. Hall, and T. Kepe. 2011. *Land Memory, Reconstruction, and Justice: Perspectives on Land Claims in South Africa*. Pietermaritzburg, South Africa: University of KwaZulu-Natal Press.

Weaver, J. C. 2003. *The Great Land Rush and the Making of the Modern World, 1650–1900*. Montreal: McGill-Queen's University Press.

Weaver, T. 2001. *Theatres of the Wild: The Parks of Peace*. Stuttgart, Germany: DaimlerChrysler AG.

Wellings, P. A., and J. S. Crush. 1983. "Tourism and Dependency in Southern Africa: The Prospects and Planning of Tourism in Lesotho." *Applied Geography* 3: 205–23.

Wells, M. P. 1996. "The Social Role of Protected Areas in the New South Africa." *Environmental Conservation* 23 (4): 322–31.

Wendt, A. 1987. "The Agent-Structure Problem in International Relations Theory." *International Organization* 41 (3): 335–70.

West, P. 2006. *Conservation Is Our Government Now: The Politics of Ecology in Papua New Guinea.* Durham: Duke University Press.

West, P., and D. Brockington. 2006. "An Anthropological Perspective on Some Unexpected Consequences of Protected Areas." *Conservation Biology* 20 (3): 609–16.

West, P., and J. Carrier. 2004. "Ecotourism and Authenticity: Getting Away from It All?" *Current Anthropology* 45 (4): 483–98.

Wheeler, K., and J. Nauright. 2006. "A Global Perspective on the Environmental Impact of Golf." *Sport in Society* 9 (3): 427–43.

Wittmayer, J. 2007. "Life Projects, Development and the State: An Anthropological Study into Land Claims in Lesotho." Master's thesis, vu University Amsterdam.

Wittmayer, J., and B. Büscher. 2010. "Conserving Conflict? Transfrontier Conservation, Development Discourses and Conflict between South Africa and Lesotho." *Human Ecology* 38 (6): 763–73.

Wolmer, W. 2003. "Transboundary Conservation: The Politics of Ecological Integrity in the Great Limpopo Transfrontier Park." *Journal of Southern African Studies* 29 (1): 261–78.

——. 2006. "Big Conservation: The Politics of Ecoregional Science in Southern Africa." Paper presented at the "Culture, Nature, Future? Perspectives on Science and Development in Africa" conference, University of Edinburgh, 12–13 April.

World Bank. 1996. *Transfrontier Conservation Area Pilot and Institutional Strengthening Project.* Report no. 15534-MOZ, World Bank, Washington, D.C.

World Bank. 2001a. "Project Appraisal Document on a Proposed Grant from the Global Environmental Facility Trust Fund in the Amount of SDR 5.6 Million to the Kingdom of Lesotho for a Maloti-Drakensberg Transfrontier Conservation and Development Project." Washington D.C., 20 August.

——. 2001b. "Project Appraisal Document on a Proposed Grant from the Global Environmental Facility Trust Fund in the Amount of SDR 6.0 Million (US$7.92 Million Equivalent) to the Republic of South Africa for a Maloti-Drakensberg Transfrontier Conservation and Development Project." Report no. 22630-SA, Washington, D.C., 20 August.

——. 2004. "Implementation Completion Report (TF-28483) on a Grant in the Amount of US$5 Million to the Republic of Mozambique for a Transfrontier Conservation Areas Pilot and Institutional Strengthening Project." Report no. 28382, Washington D.C.

——. 2005. "South Africa Maloti Drakensberg Transfrontier Conservation and Development Project (P052368): Mid Term Review, August 1–8, 2005; Draft Aide Memoire." Maloti-Drakensberg Transfrontier Project, Howick, South Africa.

Wunder, S. 2001. "Poverty Alleviation and Tropical Forests—What Scope for Synergies?" *World Development* 29 (11): 1817–33.

Young, Z. 2002. *A New Green Order? The World Bank and the Politics of the Global Environment Facility.* London: Pluto Press.

index

Consensus, 18–20, 22, 24–25, 49–50, 52, 59–60, 63–66, 68, 73, 79–81, 83, 92, 94, 110, 112–14, 125–33, 136, 148–50, 166–67, 169, 185, 192, 221–23, 225–26, 230, 232, 235n15, 241n28, 247n38; marketing, 101–6; technical, 96–101; Washington, 16, 235n16

Conservation: and development, 2, 5, 11, 14, 18–22, 38–41, 59, 66–68, 70, 80, 104, 107, 131, 167, 170–71, 178, 192–94, 203–4, 214, 218, 224, 226, 233n2; consultants in, 61–63; economy, 174–76; fortress, 11, 34–35, 39–40, 127; frontiers of, 9, 12, 42, 196, 219; plan, 112–13, 124; and spectacle, 74; telos of, 2, 50, 66, 79, 222; value of, 4, 77–78, 197–98, 226, 258n1. See also Community Based Conservation; Neoliberal conservation

Conservation International, 1, 60

Conserving Mountain Biodiversity in Southern Lesotho (UNDP project), 145

Consultants, 61–63, 95, 100, 115–16, 180–183, 211–12. See also Conservation

Convention on Biological Diversity, 100

DaimlerChrysler, 242n38

Department of Economic Affairs Environment and Tourism (Eastern Cape), 137, 142

Department of Environmental Affairs and Tourism (DEAT, South Africa), 60, 74, 76, 78, 102, 112, 118, 126–27, 138–39, 142, 191, 204, 221

Department of Tourism, Environmental and Economic Affairs (Free State), 138, 141

Department of Water Affairs and Forestry (Natal), 84

Depoliticization. See Antipolitics

Development: benefits, 37, 41, 49, 82–83, 88; capitalist, 32, 179, 219, 221; community, 44, 77, 92, 95, 199, 205; climate, 35; local, 7, 135, 217, 238n15; moral critique of, 236n18; postcolo-

nial, 28, 35, 38; spatial, 113, 165; studies, 10, 83. See also Conservation

Difaqane, 30

Discourses, 12, 22, 25, 59, 61, 64, 89, 149, 167, 169, 180, 193, 196, 215, 217, 220, 225; amplification of, 2, 65; colonial, 55; conservation, 11, 41, 87; jubilant, 5; management of, 61; Neoliberal conservation, 4; operationalization of, 92, 106; Peace park, 7, 9, 50–54, 60, 66–67, 78, 80, 91, 222, 227

Dispossession, 29, 36, 59, 237n8, 239n22; of land, 31, 40, 90; of native populations, 30; racialized, 2, 4, 11

Drakensberg-Maloti Mountain Conservation Programme (DMMCP), 84–85, 87–88, 244n11

Dual mandate, 34–35, 37, 55, 72

Eastern Cape (province), 137, 141–42, 186

Ecotourism. See Tourism

Elites, 37, 179; political and business, 44, 52–54, 59, 64

Ethnography, 3–4, 9–10, 229

European Union, 85, 89, 244n11

Ezemvelo KwaZulu Natal Wildlife (KZN Wildlife, South Africa), 102, 110, 118, 137–40, 180, 252n5

Ferguson, James, 21, 89, 146, 236n21

Foucault, Michel, 234n10

Fouriesburg (South Africa), 177

Free State (province), 138, 141, 177, 191, 260n14

Frontier, 4–5, 9–12, 27, 41–42, 64, 196–97, 201–2, 208; 219–20, 231–32, 237n3; history, 28–31; postmodern, 26

Garden of Eden (symbolism), 33–34, 72, 238n16; as marketing tool, 74, 179

Giant's Castle Nature Reserve, 85

Global Environment Facility, 7, 85, 92–96, 99, 114, 171, 189, 192, 245n25, 245n26, 246n27

Golden Gate Highlands National Park (South Africa), 138

Maloti-Drakensberg Transfrontier Project, 7–8, 11, 14, 124; components, 246n32; Giant's Castle Declaration, 91; history, 36, 39, 84–96; objectives: 94–95; preparation politics, 104–5; pre-project, 85, 87; Project Appraisal Document (PAD), 94, 96–101; in the Southern African transfrontier conservation landscape, 81–82; twenty-year bioregional plan, 125–31, 175–76

Managed Resource Areas (MRA), 136, 143–46, 252n1; 'Moteng, 151–56

Mandela, Nelson, 2, 6, 43, 53, 68, 242n38

Marketing, 22–24, 67, 70–74, 80, 101–6, 128, 169–94, 203–6, 212–17, 223–24, 227; Boundless Southern Africa, 76–79; social, 236n25. *See also* Branding

Marx, Karl, 4, 10, 67, 201

Mbeki, Thabo, 6, 49, 53, 239n20

Millennium Development Goals, 235n17

Minerals-energy complex, 32

Ministry of Finance and Development Planning (Lesotho), 121

Ministry of Local Government (Lesotho), 143, 146–47

Ministry of Tourism, Environment and Culture (Lesotho), 104, 117, 121, 143, 182, 205

Mnweni/Cathedral Peak area and catchment, 199, 215

Mokhotlong (Lesotho), 111, 123, 151

Moosa, Valli, 47, 55, 239n20

Moshoeshoe (Sotho Chief), 30

Mosse, David, 234n8

Mozambique, 44, 51, 56–58, 241n23

Mugabe, Robert, 49

Namibia, 31, 35, 51

Natal, 32, 84. *See also* KwaZulu Natal

Natal Parks Board, 84, 86, 102, 245n12, 252n5. *See also* Ezemvelo KwaZulu Natal Wildlife

National Environmental Secretariat (Lesotho), 103, 244n11

Natural resources, 31, 38, 87, 146, 155, 166, 184, 186, 216, 221: access to, 41, 210. *See also* Biodiversity; Grazing lands/areas

Neoliberal conservation, 4, 12–13, 176, 196–202, 217–19; bubble of, 26, 207–10, 225, 232; politics of, 9, 18, 24, 28, 41, 80, 89, 221–25; resistance to, 227, 259n6. *See also* Payments for Environmental Services, Tourism

Neoliberalism, 3, 11, 41–42, 201, 209; "actually existing", 13, 214; and ANC Growth, Employment and Redistribution agenda, 40, 73; beyond, 228–31; culture of, 73; definition of, 12; and modes of devolved governance, 13–16, 19, 220, 224; and modes of political conduct, 16–18, 220, 224, 228; as political ideology, 79; resistance to, 10, 18, 22, 194; roll-out, 110; and the state, 15–17, 50, 63–64, 68, 235n14. *See also* Political economy

Neoprotectionism, 39, 238n15

New Partnership for Africa's Development (NEPAD), 177

Nyakoaneng (Lesotho), 151–56, 158, 163–65, 185, 254n53

Obonjaneni (South Africa), 158–65, 185

Orange (river), 30, 84

Orange Free State, 30–32. *See also* Free State (province)

Overbeek, Henk, 19–20

Paper/policy trail, 61–62, 65, 86, 192, 225

Parks. *See* Protected areas

Payments for Environmental Services (PES), 130, 184, 195–202, 208–9, 211–14, 218

Peace, 1–2, 42, 66

Peace parks, 1–8, 11, 18, 27–28, 38, 42, 69, 70–72, 79, 91, 219–20, 225–26, 242n38, 260n2; discourse, 7, 9, 50–54, 58–60, 64–67, 78, 80, 91, 221–23, 227. *See also* Transfrontier conservation; Transfrontier Conservation Area

Peace Parks Foundation, 2, 5–7, 22, 43–44, 51–55, 60, 67–68, 71, 78–79, 81, 91, 103, 205, 210, 221–23, 227, 241n22

Player, Ian, 86, 244n12

Policy, 39, 52, 83, 95–96, 194, 210; discourse, 131; goals, 100–101, 130–31; networks, 187; oriented judgment, 188, 193; preoccupation with, 62, 241n25

Political ecology, 3, 10, 20, 196, 228–31

Political economy, 28–29, 31–34, 36, 38–40, 42–45, 72, 79, 89, 127, 133, 212, 219, 221, 225, 234n8; neoliberal, 3–5, 10, 207; postcolonial, 28–29, 39, 45; and water, 88, 199. *See also* Neoliberalism

Politics: democratic, 21; frontier, 9, 12, 18, 24, 41; and marketing, 70–71, 78, 193, 217; practices of, 61–62; of technical consensus, 96–101. *See also* Antipolitics; Neoliberal conservation

Postcolonial, 3, 11, 14, 18, 25, 28, 35, 38–40, 59, 61, 119, 143, 169, 205, 221, 233n2. *See also* Political economy

Power: decentralization of, 39, 50; diffused, 209; disciplinary, 16, 24; discursive, 41, 149, 167; emotional, 242n37; relations, 10, 40, 166, 186; resource and network, 55, 213; state, 17, 147; struggles, 20, 67

Private-sector, 176–79; operating principles, 63

Project Coordination Unit (MDTP), 109–11; differences between, 112–25, 148–50

Protected areas, 1–3, 33, 38–39, 66, 71, 87, 92, 130, 138, 151, 215; and land restitution, 90; social impact of, 11, 35

Public relations. *See* Marketing

Qacha's Nek (Lesotho), 111, 151, 186

Race, 11–12, 29, 32, 35–36, 103–4, 115–16, 118–22, 125, 141–42, 181, 192

Ramsar Convention, 97, 100

Ramutsindela, Maano, 43

Rand Water, 160–61, 176, 256n14

Range lands/areas, 114–15, 143–46, 151, 155, 195, 249n21; and biodiversity, 115. *See also* Grazing lands/areas

Range management, 146, 154, 191

Range Management Division (Lesotho), 143–44

Royal Maluti Golf Estate, 177–79, 200, 210–11, 256n15

Royal Natal National Park (South Africa), 158

Rupert, Anton, 6, 43–44, 51 69, 71–72, 224, 242n38

Schedler, Andreas, 20–21, 151

Security, 64, 67, 84, 178–79, 211, 216; border, 47; forces, 36; job, 141; water, 197

Sehlabathebe National Park (Lesotho), 97, 99, 103, 143, 205, 244n1

Settlers (Dutch and British), 29–31

Shaka kaSenzangakhona, 30

Soil erosion, 88, 151, 155, 185

South Africa: post-apartheid, 38, 40, 52, 73; relations with Lesotho, 36, 82, 84–89, 116–17; and tourism, 58; transformation process, 137–142; unionization and formal independence, 32. *See also* Apartheid

South Africa National Biodiversity Institute, 123–24

South African National Parks (SANParks), 138

Southern Africa Initiative of German Business (SAFRI), 242n38

Southern African Development Community (SADC), 49, 51, 53, 60, 77, 177

Southern African Nature Foundation, 43–44, 69. *See also* World Wildlife Fund

Sovereignty, 11–12, 29, 36, 38, 45, 51, 60, 116–18; community, 50; fragmented forms of, 56

State, 14, 37, 62–65, 95, 165, 184–85, 235n14; colonial, 34; as focal point, 53; role of the, 17, 50, 200

Swedish Water House, 212–13